Hosea, Joel, and Obadiah Through the Centuries

Wiley Blackwell Bible Commentaries

Bradford A. Anderson

WILEY Blackwell

Hosea, Joel, and Obadiah Through the Centuries

The right of Bradford A. Anderson to be identified as the author of this work has been asserted in accordance with law.

Registered Office(s)
John Wiley & Sons, Inc., 111 River Street, Hoboken, NJ 07030, USA
John Wiley & Sons Ltd, The Atrium, Southern Gate, Chichester, West Sussex, PO19 8SQ, UK

For details of our global editorial offices, customer services, and more information about Wiley products visit us at www.wiley.com.

Wiley also publishes its books in a variety of electronic formats and by print-on-demand. Some content that appears in standard print versions of this book may not be available in other formats.

Library of Congress Cataloging-in-Publication Data applied for
Hardback ISBN: 9781394239672

Cover Design: Wiley
Cover Image: © Life of William Blake (1880), Volume 2 Job illustrations by Cygnis insignis is licensed under CC BY-SAA

Set in 10/12.5pt Minion Pro by Straive, Pondicherry, India

For Georgie, Molly, Maeve, and Fionnuala Anderson
With thanks to Walter Moberly
In memory of John Sawyer and Molly Walsh

Contents

Hosea

Joel

Obadiah

List of Figures

The Blackwell Bible Commentaries series, the first to be devoted primarily to the reception history of the Bible, is based on the premise that how people have interpreted, and been influenced by, a sacred text like the Bible is often as interesting and historically important as what it originally meant. The series emphasizes the influence of the Bible on literature, art, music, and film, its role in the evolution of religious beliefs and practices, and its impact on social and political developments. Drawing on work in a variety of disciplines, it is designed to provide a convenient and scholarly means of access to material that until now was hard to find and a much-needed resource for all those interested in the influence of the Bible on Western culture.

Until quite recently this whole dimension was for the most part neglected by biblical scholars. The goal of a commentary was primarily, if not exclusively, to get behind the centuries of accumulated Christian and Jewish tradition to one single meaning, normally identified with the author's original intention.

The most important and distinctive feature of the Blackwell Bible Commentaries is that they will present readers with many different interpretations of each text in such a way as to heighten their awareness of what a text, especially a sacred text, can mean and what it can do, what it has meant and what it has done, in the many contexts in which it operates.

The Blackwell Bible Commentaries will consider patristic, rabbinic (where relevant), and medieval exegesis as well as insights from various types of modern criticism, acquainting readers with a wide variety of interpretative techniques. As part of the history of interpretation, questions of source, date, authorship, and other historical–critical and archaeological issues will be discussed, but since these are covered extensively in existing commentaries, such references will be brief, serving to point readers in the direction of readily accessible literature where they can be followed up.

Original to this series is the consideration of the reception history of specific biblical books arranged in commentary format. The chapter-by-chapter arrangement ensures that the biblical text is always central to the discussion. Given the wide influence of the Bible and the richly varied appropriation of each biblical book, it is a difficult question to determine which interpretations to include. While each volume will have its own distinctive point of view, the guiding principle for the series as a whole is that readers should be given a representative sampling of material from different ages with an emphasis on interpretations that have been especially influential or historically significant. Although commentators will have their preferences among the different interpretations, the material will be presented in such a way that readers can make up their own minds on the value, morality, and validity of particular interpretations.

The series encourages readers to consider how the biblical text has been interpreted down the ages and seeks to open their eyes to different uses of the Bible in contemporary culture. The aim is to write a series of scholarly commentaries that draw on all the insights of modern research to illustrate the rich interpretative potential of each biblical book.

John Sawyer
Christopher Rowland
Judith Kovacs
David M. Gunn

Acknowledgments

This project has been long in the making, and I would like to thank the HB series editors: David Gunn and the late John Sawyer for their encouragement and guidance through the years, and Lena-Sofia Tiemeyer and Andrew Mein for helping me bring it to completion. All of these colleagues gave invaluable feedback along the way. Research for this commentary was presented at several conferences, including the Irish Biblical Association and the Society of Biblical Literature, and I am grateful for the input and feedback from colleagues as this work progressed. The library team at Dublin City University is unfailingly helpful and resourceful, and I am immensely grateful for their help along the way, particularly Victoria Smyth for her help in tracking down some hard-to-find resources. Research for this volume was also undertaken at KU Leuven's Maurits Sabbe Theology and Religious Studies Library, as well as the library of the École biblique et archéologique française de Jérusalem—I am grateful for the hospitality shown to me at both institutions and for being given access to their wonderful collections. Colleagues in the School of Theology, Philosophy, and Music at Dublin City University have been encouraging (and long-suffering!) as I've worked on this project. Special thanks to Peter Admirand, Róisín Blunnie, Amanda Dillon, Patricia Flynn, Jonathan Kearney, Ethna Regan, and Joseph Rivera for their encouragement along the way. Funding was provided by the DCU Faculty of Humanities and Social Sciences for several aspects of this project through the years, and I'm very grateful for the support of colleagues in the faculty.

I gratefully dedicate this volume to my wife Georgie and our three children, Molly, Maeve, and Fionnuala, who keep me grounded in the present when I get lost in the past; with thanks to Walter Moberly, who taught me the value of worthy conversation partners, both the quick and the dead; to the memory of John Sawyer, whose tremendous intellect was matched by his kindness and generosity; and to the memory of Molly Walsh, who made the world a better place because she was in it.

Elements from this volume have been published previously in the following articles, and the content is used here with permission:

Anderson, Bradford A. 'The Reception of Obadiah: Some Historical, Ideological, and Visual Considerations.' *Proceedings of the Irish Biblical Association* 36 (2013): 17–35.

Anderson, Bradford A. 'Hosea's Marriage: A Brief History of Interpretation.' *Proceedings of the Irish Biblical Association* 43 (2021): 24–37.

Anderson, Bradford A. 'Family Dynamics, Fertility Cults, and Feminist Critiques: The Reception of Hosea 1–3 Through the Centuries.' *Religions* 12 (2021): 1–20.

Anderson, Bradford A. 'Visualising the (Invisible) Prophets: Artistic Strategies for Representing Joel and Obadiah in Christian and Western Traditions.' *Die Bibel in der Kunst/Bible in the Arts* 7 (2023).

Introduction

This commentary explores the reception history of three Hebrew prophets: Hosea, Joel, and Obadiah. Investigating the reception of the Bible is important for many reasons, not least because texts can (and often do) mean different things to different people. What was self-evident about a text to a first-century Jew is often very different from what a medieval monk or rabbi might have made of the same text, and the interpretation of a modern Western scholar will likely be different again. So a key element of reception history, and of this project in particular, is the exploration of how and why biblical texts have been used and understood through the years, as well as investigating the use and impact of these biblical books across the centuries.

Reception history is a broad designation that encompasses a wide range of approaches and source materials. For the present study, I understand reception history as the exploration of the interpretation, use, and impact of these prophetic texts and traditions down through the centuries, including commentaries and interpretive traditions, the use of these texts in religious communities, and the social and cultural mobilization of these prophetic works in areas ranging from literature to the visual arts. Within this broad understanding, there are several elements (and challenges) to consider.

First, using the understanding of reception history noted above, the possible forms of reception that one could engage with are seemingly endless. Indeed, the writing of this commentary has been a process of curation, which is itself a form of interpretation, and the voices that are highlighted in what follows are representations of my own location, interests, and biases as a reader and interpreter. The approach I have taken is to engage with a number of recurring

Hosea, Joel, and Obadiah Through the Centuries, First Edition. Bradford A. Anderson.
© 2024 John Wiley & Sons Ltd. Published 2024 by John Wiley & Sons Ltd.

'conversation partners'—voices ranging from antiquity to the contemporary world—which serve as guideposts through and indeed across the books under discussion. This is not an exhaustive and final word on the reception of these prophets. Rather, these voices give us snapshots of what I understand to be important and interesting trajectories in the afterlives of these prophetic books. A brief overview of these conversation partners can be found in the 'Glossary and Biographies' at the end of this volume.

Second, while the focus here is on the use and impact of the biblical texts in question, we should not assume a linear process of influence is always at work with the biblical texts serving as the sole inspiration or as the sole point of departure. In reality, the various uses of these prophetic texts are part of much larger matrices of texts and traditions that have been picked up and reused in various ways with manifold influences (for an illuminating discussion of this in relation to the second Temple period in particular, see Mroczek 2016). Thus, while we are focusing here on the use and reception of Hosea, Joel, and Obadiah, these are only soundings from what is a much larger and more intricate set of interrelationships of which these prophetic texts, their language, and their imagery are an important part.

Anyone undertaking a task such as this faces a number of ethical challenges. First, the history of recorded engagement with the Bible is dominated by men and male voices—although not necessarily the lived reality of how the Bible has actually been used, this is nonetheless what has been passed down to us. While I have attempted to incorporate women commentators, readers, and artists wherever possible, their voices remain a noticeable minority. The question is whether the approach taken contributes to the problem by reifying the patriarchal history that has shaped the use of these texts and the stories we now tell. I do not have a simple solution for this question, and it is an issue to which those of us involved in exploring the reception of the Bible will need to continue to be attentive.

Another ethical quandary revolves around Jewish-Christian relations and, in particular, anti-Jewish rhetoric that is found in the Christian reception of these prophetic texts. (Similar issues arise in relation to Protestant rhetoric concerning Roman Catholicism, and readers will note this usage, particularly in the centuries following the Reformation.) For this study, I have engaged with and included various examples of this rhetoric. While not approving of this, it remains an important part of the way in which these texts have been received and is part of the story, which is worth telling. When such cases appear, I have tried to note the potentially harmful use of language as well as the supersessionist implications of such comments in the relationship between Judaism and Christianity. However, for extensive engagement on these issues, other resources should be explored (e.g., Fredriksen and Irshai 2006; Siquans 2020).

This volume begins with a chapter situating Hosea, Joel, and Obadiah as part of the Book of the Twelve (or Minor Prophets) and the reception of these three prophetic works as part of this collection. We then move to commentaries on the three prophetic books in question. Within these, an introductory chapter offers a broad overview of the reception of each prophetic work, including (1) a brief history of interpretation; (2) key historical and literary issues in the book's interpretation; (3) important theological, thematic, and rhetorical issues that have shaped the use and impact of the book; and (4) religious, social, and cultural reception of the prophet and the book. The main body of each commentary then moves through the three books sequentially, offering chapter-by-chapter reflections. Where possible, the commentary is offered chronologically, beginning with early Jewish and rabbinic interpretation and moving to Christian and then the later critical reception of these texts. Religious, social, and cultural uses of these prophets and the books bearing their names are interspersed throughout the volume, giving a sense of the broad-ranging ways in which people and communities have engaged with these prophets.

A few notes on style and referencing will be helpful. Unless otherwise noted, translations are taken from the NRSV as a starting point. For the Hebrew text in the Masoretic tradition, I have followed *BHQ* (Gelston 2010). For the Septuagint, I have relied on Ziegler (1984) for the Greek and the New English Translation of the Septuagint (NETS 2009) for English translations. Similarly, for the Aramaic Targum, I have used Sperber (1962) for the Aramaic and Cathcart and Gordon (1989) for English translation. While I have avoided extensive use of Hebrew and other ancient languages, where important I have included Hebrew and Greek terms in transliteration, using the basic general-purpose style (SBL) for ease of use.

With regard to referencing, for the recurring 'conversation partners' and major commentaries that are used throughout the volume, I use only the author's surname; unless quoting verbatim, I have not included page numbers so as to keep the text free of unnecessary clutter. Other resources are cited by author name and year. While I have attempted to use stand-alone works and commentaries where possible, a number of anthologies and reference works have proved invaluable in this project. For rabbinic literature, the works of Neusner (2007a, 2007b, 2007c) and Montefiore and Loewe (1938) have been indispensable. References and translations of Talmud are from the open-access online collection at Sefaria (sefaria.org). Abbreviations for rabbinic and other ancient references are based on the *SBL Handbook of Style*. The references to Rashi, Radak, Ibn Ezra, Abarbanel, and a number of other important voices in Jewish tradition are usefully brought together in *Miqra'ot Gedolot*, and citations of these are drawn from Rosenberg's edition of the Book of the

Twelve (1986). Likewise, the volume on the Minor Prophets in the Ancient Christian Commentaries Series (Ferreiro 2003) is extremely helpful. Many of the references to early Christian engagement with these texts beyond the major commentaries cited can be found in Ferreiro's anthology. Several reference works have also been very helpful in the course of this research, in particular *The Bible in Music* (Dowling Long and Sawyer 2015), and the *Encyclopedia of the Bible and Its Reception* (de Gruyter 2009–).

Hosea, Joel, and Obadiah as Part of the Book of the Twelve

Before exploring the individual books of Hosea, Joel, and Obadiah, it is worth reflecting on an important aspect of their reception that relates to them collectively: their placement in the Book of the Twelve or the Minor Prophets.

1. The Book of the Twelve

Hosea, Joel, and Obadiah are part of a collection known as the Book of the Twelve or the Minor Prophets. Ben Sira 49:10 makes mention of 'the bones of the Twelve prophets', which suggests that by the second century BCE, a group of prophetic texts was known and identified as a collection (Goshen-Gottstein 2002). The notion of Twelve prophets would be found or alluded to in various sources in the following centuries from Josephus (*Against Apion* 1.8.3) to Augustine (*City of God* 18), the latter perhaps the earliest example of the use of the term *Minor Prophets*, a reference to the brevity of their works (Glenny 2016). In the Babylonian Talmud, the Sages suggest that Hosea and other smaller texts were brought together to avoid any of them being lost (b. B. Bat. 14b, 15a).

Conclusive evidence for the ordering of this collection, however, is another matter. In the tradition of the Hebrew Masoretic Text, the first half of the Book of the Twelve is ordered as Hosea, Joel, Amos, Obadiah, Jonah, and Micah, and it is this ordering that has generally been followed by the Jewish and Christian traditions. This ordering is also found in the Greek text from Nahal Hever known as 8HevXIIgr (ca. first century CE) and texts from Wadi Murabba'at

Hosea, Joel, and Obadiah Through the Centuries, First Edition. Bradford A. Anderson.
© 2024 John Wiley & Sons Ltd. Published 2024 by John Wiley & Sons Ltd.

(second century CE). However, there is a good deal of fluidity in the ordering of these books elsewhere in the ancient traditions. In the Greek tradition of the Septuagint (also found in 4 Ezra 1:39–40), the order of these initial books is Hosea, Amos, Micah, Joel, Obadiah, and Jonah, an order still followed by some Orthodox Christian traditions; the major Greek manuscripts follow this ordering, including Vaticanus, Sinaiticus, and Alexandrinus. Still other orderings represented in antiquity include the Ascension of Isaiah (4:22; Amos, Hosea, Micah, Joel, Nahum, Jonah, Obadiah), and the Lives of the Prophets (Hosea, Micah, Amos, Joel, Obadiah, Jonah) (see Sweeney). The Coptic tradition also presents variant orderings, including the LXX order, and the otherwise unattested Hosea, Joel, Amos, Micah, Obadiah, and Jonah (Bosson 2016). There are, then, a number of different ways in which these Twelve prophetic books were ordered and presented in antiquity.

Authorship of the Twelve is generally dealt with on a case-by-case basis in the traditions, and this is covered in the commentaries that follow. However, the authorship and collecting of these prophetic books have been noted in relation to the collection as a whole. In the Babylonian Talmud (B. Bat. 15a), it is stated that the Men of the Great Assembly recorded the prophecies of the Twelve, which would mean that these prophecies were not committed to writing until the return from the Babylonian exile (Rosenberg 1986). Indeed, Rashi figures that these prophets did not write their own messages as they were (relatively) short. Instead, it was Haggai, Zechariah, and Malachi—those prophets that are clearly later than the others—that wrote their own messages and combined these with the other shorter prophetic oracles.

Although definitive answers concerning the authorship and collection of these books remain elusive, there are nonetheless significant interpretive issues that emerge from the various ways in which the Twelve are presented, issues that have been noted at various points throughout history. While Hosea stands at the beginning of the collection in almost all known traditions, Joel and Obadiah are found in various positions, and their relationships with one another and other books in the Twelve have led to various reconstructions. In the MT, Joel is followed by Amos, which is then followed by Obadiah and Jonah. There are thematic resonances in this ordering, including the castigation of Edom in Joel 3 and Amos 9, which is then picked up as the main theme in Obadiah. These and other connections between the various books have been noted at various points throughout history (e.g., the fifteenth-century rabbi Abarbanel in *Miqra'ot Gedolot*). However, there is no clear chronological logic to this ordering. In the Greek tradition, meanwhile, Hosea is followed by Amos and Micah, and the next three books are Joel, Obadiah, and Jonah. In this case, the Book of the Twelve opens with three books that have clear historical markers in the eighth century BCE, while the next three are more difficult to situate historically. Reconstructions of the formation of the Twelve interpret these placements as intentional, positing that those who brought together and edited the collection wished to make thematic and theological connections or to highlight chronological factors in the example of the LXX ordering (see Wolff 1974a; Nogalski 1993). Indeed, recent research on the Twelve has suggested more complex redactional histories for this collection to account for thematic and linguistic connections across these books (Albertz, Nogalski, and Wöhrle 2012; Werse 2019). Whatever the case, it is clear that there are already interpretive moves being made as these Twelve prophets were brought together, and the ordering of this collection is one of the first aspects of the reception of these prophetic works (Dines 2012).

2. Textual Witnesses and Translations

The oldest Hebrew texts that witness to the Book of the Twelve are those which were found at Qumran (see Brooke 2006; Fuller 1997, 2017). There are up to ten possible scrolls containing texts from the Twelve prophets at Qumran, though these vary in size and some are fragmentary, and it is unclear as to whether all of these rolls would have contained all Twelve works (Guillaume 2007). Included in this are 4QXII[a] and 4QXII[b], which, dated to the middle of the second century BCE, seem to be the oldest extant textual witnesses to the Minor Prophets. Brooke notes that these textual witnesses point to the fact that diverse forms of the Twelve were circulating during this period: 'for what may be deemed to be the scriptural texts of the Twelve, there is as much variety as exists for several other scriptural compositions, such as Exodus, Jeremiah and the Psalms. Overall a strong case can be made on the basis of variant order alone that there was more than one literary edition of the Twelve' (Brooke 2006: 34). Even so, it seems that the textual traditions solidified relatively quickly: the second-century CE manuscript MurXII found at Wadi Murabba'at is close to the Masoretic traditions. The major witnesses to the Masoretic text followed by the critical editions of the HB include the important medieval manuscripts the Leningrad Codex, the Aleppo Codex, and the Cairo Codex (Fresch 2017).

The Greek translation of the Twelve, dated to the middle of the second century BCE, generally follows closely to the Hebrew, and 'many of the differences from the Hebrew text can be readily explained as translational adaptations or stylistic modifications' (Gelston 2010: 7). An important witness to this tradition is a text already noted above, 8HevXIIgr, a first-century CE Greek Minor Prophets Scroll from Naḥal Ḥever, which aligns quite closely with the Hebrew traditions (Tov 2003). Interestingly, in several Greek versions of the entire Old Testament, the Minor Prophets come before the Major Prophets (Vaticanus and Alexandrinus; see Glenny 2016). The Latin traditions, including the Old Latin and the Vulgate, tend to follow the Hebrew tradition of the MT rather than the Greek. The same is true of the Syriac Peshitta and the Aramaic Targum, though the Targum is not always a literal translation but is often idiomatic and at times expansively interpretive in ways that will be explored in the commentaries below. Indeed, the Aramaic Targum has played a significant role in Jewish tradition as both translation and exegesis as can be seen in its inclusion in the *Miqra'ot Gedelot* or Rabbinic Bible (see Figure 1), as well as its frequent use by major Jewish commentators, including the influential medieval interpreter Rashi.

3. Visual Reception of the Twelve

Throughout history, the Twelve prophets have been grouped together not just literarily but visually as well. Depictions of the Twelve pointing to Christ are common in Christian tradition, as the Hebrew prophets were understood as foretelling the coming of Jesus and the new dispensation which he would usher in (see Figure 2).

John Singer Sargent's late nineteenth-century portrayal of the Twelve prophets in the Boston Public Library again brings these prophetic figures together visually and offers a more modern take, envisioning the emotional turmoil of these prophets and the challenge of their prophetic vocation (Figure 3).

This collective portrayal can also be seen in several famous Christian churches. The Cathédrale Notre-Dame d'Amiens (hereafter Amiens Cathedral) has individual relief sculptures which depict the Twelve prophets in various ways on different sides of the building, and some of the Twelve are also represented in a well-known set of sculptures by the artist Aleijadinho on the Santuário do Bom Jesus de Matosinhos in Congonhas do Campo, Brazil (including Hosea, Joel, and Obadiah). While examples in the commentary will for the most part focus on individual representations of these prophets, their collective portrayal in various art forms is also a significant aspect of their reception as part of the Book of the Twelve.

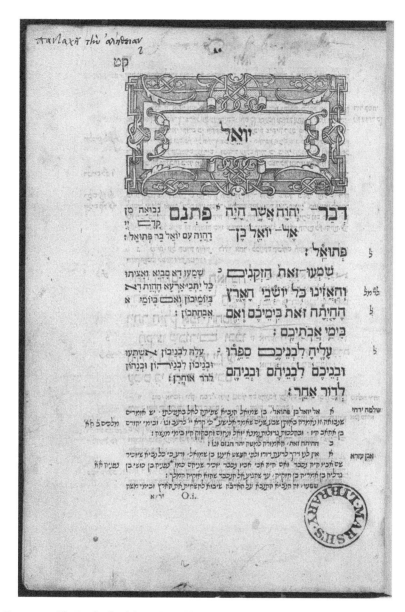

FIGURE 1   *The Book of Joel from the Rabbinic Bible with Hebrew and Aramaic text and commentaries (Geneva, 1556).*

FIGURE 2   *The Twelve Minor Prophets, pointing to Holy Family. From Histoire de l'Ancien et Nouveau Testament, par Royamount (1724).*

Used with permission from Mary Evans Picture Library.

FIGURE 3   *John Singer Sargent, Frieze of the Prophets, West Wall, Zephaniah, Joel, Obadiah, and Hosea; Boston Public Library (1890–1895).*

Used with permission from Sheryl Lanzel/Boston Public Library.

Hosea: Introduction and Overview

Because of its position at the beginning of the Book of the Twelve, and the command given to the prophet to take an unfaithful wife, Hosea is probably the most well known of the Minor Prophets. This introduction offers a broad overview of the reception of Hosea, including (1) a brief history of the interpretation of the book, including key trajectories in how it has been read and understood; (2) significant historical and literary issues in the book's interpretation; (3) important theological, thematic, and rhetorical issues that have shaped the use and impact of the book; and (4) religious, social, and cultural reception of the prophet and the book. These issues are explored further throughout the commentary.

There is diversity regarding the way in which the text of Hosea is divided in the manuscripts and traditions (see Gruber). For modern readers, this is most evident in the versification as reflected in English translations and Hebrew traditions. The table below outlines these differences—the present work follows the versification of English translations.

English versification	Hebrew versification
1:10–11	2:1–2
2:1–23	2:3–25
11:12	12:1
12:1–14	12:2–15
13:16	14:1
14:1–9	14:2–10

Hosea, Joel, and Obadiah Through the Centuries, First Edition. Bradford A. Anderson.
© 2024 John Wiley & Sons Ltd. Published 2024 by John Wiley & Sons Ltd.

A Brief History of Interpretation

The earliest textual witnesses to Hosea are found in the Dead Sea Scrolls, though these tend to be smaller sections and fragments of the book (Pajunen 2021). More insight into the early reception of Hosea can be found in the ancient versions and translations (Glenny 2021). The Greek LXX offers a translation that is relatively close to the Hebrew found in the MT even if it does have to account for the complexity of the Hebrew, which leads to some variation. Other versions—the Syriac Peshitta and Latin Vulgate in particular—also offer translations that suggest access to a Hebrew text which is quite close to the MT (see Macintosh). The Aramaic Targum, meanwhile, is an outlier. It offers a much more loose and expansive 'translation'; this is seen from the very beginning of the book, where the wife and children are removed from the text. Instead, a reading is offered which focuses solely on the issues of national infidelity that underpin Hosea's message, without any mention of the biographical aspects that are present in the Hebrew traditions.

In early and medieval rabbinic interpretation, Hosea is most often taken up in relation to halakhic matters, theological concerns, or as a proof text (see b. Pesaḥ.; Rashi; cf. Macintosh 2001). The most extended discussion of Hosea in early rabbinic literature is found in the Babylonian Talmud, tractate Pesaḥim (b. Pesaḥ). Here, and in other rabbinic texts, Hosea is discussed in relation to thematic and theological concerns, including questions of repentance and return, idolatry, and divine love (cf. PesK). In these cases, the special place of Israel and its elect status often take precedence in interpretive endeavors. Elsewhere in rabbinic literature, much is made of Hosea's references to other parts of the story of Israel (Jacob, the exodus, the wilderness), and so intertextual associations are common (Gen. Rab.). With the turn toward *peshat* and the plain sense of the text, medieval Jewish commentators such as Rashi, Ibn Ezra, and Radak began to focus on linguistic and historical issues, alongside engagement with rabbinic tradition. Within this, there is considerable diversity in how Jewish interpreters would understand Hosea's marriage with both literal and figurative approaches put forward (see commentary at Hos. 1:2).

Hosea was very influential in early Christianity, in part because the book is quoted by several New Testament writers. In the Gospels, Matt. 2:15 draws on Hos. 11:1 ('out of Egypt I have called my son'), Matt. 9:13 uses Hos. 6:7 ('I desire mercy and not sacrifice'), and Luke 23:30 picks up Hos. 10:8. In Rom. 9:25–26, Paul brings together two citations from Hosea—2:23 and 1:10—in his programmatic statement on Israel and the identity of the chosen people. Meanwhile, 1 Cor. 15:55, drawing on the LXX, employs Hosea's iconic statement from 13:14 regarding the sting of death and the victory of the grave.

A number of church fathers offered extensive commentaries on Hosea with notable contributions from Jerome, Cyril of Alexandria, Theodore of Mopsuestia, and Julian of Eclanum, among others. In line with much commentary from this era, the material on Hosea is a mixture of historical and figurative readings. For example, some saw reflected in Hosea's actions the sanctifying work of Christ (Irenaeus) or in Gomer a prefiguring of the woman who anointed Jesus's feet (Augustine). Nevertheless, there are cases where the plain sense is given consideration (Theodore of Mopsuestia), and a good deal of attention is given to the relationship of Hosea and Gomer and how this might be understood, both spiritually and morally. In the medieval era, Aquinas's engagement with Hosea in the *Summa Theologica* tends to focus primarily on moral matters such as what the book says about marriage and infidelity, though he, too, discusses the relationship of Hosea and Gomer, concluding that Gomer is a concubine rather than a wife. The medieval collection found in the *Glossa Ordinaria* traces various other approaches to this question common in this era, many of which draw on and extend readings put forward by the church fathers.

Moving to the Reformation period in the Christian tradition, we find extensive engagement with Hosea in the work of both Martin Luther and John Calvin. As is notable in his other commentaries, Luther does address the plain sense of Hosea, contextualizing the prophet and his message in the northern kingdom of Israel. However, Luther's reading of this text is also heavily Christological, laden with references to the contemporary Catholic Church, and indicates that he also struggled with the implications of God calling Hosea to marry an unfaithful woman; in the end, he argues that it must be understood figuratively. Calvin offers sustained reflection on the historical context of Hosea, along with close readings and philological comments. He, too, wrestles with the moral implications of Hosea's call, particularly the disrepute it would bring on one who was a teacher. Calvin concludes that Hosea is playing a part, taking on a character, for the benefit of Israel. Nevertheless, both Luther and Calvin draw out the tension of judgment and divine love that runs throughout the book—though, not surprisingly, their sympathies lie with God and the prophet, rather than the woman and children. In the end, both of these interpreters—and indeed most from this era—understand the book as pointing to God's gracious love and the need for humanity to respond to this love with repentance and sincerity.

The historical and philological issues highlighted by Jewish interpreters such as Radak and Christian exegetes including Calvin would take root in the modern period. Historical-critical work on Hosea would focus on a number of issues, including possible redactional layers in the book, Hosea's relationship to other traditions in the HB (e.g., Jacob and the wilderness traditions), the geographical and cultural setting of the book in the northern kingdom, and the influence of other religious traditions in this context, notably Canaanite religion and fertility cults (Rudolph 1966; Wolff; Andersen and Freedman; see discussions in Kelle 2009). More recently, theoretical and ideological reflection on the book has focused on questions of gender representation and the book's portrayal of its characters, as well as its use of metaphor (Weems 1989; Yee 1996; Baumann 2003; Moughtin-Mumby 2008). Indeed, Hosea has been front and center in the discourse questioning the ideologies of the prophetic material (Sherwood 1996; O'Brien 2008).

Historical and Literary Issues in Reading Hosea

Because of the various historical markers that are present in Hosea—including the mention of several kings and various geographical references—Hosea has long been understood to have been a prophet in the eighth century BCE and situated in the northern kingdom of Israel. These historical markers have been observed from antiquity, as readers have commented on Hosea's historical context and setting (b. Pesah.; Theodore of Mopsuestia). Commentators from the church father Jerome, to the medieval Jewish interpreter Radak, to the Reformer John Calvin would offer extensive reflections on historical matters in the text—and while they disagree on many details and historical referents, they nevertheless agree on the prophet and his message fitting within the historical milieu of the eighth century BCE in Israel. Indeed, the eighth century was a turbulent one in the northern kingdom—politically and religiously (Davies 1992). Thus, palace intrigue, political alliances with foreign neighbors, and Israel's relationship with Canaanite religious traditions have all played a central role in historical reflections and reconstructions.

Historical concerns would take on further significance in the early modern period as questions concerning the unity of the book as well as the implications of its northern provenance would take center stage. Several centuries of such critical examination have led to broad agreement that the book of Hosea had a lengthy redactional history with Judean, southern influence (see, e.g., Wellhausen; Buss 1969; Jeremias 1983; Emmerson 1984). A common suggestion is that Hosea's prophecies initially took shape in the northern kingdom and were taken south to Judah after the fall of the northern kingdom in 721 BCE, where editing began to take place (Willi-Plein 1971). Some have recently argued that the book as a whole should be understood as a later (Judean or Persian-era) creation (Trotter 2001; Rudnig-Zelt 2006; Bos 2013). Ben Zvi offers one such reading, suggesting that the book was composed in the post-exilic period for a Persian-era literati, and the prophet is a 'literary and ideological character that lives within the world of the book' (2005: 6). However, many modern commentators still hold that the book is related in some way to a historical prophetic figure based in the eighth century BCE even if some assign more (Andersen and Freedman; Macintosh) or less (Yee 1996) of the book to the historical prophet. It is also worth noting the frequent references in the book to other parts of Israel's story (Jacob, exodus, wilderness). This feature has not only played a role in the understanding of how the book itself took shape but has also ensured that Hosea has been an important element in reconstructions of the formation of other parts of the Hebrew Bible, including the Torah.

Along with the issue of authorship and redaction, other literary issues relevant to Hosea include the structure of the book, its poetry, and the nature of the Hebrew that is found in the text. In terms of structure, readers have long noted chapters 1–3 as distinct from chapters 4–14 (see Jerome), in part because of the biographical material in the early chapters. While diverse suggestions abound, one common approach is to see the structure of the book as consisting of three main sections: chapters 1–3, 4–11, and 12–14 (Ben Zvi 2005; Yee 1996). In spite of the many points of disjuncture that readers find in Hosea, there are also cross-references that stitch the book together and give it a sense of coherence as a whole in its final form (Landy).

The poetry that permeates the book has also received attention in recent years. While consisting primarily of prophetic oracles, the poetic form of the material means that issues such as wordplay and rhetoric are important to consider (see, e.g., Lundbom 1979; Morris 1996). The fact that much of the book is addressed to Israel, its kings, and princes has led some to suggest that the poetry has a performance-like quality to it—almost bardic in nature (Landy). Beyond the form that it takes, the Hebrew of Hosea is notoriously difficult, a point that has been noted throughout history (Jerome; Radak; Luther). With the rise of critical biblical studies, it came to be assumed that the text was corrupt and in need of emendation (Wellhausen; Harper). In the twentieth century, scholars began to suggest that the book might reflect a northern dialect of Hebrew as opposed to being hopelessly corrupt (Mays 1969; Macintosh; Yoo 1999).

Theological, Thematic, and Rhetorical Issues in Interpreting Hosea

A number of themes and issues have been noted as central to the book of Hosea down through the centuries. Many of these stem from the marriage imagery found in chapters 1–3.

From antiquity, readers have struggled with how to understand the call for Hosea to take an unfaithful wife with both literal and figurative approaches common in Jewish and Christian traditions (Bitter 1975). The Talmud (b. Pesaḥ.) and Targum exemplify distinct approaches—the Talmud suggesting that the command given to Hosea should be taken at face value and the Targum understanding it as figurative and removing the woman (and children) from the text altogether. These same interpretive trajectories are also found in the Christian tradition and indeed have been represented throughout history. (For a fuller discussion of how the marriage has been interpreted, see the commentary on Hos. 1:2 and 3:1.)

How, though, should the figurative elements of the book be understood? What is the significance of Hosea's marriage, and how does this relate to the rest of the book? A common understanding in antiquity was that Hosea's message was broadly concerned with idolatry and religious infidelity on the part of the Israelites. Within the traditions of Judaism and Christianity, the book and its figurative elements have been understood as a reflection on repentance and return, as well as divine love and fidelity. As such, the call to return to YHWH is an invitation to return to a commitment to God and his ways, including following Torah (Targum). Over time, this religious framing has been refined and revisited. One such interpretation—which became influential in the twentieth century—is that Hosea's polemic is directed at Canaanite religious traditions and the Baal fertility cult in particular (Wolff; Mays). In this reading, Gomer's promiscuity not only reflects religious infidelity but also points to actual sexual practices that were part of Canaanite fertility rites. While the sexual dimensions of this interpretation have fallen out of favor, the assumption that Hosea is critiquing Israelite engagement in Canaanite traditions, or syncretistic practices that combine Baal and YHWH worship, has remained popular (Andersen and Freedman; Macintosh). However, in recent decades, commentators have given increased attention to the metaphorical language and imagery in the book. In doing so, the dominant 'religious' and cultic framing of Hosea's critique has been challenged. Thus, readers have suggested that socioeconomic (Keefe 2001) or political (Kelle 2005) issues should be given more consideration as being at the heart of Hosea's message even if religious apostasy may also have been in view.

In spite of these varied interpretations of the figurative aspects of the book, the use of the marriage as a means of communicating Israel's infidelity was not seen as problematic for much of history. Feminist scholars have brought fresh perspective to this question in recent decades, interrogating Hosea in relation to issues of gender and sexuality (Weems 1989; Yee 1992; Sherwood 1996; Adler 1998; Wacker 2012). Feminist scholarship has been an important development in biblical interpretation and one of the most impactful aspects of the reception of the Bible over the past half century. Nowhere has this been clearer than in the reception of Hosea (Brenner 1995).

One key issue that feminist readers have noted is that the book of Hosea is unequivocally male-centered. In the analogy with Israel, the male figure is equated with God, while the woman is equated with the sinful people. The book also critiques the woman's sexuality, while leaving the man's sexuality uninterrogated—a significant double standard. Yee frames the issue in this way: 'if Hosea had been a woman, commanded to marry a promiscuous man, what form would *her* prophecy have taken? In what would *her* tragedy consist? What kinds of personal grief, disappointments, or sorrows would *she* experience?' (1996: 220). Another issue noted by feminist readers is that Gomer has little agency and no voice in the text (Wacker 2012). God or the husband is always speaking on her behalf (Sherwood 1996). Further, as the text unfolds, we encounter threats of violence and shaming of the woman, scenes that are all too common for many women. Indeed, the account in Hosea 1–3 correlates quite closely with patterns of abusers: emotional and verbal abuse, isolation, threats, and blaming are followed by a honeymoon period where all is forgiven (Graetz 1995; O'Brien 2008). For some, the reconciliation comes too soon with too little thought for the woman (Weems 1989).

In spite of these recurring themes, critiques of Hosea from feminist perspectives are diverse and wide-ranging (for discussion and critique of various feminist readings, see Keefe 2001; Sherwood 1996). One approach highlights the problematic nature of the text while attempting to hold on to its place as Scripture (Weems 1989; Yee 1996). Such readings approve of the underlying message of divine love and repentance but criticize the vehicle (i.e., the marriage metaphor) as inappropriate. Other feminist readings have focused on the interrelationship of the text and its reception. Thus, one interpretive stream suggests that the marriage and sexual imagery of Hosea have been misconstrued because of social and theological biases; closer examination reveals that the prophet is ultimately offering a critique of social, economic, and political issues, but the patriarchal nature of the text's interpreters has kept the focus on sexual matters (Keefe 2001; Yee 2001). A related approach focuses on the fact that men were likely the primary intended hearers of this text—in which case they were to identify themselves with the unfaithful woman (Winn Leith 1989). This 'feminizing' of the male audience is often missed in the interpretive traditions. 'To call the people of God "woman", and even more disturbingly "promiscuous woman", is, in a patriarchal context, to give offence. … In resisting identification with the woman, androcentric commentators support the ideology of the text but resist its symbolic roles' (Sherwood 1996: 263–64). One further approach is worth noting as it offers a feminist reading but from a very different perspective. Wacker and others see in Gomer a subversive, powerful figure, who may even be a symbol of (repressed) goddess worship in ancient Israel (Balz-Cochois 1982; Wacker 1996). These readings try to liberate the woman in the text from traditional interpretations, while assigning some agency and power to the character, drawing on ANE traditions.

There are, then, a variety of ways in which the message of Hosea's marriage has been understood through the years. What has long been understood as a text focusing on divine love and an invitation to repentance and return in the traditions of Judaism and Christianity, or as a critique or religious syncretism with Canaanite fertility rituals in modern scholarship, is an increasingly difficult and problematic text for contemporary readers who are grappling with the rhetoric of the text and the portrayal of both God and the human characters in its pages.

Liturgical and Cultural Engagement with Hosea

Beyond the world of commentary and the history of interpretation, Hosea has played an important role in religious traditions, as well as in broader social and cultural contexts.

Religious and Liturgical Traditions

Hosea has long been a significant prophet in Jewish liturgical practices. One might first note that Hos. 2:19–20 is one of the prayers recited while putting on *tefillin*, reiterating the special relationship between Israel and God. The book also features as a *haftarah* reading in several places: Hos. 2:1–22 is the *haftarah* for *Bemidbar* (Numbers 1–4); Hos. 12:13–14:10 is the paired reading for the Jacob cycle in Genesis 28–32 (in the Ashkenazic rite; 11:7–12:12 in Sephardic tradition); and Hos. 14:2–10 is one of the readings for *Shabbat Shuva*, the Sabbath preceding Yom Kippur, a service known for encouraging repentance. Along with intertextual resonances with the stories of Jacob and the wilderness, these liturgical settings focus on repentance and return, themes that, as noted above, have been common in the religious appropriation of Hosea through the centuries.

Hosea also has a long and varied history in Christianity, beginning with usage in the New Testament (Matt. 2:15, Rom. 9:25–26, Rev. 6:16, among others). Hosea also appears in Christian worship in both the Revised Common

Lectionary (uses include Hos. 1:2–10; 2:14–20; 5:15–6:6; and 11:1–11) and the Catholic lectionary (Sunday readings include Hos. 2:16b, 17b, 21–22; 6:3–6; 11:1, 3–4, 8c–9). The focus of the book on God's passionate love for his people has meant that Hosea has been popular in preaching and exhortation about these issues. A number of these liturgical and homiletical uses are explored further in the commentary that follows.

Hosea is not mentioned in the Qur'an, but the book is noted as being written by one of the prophets by some scholars in Islamic tradition (Abū Nasr Mutahhar b. Tahir al Maqadisi, 10th century CE; see Wheeler 2021). The prophet is also invoked in some Muslim commentary and apologetic writing (see commentary at 9:6 and 13:5).

Visual Representations

As is the case with other Hebrew prophets, the depictions of Hosea are varied in visual art, including images that depict the prophet with others from the Twelve, as well as those that present the prophet in light of aspects related to the message of the book. Notable representations of Hosea among the prophets include Raphael's sixteenth-century image of Hosea and Jonah (1510), where the prophet holds and points to a scroll containing his message, a common iconographic trope in depictions of the prophets (Figure 4).

Images that capture elements of Hosea's message include Duccio di Buoninsegna's portrayal (1311) of Hosea carrying a scroll with the text from the book which is quoted in Matt. 2:15, 'Out of Egypt I called my son'. As discussed in the commentary below (Hos. 11:1), this text was particularly popular among Christian exegetes when discussing Hosea, because of its use in Matthew's Gospel, and the typological connection of the Egypt traditions with the story of Jesus and the holy family. Amiens Cathedral, meanwhile, has several portrayals of Hosea, each of which has him alongside the woman from the text, highlighting narrative and biographical elements in the book (see Figure 5). Numerous woodcarvings and other artistic depictions also focus on Hosea and his family (see commentary on chapter 1).

As noted above (Figure 3), John Singer Sargent's depiction of the Twelve in the Boston Public Library portrays Hosea in a panel alongside Zechariah, Joel, and Obadiah. Rather than the triumphal and text-based portrayals of earlier eras, Singer Sargent offers a more introspective (and even menacing) Hosea. Here the prophet is clothed in white, perhaps signifying his purity (in opposition to Israel's unfaithfulness) and signaling the call for fidelity found throughout his book.

FIGURE 4   Raphael, The Prophets Hosea and Jonah (1510).
National Gallery of Art.

FIGURE 5   Hosea and Gomer, Amiens Cathedral, France.
Used with permission from Stuart Whatling.

Literature, Film, and Music

Hosea has fared better than many of the Minor Prophets in popular culture—again owing much to the marriage relationship, which has proven to be a fruitful source for creative endeavors. Hosea marrying a woman of ill repute is a trope that has been picked up by many important writers (explicitly and implicitly) from Shakespeare to William Blake to Thomas Hardy (Krier 2016). More recently, Hosea's marriage to Gomer is invoked in Min Jin Lee's 2017 novel *Pachinko*, where a young Protestant pastor in Korea draws inspiration from Hosea and takes a young pregnant woman as his wife.

Popular Christian media has also drawn on the story of Hosea (see McEntire 2021). Some retellings in literature and film attempt to situate the story of Hosea in its ancient historical context even if in a fictionalized form. Larry Christenson's *Hosea: A Novel* (2013) offers one such example, retelling the story of Hosea and Gomer and contextualizing it in the northern kingdom of Israel. Other Christian retellings make use of the story by resituating the story of Hosea and Gomer in more contemporary contexts. A popular fictional retelling of the story in this vein is found in Francine Rivers's *Redeeming Love* (1997). (These and other examples are discussed further in the commentary on Hosea 1.)

Stage productions have also drawn from and retold the story of Hosea. A prophetic character named Hosea plays a role in the 16th-century morality play *A Looking Glass for London and England*, and Hosea is also invoked in significant ways in Marc Connelly's play *Green Pastures* (1930), which was subsequently adapted for film (1936). Connelly's play was based on Roark Bradford's 1928 collection of stories, which envisioned the Old Testament from the perspective of a young Black girl from New Orleans. In Connelly's play, all of the characters, including God, are played by African-Americans from the American South. Exploring various stories from the Old Testament, the play offers a picture of both God and his people developing over time and learning from one another. The prophet Hosea plays a key role in this: over time the people come to worship the 'God of Hosea', who is a God of mercy, rather than a God of vengeance, such as the God of Moses. In this retelling, Hosea's message of God's love and mercy is seen as a new dispensation and signals a change in development in the portrayal of God within the Old Testament itself.

Hosea is also well represented in music. Bach's 1723 cantata 'Was soll ich aus dir machen' ('What Shall I Make of you, Ephraim?') draws on Hos. 11:8, while David Harris's 1976 choral piece is entitled 'Come Let Us Return to the Lord', drawing inspiration from Hos. 6:1 (see Dowling Long and Sawyer 2015). These settings of Hosea focus on larger themes within the book, rather than the prophetic character of Hosea: Bach's cantata draws on the text to discuss the sinfulness and waywardness of humanity, while Harris's choral work finds inspiration in the book's themes of repentance and return. Meanwhile, contemporary Christian songwriters have also found the prophet's story to be generative. Both Michael Card's 'The Song of Gomer' (1992) and Andrew Peterson's 'Hosea' (2008) offer accounts of the marriage relationship from Gomer's perspective, highlighting Hosea's love and patience. In retelling the story of the married couple, both of these contemporary songs give voice to Gomer, who offers a sense of wonder at Hosea's (and God's) fidelity in spite of her unfaithfulness.

Hosea 1

The first three chapters are the most well-known parts of Hosea and are linked together by the account of the prophet and his family. From antiquity, readers have tended to group chapters 1–3 as a separate unit within the book (Jerome; cf. Rudolph 1966). Helpful entrees into the vast reception of Hosea 1–3 can be found in Rowley (1956), Sherwood (1996), Macintosh, and Kelle (2009).

In Hosea 1, we are introduced to the prophet, his family, and the symbolic issues related to the command given to Hosea. While Hosea 1 has nine verses in the Hebrew traditions, most English translations end the chapter after eleven verses (see discussion in Andersen and Freedman). This commentary follows the English ordering, as outlined in the Introduction and Overview to Hosea (e.g., Eng. 1:10 = Heb. 2:1).

1:1a

The book of Hosea begins by noting that the 'word of the LORD' came to the prophet. The centuries-long discussion of this prophetic work begins with this initial clause: To what does this 'word of the LORD' refer? The fourth–fifth-century church father Theodore of Mopsuestia takes this divine word as indicative of divine force, such as seen in Ps. 33:6. His contemporary Jerome, meanwhile, begins his commentary with a Christological connection: 'The word of the Lord (which was in the beginning with God the Father, and the Word was God)' (151). For others, the divine origin of this word is a reminder that

Hosea, Joel, and Obadiah Through the Centuries, First Edition. Bradford A. Anderson.
© 2024 John Wiley & Sons Ltd. Published 2024 by John Wiley & Sons Ltd.

this message comes from God rather than humanity; the nineteenth-century English clergyman and Oxford professor E. B. Pusey notes 'that word came to [Hosea]; it existed then before, in the mind of God. It was first God's, then it became the Prophet's' (19). In modern scholarship, it has been pointed out that the superscription with which the book begins resembles other prophetic texts (Joel 1:1; Mic. 1:1; Zeph. 1:1). This similarity of form has led to speculation that a school or tradition—perhaps Deuteronomistic—might be responsible for editing these prophetic works (Wolff; Andersen and Freedman).

The initial 'v' of the Latin term for 'word', *Verbum*, figures prominently in illuminated medieval manuscripts. In an exquisite example from the thirteenth-century Marquette Bible, the prophet and his wife are placed within the initial 'v' with gold leaf in the background. Here, the prophet is holding a codex rather than a scroll (see Figure 6).

The name 'Hosea' (Heb.: *hoshea*) comes from the root word meaning 'salvation' and is the same name originally assigned to Joshua in Num. 13:8, 16 (see also 1 Chron. 27:20). The lexical similarities that Hosea shares with the names Joshua and Jesus have been a launching point for reflection on possible

FIGURE 6   *Initial V: Hosea with Gomer, Marquette Bible, ca. 1270.*
Courtesy of Getty's Open Content Program.

connections: the eighteenth-century Baptist John Gill, for example, comments that Hosea's name 'is the same with Joshua and Jesus, and signifies a saviour; he was in some things a type of Christ the Saviour'.

The prophet is identified as the son of Beeri. In rabbinic tradition, this Beeri was equated with Beerah, the leader of the Reubenites taken to Assyria by Tiglath-Pileser (1 Chron. 5:6). The Sages believed that if in Scripture a father was noted alongside a prophet, the father was also a prophet. In this case, Hosea's father was thought to have prophesied just two verses, Isa. 8:19–20; these verses were added to the book of Isaiah as they were not enough to stand on their own. In this reading, Beeri's words in Isaiah speak of the exiles from the north, who were taken into exile by the Assyrians (PesK; Lev. Rab. 6:6; cf. Rosenberg). The name Beeri is related to the Hebrew term for 'well' or 'spring'. Pusey comments that the name of Hosea's father, Beeri, is appropriate as 'from the fountain of life, Hosea drew the living waters, which he poured out to the people' (19).

The book gives no specific geographical location for Hosea even if the book as a whole seems to be largely focused on the northern kingdom. Genesis Rabbah, a midrash on Genesis from the Talmudic era, states that Hosea came from the tribe of Reuben (84), while in the *Lives of the Prophets*, an early collection of Jewish legends, he is said to come from the northern tribe of Isaachar, specifically Belemoth, an otherwise unknown location, where he was also said to be buried (Hare 1985). Other traditions state that Hosea died in Babylon but was returned in order to be buried in Safed (Ginzberg 1909: 4.261).

1:1b

The book situates Hosea during the reigns of the Judean kings Uzziah, Jotham, Ahaz, and Hezekiah, as well as that of Jeroboam II (son of Joash) in the northern kingdom of Israel. This list of kings has caused some confusion, and several issues have vexed readers.

First, how do these kings relate to the context and length of Hosea's ministry? Jerome offers a full history of the kings that are noted and deduces that these rulers would situate Hosea's ministry both before and after the fall of the northern kingdom: Hosea 'announced it when it was to come and lamented it when it befell, and disclosed its meaning for Judah's correction when it was past' (152; cf. Cyril of Alexandria). Theodore of Mopsuestia says that the mention of these different kings suggests Hosea 'did not compose the book in one exercise' (39–40) but received revelation at various times just as David composed psalms at different times. Rashi draws on the Talmud to explain that Hosea outlived four kings of Judah, which proves the proverb 'Woe is to authority, for it buries its holders' (cf. b. Pesaḥ. 87b).

John Calvin tallies up the years of the kings and figures that Hosea must have prophesied for over sixty years, perhaps over seventy; John Gill does similar math and concludes that the years of his service may have reached eighty. These extreme lengths of time were not problematic for these commentators; rather, they point to the invigorating power of God and the exceptional patience of Hosea. Those modern commentators who assume that Hosea was a historical figure are generally less convinced of the prophet's longevity with some debate as to whether his career came to an end before or after the fall of the northern kingdom in 722/1 BCE (Blenkinsopp 1996; Macintosh). Others have argued that there is very little of historical value of the prophet that can be reconstructed from the ancient text as the book as a whole is likely a later creation (Ben Zvi 2005).

A second question raised by readers down through the centuries has been why only Jeroboam II is mentioned among the kings in Israel; not only was he an 'ungodly' king, but other rulers who came after him seemed to be a better fit within the time frame of Hosea's ministry based on the Judean kings that are mentioned (Ben Zvi 2005). According to the Babylonian Talmud, Jeroboam was listed along with the more righteous kings of Judah because when Amaziah, the priest of Bethel, made accusations against Amos (Amos 7:10–11), the Sages say that Jeroboam did not believe the false report (b. Pesaḥ. 87b). Other commentators understand the reference to Jeroboam, but not his successors in the north, as evidence that the prophet is speaking a hard truth at a time of wealth and strength in Israel under Jeroboam (Luther; Calvin; Pusey). The fact that the kings of Judah are mentioned first has been a key element in the suggestion that this superscription came at a later time (Harper). While the northern kingdom is most often in view, aspects of the book have a distinctly pro-Judean tenor (Emmerson 1984).

1:2

Verse 2 commences by noting that 'when the LORD first spoke through Hosea …' The Hebrew can be rendered in various ways. Some rabbis took this to mean that Hosea was the first of the written prophets to receive prophecy, followed chronologically by Isaiah, Amos, and Micah (b. Pesaḥ. 87a; Gen. Rab. 82:11). However, Rashi notes that the plain meaning of the verse seems to be that this refers to the beginning of God speaking to Hosea.

God commands Hosea to 'take' (*laqah*) a wife of harlotry (*zenunim*) and to have children of harlotry. This unlikely directive has been understood in wide-ranging ways through the centuries as readers have tried to make sense of such a command coming from God. To begin with, the Hebrew term used to describe Hosea's future wife, *zenunim*, has been translated in various ways. The LXX renders this with the root *porneia*, the Peshitta offers 'prostitution', while the Vulgate uses the term *fornicationum*. More recent translations describe the woman with terms such as *harlotry* (RSV; NASB), *whoredom* (KJV; NRSV), *promiscuity* (NIV), *unfaithful* (GNT), and *prostitution* (NLT; AMP). And yet, contrary to popular opinion, the text does not refer to Gomer as a *zonah*, the technical term for a prostitute; rather, her promiscuity signals sexual activity beyond the marriage relationship (Wacker 2012). This was noted as far back as Isho'dad of Merv, the ninth-century bishop and theologian of the Eastern Church, who commented that the wife-to-be is not referred to as a 'whore' but as one who gives herself to whoredom, which he takes to mean 'consorts with men and idols' (Ferreiro).

Similar issues emerge in attempts to understand what it means for Hosea to have 'children of harlotry'. Jerome comments that the term can mean either that Hosea took in the woman's previous children born out of promiscuity or that he would have children with the woman who would nonetheless carry a label similar to their mother. Isho'dad understands this as indicating that the children will follow in the mother's footsteps. Pusey notes that the children, even though Hosea's, share the mother's description because in some way sin is passed down from generation to generation (cf. discussion in Davies 1992).

The text connects the command given to Hosea with the fact that 'the land commits great whoredom by forsaking the LORD'. It is clear that there is a symbolic element to the directive given to Hosea; however, what is the relationship between the command given to the prophet and the figurative explanation that God gives to him?

In parts of Jewish tradition, the command to take a wife was understood as a literal injunction given to Hosea to illustrate Israel's unfaithfulness (b. Pesaḥ. 87a; Rashi). As the nineteenth-century rabbi known as the Malbim notes, God at other times commands his servants to perform unusual acts such as the actions of Ezekiel, and so this is not out of the ordinary (see *Miqra'ot Gedolot*). In the Talmud, this divine command has a controversial backstory. God had commanded Hosea to go and preach to the people, but Hosea refused because the people had been unfaithful, and he told God to take another people as his own. Because Hosea refuses to deliver this message, and because God is unwilling to forsake his people, he commands Hosea to take an unfaithful spouse, just as God himself has done (b. Pesaḥ. 87a). Conversely, in the Targum, this entire narrative frame is absent—the marriage, woman, and children are removed altogether in the Targum, and Hosea is instructed to teach the unfaithful people to turn back to God. Still others, including the influential medieval Jewish commentators Ibn Ezra and Radak, suggest that this is a prophetic vision and that Hosea receives this command only in a dream (cf. Maimonides).

There were similar interpretive impulses at work in early Christianity. Cyril of Alexandria, the fourth–fifth-century church leader and theologian, pushes back against those (such as Origen) who want to only read these verses figuratively and who claim that a prophet would never act in such a manner. Cyril instead praises Hosea's obedience: 'He takes Gomer, not acting out of lustful passion, but discharging a task of obedience and service' (45; cf. Julian of Eclanum). A common interpretive move in early Christianity was to understand the marriage as literal, while also highlighting the figurative nature of the relationship—though, not surprisingly, these readings often move beyond Israel's infidelity to explore various Christocentric and ecclesiological dimensions. Irenaeus, the second-century theologian and bishop of Lyon, offers a symbolic reading regarding the church which takes the marriage at face value: just as the woman was made holy through her marriage to the prophet, so the church is made holy through union with the Son (*Against Heresies* 4.20.12; Ferreiro). Theodore of Mopsuestia views the marriage as not only a teaching opportunity for Hosea but an example of divine condescension as God has chosen to work through undeserving people. Jerome sees in this story a prefiguration of Jesus's engagement with sinful women, including the one who washed his feet, as well as the relationship between Jesus and the church. In the medieval period, the question of Hosea's marriage would remain a lively one as seen in the collection known as the *Glossa Ordinaria*, where diverse understandings of the relationship are noted.

For these readers, Hosea's union did lead to considerable ethical and moral reflection regarding husband and wife. Several church fathers would go to great lengths to argue that the woman does not defile the prophet by association; rather, the prophet is to be applauded for 'converting the prostitute to chastity' (Jerome: 153). On the other end of the spectrum, Tertullian, the second–third-century author from Carthage, uses Hosea's marriage to a 'base prostitute' as part of a catalog that indicates why Jesus, and the new dispensation that he inaugurated, is a better moral guide for discipleship than is the Old Testament and its sordid stories (*On Modesty*). Thomas Aquinas, meanwhile, uses Hosea as part of the larger discourse on natural law in his magisterial *Summa Theologica*. As a response to those who say that Hosea is an example that natural law can be changed—as the prophet took a wife of fornications thereby being party to adultery—Aquinas answers that what is commanded by God is, by definition, right and natural (*ST I-II*, q. 94, a. 5).

The literal understanding of the marriage became unfashionable in Christianity in the Reformation period. The German reformer Martin Luther, for example, argues that Hosea's wife did not actually act as a harlot; rather, this is stagecraft, and she allows these descriptors for herself and her children for the sake of Hosea's message. Calvin explicitly pushes back against Jerome and Aquinas and suggests (like some Jewish forebears) that this was a vision, and Hosea assumed a character when going before the people to relay the message. The eighteenth-century Baptist John Gill notes that Hosea is commanded to take 'a wife of whoredoms … a notorious strumpet'; however, if this were to have actually happened, it would look like 'countenancing whoredom', while also being 'very dishonourable to the prophet'. Gill thus prefers to understand this as a parable, following the Targum.

Over time, the consensus would return to favoring a literal understanding of the marriage and to biographical reconstructions of Hosea and his family. In the nineteenth century, Pusey notes the plural form of the term *zenunim*, which points to the ongoing nature of the woman's unfaithful activity: 'She must … have been repeatedly guilty of that sin, perhaps as an idolatress, thinking of it to be in honour of their foul gods' (20). We see here the notion that Gomer might in some way be connected to cultic or ritual prostitution, an idea that would become popular in the twentieth century (Mays). Readers also became interested in the question of *when* Hosea became aware of his wife's misdeeds: Did he know beforehand, or was her unfaithfulness only made plain after the union had been joined? The nineteenth-century German scholar Julius Wellhausen suggested that Hosea came to his calling through his marriage, not knowing of her unfaithfulness before the union, an idea that would be followed by several others (Paton 1896; Harper; Andersen and Freedman; Macintosh). However, in his extended study on the marriage, the twentieth-century English scholar H. H. Rowley (1956) comes to the conclusion that the unfaithfulness was prior to the marriage, which strengthened the message to Israel concerning God's fidelity to an unfaithful people: both God and Hosea knew what they were getting themselves into.

Scholars in the early twentieth century began to focus on identifying the infidelity of 'the land' referred to in the second half of verse 2. A common interpretation was that this national 'whoredom' related in some way to a sexualized Baal cult in eighth-century Israel (May 1932) and that Gomer herself may have been a cultic prostitute (Mays) or was in some way engaged in a sexualized Baal fertility cult (von Rad 1968; Wolff). In this interpretation, Gomer's infidelity is both religious and sexual as is the broader unfaithfulness of Israel as a whole. This connection of the critique found in Hosea with a Canaanite Baal cult would hold sway for much of the twentieth century even if, over time, scholars became less sure of how confidently they could comment on the biographical dimensions of Hosea and his marriage (Andersen and Freedman; Jeremias 1983) or the sexual dimensions of religious activity in ancient Israel (Bird 1989; Gruber). Indeed, Keefe and others have argued that the assumption that a sexualized fertility cult is at the root of Hosea's concerns can be 'traced to the biases of a theological agenda within which Canaanite religion is gendered as the seductive and degenerate "other" against which biblical religion defines itself' (2001: 11; cf. Anderson 2021).

Literary, rhetorical, and ideological concerns would take center stage in the latter parts of the twentieth and early twenty-first centuries. Studies began focusing on rhetorical elements of the text, eschewing almost all attempts at biographical reconstruction of the prophet and his personal life (Landy; Ben Zvi 2005). Along with this, readings that have given attention to metaphor theory have proliferated precisely because the text itself points to the figurative nature of the marriage in the second half of verse 2 (see Kelle 2009). Here, readers have revisited the metaphors in these verses (and chapters 1–3 more broadly) as they relate to religious, social, political, and economic realities in ancient Israel and later Judah (Yee 2001; Keefe 2001; Kelle 2005).

The most significant and influential development of the late twentieth and early twenty-first centuries has been the rise of feminist readings of Hosea (Weems 1989; Brenner 1995; Yee 1996; Sherwood 1996; Baumann 2003). Along with exploring and challenging the book's marriage imagery, such studies have also examined the broader rhetoric of the text and its reception. Feminist readings have noted a number of issues that have often been overlooked in the history of interpretation (for more on this issue, see 'Hosea: Introduction and Overview'). First, in the analogy with Israel, the male figure is equated with God, while the woman is equated with the sinful people, perpetuating androcentric perspectives. Relatedly, the book also critiques the woman's sexuality but not the man's—creating a significant double standard. Further, the woman has little agency and no voice in the text as God or the husband is always speaking on her behalf. Taken together, feminist interpreters have argued that the marriage imagery, which begins in Hos. 1:2, is not the divine love story that it is often made out to be, and readers are encouraged to reexamine the suppositions that underlie such a metaphor.

The unusual depiction of Hosea's marriage has meant that this verse has had far-reaching influence. In Christian traditions, Hos. 1:2 is the beginning of a lectionary reading that extends through verse 10. This reading, on the seventh Sunday after Pentecost in Year C of the Revised Common Lectionary cycle, is paired with Psalm 85, Gen. 18:20–32, Psalm 138, Col. 2:6–15(19), and Luke 11:1–13. The readings from Psalm 85 and Genesis 18 deal with issues of God's judgment and mercy, while the Gospel reading includes the Lord's Prayer and the reminder that God is responsive to his people—themes that have been prominent in the way in which Hosea has been read and understood down through the centuries.

Hosea's marriage has also been the subject of considerable attention in social and cultural contexts. An interesting example is found in Min Jin Lee's 2017 novel *Pachinko*, where a young Protestant pastor in Korea, Isak, draws inspiration from Hosea in his decision to take a young pregnant woman, Sunja, as his wife. In this story, Sunja has helped nurse Isak back to health from a near-death experience, and he knows that, as a young pregnant woman, she is in a vulnerable position. In explaining his decision to a more senior pastor, Isak comments that Hosea's marriage to Gomer is an example of God's steadfast and enduring love for his people even when they do not deserve his love. Thus, Isak will also take for his own someone who may be undeserving. Hosea's marriage in this case is an inspiration for Isak's decision to marry Sunja, but it also serves as a rationale for his decision that is meant to convince his coreligionists of the propriety of the relationship.

Popular Christian culture has also drawn on the story of Hosea and his marriage in recent years, where it is seen as a story of redemption. Some approach this by retelling the story of Hosea and Gomer in more contemporary contexts. A popular fictional retelling in this vein is found in Francine Rivers's *Redeeming Love* (1997). Based on the biblical story of Hosea, Rivers tells the story of a woman named Angel set in 1850s California. Angel was sold into prostitution as a child and has faced abuse all of her life until she meets a man named Michael Hosea. Michael, a deeply religious man, follows God's call to marry Angel. As the story unfolds, Angel must come to accept the love of her husband and that of God. Rivers's retelling is beloved by many readers as a 'historical romance', but it also highlights themes that are common in evangelical engagement with the book of Hosea, including God's endless love and pursuit for his people. While the novel makes clear that Angel has suffered significant abuse throughout her life, it does not make any connection with feminist scholarship on Hosea, which has noted the problematic rhetoric and abusive imagery found in the biblical text itself. Similar approaches can be found in Christian films such as *Oversold* (2008), which offer more contemporary retellings of the Hosea story for modern audiences. In *Oversold*, we find the story of a pastor who falls in love with a Las Vegas stripper and the journey this woman takes toward redemption. Meanwhile, the stage play *Whipped* (Bonnick 2017) offers a modern-day retelling of the biblical story in a Black American church context. Here, an African-American pastor is struggling to lead his church with a wife who is not supportive and has a checkered history.

In all of these contemporary retellings, there is a sympathetic 'Hosea' figure, often a religious leader or deeply religious person, and a wayward woman in need of being rescued and redeemed.

Other retellings in literature and film attempt to situate the story of Hosea and his wife in its ancient historical context. Larry Christenson's *Hosea: A Novel* (2013) offers one such example, retelling the story of Hosea and Gomer in the northern kingdom of Israel just as Assyria is coming to prominence in the ancient Near East. Christenson's novel focuses on Israel's religious infidelity during this period, as well as the challenges of Hosea's marriage due to Gomer's unfaithfulness. In Christenson's retelling, the story of Hosea is an ode to God's enduring love for his wayward people in the Old Testament, as well as a practical reflection on the challenges of marriage. Another retelling, which bridges the ancient context with a contemporary setting, is the 2012 film *Amazing Love*, starring Sean Astin. Astin plays a youth leader who retells the story of Hosea to his youth group during a camping trip. The scenes in the film alternate between the camp setting and ancient depictions of the story of Gomer and Hosea. In this retelling, the intention is to highlight God's unconditional love and forgiveness, both in biblical times and in the present, which should serve as a model for these young Christians.

Contemporary Christian songwriters have also found the prophet's marriage to be generative. Both Michael Card's 'The Song of Gomer' (1992) and Andrew Peterson's 'Hosea' (2008) offer accounts from Gomer's perspective, highlighting Hosea's love and patience. In retelling the story of the married couple, both songs give voice to Gomer, who offers a sense of wonder at the prophet's (and God's) love. This is an interesting juxtaposition with feminist scholarship on Hosea, which often highlights Gomer's lack of voice and agency and the text's implicit approval of Hosea's actions. In these musical retellings, Gomer is given a voice, but her words reinforce the traditional interpretation and use of the book rather than pushing back on some of the more challenging elements which have been highlighted by contemporary interpreters.

Finally, visual depictions of Hosea often include his wife. From engravings at Amiens Cathedral (see Figure 5) to Reformation-era woodcuts, to Marc Chagall's provocative rendering, we see how artists have also been drawn to this couple, sparse as the details might be, in order to bring to life the prophet and his message. Many ancient and premodern depictions of Hosea and his wife portray a genteel relationship between the two, with Hosea often portrayed as tenderly touching his wife (see Figure 7).

However, some contemporary depictions, particularly those created for Christian audiences, increasingly offer a picture of a masculine Hosea who serves as a savior for a weak and wayward woman who needs to be rescued,

Figure 7   Hosea and Gomer, detail from the Bible Historiale, Den Haag, NMW 10B 23 426r (1372).

Museum Meermanno/Wikimedia Commons/Public Domain.

often from some sort of servitude. This shift may reflect trends in interpretation in the twentieth century, where Gomer's status as a prostitute or cultic sexual figure was highlighted. These portrayals are particularly common in depictions that include Hosea's presumed buying back of Gomer as recounted in Hosea 3. (See the commentary on chapter 3 for further discussion.)

1:3

In verse 3, we learn the name of Hosea's wife: Gomer, daughter of Diblaim (on the question of whether or not the woman in Hosea 3 is to be identified with Gomer, see comments on chapter 3). While the text is silent regarding biographical details of the woman's life, Jewish and Christian readers are suspicious of Gomer from the outset. Some claimed that Gomer was a well-known harlot at the time (Radak), while others attempted to connect her name to her reputation through wordplays and homonyms (b. Pesaḥ 87a; Rashi; Calvin; Gill). Theodore of Mopsuestia states that the reference to Gomer's father is given 'lest what was said should seem some trifling fiction and not a true record of events' (42).

Gomer gives birth to a son. In the Hebrew text, we are told that she bears this child for Hosea. With the subsequent children, however, no mention is made of the prophet. Thus, some readers have inferred that this first child was Hosea's, while the second and third were the fruits of Gomer's infidelity (Rowley 1956). As with the marriage itself, some have struggled with the depiction of the prophet having children with Gomer. Calvin notes that if Hosea did not really marry a harlot, neither did he have children with her. Pusey, however, offers an opposing view: if Scripture relates these events as having happened, then we must take them as such. Just as Jesus was the 'friend of publicans', so Hosea's family does not detract from his message or status. For Pusey, the mere presence of these children among the people means that they, too, were vehicles of the prophet's message even if only through their names (cf. Mays). Rudolph (1966) offers a historical-critical alternative: the original command to Hosea was to marry a woman and have children with her, giving them symbolic names; the reference to a promiscuous wife was added later as the first chapters were brought together.

1:4–5

Hosea is commanded to name this son Jezreel because the house of Jehu will be punished for the blood of Jezreel (v. 4). The use of the name Jezreel has been interpreted in various ways. The Targum continues its figural reading, removing any reference to the birth of the son and replacing the name Jezreel with 'the scattered ones', playing on the Hebrew root indicating 'seed' or 'sowing' (*zara'*). Other Jewish readers would offer more specific interpretations, including those that equate the son with Jeroboam (Radak) or the generation that followed him (Ibn Ezra). Noting that the name Jezreel is related to 'sowing', Cyril of Alexandria comments that the relationship of Hosea, Gomer, and Jezreel is similar to that between Moses, Israel, and Christ: a prophet is called to lead a wayward people, culminating in the 'seed of God', the true first son. Citing the similarity between the names 'Jezreel' and 'Israel', Calvin ascribes the following to God: 'They call themselves Israelites; but I will show, by a little change in the word, that they are degenerate and spurious, for they are Jezreelites rather than Israelites' (34).

The reference to the house of Jehu and the blood of Jezreel has also been interpreted variously in the traditions. This clause is most frequently understood as related in some way to the events of 2 Kings 9–10, where Jehu slays Ahab at Jezreel. A difficulty, however, is that 2 Kings suggests that Jehu's actions were supported by Elisha and, thus, by God. How do we reconcile this with the 'blood of Jezreel'? Andersen and Freedman put forward a minority view: they see Hosea's critique as aimed at the Omride dynasty rather than at Jehu. 'Hosea is saying that what God did to Ahab and his brood by means of Jehu is exactly what he will now do to Jeroboam and his family, *and for similar reasons*. ... Hosea thinks that Jeroboam is following in Ahab's footsteps' (181; italics in original). A more popular reading, however, has been that the blood OF Jezreel refers to the blood of Ahab and is a critique of Jehu and his actions (Targum; Jerome; Theodore of Mopsuestia; Radak; Rashi; Abarbanel). A number of readers overcome the interpretive obstacle of Jehu's divinely ordered conduct by doubting Jehu's sincerity, suggesting that his motivations were for his own gain rather than divine obedience (Cyril; Gill; Pusey; Ewald; Wellhausen).

Calvin attempts to resolve this issue by noting that it was the short-lived nature of Jehu's reformation to which the prophet refers—and, with a contemporary allusion, he illustrates this with reference to the short-lived zeal for religious reform likewise found 'under Henry King of England' (35). In a similar reading, Wolff suggests that the blame pointed at Jehu could point to the fact that he did not resist the 'Canaanization' of Israel's religion during his reign. 'Hosea's first child, named Jezreel, is to be a constant reminder that the reigning dynasty—from the hour of its founding onward—is not in accordance with God's will. A monarchy in Israel that bases its power upon bloodletting can expect a "No" from Yahweh' (Wolff: 18). Sweeney expounds on some of the theological implications of this intertextual link between Hosea and 2 Kings: while we often think of Israel's prophets (and, indeed, the broader corpus of the HB) as having a unified theological viewpoint, in fact, there is great diversity with regard to interpreting the divine will—Hosea's disagreement with other traditions concerning Jehu is a case in point.

1:6

Gomer, we are informed in verse 6, next bears a daughter who is to be named Lo-ruhamah ('no pity'; Vulgate: 'without mercy'). This is because God will no longer have pity on or forgive Israel. The term *ruhamah* means much more than pity; it also implies love, particularly the tenderness of a parent to a child (Pusey; Mays). In rabbinic tradition, the mention of a daughter was seen as symbolic of the weaker generations that followed Jeroboam, in particular Zechariah, who was on the throne for only six months (Radak). Rather than pointing to an individual, Rashi and Ibn Ezra see in the language of 'no mercy' a prediction of the coming judgment, including the coming exile (so too Cyril of Alexandria). In the same vein, others have noted the distinct change in relationship which this name implies. Calvin, for example, comments that divine favor has been removed from the people—the election freely given has been taken away. Sweeney similarly notes that this is a significant change in relationship from care under the God who is known for showing mercy to his people (e.g., Exod. 34:6) to a state where such mercy will now be withheld.

Artistic renderings of Hosea 1 often include Hosea and Gomer, or the couple with all three children. An exception is a drawing of Hosea and Gomer with just two children in a fifteenth-century German Bible (Figure 8). In this image, the younger child, presumably Lo-ruhamah, is still being breastfed and so has not yet been weaned, an element that is introduced a few verses later in Hos. 1:8.

FIGURE 8   *Hosea and family from German Bible by Johann Dietenberger (1475–1537).*
Courtesy of Pitts Library Digital Archive/Emory University.

1:7

In verse 7, we read, 'But I will have pity on the house of Judah, and I will save them by the LORD their God; I will not save them by bow or by sword or by war or by horses or by horsemen.' The introduction of Judah in this verse has led to some disagreement regarding how to understand this reference. Andersen and Freedman see it as a continuation of verse 6: just as God will not show mercy on Israel, neither will he save Judah. They read the first clause of verse 7 as negative 'even though the negative particle is not explicit' (194). In contrast to this, most readers interpret verse 7 as stating that Judah will be spared in juxtaposition to Israel. Because the text states that this salvation will not come by war but, seemingly, by divine intervention, a common interpretation has been that this refers to Sennacherib's attack on Jerusalem as described in 2 Kings 18–19 and Isaiah 36 (Theodore of Mopsuestia; Ibn Ezra; Radak; Luther). Modern readers have pointed out that if this is indeed the case, then this is likely a later Judean interpolation (Wellhausen; Mays; Yee 1996). Jerome and other Christian readers understood this deliverance figuratively: the Gospel likewise demonstrates God's saving power apart from the might of humanity. Cyril of Alexandria goes further and identifies Judah with 'the children of the tribe of Judah born to Christ'—it is these that are shown God's mercy (56; cf. Pusey).

1:8–9

The final verses of the chapter introduce one further child. After weaning Lo-ruhamah, Gomer bears another son; this one is to be named Lo-ammi, 'not my people'. Weaning in ancient Israel usually took place after three years, which may indicate the passing of some time before this final threat (Pusey; Wolff). The Targum renders both elements here figuratively—the weaning refers to the generation that will pass away while in exile, and the reference to a further son indicates that the people continued on in their evil ways, forsaking the Torah (cf. Ibn Ezra; Malbim). Rashi, however, states that the plain meaning of the text is the best reading: Hosea's wife bore another son.

In Christian tradition, Jerome comments that weaning refers to the people of Israel being deprived by God of those things that sustain them (cf. Pusey). Alternatively, Calvin sees the weaning as evidence of God's patience and forbearance with the people—sustaining them long after it was deserved. Another perspective has been offered by Sherwood (1996), who notes that the breastfeeding of 'no mercy' is a dissident action by Gomer; that is, the images of childbirth, mothering, and familial care in fact undermine the text and its message of God's rejection of Israel.

The naming of the third child 'not my people', according to Theodore of Mopsuestia, refers not to a person but to the coming trouble at the hands of foreigners. Cyril offers both a literal and a figurative reading: the historical meaning of the text refers to when the people were carried off by the Assyrians. The spiritual meaning refers to the Jewish people who, rejecting Jesus, forfeited their status as the chosen people—and in Cyril's view the church has assumed this place. An interpretation with similar anti-Jewish sentiments is offered by Luther, who sees here a connection between 'the prophecy of the temporal kingdom with that of the eternal kingdom' (6) and a firm rejection of the synagogue. Both Cyril and Luther employ strong supersessionist language in their comments on these verses. Calvin uses less-inflamed rhetoric but a similar idea, noting that 'not my people' indicates the Jewish people would essentially now be no different from profane Gentiles.

The increasing chastisement involved in the names of the children is noted by several commentators (Yee 1996). Pusey writes, 'As the *scattering of God* did not involve the being wholly *unpitied*; so neither did the being wholly *unpitied* for the time involve the being wholly rejected, so as to be *no more His people*' (24). This negation of a key aspect of Israel's identity in the HB—'*ammi*, 'my people' (Exod. 6:7; Lev. 26:12; Jer. 7:23)—has been noted by a number of scholars, indicating that the negative consequences related to the covenant relationship will now come into effect (Mays).

Verse 9 concludes with what seems like an ellipsis: 'and I will not be yours (*lo'-'ehyeh lakem*) …' Ibn Ezra comments that God's anger was so fierce that he omitted the final word (cf. Pusey, 24: 'the words say the more through their silence'). Mays and Wolff, among others, suggest that there might be a reference here to the revelation of the divine name in Exodus 6 with the use of the term *ehyeh*. Thus, the clause can be read, 'You are not my people, and I am not your "I am"' (cf. the LXX).

In spite of the unusual depiction of the family and children in these verses, most artistic depictions of the family present an idyllic picture of Hosea, Gomer, and the children (see Figure 9). However, sympathizing with Gomer and the children, Landy notes, 'It must have been difficult to be married to Hosea. Gomer tries to keep the family together, while he insists on calling the children horrible names, on excoriating her as an example of Israel's infidelity' (23). Landy's comments resonate with a number of important issues raised by feminist readers concerning Gomer and her children in these verses. One is that while God is in communication with Hosea about the children

FIGURE 9   *Hosea and family from Latin Bible printed by Friedrich Peypus (1485–1534).*
Courtesy of Pitts Library Digital Archive/Emory University.

and their future, Gomer remains without agency—while she gives birth to and sustains the children, she nevertheless has no voice in the conversation regarding their names. Wacker suggests that the feud in the text is really between Gomer and Yhwh: 'Do the children belong to the side of Gomer, the *ʾēšet zĕnûnîm*, who brings them into the world and nourishes them, or to the side of God, who gives them calamitous names and declares them to be living metaphors of the wicked Israel?' (2012: 372). These issues come into sharper focus in the following verses and into chapter 2, where the 'rehabilitation' of the children is envisaged.

1:10–11

In the first nine verses, Hosea's marriage and family life point to Israel's unfaithfulness. The tone shifts abruptly beginning in Hos. 1:10 (Heb. 2:1), as a positive future for the people is outlined. This change of tone has been the source of significant reflection from antiquity to contemporary scholarship. Drawing on the Talmud, Rashi notes how passages that seem at odds can be placed next to one another, and here we find an example of such a juxtaposition. Rabbi Joseph Kara, the medieval Jewish exegete from Troyes, likewise comments that a pattern can be seen in Scripture where texts of retribution are juxtaposed with those of salvation (see *Miqra'ot Gedolot*; cf. Theodore of Mopsuestia; Calvin; Pusey). In modern biblical studies, this change of tone is often seen as signaling some sort of editorial work (Wellhausen; Yee 1987).

Verse 10 begins by noting that the people will be as numerous as the sand of the sea, and instead of being 'not my people', they will be called 'sons of the living God'. The reference to the sand of the sea has drawn the attention of commentators both to the promises to the ancestors (Calvin; Wolff; Mays) and to the language of Isa. 10:22 (Cyril of Alexandria; Luther). This imagery is also used in the late-nineteenth-century hymn by Francis A. Blackmer, 'Numberless as the Sands'. While Blackmer's hymn draws on the imagery of Hos. 1:10, the image is transposed to a different context—the song is about a reunion of the saints in heaven, and the imagery of 'numberless as the sands' refers to the 'ransomed host' who are now together:

> Numberless as the sands of the seashore,
> Numberless as the sands of the shore!
> O what a sight'twill be
> When the ransomed host we see,
> As numberless as the sands of the seashore!
> (Francis A. Blackmer, 'Numberless as the Sands')

What is at the heart of the reversal and restoration noted in verse 10? The Targum tries to clarify the text with additions that refer to the exile—the reenvisioned future outlined in Hos. 1:10 refers to the restoration of the people following their time away from the land. In Christian tradition, interpretation of this verse has been heavily shaped by the fact that it is quoted twice in the NT—in Rom. 9:26 and 1 Pet. 2:10. In both places, the clause 'children of the living God' is used as part of a larger discourse related to the newly constituted people of God that has taken shape through the work of Christ. This use by the NT writers, particularly Paul, would be taken up by other Christian writers. The influential patristic theologian Augustine of Hippo, for example, cites the apostles and their use of this text to suggest that this verse is 'a prophecy of the calling of the Gentiles, who were previously not God's people' (*City of God* 18.28; cf. Jerome). A number of Christian commentators see in Hos. 1:10 a reference to both Jews and Christians, who together constitute the new people of God, though with the caveat that this is through Christ (Calvin; Gill; Pusey). As Luther comments, 'the kingdom of Judah was never destroyed but was transformed into a better one. The kingdom of Christ is the preservation of the kingdom of Judah' (6).

The phrase 'children of the living God' has been taken up in other contexts, particularly in evangelical Christianity, where notions of God as father are prominent. Sinclair Ferguson authored a book entitled *Children of the Living God: Delighting in the Father's Love* (Banner of Truth, 1989). Starting from the premise that Jesus taught his followers to call God 'our Father', Ferguson explores a number of issues related to being a child of God, including new birth, adoption, and fatherly discipline. The Christian singer-songwriter Fernando Ortega has a song of the same title (1997). In this song, Ortega uses the phrase 'children of the living God' as a summons to praise and a call to sing of God's mercy and forgiveness. While there is little engagement with the prophet or the message of the book itself, both of these examples draw on Hosea's imagery and demonstrate the broad-ranging appeal of the book's themes.

Verse 11 states that the children of Judah and the children of Israel will be gathered and will appoint one head. A common interpretation is that this 'one head' refers to the house of David (Targum; Rashi; Sweeney) or, perhaps, a Moses-like figure (Andersen and Freedman). Not surprisingly, however, figurative and eschatological understandings are frequently encountered. Radak notes that this must refer to a future messianic age because, in the second Temple period, it was only the Judean exiles, and not those of the tribes of Israel, that were restored to the land. In the Christian tradition, this has often been read Christologically—Jesus is the head who will rule over all (Cyril of Alexandria; Luther; Gill). Many of these commentators extend this figurative reading to include the 'day of Jezreel', which is understood to add an eschatological dimension to the prophet's message.

Although we see in Hos. 1:10–11 the beginning of the transformation of Hosea's children ('not my people' becomes 'children of the living God'), Gomer is again conspicuously absent in these verses and in the promises of restoration (Wacker 2012). An interesting retelling of this story that notes these tensions along with the issue of agency is found in Rabbi Milton Steinberg's unfinished novel, *The Prophet's Wife*. Here, Gomer is depicted as a strong and independent woman who is unhappy with the unfair life that has been assigned to her as a woman. In fact, her true love is the prophet's brother, and it is in this context that the infidelity takes place. While unfinished at the time of Steinberg's untimely death in 1950, the novel nonetheless raises a number of pressing questions about the biblical account and foreshadows many of the concerns that would arise in feminist readings in the ensuing decades, particularly those related to Gomer's voice and agency—or lack thereof—in the text (e.g., Fokkelien van Dijk-Hemmes 1989).

The first three chapters of Hosea are often read as a unit with chapter 2 understood to be one long speech explaining the figurative elements at work in the more biographical sections of chapters 1 and 3 (Harper). Within the traditions of Judaism and Christianity, the theme of chapter 2 has long been understood as repentance and return to Yhwh (so stated the twelfth-century Jewish philosopher Maimonides in his *Mishneh Torah*; cf. Luther). However, as we will see below, the rhetoric and the perspective of the text raise a number of difficult issues (Yee 1992).

Although not always linear in its presentation, scholars frequently note the coherence of chapter 2 as a unit (Wolff; Andersen and Freedman; Kelle 2005). Mays situates this speech early in Hosea's ministry during the final years of Jeroboam II: 'Abundant prosperity (vv. 5, 8) and a confident cult (vv. 11, 13) point to prosperous, untroubled times' (36).

2:1

In Hos. 2:1 (Heb. 2:3), the frame of reference shifts to brother Ammi and sister Ruhamah—here the negative particles attached to the names in chapter 1 have been removed. A key interpretive issue has been how these characters should be identified in relation to the larger metaphor. If the husband is God and the wife is wayward Israel, who do Ammi and Ruhamah represent in this symbolic world? The Targum addresses this issue by (again) removing the persons from

Hosea, Joel, and Obadiah Through the Centuries, First Edition. Bradford A. Anderson.
© 2024 John Wiley & Sons Ltd. Published 2024 by John Wiley & Sons Ltd.

the text, calling instead on the collective people to return to the law. Here the references to 'whoring' and 'adultery' are replaced with 'evil deeds' and 'worship of idols' (cf. Rashi). Luther takes the entirety of chapter 2 as addressed to both Jews and Christians who have received mercy, while the mother refers to the Jewish people ('the synagogue') more broadly (Luther; Pusey). Gill suggests that the reference to Ammi and Ruhamah can refer either to Judah and Benjamin, who are to speak to wayward Israel, or to the faithful among the ten tribes. Wellhausen would follow this latter idea: individuals are here asked to oppose the wrong direction of the larger whole, the mother (cf. Mays).

2:2

These siblings are to plead with their mother 'for she is not my wife, and I am not her husband' (2:2). The call for the children to plead with their mother has been understood in various ways. Jerome notes that there is a change in perspective of these verses as the children discussed in chapter 1 are now directly addressed: perhaps they can succeed where the husband has failed in calling their mother to reform. Calvin, meanwhile, would remark that in a divorce, children often side with the mother. When viewed from this perspective, this discourse can be seen as an explanation to the children for God's actions: in essence, 'your dispute is not with me', should they wish to blame God.

In the modern era, commentators began to note the similarities in language and style with courtroom and legal matters. Of particular importance here is the Hebrew term *rib*, often translated as 'plead with'. This term is more confrontational and hostile than 'plea' would seem to indicate, and other suggested translations have included 'accuse' or 'argue with' (Andersen and Freedman; cf. Latin Vulgate). The use of the Hebrew *rib* has led to some speculation that this section may have originated as part of legal proceedings. Indeed, the language of the following clause ('for she is not my wife, and I am not her husband') has led to similar conjecture (see Kelle 2009). By the eighteenth century, John Gill was suggesting that these verses indicate an official bill of divorce. This notion would gain greater credence in the ensuing centuries as further ANE texts and traditions—and thus potential parallels—were discovered. In the twentieth century, a number of scholars were confident that this statement reflected an actual divorce formula as seen in other ANE texts such as those from Elephantine (Gordon 1936; de Vaux 1961). Over time this assuredness faded; while some relationship to divorce might be in view, the notion of a technical declaration of divorce would fall out of fashion (Wolff; Macintosh).

The children are to plead with their mother to 'put away her whoring from her face, and her adultery from between her breasts' (2:2). The allusion to the face and breasts has most often been understood as a reference to the custom of prostitutes making up their faces and perfuming themselves for their lovers (see, e.g., the medieval Christian commentator Nicholas of Lyra, whose comments are found in the *Glossa Ordinaria*; cf. Yee 2001). Calvin comments that while the reference to the face and breasts alludes to the 'meretricious finery' of harlots, it is the shamelessness of the people in their apostasy that is in view. Various figurative readings have also been put forward. Radak notes that the face may be understood as symbolic of the prophets and the breasts as figurative of the Torah, both of which are substituted with false prophets and false statutes. Some early Christian writers understood the removal of the harlotry and the adultery as referring to Israel's removal into captivity, at which point the unfaithfulness and idolatry would be rooted out (Theodore of Mopsuestia). With the rise of modernity, readers began to focus on the exact nature of the infidelity in question. For many, this betrayal refers to Israel's worship and religious life, specifically Baal worship—not least because Baal is mentioned later in the chapter (2:17; so Wellhausen; Mays). Wolff goes so far as to say that the adornment of the woman's face and breasts may refer to jewelry worn as part of the Baal cult.

2:3

In 2:3 we read that if this mother figure does not change her ways, she will be stripped naked and laid bare like a wilderness. Readers have engaged with the problematic language of 'stripping her naked' in various ways. The Targum renders this as removing the Shekinah from the people and thus taking away their glory. According to Mezudath David, the commentary of the seventeenth–eighteenth-century rabbi David Altschuler from Prague, this language is used because Israel is compared to a harlot, and so 'he depicts her shame as that customarily inflicted upon a harlot' (see *Miqra'ot Gedolot*; cf. Wellhausen and Mays who both draw on Ezek. 16:36ff).

Rashi notes the language of being naked 'as on the day she was born' is similar to that in Ezek. 16:4–5 and suggests that this refers to when the people were saved from Egypt (cf. Abarbanel). Jerome likewise draws on points of contact with Ezekiel 16, including the reference to fine clothing and ornaments. The fine things that were given to the people after Egypt will be taken away, and Israel will again be without a husband as she was in Egypt (others who draw on

Ezekiel 16 or who make an intertextual link with Israel's time in Egypt include Theodore of Mopsuestia; Cyril of Alexandria; Calvin; Gill; Pusey; Mays; Andersen and Freedman; Yee 2001). Others, meanwhile, interpret the stripping naked as a reference to the Babylonian exile (Nicholas of Lyra; Luther). Offering a spiritual reading, Pusey suggests that there is both an inward and an external nakedness. 'The invisible nakedness is, when the soul within is bared of the glory and the grace of God.' The outward, physical stripping is a reflection of the internal, spiritual state as seen in Genesis 3 (28).

In the twentieth century, a number of potential parallels from the ANE and the HB were used to make sense of this reference to stripping. Texts from Babylonia and Nuzi were used to argue that stripping was used as part of divorce proceedings (Kuhl 1934; see critique from Day 2000). Others pointed to Exod. 21:10, which notes a man's legal responsibility to clothe a wife; on this basis, Wolff and others argue that the stripping of the woman is a declaration of freedom from that legal obligation (cf. Sweeney). More recently, comparison with other ANE traditions has focused more broadly on the economic issues related to inheritance and gift-giving related to marriage in the ancient world (Kelle 2005).

The Targum understands the reference to the wilderness in the second half of verse 3 as referring to the wilderness wanderings of the generations that left Egypt—thus, according to the Aramaic, 'My anger will fall on her as it fell on the people of the generation that transgressed my law in the wilderness.' Variations in this connection to the wilderness traditions have been noted by ancient as well as more contemporary readers (Jerome; Rashi; Andersen and Freedman). Others, such as Cyril of Alexandria, see this as a spiritual wilderness, connecting Hosea to texts such as Amos 8:11–12 and Jer. 6:7–8. Meanwhile, according to Mays, the invocation of the wilderness and the parched land again points to the Canaanite fertility cult, in which 'the land was considered the female to be fertilized by the rain of Baal' (38; see rebuttals from Andersen and Freedman; Keefe 2001).

In recent decades, feminist voices have pointed out the disturbing nature of Hos. 2:3, including its escalating series of threats (Yee 1996). The language of stripping has come in for particular criticism. In 1985, Setel labeled the first two chapters of Hosea as pornographic in that the text depicts female sexuality as negative (as opposed to the neutral, positive depiction of male sexuality), it degrades and humiliates women, and it regards female sexuality as the possession of men. The language of stripping, exposing, and killing with thirst is part of the rhetoric that Setel sees as fitting this profile. To assume that such a text can be read as normative and authoritative, according to O'Brien (2008), is both problematic and potentially dangerous.

2:4

The castigation of the woman continues in the following verses, focusing on the fact that she has chased after other lovers; however, verse 4 includes the children in this rebuke as mercy will also be withheld from them. One common interpretation sees the mother as representing the nation as a whole and the children as representing individuals. Thus, while the collective nation has turned away, so too have individuals (Radak). John Calvin would put a contemporary spin on this verse, equating the children with Papists who are guilty by association with the 'Mother' church: 'In vain then they boast themselves to be the children of God, and that they have the holy Mother Church' (67). In relation to the question of how the children might be implicated in these matters, Cyril of Alexandria invokes Ezekiel 18 and the question of intergenerational guilt to suggest that the children must themselves be guilty of spiritual prostitution. Whatever the case, the legitimacy of the children is suspect because of the mother's infidelity.

2:5

The use of the term *lovers* to refer to adulterous lovers is found only in Hosea, Jeremiah, and Ezekiel. The identification of the lovers in Hos. 2:5–7 (Heb. 2:7–9) has been the subject of wide-ranging commentary. In Jewish tradition, these lovers have been understood as idol worship (Targum; cf. Abarbanel, the fifteenth-century Jewish philosopher and commentator) or having to do with following after foreign nations (Rashi; Radak). These same options are found in the Christian tradition as well: Jerome notes that the literal sense refers to Israel's engagement with the Assyrians, Babylonians, and Egyptians while Calvin sees these lovers as false gods. However, other spiritual readings have also been put forward. These lovers have been equated with demons or the devil (Theodore of Mopsuestia; Pusey), as well as following after sensual pleasures rather than the more difficult way of 'devout doctrine' (Luther).

In the modern era, the focus of interpretation shifted to the presumed cultic and agricultural elements at work in these verses (Macintosh). A key element here is that the lovers are said to give the woman 'my bread and my water, my wool and my flax, my oil and my drink' (2:5). Many modern readers have taken this to indicate an assumption that life's material blessings come from these lovers, that is, false gods (Ewald). Indeed, a common interpretation has been that this relates to the land-focused Canaanite cult and the local god, Baal (Wellhausen; Mays; Wolff). However, the identity of these lovers is not made clear; in fact, the only explicit identification of lovers in Hosea comes in chapter 8, where the text refers to the lovers as those nations with whom Ephraim has made treaties. Thus, an alternative reading is that these lovers should be understood as foreign nations, an idea that has ancient roots, as noted above. In this case, the supply of material goods—bread, water, wool—could refer to trade with these nations and the assumption that provision comes from these other nations rather than being provided by Israel's God (Yee 2001). Brad Kelle offers a more specific interpretation of these metaphors as political: the lovers refer to political allies, and the chapter as a whole is concerned with Samaria's political situation at the end of the Syro-Ephraimitic war (Kelle 2005).

2:6–7

The husband vows to 'hedge her way with thorns, and build a wall against her' (2:6). The thorns have led to various figurative readings; Gregory the Great, the sixth–seventh-century Pope and theologian, understands the thorns as those adversities which push us back toward God (*Morals on the Book of Job* 6.34.3; cf. Jerome). Cyril of Alexandria interprets these historically as referring to the wars, captivity, and servitude that encourage people to return to God. More recently readers have noted that this language paints a picture of a wandering animal that must be contained (Mays; Andersen and Freedman). Feminist voices, meanwhile, have pointed to the potentially problematic nature of this language: the husband's actions in these verses suggest a strategy that 'reflects the social methods of the patrilineal, honor/shame culture … to control women's sexuality' (Yee 1992: 199). In verse 6 we see the first stage of such control, which begins with seclusion and isolation as the thorns and wall hedge the woman in (to be followed by withholding food and material goods and then social/psychological abuse).

The woman, so the text indicates, will eventually come to the realization that these lovers do not provide the comfort of her original husband, to which she will return. A number of commentators have noted the similarities between the woman's return to her first husband and the Prodigal Son's return to his past life in the parable found in Luke 15 (Pusey; Mays). However, Wacker (2012) points out the continued lack of agency on the part of the woman: even when she does speak in the text, these words are put in her mouth by the male protagonist and are not really hers at all.

2:8-13

Verses 8–13 continue to lay out the case against the woman, who does not know the true source of her material possessions; this idea is echoed in verse 13, which says Yʜwʜ has been forgotten. Hosea seems to come from a tradition that ascribes the good things of the land to Israel's God, a sentiment common in Deuteronomy (e.g., Deuteronomy 26; see Mays). Parts of Jewish tradition understood this 'not knowing' as a reference to the leaders of Israel, who led the people to believe their material provisions came from the heavenly bodies (Radak). Calvin's reflections are harsher: not recognizing the source of their good things, after all that had been done for them, points to the 'inexcusable stupidity' and ingratitude of the Israelites. Because of this, these good things and possessions will be taken away.

In verse 8 we have the first explicit mention of 'Baal' in Hosea, a term that originally meant 'lord', but which by the late Bronze Age had come to be used as a title for various gods. Texts from the ancient site of Ugarit mention Baal and have offered important information for our understanding of Baal in antiquity (Davies 1992). Readers have made sense of the reference to 'Baal' in different ways, a tradition that extends back at least to the Dead Sea Scrolls (see Figure 10). In 4Q166—or 4QpHos a, the Hosea pesher or commentary—we find a political reading, where 'Baal' is replaced with the nations on whom the people of Israel relied during Hosea's time, along with a chastisement for blindly following them like gods. The Targum, meanwhile, replaces the term *baal* with *idols*, while Jerome sees Baal as referring to the 'demon of the Sidonians' or perhaps Bel of the Babylonians.

The plural use of *baalim* in verse 13 has led to further speculation. Some have suggested that this points to many local gods in Canaan—Baal-Berith, Baalzebub, and so on—even if Baal over time came to be understood as the chief god (Pusey; Wolff). Others have posited that the plural form indicates various shrines where the one Baal was worshipped. Some contemporary readers have pushed back against these deity-related interpretations, suggesting instead the term *baal* points to political allies and overlords, an idea that, as noted above, extends back to antiquity and the Dead Sea Scrolls (Kelle 2005).

An element singled out in verse 8 is that silver and gold were lavished upon the woman, but these were used for Baal. The reference to gold in proximity with Baal led the rabbis to draw a parallel with the golden calf episode (Exodus 32), and the Sages noted in the Talmud that the abundance of gold and silver led to the sin of the golden calf (b. Ber. 32a; cf. Ewald). Others would suggest that this refers to the gold and silver later used in idolatrous worship in Israel,

FIGURE 10   *Fragment of 4Q166, Hosea Commentary Scroll (Pesher Hosea),*
Dead Sea Scrolls.
United States Library of Congress.

closer to the time of the prophet (LXX; Ibn Ezra; Nicholas of Lyra). Pusey, for
example, understands this as the gold that was actually fashioned into Baal
idols, and ties this into Baal worship, which was introduced by Jezebel and then
developed further in the northern kingdom.

In verses 10–13, the speaker vows to uncover the woman's shame, as well
as doing away with her feasts and festivals, and laying waste to her land. This
devastation has, since antiquity, been understood as a reference to the con-
quests of the Assyrians and the Babylonians (Jerome; Cyril of Alexandria;
Radak; Nicholas of Lyra) or even the Romans (Gill). In the modern era, the
threat to the harvest and produce came to be seen as a critique of the northern
adoption of the Baal cult with its focus on fertility (Wolff). However, the
threat to uncover the woman's shame 'in the sight of her lovers' can also be
understood in political terms with some positing that Assyria will see the
weakness of Israel during this time of deprivation (Andersen and Freedmen).
Focusing on socioeconomic matters, Yee (2001) suggests that the critique of

feasts and festivals is not related to their sexualization but to socioeconomic factors as these were profitable events for the elite.

In these verses we read that while the Israelites presume that their material goods come from Baal, the deprivation of these same goods will make clear that these came from YHWH. For most of history, the dominant voices within the interpretive traditions have not questioned the morality of this episode or God's/the husband's right to act in such a manner. Calvin, remarking on 2:13, suggests that the punishment of God was not only just but was necessary. However, recent decades have seen these assumptions scrutinized. As Renita Weems (1989) has noted, the uncovering/stripping in 2:10 speaks of sexual humiliation. For many, these are problematic images not least because 'they facilitate the development of an image of God who is ready to use violence that then is misused to legitimate male and especially marital violence against women' (Wacker 2012: 374). Indeed, a number of feminist readers have highlighted that these verses indicate an escalating series of punishments for the woman: withholding food and clothing (2:9), exposing her to lovers (2:10), putting an end to celebration and happiness (2:11), and destroying land and produce (2:12). When read in light of abusive relationships and cycles of violence, these are troubling images, whatever their intent (Yee 1996).

2:14

The tone of the chapter seems to change abruptly beginning in verse 14 (Heb. 2:16) as the husband speaks about the restoration of the fractured relationship. Verses 14–15 use evocative imagery with the husband promising to 'bring her into the wilderness and speak to her kindly'. The wife will then respond 'as in the days of her youth' just as when she came out of Egypt. The LXX, however, offers a substantially different reading. Instead of bringing the woman into the wilderness, the Greek states that 'I will deceive her', and rather than responding positively as in the days of her youth, it says that 'she will be brought low as in the days of her infancy'. The Latin Vulgate is closer to the Hebrew as the husband will 'allure' the woman, and she will 'sing' as in the days of her youth coming from Egypt (v. 15).

The reference to the wilderness in verse 14 has led to various readings. Radak and other Jewish commentators note that the wilderness here might refer to exile (cf. Theodoret of Cyr, fifth-century Christian bishop and commentator). Nevertheless, because Egypt is also mentioned, the most common assumption is that this refers to the exodus traditions (see the discussion of this connection in Jewish liturgical tradition below). The woman's response, as in the days of her youth, is most often likened to the song of Moses after the crossing of the Red Sea (Rashi; cf. Nicholas of Lyra; Calvin; Gill). Wolff notes that Hosea seems to be unaware of those aspects of the wilderness wanderings that connect the desert with murmuring and complaining; for this prophet, the wilderness is only a place of growth and restoration.

Christian readers have gone to great lengths to explain how the 'alluring' (or 'deception', LXX) of the husband is in fact a good thing. Cyril of Alexandria notes that the 'seducing' of the woman actually helps in turning her away from things that are shameful and harmful. Theodore of Mopsuestia likewise sees the 'seducing to the wilderness' as something difficult that leads to a positive outcome, as happens often in Scripture. Pusey offers a similar reading: 'God uses, as it were, Satan's weapons against himself. As Satan had enticed the soul to sin, so would God, by *holy* enticements and persuasiveness, allure her to Himself. God too hath sweetnesses for the penitent soul' (35). Jerome, meanwhile, makes a Christological connection. After all the hardship that will come upon Israel, he writes, 'then—that is, at the advent of Christ his son—he will open the hope of salvation and will provide an opportunity for repentance and will flatter her; for this is the meaning of *I will allure her*' (165). Luther, too, sees the 'allure' of Hosea as a reference to the Gospel: 'Through my apostles I will teach you a sweet doctrine that is different from the Law' (11). However, as O'Brien (2008) and other readers have noted, this alluring to the wilderness can also be read as yet another phase in the cycle of abuse as the husband now attempts to placate the woman after the physical and psychological abuse noted above.

The relational imagery from Hosea has been picked up in other contexts, which highlight the complexity of the text and its reception. One interesting example is John Donne's 'Holy Sonnet XIV' ('Batter my heart, three-person'd God'). An excerpt reads:

> Batter my heart, three-person'd God, for you
> As yet but knock, breathe, shine, and seek to mend;
> That I may rise and stand, o'erthrow me, and bend
> Your force to break, blow, burn, and make me new.
> ...
> Take me to you, imprison me, for I,
> Except you enthrall me, never shall be free,
> Nor ever chaste, except you ravish me.

In this sonnet, Donne (1572–1631) draws on imagery from the Bible, including Hosea, to graphically describe his relationship with the Trinity. 'Hosea's wife ... is to Hosea as Israel is to Yahweh and as Donne is to the Trinity'

(Mueller 1961: 314). However, Donne's language is unsettling, and the use of imagery similar to that found in Hosea forces the reader to contemplate the force of this imagery and rhetoric, both in the poem and in the biblical text.

An interesting aspect of verse 14 is that, as part of the restoration, the Valley of Achor will be made into a 'door of hope'. This reference to Achor alludes to Joshua 7 and the story of Achan who, along with his family, was stoned in Achor for taking and keeping items for himself during the conquest of Jericho. Verse 14 states that this valley will now become a 'door of hope' (*petah tikvah*). This name—Petah Tikvah—was given to one of the first Jewish agricultural villages in modern Palestine formed in 1878. The founders had intended to form a settlement in the Achor Valley near Jericho. When this location fell through, the settlers retained the name Petah Tikvah in the new location, east of Tel Aviv. A large city of the same name is still found there today. The title 'Door of Hope' has also been used by Christians in the last several centuries in relation to homes for unwed mothers and is also a popular name for contemporary churches, often evangelical (Gruber).

The second chapter of Hosea (Eng. 1:10–2:20; Heb. 2:1–22) is the *haftarah* reading for *Be-midbar*, Num. 1:1–4:20, in both the Ashkenazic and Sephardic liturgical traditions. There are a number of thematic connections between these texts, including the reference to the time in the wilderness after coming out of Egypt in verses 14–15. As Fishbane notes,

> Following the covenant and the apostasy of the Golden Calf, this wandering with the Ark could thus be perceived as a time of purification prior to the nation's entrance into the Land. … The desert (*midbar*) serves a similar function in the haftarah. Speaking of a subsequent time, the prophet Hosea first shows how the seductions of idolatry have (again) perverted Israel's worship and deformed its religious consciousness. He then portrays how reconciliation will come about through God's tender speech to the people in the 'wilderness'. … The desert thus serves as a physical realm marking the transformation of the nation from bondage to freedom and a symbolic realm marking this same passage as a spiritual journey of rebirth. In both cases, the desert has a paradigmatic status in the life of the nation, marking change, transition, and new beginnings.
>
> (Fishbane 2002: 158)

However, the use of this text in the liturgy is not without problems, in part because the *haftarah* reaffirms the androcentric perspective of the text. A number of readers have noted that marriage imagery that cannot be accepted by both women and men is not a helpful metaphor in contemporary liturgical contexts (Graetz 1995).

2:15–17

In the final verses of the chapter, the imagery switches back and forth between YHWH/Israel and Hosea/Gomer: 'Both are always present, but at some points the prime reference is to Yahweh, while at others the human situation is more to the fore' (Andersen and Freedman: 289).

Verses 16 and 21 both begin with the phrase 'On that day', which has been understood as introducing an eschatological thrust to the passage (Wellhausen; Mays). At this time, God notes, 'you will call me "My husband" (*ishi*) and no longer will you call me "My Baal" (*baali*)'. Various readers have noted wordplay at work here as the use of 'my Baal' can refer both to the role of husband as well as the god of the same name. The terms *ishi* and *baali* can both be used in Hebrew to refer to the husband in both ancient and contemporary usage (Jerome; Cyril of Alexandria; Luther; Pusey). A number of commentators have noted that *ishi* is a more personal title, while *baali* is based on a master-servant relationship predicated on fear (Rashi; Gill). Implicit in this rhetoric, however, is also a critique of Baal as an alternative to YHWH (Wolff; Sweeney; cf. Targum). Modern interpreters have noted the allusions to syncretism here, as Israel's God seems to have been called Baal, and thus 'a constant and dangerous erosion of the distinctive understanding of Yahweh set in' (Mays: 48). Personal names from the era—found, for example, on ostraca—appear to bear this out, reflecting both the titles YHWH and Baal (Wolff).

2:18–20

In verse 18 we are told of a covenant that will include animals and the abolition of war. The inclusion of animals here seems to reverse the damage done by animals earlier in the chapter (2:13; cf. Theodore of Mopsuestia; Ibn Ezra; Wolff). The animals listed also seem to recall those described in Genesis 1 (Andersen and Freedman; Sweeney).

The term *betrothal* (*'eras*; 'take you for my wife', NRSV) recurs three times in verses 19–20. Christian readers have made much of the betrothal imagery. Jerome remarks on the unique nature of God's love: 'see how the union of God and men differs; when a man takes a wife, he makes of a virgin a woman, that is, not a virgin; God, even when he is united to prostitutes, changes them into virgins' (169; cf. Calvin). Still others note that this betrothal symbolically represents the church as the bride of Christ (John 3:29; 2 Cor. 11:2) or points to the marriage supper of the lamb (Rev. 19:7; Gill).

Verses 19–20 (Heb. 21–22) have a unique place in Jewish prayer rituals. These verses are recited when putting on tefillin, specifically when wrapping the strap around the middle finger of the left hand, signifying the person's commitment and 'betrothal' to God. This tradition dates back to at least the sixteenth century (Gruber; Nulman 1993).

2:21–23

The chapter ends by returning to the children noted in chapter 1 and attempts to bring some resolution to the issues introduced with them. The reference to Jezreel is again used in conjunction with a reference to sowing in the land, and the plain meaning, as Radak notes, is that the people will increase. The Targum, however, replaces Jezreel with a reference to those in exile (cf. Rashi). This idea is picked up in the Talmud, where we are told that Israel was exiled to the nations only to bring in converts. "'I will sow her to the land: Does a person sow a *se'a* of grain for any reason other than to bring in several *kor* of grain during the harvest? So too, the exile is to enable converts from the nations to join the Jewish people." Rabbi Yohanan continues: "Even those who were initially 'not my people', i.e. gentiles, will convert and become part of the Jewish nation'" (b. Pesah. 87b).

Christian readers also made much of these final verses and the reconstituted names of the children. In Rom. 9:25–26, Paul brings together two citations from Hosea—2:23 and 1:10—to highlight the fact that God has called both Jews and Gentiles:

[25] As indeed he says in Hosea,

'Those who were not my people I will call "my people",
and her who was not beloved I will call "beloved".
[26] 'And in the very place where it was said to them, "You are not my people",
there they shall be called children of the living God.'
(Rom. 9:25–26, NRSV)

Paul's appropriation of the renaming of Lo-ammi to 'my people' and 'children of the living God' was very popular, particularly among the church fathers. The reference to those who were 'not my people' but are now 'my people' is seen as a clear reference to the calling of the Gentiles and the foretelling of the church (Ambrose, *On the Holy Spirit* 2.10.101; John Chrysostom, *Homilies on Romans* 16; Bede, *Commentary on 1 Peter* 2:10; Origen, *Homilies on Jeremiah* 9:4; see Ferreiro). In a sermon preached in London in 1893, Charles Spurgeon would also highlight the connection between Hos. 2:23 and Rom. 9:25. Spurgeon does not speak about the context or broader message of either Romans or Hosea. Rather, for Spurgeon, these verses relate general truths about the spiritual states in which people live: all of us were once not God's people, but through Jesus there is the possibility of becoming a child of God (Spurgeon 1893).

———

As outlined above, the imagery of this chapter has been generative for inter-preters down through the centuries. In both the Jewish and Christian tradi-tions, the common refrain has been that this chapter is a picture of divine love. Luther speaks for many within the traditions when he says, 'There is on earth no love more ardent than that between a groom and his betrothed' (13). The usefulness of this imagery seems evident in the employment of this chapter in both the Jewish and Christian liturgical traditions, where the allusions to both the wilderness and marriage motifs have served as a basis for intertex-tual reflections. As noted above, the second chapter of Hosea (Eng. 1:10–2:20; Heb. 2:1–22) is the paired reading for the Torah reading *Bemidbar*, Num. 1:1–4:20, in both the Ashkenazic and Sephardic traditions. Meanwhile, Hos. 2:14–20 is the Old Testament reading for the eighth Sunday after Epiphany in Year B of the Revised Common Lectionary, where it is paired with readings that include Mark 2:13–22, where Jesus speaks of himself as the bridegroom. Hos. 2:18–23 is also used as part of a ritual for the 'Blessing of an Engaged Couple' (Catholic Bishops' Conference of England and Wales 2015, Order of Celebrating Matrimony). Thus, this chapter has been a focal point for reflection on human and divine love within the liturgical traditions of both Judaism and Christianity.

In modern scholarship, the dominant frame for understanding the metaphorical elements in this chapter has been religious infidelity with more specific reconstructions related to Canaanite or Baal fertility cults coming to the fore in the twentieth century (see, e.g., Wolff). However, this consensus has been challenged in recent decades as scholars have questioned the major underpinnings of cultic sin related to Baal fertility rituals. In its place, scholars have suggested that social or socioeconomic critiques may actually be at the heart of the chapter's figurative sexual imagery, challenging Israel's political and religious leaders, as well as the emerging socioeconomic context in Israel (Keefe 1995; Yee 2001). Others have suggested that more concrete political issues are at the center of Hosea's imagery in chapter 2 (Kelle 2005). Readers have also begun noting the interrelationship of humanity and the natural world in this chapter as the themes of land and people are interwoven (Marlow 2009).

Thus, assumptions concerning the connection between the chapter's sexual imagery and Israel's religious infidelity are not as dominant as they once were.

Along with the metaphorical language, the rhetoric of this chapter has led to some ethical concerns, particularly in the contemporary era. As a number of interpreters have observed, the actions in this chapter correlate quite closely with patterns of abusers, particularly within marriage or male-female relationships: emotional and verbal abuse, isolation, threats, and blaming are followed by a honeymoon period where all is forgiven (Graetz 1995; O'Brien 2008). Again, the woman's voice is silent in this chapter as the husband speaks for her (Wacker 2012). For these and other reasons, contemporary readers have encouraged us to pause and reflect on the rhetoric of this chapter, as well as its potential real-world impact (Landy; Yee 1992).

Hosea 3

3:1

In Hosea 3, the text returns to narrative form. Hosea is instructed by God to 'Go, love a woman who has a lover and is an adulteress, just as the LORD loves the people of Israel'. A recurring question has been how this command relates to what has gone before in chapters 1 and 2. Do these verses again refer to Hosea and Gomer, or is another woman in view? The confusion on this matter is evident already in the ancient versions, which approach the issue in different ways (see discussion in Gill; Ewald).

As was the case with Hosea 1, there are some traditions that interpret this scene figuratively, and so the identity of the woman is left unexplored. In the Targum, for example, all references to an actual woman are erased and instead we read: 'speak a prophecy concerning the house of Israel, who are like a woman loved by her husband, but she betrays them'. A number of church fathers also gloss over the identity of the woman and instead highlight the symbolic reference with which the text is concerned, namely Israel (Jerome) or Judah (Theodore of Mopsuestia).

Another approach understands chapter 3 as introducing another woman. This reading also has ancient roots in both Jewish (Ibn Ezra and R. Joseph Kara; see *Miqra'ot Gedolot*) and Christian traditions (including Cyril of Alexandria and Luther). In many of these readings, it is assumed that Hosea purchases a prostitute after the failure of his first marriage with Gomer (John Gill; Rudolph 1966).

Hosea, Joel, and Obadiah Through the Centuries, First Edition. Bradford A. Anderson.
© 2024 John Wiley & Sons Ltd. Published 2024 by John Wiley & Sons Ltd.

The above examples notwithstanding, the majority of readers have assumed that this account refers again to Hosea and his wife Gomer. Within this, some see chapter 3 as a first-person retelling of the events from Hosea 1 (see the church father Ambrose, *Letter 50*; Calvin; Gordis 1954). However, many interpret this as a subsequent scene between Hosea and Gomer (Ewald; Wellhausen; Pusey; Harper; Rowley 1956; Mays; Yee 1996). In this reading, 'Gomer was an originally faithful bride, who subsequently committed adultery, underwent divorce and perhaps descent into slavery, but was eventually taken back by Hosea as a symbol of Yahweh's love for apostate Israel' (Kelle 2009: 190).

Within these theories, there are many variations. Some modern readers posited that while the account of chapter 1 is based on historical circumstances, chapter 3 is allegorical or a secondary addition (Volz 1898; Batten 1929). Another reading suggests that the same woman is in view in both chapters, but that chapter 1 refers to a time when Hosea was a client of Gomer's, while chapter 3 refers to Hosea purchasing and marrying Gomer (Davies 1992, 1993).

3:2

In verse 2 we read that Hosea purchases the woman (LXX: 'hired her for myself') for fifteen shekels of silver, as well as a quantity of barley (and, according to the LXX, some wine; cf. NRSV). The numbers and quantities noted here have led to considerable conjecture, and spiritual and intertextual connections were common. The Targum, in line with Talmudic tradition, understands the specific reference to fifteen as pointing to another redemption, the date for Israel's exodus from Egypt: 'I redeemed them by my Memra on the fifteenth day of the month of Nisan' (cf. Rabbi Yohannan in b. Ḥul. 92a). In the medieval period, Ibn Ezra would suggest that the fifteen refers to the fifteen kings of Judah, while Radak says it refers to the twelve tribes along with Abraham, Isaac, and Jacob. In the patristic era, note was made of the fact that fifteen is made up of eight and seven: seven refers to the time of the law and the celebration of the Sabbath on the seventh day while eight points to the resurrection of Jesus on the eighth day (Ambrose, *Letter* 50; Cyril of Alexandria).

In the Talmud, the Sages would also expand on the reference to the quantity of barley, again offering a figural reading:

The verse states: 'A Ḥomer of barley, and a half-Ḥomer of barley.' A Ḥomer equals thirty se'a, and a half-Ḥomer equals fifteen se'a, totaling forty-five se'a; these are the forty-five righteous individuals in whose merit the world continues to exist. (b. Ḥul. 92a)

Jerome would offer his own reading in this vein, taking account of both the numbers, fifteen and forty-five: Israel is freed on the fifteenth of Nisan and arrives at Sinai on the forty-fifth day (cf. Nicholas of Lyra). Calvin is not impressed with Jerome's exegesis; these are, he says, 'puerile trifles' (127).

For others, the precise amounts of silver and barley delineated are seen as proof of an actual transaction (Theodore of Mopsuestia; cf. Wolff). Fifteen shekels of silver is noted as half the price of a common slave (Exod. 21:32), and so the woman is worth less than a slave (Gill; Pusey; Mays). Wolff and Gruber suggest that the silver and barley together equal thirty pieces, and so in sum the payment may be equal to the price of a slave as noted in Exodus.

Why does Hosea need to pay at all? If this is his wife, it seems unnecessary that he should need to purchase her (Landy). According to Calvin, Hosea gave these quantities as an arrangement to his wife on which she might live. This is an allowance as she is already his wife. In this sense, he bought her allegiance, though it is a meager allowance (cf. Pusey). Others suggest that Hosea is paying for exclusive rights for a prostitute (Rudolph 1966) or that the woman has become someone else's personal slave, and so he must buy her back (Budde 1925).

The visual reception of this scene highlights the diverse ways in which this payment has been understood, while also pointing to the way in which readers have visualized the characters in this vignette. One of the images of Hosea in Amiens Cathedral depicts Hosea handing over what seems to be coins to the woman, a depiction that would seem to align with the understanding that the woman herself is being paid, either as an allowance or as a fee (Figure 11).

Other representations of this scene paint a different picture with Hosea seemingly buying Gomer out of slavery or sexual exploitation. This is particularly common in modern Christian depictions. An interesting element in such images is the portrayal of Hosea as a masculine, savior figure, redeeming the woman who is in need of rescuing (see Figure 12). Here the genteel, tender depictions of Hosea and Gomer, common in earlier eras, are replaced by those in which Hosea is portrayed as a masculine, heroic figure.

3:3–4

The next verses present a speech from Hosea to the woman and an explanation of the scene. The reported speech from Hosea states that the woman is to refrain from playing the whore, and she is not to have intercourse, even with the prophet. This, we are told, points to a time when Israel will be without

FIGURE 11   *Hosea paying Gomer, Amiens Cathedral, France.*
Used with permission from Stuart Whatling.

their leaders or elements of worship. This time of refraining and withholding has been interpreted as a reference to exile (Theodore of Mopsuestia; Rashi; Luther) or the destruction of the Temple in 70 CE (Origen, *On First Principles*, 4.1.3; Ferreiro).

3:5

Verse 5 begins by stating that 'Afterwards the Israelites shall return and seek the LORD their God, and David their king.' Through the centuries, the traditions have spent significant energy on the reference to David in this verse. Following the Sages, Rashi offers a plain reading that sees this as a critique of the northern kingdom and their rejection of the Davidic line (cf. Ben Zvi 2005). In the Christian tradition, Theodore of Mopsuestia also offers a thorough historical reading, noting that this passage refers to the Babylonian exile, and the mention of David refers to the restoration of the people under the leadership of Zerubbabel. Nevertheless, a large number of readers have offered messianic and

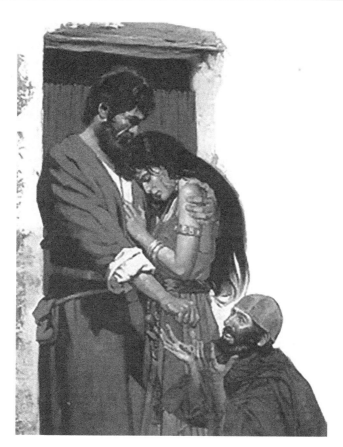

FIGURE 12   Hosea and Gomer.
Unattributed image.

Christological interpretations. The Targum adds an explicit reference to the messianic era in verse 5, stating that the people of Israel 'will obey the anointed One son of David their king' (cf. Ibn Ezra). Augustine, meanwhile, states, 'You will never find a prophecy plainer than this, for the name King David means Christ' (*City of God* 18.28; cf. Jerome; Nicholas of Lyra; Luther). In the modern period, a common refrain is that much of verse 5, notably the reference to David and the latter days, points to a later Judean interpolation (Wellhausen; Wolff; Mays).

The chapter seems to end on a positive note of Israel returning, counteracting the harsh language and punishment in the previous verses. Many readers have thus read this chapter in a positive light as a picture of divine love calling us to repentance. The time of withholding is like a widowhood for the people, but this is in fact a kindness of God that leads to restoration rather than the outright destruction that is deserved (Calvin; Gill). In the words of Wolff, 'the woman, who could no longer resist temptation, was saved from it. Thus love dominates these severe measures' (62).

However, others are less convinced of a positive framework. Baumann, for example, suggests that as long as we hold on to the metaphor, we are reinforcing the patriarchal nature of the imagery; it is an untenable metaphor for reflection on God (Baumann 2003). Yee concurs: as was noted in relation to chapter 1, while men may be able to relate to God's wounded heart, it is more difficult for women as this scene again 'absolutizes and elevates male experience as "human" and overlooks women's distinctive circumstances' (Yee 1996: 232).

Hosea 4

In chapter 4 the broad narrative framework of Hosea 1–3 comes to an end, and from this point, the reader encounters a series of oracles cataloging Israel's unfaithfulness along with a call to return that extends through much of the rest of the book (Calvin; Wellhausen). Modern critics often designate chapters 4–11 as an addition to the earlier account of Hosea and his wife even if some oracles are traced back to the prophet himself (Wolff; Ginsberg 1971). Regardless of their redactional history, these chapters are filled with creative imagery and forceful metaphors; as with the preceding chapters, these pose challenging questions for readers, both ancient and modern (Moughtin-Mumby 2008). For an overview of the modern interpretation of chapters 4–14, see Kelle (2010).

4:1–3

Chapter 4 begins with an indictment against the people of Israel and the inhabitants of the land. This accusation includes a lack of faithfulness, loyalty, and knowledge of God, the converse of which is the ongoing swearing, lying, murder, stealing, and adultery. Because of this, we are told, the land mourns, and its inhabitants (including animals) languish.

This section takes the form of a lawsuit, a courtroom accusation, based on the use of the term *rib*, 'to strive, or contend' (Pusey; Sweeney; Mays; Davies 1992). The Targum clarifies these initial verses by making some of the abstract comments more concrete. Thus, 'swearing' becomes 'swearing falsely', and

Hosea, Joel, and Obadiah Through the Centuries, First Edition. Bradford A. Anderson.
© 2024 John Wiley & Sons Ltd. Published 2024 by John Wiley & Sons Ltd.

'adultery' becomes 'begetting children by the wives of their companions' (cf. Rashi; b. Qidd. 13a). Radak sees here a reference to the covenant relationship that God made with Israel. Since Israel has done the opposite of what they promised to do, so now God will do the opposite and will abandon his people. Wolff refers to this list of sins as 'the opposite side of the flourishing economy at the time of Jeroboam II … that produced a social crisis of the first order, without which the subsequent political crisis cannot be comprehended' (Wolff: 68; cf. Harper). While the points of contact with elements in the Decalogue in these verses were not often commented on in antiquity, Gill notes this connection in the eighteenth century as do a number of modern commentators (Macintosh; Sweeney; Gruber).

The imagery of the natural world in these verses has been understood variously. Some understand the animals as a figurative reference to humanity (Theodore of Mopsuestia; Cyril of Alexandria), while others see the land-related language as drawing on fertility imagery and the Baal cult (Sweeney). More common, however, has been reflection on the interplay of humanity and the created world. One interesting factor is the possible connection here with the language of creation as beasts, birds, and fish resonate with the creation account of Genesis 1; this punishment is in a sense an undoing of God's good creation (Pusey; Andersen and Freedman). A number of other commentators throughout history have used these verses to discuss the way in which nature suffers for humanity's sin (Targum; Calvin: Ewald; Mays). Related to this, readers have begun examining these verses in light of ecological issues and concerns. Here focus is placed on the interconnectedness of humanity and the created world, and the reality that human actions have repercussions for the land and animals. This has proved useful for some readers in relation to thinking about the present environmental crisis (Loya 2008; Marlow 2009; Keefe 2016). Wacker (2012) points out that the land is represented in a different manner here than it is in chapter 1; while in the former the land has abandoned YHWH, here it seems to align with God against the people as it mourns and dries up, withholding life-giving elements.

The imagery of verses 1–3 has also been picked up in less mainstream forms of interpretation. One example understands these verses as a prophecy being fulfilled in the present time. Drawing on Hos. 4:3, where we read that 'together with the wild animals and the birds of the air, even the fish of the sea are perishing', Holm (2014) argues that the unprecedented death of animals throughout the world should be interpreted as part of God's indictment on the world for humanity's sin and as a harbinger of the end times. The author presents over 250 'mass death' events of animals from around the world—from bees, to chickens, to fish—as evidence that Hosea's prophecy is being fulfilled in the present. This is to be understood as a warning and a call to repentance in these last days.

4:4–5

The Hebrew of the following verses is notoriously difficult, and this has led to diverse interpretations on matters both large and small. Contemporary scholarship has offered a number of reconstructions of the Hebrew, as well as suggestions regarding potential redactions within this section (see Wolff).

A key question in verses 4–10 is whether the critique offered here is aimed at the priests, the people of Israel, or both. The Hebrew is hard to decipher on this matter. The Septuagint sees the people as a whole in view, noting that the people are like a priest being contradicted. The complicated relationship between the people and the priests is picked up in the Talmud: both b. Šabb. (149b) and b. Qidd. (70b) draw on Hos. 4:4 when noting that some Sages say priests are naturally quarrelsome and cantankerous. The Targum agrees that the people as a whole are being critiqued but, instead of comparing the people to the priests, suggests that the people 'argue with their teachers' (cf. Vulgate: contradict the priest). Rashi incorporates this into his commentary, noting that the priests were seen as teachers and instructors (Deut. 33:10). The people do not like to be taught, and their lack of knowledge will mean that they will no longer be a royal priesthood (Rashi).

Early Christian interpreters likewise agreed that the whole people of Israel are being confronted in verses 4–6 either because they contradict the priests (Jerome) or because they are like a priest who is under attack and is losing respect (Theodore of Mopsuestia; Cyril of Alexandria). Luther and Calvin also see the people being denounced in these verses. Luther says, 'They are the kind of people who accuse the denouncer and accuser in return' (20). Pusey concurs, suggesting that this depiction of the people as quarrelsome is a reflection of the 'national character' of northern Israel, which had broken off from Judah and Jerusalem.

In the modern period, and drawing on extensive reconstructions of the text, scholars began to argue that the entire unit is concerned with priests, likely those related to the northern cult (Wellhausen; Wolff), or a particular (perhaps chief) priest (Jeremias 1983; Andersen and Freedman). The notion that these verses are concerned with priests (rather than the people as a whole) continues to be the consensus in scholarship (Mays; Macintosh; Sweeney; Tiemeyer 2006).

4:6–7

In verse 6 we are told that it is a lack of knowledge that will destroy God's people (Targum: 'My people have become stupid for lack of knowledge'). Some have tied this lack of knowledge back to the priests and northern schismatic priests in particular (Ibn Ezra). Such priests are to blame for the damage done in terms of the people no longer having proper knowledge of God (Calvin; Wellhausen). Others have suggested that this knowledge refers to an inward disposition or heartfelt devotion toward YHWH (Lohfink 1961). More common, however, is the understanding that this knowledge of God relates to God's revealed will and his Torah—the people have been deprived of such understanding (Targum; Jerome; Wolff; Andersen and Freedman). This notion of God's people being destroyed because of a lack of knowledge has again become popular in recent decades, particularly in Protestant evangelicalism, where it is especially popular in sermons and other devotional settings. Here the idea of 'knowledge' seems to be similar to that of Lohfink (1961) noted above—the lack of relational knowledge of God is seen as being at the heart of many of society's ills (Jackson 2020; cf. comments below at 4:13).

Verse 7 states that 'the more they increased, the more they sinned against me', changing glory for shame. The Aramaic Targum attempts to clarify this increase, stating that 'the more I increased their income, the more they sinned before me'. However, most interpreters see this increase as a reference to Israel's growing impiety either in relation to the priests (Macintosh) or the religious leaders and people alike (Calvin). Rashi offers another understanding: the more the prophets called after the people and rebuked them, the more they turned away and increased their wickedness.

4:8–10

In verse 8 we read that 'they feed off the sins of my people'. The most common understanding of this is that it is the priests who are feeding off of the people's sins (Calvin). Origen sees this as positive, noting that as the priests are said to eat the sins of the people, so Christ is the priest who devours our sins (*Homilies on Leviticus* 5.2). Most interpreters, however, see here collusion between priest and people, perhaps with the priests consenting to the people's sins (Jerome) or profiting from their sins by gaining from their continual sacrifices (Gill; Pusey). This 'satirizes and inverts the priest functions' as outlined in the Torah, where the priests consume the people's sins so as to restore purity and holiness (Landy: 57).

The theme of unfaithfulness returns in verse 10 as we are told that 'they shall play the whore', and they 'devote themselves to whoredom'. Most often this harlotry has been interpreted as religious infidelity. Jerome suggested this fornication refers to the idols of Jeroboam, while many modern commentators have understood this as another reference to syncretism (Mays). Wolff goes so far as to say that the use of the Hebrew word *'azav*, 'forsake', is likely the first use (perhaps in the history of religion!) of the notion of apostasy. However, as will be seen in the next section, a number of different proposals for understanding this theme of infidelity have been put forward in recent years.

4:11–14

The next verses of this chapter focus more intently on Israel's infidelity, calling into question a number of the people's actions. Verse 11 first notes that wine takes away understanding. Luther comments that harlotry and wine make fools in every culture—especially popes and monks. Pusey concurs; these fleshly sins lead man to be 'brutish and irrational' (51). However, Ben Zvi offers a reminder that in Hosea, 'drunkenness and sexual promiscuity … do not stand by or for themselves, but rather serve to convey a sense of wrongful cultic behaviour' (2005: 104).

The people, we are told, also consult wood and rod. There has been considerable debate as to what these might refer to. The LXX uses 'divining rods' here, suggesting that some form of divination is in mind (cf. Luther). According to Cyril of Alexandria, the wood and rod refer to a staff used for divination, such as used by Nebuchadnezzar for casting lots in Ezek. 21:21–22. Others have understood wood here as a reference to idols made of wood (Calvin; Rashi) or more specifically to the customs of Baal worship in Canaanite rituals (Wolff). Sweeney has argued that the wood and rod refer to the traditional Levitical rod or staff, questioning its efficacy in the northern cult (Num. 17:1–12).

The castigation continues in verse 12, remarking that 'a spirit of whoredom has led them astray'. This 'spirit of whoredom' (*ruach zenunim*) has been understood in various ways. Theodore of Mopsuesatia saw this infidelity as turning to idols and their vices, and others have also suggested this refers generally to apostasy and idolatry (Macintosh). In the modern era, Andersen and Freedman have suggested that this *ruach zenunim* may refer to a goddess known in antiquity. A similar claim has been made by Wacker (2012) in relation to the giving of offerings under various types of trees noted in verse 13. She suggests that the reference to trees may indicate the presence of female deities in Israel, particularly tree goddesses, as there is a close connection of tree symbolism and female deities elsewhere in the ANE. Several centuries earlier, Gill had compared this reference to trees with pagans, such as Druids in Britain, who have sacred groves.

The prophet uses strong language in the following clauses, noting that 'your daughters play the whore, and your daughters-in-law commit adultery'. However, God will not punish these discretions, we are told, because the men themselves have been unfaithful (vv. 13b–14). The Targum offers some explanation, clarifying that this refers to the daughters whom you have 'from the daughters of the nations' and daughters-in-law 'from the nations whom you have taken for your sons'. More problematic has been how to understand the final term used to designate with whom the men have been unfaithful (*ha-qedeshot*). The LXX renders this term as *initiates*, suggesting the people in view have a cultic role. The Vulgate, meanwhile, translates this clause as 'sacrificed with the effeminate (*effeminatis*)'. Jerome expands on this translation in his commentary, where he equates the *effeminatis* with eunuchs, which in this case he thinks refers to sacred prostitutes (cf. Cyril of Alexandria). While not everyone has agreed with Jerome's rendering, the notion that sacred prostitution is here in mind has held significant sway throughout history (Nicolas of Lyra; Pusey). Drawing on accounts from Herodotus, Wolff argues that the sexual rites outlined here are similar to examples of sacred prostitution found throughout the ancient world (cf. Davies 1992). In this case we have temple prostitutes who are active among the Israelites, again mimicking Canaanite Baal rites (Mays).

Not everyone, however, has subscribed to this theory. In his notes, Luther specifically counters Jerome's understanding of eunuchs or sacred prostitutes, suggesting that the term simply means 'harlots', as it stands in parallel here with the more common term for such practices, *zenunim*. Others have suggested these *qedeshot* might be 'cult women' attached to the holy places but not necessarily prostitutes themselves (Macintosh; Wacker 2012). Indeed, the notion of sacred prostitution and its practice in antiquity has been called into question in relation to both the Bible (Bird 1989; DeGrado 2018) and also the wider ancient world (Budin 2008). Thus, alternative readings have suggested that the parallel between prostitutes and *qedeshot* is metaphorical as holy women are scandalously depicted as prostitutes (Moughtin-Mumby 2008).

Why are the daughters and daughters-in-law not punished for their harlotry? In the Christian tradition, one answer to this question is that the sins are not corrected because God wants the infamy of the people to be seen by all (Calvin). In the Jewish tradition, an interesting connection is made here with the Soṭah in Numbers 5, the ritual to be undertaken if a husband suspects his wife of adultery. In the Talmud, we read that the bitter waters test (Numbers 5) becomes worthless when immorality is prevalent; thus, the Sages note, after Hosea this practice was discontinued (b. Soṭah 47b). Rashi expands on this, explaining that the outcome of the test depends on the husband's moral purity. Thus, according to the Sages, the daughters in Hosea 4 are not judged because the men have likewise been unfaithful—and the bitter waters test is no longer valid because immorality is widespread. This connection was the basis for a reading in the triennial cycle of the Torah, practiced in Judaism before the twelfth century CE, where Hos. 4:14–5:2 was paired with Num. 5:11–6:21 (Mann and Sonne 1966).

Sermons and homiletical reflections on Hosea 4 are plentiful, particularly in Christian tradition, where the sexual immorality of the chapter is highlighted. A common point of emphasis is the connection of the 'lack of knowledge' noted in 4:6 with the spiritual and sexual infidelity described in 4:11–19. An example of this can be seen in Michael Stark's sermon entitled 'The Root of Immorality' (2020), where he suggests that the contemporary Western world is in a state of spiritual and moral decline. Hosea 4 is used as one of many examples in the Bible where moral (primarily sexual) decline follows on from spiritual decline in a society, and both of these are seen as stemming from society turning from the knowledge of God. Just as Israel was unfaithful to YHWH and adopted the moral baseness of its neighbors in Hosea, Stark argues, so have nations such as the United States and Canada turned from knowledge of God and adopted the immorality of the contemporary secular world.

4:15–16

We find a reference to Judah in verse 15, which calls on the southern neighbor to not be caught up in Israel's idolatry, and modern commentators have thus suggested that this section is a later Judean insertion (Budde 1926; Emmerson 1984). More interesting to commentators throughout history, however, has been the injunction in this verse not to go up to Gilgal or Beth-Aven. Gilgal was a place where Israel's crossing of the Jordan under Joshua was commemorated (Joshua 4–5). Beth-Aven is less clear. While there does seem to be a place bearing this name (see Josh. 7:2), in the LXX this name becomes 'House of On'. The Targum clarifies the text by replacing Beth-Aven with Bethel, a reading that most interpreters have adopted. Beth-Aven ('house of iniquity') is a pejorative name for Bethel in Amos 5, and thus it is assumed the same idea is at work here due to Jeroboam's setting up of the golden calf at Bethel (see Rashi; Radak; Nicolas of Lyra; Calvin). In the modern period, questions began to be raised about the origins of this idea with a number of scholars indicating that Hosea may have in fact borrowed this wordplay from Amos 5:5 (Ewald; Wellhausen; Davies 1992).

The Hebrew of verse 16 states that Israel is stubborn like a stubborn heifer. The ancient translations rendered this in various ways. The Greek LXX says that Israel was 'like a frenzied heifer that went into a frenzy', while the Targum likens Israel to an ox that has become fat, in this case a reference to their wealth (cf. Rashi). The verse concludes with a reference to God feeding the people as lambs on a wide pasture. While some take this statement at face value, referring to God's provision for the people in spite of their infidelity (Yee 1996), this is more commonly understood as a rhetorical question—given that Israel is so stubborn, should YHWH feed them as innocent lambs (NRSV; Macintosh)?

4:17–19

In verse 17 we read that 'Ephraim is joined to idols—let him alone'. Here the designation Ephraim is used to denote the entire northern kingdom and its 'addiction' to idolatry (Targum; Macintosh). Calvin suggests that the term *joined* may be an allusion to Hosea's marriage as Israel has made an alliance with foreign peoples and gods.

How should we understand the clause 'let him alone'? Rashi argues that this is God speaking to the prophet, telling Hosea to refrain from rebuking Israel since it will do no good. Similar sentiments are found in a sermon from the nineteenth-century Baptist preacher Charles Spurgeon. In a sermon entitled 'Let Him Alone', Spurgeon warns his London congregation that if they are not careful, they will become lost causes in the eyes of God. The sin that leads to being left alone is continual idolatry, as seen in the northern kingdom and their worship of calves and idols. In the world of nineteenth-century England, Spurgeon equates this with drinking, profanity, and debauchery, and he calls out in particular those who refuse to respond to their conscience or change their ways. 'Where a man becomes guilty of despising the chastisements of God,' the preacher notes, 'and perseveres in his wickedness after having suffered for it, there again the guilt assumes a double dye' (Spurgenon 1951: 437). Being left alone means being cut off from God, the church, and those who love us—and the ultimate end of such a life, Spurgeon concludes, is destruction.

The enumeration of Israel's sins continues in verse 18 with reference to drinking, orgies, and lewdness. The Hebrew of this verse is very difficult, which has led to wide-ranging translations and commentary. The Targum suggests that the leaders have multiplied banquets through the oppression of others, bringing together moral and socioeconomic critique. Calvin comments that this verse points to Israel's 'shameful and beastly excess' (178). The chastisement of these feasts and gatherings may refer to the leaders of the people (Jerome) or to inappropriate behaviors happening more broadly at the sanctuaries (Macintosh).

The final verse of the chapter has also proven difficult to interpret. The NRSV translates 4:19 with the following: 'A wind has wrapped them in its wings, and they shall be ashamed because of their altars.' One stream of interpretation has understood the 'wind' in this verse as a 'spirit of lust', a reading that has ancient roots (Andersen and Freedman; Yee 1996; cf. Jerome). Others have suggested that this wind is more generally the spirit of idolatry, in which Israel has now been caught up (Ibn Ezra; cf. Lipshitz 1988). One further interpretation sees the wind as a reference to being driven into exile (Rashi; Jeremias 1983; Eidevall 1996). Here the wind is a vehicle of God's judgment, a theme found elsewhere in the book of Hosea (e.g., 8:7; see Macintosh).

What is the theme of this chapter? From antiquity, readers have understood spiritual infidelity and apostasy as the key issues being addressed (Targum; Jerome; Calvin; Pusey). As noted above, for many, this apostasy is expressed as infidelity, which ties this chapter back to the account of Hosea and Gomer in the first chapters of the book (Sweeney). In the twentieth century, scholars became increasingly convinced that, as in chapters 1–3, this chapter offers a critique of Israel's adoption of the Baal cult and Canaanite religious practices, and particularly the priests who are responsible for this abandonment of Israel's God (Wolff). However, as the Baal fertility cult reading has become less popular, various alternative interpretations have been put forward. Moughtin-Mumby, for example, has highlighted the textured use of the term *prostitute/prostitution* in chapter 4 and beyond. She argues, 'Far from being limited to straightforward allusions to a historical practice, "prostitution" gathers a wide range of associations within this provocative poetry, including those of separation, estrangement, unfaithfulness, incongruous behaviour, unacceptable cultic practice, and cultic defilement' (2008: 75). She notes that the metaphorical use of this idea is complex and multilayered in Hosea and that readers should proceed with caution if tempted to pin this idea down to one explicit reference. The multilayeredness of Hosea's metaphorical language, as we shall see, continues in the following chapters.

In Hosea 5 the castigation of Israel continues with attention given to the actions of the priests, the king, and the people as a whole. The continued sins of Ephraim are singled out as is the coming punishment for Ephraim's infidelity. The chapter ends with a call for the people to acknowledge their guilt and turn to God, a theme which will be picked up in Hosea 6.

5:1–2

Verse 1 singles out the priests, the house of the king, and indeed the whole house of Israel. A number of church fathers took this as a chance to reflect on pastoral duty and the role of shepherds in guiding their flocks (Clement of Alexandria; Gregory the Great; see Ferreiro). Other commentators have tried to more closely identify the parties in question. The priests, for example, have been equated with false priests of the northern kingdom who bought their way into the priesthood (Cyril of Alexandria) or priests from Judah who should have helped their northern kin turn from their ways (Radak). The house of the king, meanwhile, has been associated with the Jehu dynasty (Wolff), Menahem (Gill), as well as 'unhappy Zechariah, a weak, pliant, self-indulgent, drunken scoffer' (Pusey: 55). Whatever the case, it seems clear that particular blame is laid at the feet of the priests and leaders for the people's behavior (Calvin; von Rad 1968; Moughtin-Mumby 2008).

Hosea, Joel, and Obadiah Through the Centuries, First Edition. Bradford A. Anderson.
© 2024 John Wiley & Sons Ltd. Published 2024 by John Wiley & Sons Ltd.

In verses 1b–2a we are told that these groups face judgment, with the NRSV offering 'for you have been a snare at Mizpah, and a net spread upon Tabor, and a pit dug deep in Shittim'. However, the Hebrew of these verses is complicated as the history of interpretation makes clear. In the LXX, for example, we read, 'because you have become a snare to the lookout and like a net stretched over the Itabyrion, which the game hunters firmly set' (see also Jerome). In the Targum, meanwhile, there are no place names mentioned at all as Mizpah becomes 'teachers' and Tabor a 'high mountain'. Nevertheless, the identification of Mizpah and Tabor in verse 1 does have ancient roots. An interpretation from Jewish tradition held that guards were stationed on the mountains of Mizpah and Tabor to stop pilgrims from the north from going to the Temple in Jerusalem; indeed, anyone who did go to Jerusalem was put to death, so this tradition maintains (b. Sanh. 102a; cf. Rashi; Ibn Ezra). This reading was also known in Christian circles as seen in Jerome's commentary, where he cites Jeroboam's fears as outlined in 1 Kgs 12:27.

Reading Mizpah as forming a parallel with Tabor became more common in the early modern period (Luther; Calvin; Gill; Ewald). The modern era also saw a number of reconstructions of the text, the most famous being the reading of 'Shittim' as a third place name in verse 2 to go with Mitzpah and Tabor (Wellhausen). This would become the predominant reading in the modern period as seen in most contemporary translations and commentaries (NRSV; Wolff; Macintosh). In line with their interpretation of earlier chapters in the book, some form critics have suggested that these three cities may have been connected to the Baal cult in some way (Mays). Others have noted the play on the word *trap* as these places refer to various places where Israel succumbed to traps in their history, including the fornication with Moabite women at Shittim in Num. 25:1 (Sweeney).

Verse 2 ends by noting that 'I will punish all of them'. This clause is included on the image of the prophet Hosea found in the Augsburg Cathedral (Figure 13). In this twelfth-century stained glass image, the prophet holds a scroll with his words in Latin. The Latin text states that he has been a 'rebuker' or 'teacher' of them all. While the context of chapter 5 seems to indicate that the priests and leaders are under judgment, its use in this stained glass implies that this statement is a synthesis of the prophet's message, teaching Israel regarding its unfaithfulness.

5:3–6

In verse 3, God says that 'I know Ephraim', but Ephraim has 'played the whore' and is defiled. While Ephraim is a common designation for the northern tribes of Israel, some readers have offered more specific readings, suggesting that

Figure 13   *Prophet Hosea in Augsburg Cathedral, stained glass window (ca. 1135–40).*
Allie_Caulfield/Wikimedia Commons/CC BY 2.0.

Ephraim here refers specifically to Jeroboam and the erecting of the golden calves (Radak). The use of 'knowing' and promiscuity language ties into related themes that were used in previous chapters (Pusey; Andersen and Freedman). Wacker (2012), however, notes that while the use of the root *znh* (prostitution or fornication) resonates with chapters 1–4, it is used here in the masculine form, pointing to those whom the text understands as guilty of this infidelity. As with other uses of sexual imagery, it is not always clear whether the prophet has in mind sexual offenses or if this language is part of his polemical rhetoric and points to broader issues and transgressions (cf. Yee 1996; Moughtin-Mumby 2008).

In verse 6 the text mentions the people going with their flocks and herds to seek Yhwh. This imagery has long been understood as referring to ineffectual sacrifices (Jerome; Theodore of Mopsuestia; Rashi; Radak; Nicholas of Lyra). John Calvin comments that these sacrifices, which God will not accept, are much like those of the Papists of his own day with their many rituals. Wolff, meanwhile, suggests that these refer to sacrifices associated with the Baal cult.

5:7

Verse 7 contains several issues that have interested readers. To begin with, we are told that strange or illegitimate children have been born. The LXX renders this as 'foreign children', suggesting intermarriage with surrounding nations. A similar idea is found in rabbinic tradition, which speaks of pagan children, the offspring of betrothal with Gentiles (b. Yebam. 17a; Targum; Rashi). Comparable ideas are found in the Christian tradition with these 'strange children' seen as illegitimate children born of illicit relations with other nations (Theodore of Mopsuestia; Pusey). Spiritual understandings were also put forward with these children referring to those led astray by false gods or consecrated to idols (Jerome; Cyril of Alexandria; Luther; Calvin). In the modern era, the children have been equated with the offspring of the pagan cult in Israel (Wolff) or, focusing on literary and rhetorical issues, as pointing back to the story of Gomer and the children in the earlier chapters (Sweeney).

Another difficult issue in verse 7 is the statement that 'the new moon shall devour them'. In Jewish tradition, the reference to a moon was thought to refer to a specific month and was thus seen as pointing to the month of Av, when the temple was destroyed (Targum; Rashi). Others have suggested that the reference may indeed be to a month but that this refers to a short period of time before destruction comes, rather than a specific month (Gill; Pusey; Rudolph 1966). Still others have posited that this refers to the new moon festival of the priests—in this reading, destruction is coming because of the priests' actions (Andersen and Freedman).

One final issue worth noting in relation to Hos. 5:1–7 is the coherence of the section. These verses form a separate section in textual witnesses of the MT and Greek traditions as seen in the Aleppo Codex and Codex Vaticanus (Gruber). However, readers have long struggled to know how this oracle relates to others in the book. Martin Luther, for example, noted that Hosea did not prophesy or write everything down at the same time. This, he says, helps us understand the book, which covers a long period of time; this particular prophecy he thus places after the Assyrian captivity. Others have placed this oracle much earlier in Hosea's ministry (Wolff). However, the reference to Judah 'also stumbling' in verse 5 has elicited questions about the potential redaction of this section. While earlier readers saw the mention of Judah as a warning as to what was to come for the southern kingdom (Jerome; Calvin; Gill; Pusey), modern readers have suggested that this reference is a later Judean interpolation even if in the final form this indicates that the message is to serve as a warning to Judah as well (Sweeney).

5:8–11

The second half of chapter 5 points to coming desolation and destruction. There is general agreement that 5:8 is the beginning of a new section, which some see extending as far as 7:16 (Wolff; Sweeney). A number of commentators note a shift in the book at this point to a new situation with cultic concerns being replaced with social and political issues in Judah and Israel (Wellhausen; Mays).

A recurring subject in these verses is Ephraim, which is Hosea's preferred name for the northern kingdom. However, this section begins (vv. 8–9) with a warning given to a number of places near the border of Israel and Judah—Gibeah, Ramah, Beth-Aven, and Benjamin. As was the case with verses 1–2, early traditions rendered the Hebrew in various ways. The Greek of the LXX, for example, speaks of the hills, high places, and the house of On (the latter mirroring the Greek translation of Beth-Aven in 4:15). Some church fathers would follow the LXX (Theodore of Mopsuestia). However, Jerome pushes back against the LXX and renders Gibeah, Ramah, and Beth-Aven as place names with Beth-Aven referring to Bethel. This would go on to become the standard understanding (Nicholas of Lyra; Luther; Ewald).

Why are these specific places mentioned? The Targum inserts references to various biblical events and people connected to the places in question:

Prophesy that murderous nations will come against them because they made Saul of Gibeah king over them. Cry aloud as you sound the trumpet; say that kings and their armies will come against them, because they did not listen to the words of Samuel, the prophet from Ramah. Announce to them the alarms of the warriors because they acted faithlessly with my Memra, and they turned backwards from my worship and did not worship before me in the Sanctuary which is in the land of the tribe of Benjamin. (cf. Rashi)

More common has been the assumption that some sort of military action is in view. There is a clear geographic trajectory in this list of places, moving northward from Jerusalem toward Ephraim (Sweeney). A complicating factor is the question of whether the tribal lands of Benjamin were at this period part of Israel or Judah—depending in part on where one locates this oracle historically (Jeremias 1983; Landy). The medieval Jewish exegetes assumed that the enemy had conquered Ephraim and was now coming for Benjamin and thus Judah; the sounding of the shofar is a warning of a coming attack (Radak; Rashi, following Lam. Rab. 6). Others would posit that Benjamin was already part of Ephraim (Calvin; Sweeney). Taking on board the reference to the movement of boundary markers in verse 10, other scholars would suggest that the south-to-north movement from Gibeah to Bethel refers to Judah's encroachment into the heart of Israel (Wolff; Mays; Gruber).

In verse 10 we are told that 'the princes of Judah have become like those who remove the landmark'. Readers frequently point out the similarity here with Deut. 19:14, which legislates against moving a neighbor's boundary markers and in doing so claiming their land for your own (Theodore of Mopsuestia; Mays). Some have understood this as a literal injunction against stealing fields (Rashi), but more common has been the understanding that this refers to Judah claiming Israel's land for its own and in particular those who were eager for the downfall of Israel for this reason (Jerome; Luther; Pusey; Wolff).

5:12–15

The following verses return to the oppression of Ephraim and Judah. Verse 12 states, 'I am like maggots to Ephraim, and like rottenness to the house of Judah' (NRSV). The LXX translates maggots and rottenness as 'confusion' and 'a goad' (cf. Cyril of Alexandria), while the Targum offers 'moth and decay'. Radak follows the Targum, suggesting that the oppression is like a moth that slowly eats clothing (cf. Nicolas of Lyra), while Rashi envisions 'a worm which eats the wood and pulverizes it'. Jerome also translates this verse as moth and rottenness, 'one consuming clothing, the other wood'. Why are these attributes given to God? 'Not because God is a moth or rottenness, or a "disturbance" or a "goad", but because, to those bearing the punishments, he seems to be all these things' (Jerome: 190). Calvin proffers moth and grub as a potential translation, and he notes that 'the meaning of the Prophet is by no means obscure … that the Lord would by a slow corrosion consume both the people' (205; cf. Gill; Pusey; Wellhausen).

The section continues by noting that 'when Ephraim saw his sickness, and Judah his wound, then Ephraim went to Assyria, and sent to the great king (*melek yarev*). But he is not able to cure you …' (5:13; NRSV). The meaning of *melek yarev* is unclear in the Hebrew and has led to considerable debate. The LXX translates this as King Jarim, assuming this is a name (cf. Calvin). Jerome critiques the LXX and, following Aquila and Theodotion, prefers 'avenger', or 'avenging king' (cf. Cyril of Alexandria; Pusey), while others suggest that 'Yarev' refers to a place (Gill). In the modern era, the consensus has been that this refers to a 'great king', drawing on ANE parallels that use similar designations for Assyrian kings (Andersen and Freedman; Davies 1992).

The reference to Assyria in this verse has led to various historical reconstructions in which Hosea's message might be situated. While some have been content to see this as a looming threat from Assyria (Luther), a number of more specific interpretations have been put forward. The most common understanding is that this refers to the reign of Tiglath-Pilesar and the aftermath of the Syrian-Ephraimite war, ca. 733 BCE. This was put forward in an influential article by Alt (1919) and was followed by a number of scholars (Heschel 1962; Mays; Macintosh; Blenkinsopp 1996), though similar sentiments had previously been suggested (Gill; Radak; Rashi). This idea has been called into question in recent decades by scholars who feel that Alt read too much into the passage (Andersen and Freedman).

The chapter ends with God saying that he will return to his place until the people return to him and seek his face (5:15). There is a clear change of subject here from wrath to repentance. A number of Christian readers made Christological connections, particularly with the reference to seeing God's face. Cyril of Alexandria, for example, notes that when people are distressed they will seek God's face; this, for Cyril, refers to Christ: 'The Son, then, is the true face of the God and Father, especially if recognized as such; "whoever who has seen him has seen the Father"' (137; cf. Luther). For Calvin, this verse speaks to the true meaning of God's discipline: to bring repentance.

Hosea 6

The theme of returning to God, introduced at the end of chapter 5, continues in the first part of Hosea 6. However, as the chapter progresses, we are reminded that Israel (along with Judah) has not been responsive to God but has continued in its sinful ways. The chapter has a number of themes and images that have been influential in both Judaism and Christianity, including the call to return to YHWH (v. 1), the imagery of being raised up on the third day (v. 2), and the reminder that God desires mercy and not sacrifice (v. 6).

6:1

The chapter begins with a first-person invocation, 'Let us return (*nashuvah*) to YHWH.' The significance of the root *shuv*—to turn or repent—has been noted by a number of readers as crucial to the message of the book of Hosea as a whole (Mays; Yee 1996). The call to return is based on the hope-filled belief that Israel's God can both tear the people down and heal them. Calvin is representative of many when he notes that punishment from God is for the purpose of salvation and always leaves room for grace.

The imagery of returning to God found in Hos. 6:1 has been inspirational for artists and musicians as well. The American Roman Catholic songwriter Gregory Norbet wrote a piece in 1972 entitled 'Hosea (Come Back to Me)'. Often used in Lent, this song draws on imagery from Hosea as a call to repentance and return to God: 'Come back to me with all your heart, Don't let fear

Hosea, Joel, and Obadiah Through the Centuries, First Edition. Bradford A. Anderson.
© 2024 John Wiley & Sons Ltd. Published 2024 by John Wiley & Sons Ltd.

keep us apart.' Hosea's imagery is also used in an eighteenth-century hymn from the Scottish hymn writer John Morrison. Entitled 'Come Let Us Return to the Lord Our God', this song also implores the singer to return with a contrite heart to God, who is gracious and compassionate. In both of these examples, the imagery of returning to God is understood as a call to repentance, while God's attributes of mercy and compassion are also highlighted.

6:2

The hopeful refrain continues into verse 2, where we are told that 'After two days he will revive us; on the third day he will raise us up.' This reference to two and three days has led to considerable commentary in both Jewish and Christian traditions. Some in the Jewish tradition have read this verse in a literal manner. Radak, for example, says that this text is indicative of the fact that if we are ill for two days, God will heal us on the third day. However, figurative and spiritual readings have been more common. In the Babylonian Talmud, this passage is used in a discussion concerning eschatological matters:

> Rav Ketina says: Six thousand years is the duration of the world, and it is in ruins for one thousand years. ... Abaye says: It is in ruins for two thousand years, as it is stated: 'After two days He will revive us; in the third day He will revive us, and we shall live in His presence' (Hosea 6:2). (b. Sanh. 97a; cf. Esth. Rab. 9:2)

Rashi also gives an eschatological reading, relating this verse to both the history and the future of Israel: the two days refers to the destruction of the two sanctuaries; the third day points to the construction of the third temple still to come. The Targum removes the specific references to two and three days and instead speaks of 'days of consolations' and 'day of the resurrection of the dead'. Here the text is explicitly linked with resurrection and may have messianic overtones (Cathcart and Gordon: 41). However, the Targum's removal of the number of days is noticeable, and this change may have been done to avoid giving credence to Christian appropriation of this verse. Other traditions were more forthright in connecting this text to resurrection without the reservations seen in the Targum, drawing a clear connection between 6:2 and the resurrection of the dead on the third day (Gen. Rab. 56:1–2). The famous rabbinic blessing in the Mishnah ('Blessed are You ...who has revived us and made us rise up,' m. Ber. 9:3) may in fact be based on Hos. 6:2 (Gruber).

Not surprisingly, this verse has provided fertile ground for commentary in the Christian tradition. Two New Testament texts that speak of resurrection on the third day—1 Cor. 15:4 and Luke 24:7—employ language that is very similar to the Greek of Hos. 6:2 in the LXX. It has long been assumed that these NT texts and traditions were drawing on the language and imagery of Hosea (Luther). Some church fathers do in fact show restraint in their interpretation of Hosea; Theodore of Mopsuestia notes that 6:2 refers to the fact that God acts quickly to restore his people, and his commentary does not even mention resurrection. However, this is the exception to the rule. In *City of God* (28), Augustine comments that Hosea in this verse foretells Christ's resurrection (cf. Jerome). Others added further detail to the account—a popular interpretation was that the reference to the second day points to Christ's descent into hell, with the third day speaking of his resurrection (see Origen, *Homilies on Exodus* 5 [Ferreiro]; cf. Pusey). This same idea would be prevalent in the medieval and Reformation eras (Nicholas of Lyra). In his reflections, Luther says this text clearly refers to Christ's resurrection: 'This is so magnificent that it cannot refer to the temporal kingdom of Judah' (31). Calvin offers a more nuanced interpretation, noting that in these verses God is exhorting patience in his people. In his reading, Christ is 'illustrious proof' of this prophecy even if it was not written concerning him.

Over time we begin to see a shift toward more historical interpretations of 6:2. John Gill notes that the text is mainly concerned with the restoration of Israel, and with God one day is like a thousand years, so this can be understood as referring to long periods of time and Israel's eventual restoration. Wellhausen pointed out that the theme of something good happening in two or three days is common in Greek literature (such as Demosthenes), suggesting an ancient trope. Others would argue that this passage may draw on the ancient Near Eastern concept of the death and resurrection of fertility gods, which corresponded with the seasons and harvest in antiquity (Sweeney). Wolff understands the reference to both the second and third day as pointing to a short period of time; this is not a reference to raising the dead but to raising up those who are sick and wounded, in this case Israel (cf. Mays). Andersen and Freedman note similarities between Ezekiel 37 and the notion of national resurrection—as in the exilic prophet's vision, here Hosea speaks of the eventual restoration of the people in the language of resurrection.

These initial verses of Hosea 6 play an important part in liturgical traditions. In the Revised Common Lectionary, Hos. 5:15–6:6 is read in Year A in the Season after Pentecost (Proper 5) (Proper 10 in the Roman Catholic tradition), where it is paired with, among other texts, Matthew 9 and the story of Jesus raising the official's daughter from the dead. Hosea 6:1–6 is also read liturgically in Lent, on Saturday in Week Three, which again draws out the significant resonances with death and resurrection and the imagery of being raised up after three days.

6:3

In verse 3 we are told that YHWH will come to his people like the latter and former rains. Some readers have offered spiritual readings of this imagery; Pusey says this points to Christ, who, like the latter and former rain, is the beginning and end of our spiritual life. More common is the description of the seasonal rains in the Levant, which were so important for harvest (Gill; Wolff). Form critics took this reference to rain as a further critique of the Canaanite fertility cult, for which the rain was significant (Mays).

The imagery of rain in the Hebrew Bible has long been associated with the Holy Spirit in Christianity. This would take on particular significance in the late nineteenth and twentieth centuries with the rise of the 'latter rain' movement, a holiness movement that began in the United States. Along with texts such as Joel 2:23, the imagery of rain in Hos. 6:3 was seen as pointing to an outpouring of the Holy Spirit, which was first given at Pentecost (Acts 2) and was believed to be happening again in the modern world. These revivalist movements began as nondenominational but would lay the foundations for Pentecostal and holiness denominations and movements in the early twentieth century, including the Foursquare church and the Assemblies of God. The 'latter rain' movement would see a revival in the mid-twentieth century, with new leaders such as Oral Roberts stressing supernatural experiences, signs and wonders, and modern-day prophecy. The impact of this renewal movement can be seen in contemporary charismatic and prophetic groups, who continue to teach that we are living in the end times that are ushered in by the 'latter rain' of the Holy Spirit (see Robeck and Yong 2014).

6:4–5

In verses 4–11, the hopeful picture of the previous verses comes crashing back to reality as the text returns to the castigation of Ephraim and Judah because their love (*hesed*) is fleeting. The use of the term *hesed* in verse 4 is important in this section as it recurs in verse 6. While the LXX renders both instances as 'mercy', the term is often translated in different ways in verses 4 and 6 (see, e.g., Targum and NIV).

Because of the people's lack of loyalty, in verse 5 God notes that 'I have hewn them by the prophets, I have killed them by the words of my mouth'. Some, following the Greek LXX, understand this as pointing to the prophets being cut off. In this reading it refers either to prophets who were killed because of their message (Radak) or to false prophets, such as those who served under Ahab and Jezebel (Cyril of Alexandria). More common are those readings that understand the prophets and their words as the instruments of hewing that takes place (Rashi; Jerome; Calvin; Macintosh). As Wolff notes, the words of the prophets are portrayed as 'deadly weapons' (120). For Charles Spurgeon, this verse speaks of 'the rough hewer', who uses 'cutting providences' to bring people back to himself, including prophets, but also the Bible (1951: 454).

6:6

In 6:6 we are told what God wants: he desires 'steadfast love (*hesed*) and not sacrifice, the knowledge of God rather than burnt-offerings'. This is yet another evocative verse that has elicited significant commentary through the centuries. The Targum translates the first clause as 'those who do acts of kindness are more desirable'. Here 'the apparent outright rejection of sacrifice is neatly avoided' (Cathcart and Gordon: 42). Other Jewish traditions, however, did not shy away from critiquing sacrifice. One rabbinic text notes that Hos. 6:6 shows that merciful acts replaced temple sacrifice when the temple was destroyed (*Fathers According to Rabbi Nathan* 4:5; see Neusner). Abarbanel states that the people were not saved by sacrifices but by loving-kindness and observance of the Torah.

Hosea 6:6 is quoted twice by Jesus in the book of Matthew—once when eating with tax collectors and sinners (9:13) and subsequently when questioned over Sabbath observance (12:7). In both cases, Jesus draws on Hosea to challenge his detractors. These quotations, put on the lips of Jesus, have shaped the reception of this passage in the Christian tradition. In the Catholic lectionary, Hos. 6:3–6 is read on the 10th Sunday in Ordinary Time (Year A), where it is paired with Matt. 9:9–13. This is a tradition with ancient roots. Early Christian theologians such as Tertullian, Clement of Alexandria, and Ambrose note the connection of Hos. 6:6 with Matt. 9:13 and the importance of repentance and God's mercy (see Ferreiro).

Others have focused their attention on what is meant here by sacrifice and mercy. Jerome is less sparing in his comments than many of his contemporaries: sacrifices are for show, he says; what God wants is repentance. Calvin, meanwhile, equates sacrifices with all 'outward worship of God, and all legal ceremonies'. Mercy, conversely, incorporates 'faith or piety towards God, and love towards neighbours' (230–31). He also makes clear that mercy and knowledge of God stand in parallel in this verse.

Not surprisingly, a number of readers through the centuries would draw out Christological and spiritual connections. For Cyril of Alexandria, mercy rather than sacrifice refers to Christ who brings God's mercy. Pusey agrees: the notion of mercy being better than sacrifice points to the coming of Christ, who is the final sacrifice. However, mercy is not juxtaposed with sacrifice. 'If we were to say "Charity is better than church-going," we should be understood to mean that it is better than such Church-going as is severed from charity' (Pusey: 67).

Modern readers have noted both intertextual and linguistic issues in this verse. One intertextual resonance that has been commented on is found in 1 Sam. 15:22, where Samuel tells Saul that God desires obedience over sacrifices (Wellhausen; Andersen and Freedman). Wolff, meanwhile, focuses on the meaning of the term *hesed* as relating to loyalty and devotion. In this light, loyalty to the covenant relationship with Yhwh is what pleases God, and empty pious rituals do not satisfy. Mays agrees: love together with knowledge points to loyalty to the covenant, 'a knowing which becomes a state of being' (98).

The notion of God desiring mercy over sacrifice has been an important concept in Christianity, inspired in no small part by Jesus's use of this concept in Matthew 9. In his observations on Hosea, the seventeenth-century Puritan preacher Jeremiah Burroughs offers extensive reflections on this verse. For Burroughs, this verse is a rebuke of those people who trust in 'instituted religion' while living with carnal hearts and with cruelty toward others—that is, those that use religious observance as a pretense. But it is also a reminder of God's preference for mercy over sacrifice in religious practice and of our duty to show mercy to others even when it seems to conflict with religious observance. Indeed, Burroughs notes, this extends to disputed matters of truth and doctrine—even here, mercy should prevail. The connection of mercy and the knowledge of God in this verse is a reminder that knowing God and being inclined to mercy go hand in hand (Burroughs 1863: 332).

In other streams of Christianity, we see a different emphasis when interpreting this text. In a homily on the relationship of Hosea 6 and Matthew 9 in the Roman Catholic liturgy, Father Raniero Cantalamessa, then the Pontifical Household preacher, offered a number of observations about Hos. 6:6. Cantalamessa notes that some may take this verse as a wholesale rejection of ascetic

Christianity with its focus on living sacrificially. However, citing Thomas à Kempis's statement in *The Imitation of Christ* that 'one does not live in love without suffering', Cantalamessa posits that there is no love or mercy without suffering. Cantalamessa concludes,

> Sacrifice and mercy are both good things but they can become bad if misapplied. They are good things if—as Christ did—we choose sacrifice for ourselves and mercy for others; they can become bad things if on the contrary we choose mercy for ourselves and sacrifice for others, that is, if we are indulgent with ourselves and rigorous with others.
>
> (Cantalamessa 2008)

6:7

In verse 7 Hosea returns to the sins of the people. The text of verse 7 is difficult as the transgression of the covenant is linked with the Hebrew term *adam*. The LXX understands this as the generic term for man: 'They are like a person …', and this interpretation is followed by others, including Calvin. Others render this as the proper name Adam, a reference to the breaking of the first covenant (Gen. Rab. 19:9; Cyril of Alexandria; Rashi; Pusey; Landy). More recently, scholars have increasingly understood this as a reference to a location— perhaps the same 'Adam', which is noted in Josh. 3:16. This is then understood as the first of a series of locations, which will be mentioned in the following verses (Mays; Macintosh; Sweeney).

6:8–11

The rest of the chapter continues to outline what Mays calls a 'geography of treachery' (99), naming a number of places where wrongdoing has taken place. Of particular note is verse 9, which states: 'As robbers lie in wait for someone, so the priests are banded together; they murder on the road to Shechem, they commit a monstrous crime.' While Theodore of Mopsuestia sees here an allusion to the murderous attack by Jacob's sons Levi and Simeon in Genesis 34, a more popular reading suggests that this refers to priests who stopped pilgrims from the northern kingdom from going to worship at the Jerusalem temple (Jerome; Cyril of Alexandria; Luther).

Although most readers have focused on religious and political issues in this chapter, in verse 10 we have another reference to Ephraim's whoredom, which is said to 'defile' Israel (6:10). The metaphor of unfaithfulness is again used to critique the people and their leaders (Yee 1996). This usage is another reminder that these themes recur throughout the book, are used in diverse ways, and are never far from the surface in Hosea (Moughtin-Mumby 2008).

The chapter ends with God declaring that a harvest is appointed for Judah and that he will 'restore the fortunes' of his people (6:11). In the LXX, this is interpreted as 'return the captivity of my people', and similar sentiments are found in the Targum and elsewhere, often in relation to the Babylonian exile (Jerome; Pusey). The fact that Judah is mentioned in this way has led modern scholars to suspect a Judean gloss (Emmerson 1984; Macintosh).

Hosea 7

Chapter 7 continues to explore the main themes found in chapter 6, focusing on the transgressions of Ephraim (for a discussion on the ending of chapter 6 and the beginning of chapter 7 in the textual traditions, see Gruber). The Hebrew of chapter 7 is notoriously difficult—this is reflected in the translations and the major interpretive traditions and is often noted by commentators (Luther; Wellhausen; Yee 1996).

7:1–3

In 7:1 we are told that while God seeks to heal Israel, its wickedness and corruption are revealed instead. Calvin sees here a spiritual point: God is like a physician who, when he goes to heal someone, exposes even more serious issues. For some interpreters, the reference to Israel's wickedness is yet another chance to cast aspersions on Judaism. Thus, for Pusey, Samaria's wickedness is a type, foreshadowing the mistreatment of Jesus by the Jews of his day. The corruption of Ephraim and Samaria is condemned here in parallel, similar to the Jerusalem/Judah pairing that we find elsewhere in the HB (Wolff).

In verse 3 we read that in their wickedness 'they make the king glad'. A common understanding is that this refers to Jeroboam I, when the people joined with him in the matter of the calves, thus following his apostasy (Jerome; Cyril of Alexandria; Radak; Calvin). The LXX renders this with the plural 'kings', and this is followed by a number of readers who see this as a reference to

Hosea, Joel, and Obadiah Through the Centuries, First Edition. Bradford A. Anderson.
© 2024 John Wiley & Sons Ltd. Published 2024 by John Wiley & Sons Ltd.

the people pleasing the various wicked kings in general (Gill). Others take this as a reference to foreign nations and their kings taking pleasure in Israel's sin or its eventual downfall (PesK 9:7 [Neusner]; Theodore of Mopsuestia). Another interpretation argues that the reference to the king along with royal officials points to Baal and his court and so indicates Israelite participation in Baalism (Östborn 1956). More recent interpreters have identified later historical points of reference in Israel's history, as well as dysfunction in the royal court, as possible points of reference for this verse's mention of treachery—notably King Hoshea's rise to the throne and murder of (the anti-Assyrian) Pekah (Wolff; Sweeney; Wacker 2012).

7:4

The language of infidelity returns in 7:4 where we are told that 'they are all adulterers', though it is not entirely clear who is the subject of this clause. The Aramaic Targum interprets the adultery language literally, noting that 'They all desire to commit adultery with the wives of their companions.' Similar approaches are found in Christian tradition; Caesarius of Arles, the fifth-sixth-century theologian, takes these verses as a condemnation of adultery and the hypocrisy of adulterers in general (*Sermon 43* [Ferreiro]). However, more common is the understanding that this adultery refers to idolatry, with many suggesting Jeroboam's calves as the intended focus of this critique (Cyril of Alexandria; Nicholas of Lyra; Calvin; Mays).

We next read in 7:4 that 'they are like a heated oven, whose baker does not need to stir the fire'. This oven motif extends through verse 7, and interpreters have long struggled with how to understand the imagery and coherence of this section (see, e.g., Wellhausen; Harper).

In parts of Jewish tradition, the oven imagery in verse 4 is taken as a reference to the coming exile (Targum). Rashi disagrees with this, arguing that the picture is meant to indicate that even when resting, the people are planning evil (cf. Radak). Early Christian readers often employed a spiritual and moral lens to understand this imagery; Jerome likens the oven to those that are kindled 'to bake the bread of impiety' (199), similar to Jesus's warning in Matt. 16:6 concerning the leaven of the Pharisees. In the Reformation era, Luther would offer a similar reading but one that is focused on the people of Ephraim in particular: wicked teachers 'kindle this oven...they prepare and inflame the heart of this people' (36; cf. Gill).

To what might the baker refer? It is possible to interpret the baker as a literal person, a coconspirator who perhaps had a hand in the palace intrigue; it might also just be figurative language (Andersen and Freedman). If understood literally, professional bakers would have been relatively rare in the ancient world, and so it is assumed that reference to a baker in this context indicates a commercial or, more probably, a royal setting (Mays; Wolff). Figurative readings, meanwhile, have included interpreting the baker as a king. More specifically, some see this as a reference to Shallum, who conspired against Zechariah (Wolff).

7:5–8

Verse 5 comments that 'On the day of our king the officials became sick with the heat of the wine'. Readers have often equated the 'day of our king' with a coronation (Rashi) or perhaps the king's birthday (Calvin; Gill). The 'heat of the wine', Abarbanel suggests, refers to the fact that the kings are only interested in pleasure, not their duties.

In 7:7 we read that 'they devour their rulers. All their kings have fallen; none of them calls upon me'. In Lev. Rab. 36:3 this verse is used as a proof text that Ahaz and other Israelite kings have no part in the world to come (see Neusner). A similar sentiment is put forward by Pusey, who explains that the kingdom of Israel was established in sin, and so its kings were doomed from the outset. Rashi, meanwhile, draws on the Talmud to suggest that this refers to those leaders who acquiesced in helping Jeroboam raise idols and who justified and gave cover to this action by doing away with judges and leaders who might stand in the way (y. 'Abod. Zar. 1:1). In the modern period, the reference to all of the fallen kings is often seen as pointing to the various intrigues in the northern kingdom which followed the reign of Jeroboam II (Harper; Mays; Macintosh).

Ephraim, we are told, mixes with the people; it is like a cake that has not been turned (7:8). This mixing with the peoples has normally been understood as a reference to either mixing in exile (Rashi), or mixing with other peoples in Israel, including intermarriage and adopting local customs (Gill; Pusey). Some bring these ideas together: just as Israel mingled with foreigners, so foreigners would overtake them (Theodore of Mopsuestia; Luther). In the modern era, this mixing has increasingly been understood as political in nature, including Hoshea's turn to Assyria after the assassination of Pekah (Harper; Mays; Wolff). An alternative rendering is offered by Shalom Paul, who renders the clause as 'Ephraim will be kneaded among the nations', continuing the bread-and-oven theme (Paul 1968).

The image of the unturned cake is difficult to interpret. Commentators often understand it as referring to the mixing mentioned in 7:8a; in this reading, because Israel has mixed with others, it is consequently like a cake that is unturned: burned on one side but uncooked on the other. It is neither dough nor bread, thus good for nothing (Gill). In this sense, the imagery is a 'mournful derision at a people who never fulfilled their destiny' (Mays: 108). Others have interpreted this spiritually: the unturned cake is like an unconverted mind that has not been turned to God (Gregory the Great, *Morals on the Book of Job* 3.6.16 [Ferreiro]; cf. Jerome). Interestingly, the image of an unturned cake is also used in the Jewish liturgy for the Day of Atonement, 'in the penitential narrative concerning the ten Rabbinic sages martyred by Hadrian' (Gruber: 321). Gruber draws on this to interpret the clause as indicating that the bread (Israel) will be devoured hastily before it is even finished being baked (cf. Goldschmidt 1970).

7:9–10

Another interesting yet enigmatic image is found in 7:9, where we read that 'grey hairs are sprinkled upon him, but he does not know it'. For some, this points to the fact that even after a long time, Israel still did not learn how to avoid this unwelcome fate (Cyril of Alexandria; Calvin). Israel is, according to others, gradually becoming weaker and is thus at the mercy of others (Ewald; Landy). Wolff, however, suggests that this indicates that Israel quickly aged from fear (Wolff). Andersen and Freedman note that gray hair was worn with pride in antiquity, so the sense that this is used derisively is not followed; rather, they understand the reference to gray hairs as mold, which grows on food like hairs, continuing the food/bread theme from the preceding verses (Andersen and Freedman; cf. Gruber).

The nineteenth-century English preacher Charles Spurgeon draws on Hos. 7:9 in a sermon focused on these 'grey hairs'. Following those who understand this imagery to refer to weakness, Spurgeon uses this verse in a moralistic way as a launching point for reflection on spiritual decay and weakness within individuals—though any discussion of the book of Hosea or the context of the Israelites is conspicuously absent in Spurgeon's use of the text. He posits that for individuals, these gray hairs can refer to a lack of repentance, indulgence of minor sins, covetousness, worldliness, and pride, as well as a neglect of prayer and reading God's Word. There are various reasons why people may not notice these spiritual gray hairs, Spurgeon suggests: people lack introspection and do not know their own soul; they do not want to know any evil within themselves and refuse to look in the mirror; or they cannot see the gray because they 'dye themselves so thoroughly' with hypocrisy! The antidote, he preaches, is regular self-examination and supplication (Spurgeon 1951: 457–62).

We encounter the theme of 'return' (*shuv*) again in verse 10. In spite of all that has been recounted, Israel does not return to their God or truly seek him. The commentators do not hold back in their estimation of Israel: according to Cyril of Alexandria, Ephraim's crime was one 'of utter insensitivity, and clear proof of inveterate stupidity'.

7:11–12

The second part of chapter 7 focuses on Ephraim's engagement with the nations, specifically the fact that they call on Egypt and Assyria. In this context, Ephraim is compared in 7:11 to a dove, silly and 'without heart' (*'eyn lev*; NRSV: 'without sense'). The comparison to a silly and senseless dove has most often been understood as a reference to Israel's lack of understanding, discernment, and intelligence in going back and forth to Egypt and Assyria for help (Rashi; Calvin; Andersen and Freedman). Pusey quotes an eastern proverb which states that 'There is nothing more simple than a dove' (Pusey: 76). Further characteristics of doves that are noted by interpreters include the fact that doves do not grieve for their offspring, and they neglect their own safety (Jerome; Theodore of Mopsuestia). Further, doves are easily taken by trappers and easily led astray (Nicholas of Lyra; Luther; Gill). Several Christian commentators note Christ's instruction to be innocent as doves but also wise as serpents (Calvin).

The reference to Egypt and Assyria in the second half of verse 11 is interesting, not least because these two nations are mentioned seven times in parallel in Hosea; these were obviously the main political forces of the time (Andersen and Freedman). The Targum interprets the reference to these two powers as an explanation of Israel's exile to Assyria as punishment for going to Egypt for help. A more specific reading connects this passage to the time of King Hoshea in 2 Kings 17, who went to Egypt for help but ended up defeated by Assyria (Cyril of Alexandria; Gill; Wolff). Whatever the case, readers have been quick to point out Ephraim's confidence in human rather than divine deliverance (Nicholas of Lyra; Luther).

7:13

The text continues in 7:13 with a statement of 'Woe', declaring that the people have strayed from God—and because of this, destruction is coming. In 7:13b we read, 'I would redeem them, but they speak lies against me'. Some have suggested that the straying refers to Israel neglecting the Temple and worshipping Jeroboam's calves instead (Radak). For others, the proximity of Egypt in the surrounding verses indicates that it was Egypt to which Ephraim has fled, a reading that fits with the time of Hoshea, as noted above (Ibn Ezra; Rashi, citing Jer. 43:2). Further, the language of 'redemption' in this verse has led to connections with the exodus, not least because the same term is used in Exod. 15:13 and Deut. 7:8 to refer to God's deliverance of his people from Egypt (Mays). God has redeemed them, yet the people forget (Theodore of Mopsuestia; Harper; Gruber). Sweeney suggests that here God 'indulges in some self-pity' (82), noting how he has been ignored and scorned in spite of past deliverance.

7:14–16

The people do not truly cry from their hearts, we are told in 7:14, 'but they wail upon their beds; they gash themselves for grain and wine'. The first part of this verse is seen as indicating a lack of sincerity; if the people do cry out, it is done hypocritically (Calvin; Gill; Harper; Yee 1996). This chastisement for lack of sincerity is seen elsewhere in the ANE, with similar language used in Assyrian treaties to describe loyalty in political relationships (Wolff). The second half of the verse is not entirely clear, but this has not stopped interpreters from trying to make sense of it. The reference to wailing on their beds has most often been understood as referring to sexual activity (Gruber), though sometimes in not so many words: Cyril of Alexandria describes this as 'an example of vile habits, an unchecked inclination to debauchery' (161). The reference to grain and wine, meanwhile, has most often been seen as referring to local religious customs (Theodore of Mopsuestia; Gill). Wolff and others have suggested that all of these elements—the wailing on beds, lacerating oneself, and food and wine—may be connected to elements of the Baal cult (Wolff; Andersen and Freedman; Sweeney).

The chapter ends in verse 16 with a series of clauses that Wellhausen describes as 'incomprehensible and largely corrupt' (117). The leitmotif of 'turning' (*shuv*) recurs in the first part of this verse. Here, however, we are told that 'they turn to that which does not profit; they have become like a defective bow' (7:16). This defective bow has been understood as an unstretched and useless bow (Theodore of Mopsuestia) or else one that is bent and deceitful, which does not fly where it should (Jerome; Calvin). Israel turns in various directions but like a bent bow, not in the appropriate direction (Wolff). In this sense, Israel's turning is both geographical and theological—they turn to foreign powers for help and, in doing so, turn away from God (Andersen and Freedman).

The concluding clause is an enigmatic statement regarding Egypt. The LXX translates this as 'this will be their contempt in the land of Egypt' (cf. NASB: 'their derision in the land'). In this reading, the wickedness of Ephraim and the repercussions of this will lead to contempt from those to whom they have gone for help (Radak; Rashi; Calvin). Others have suggested that the Hebrew term *la'ag* has to do with unintelligible speech (Gruber; Paul 1995: 'gibberish jabber'). Thus, the NRSV translates this as, 'So much for their babbling in the land of Egypt' (NRSV). Whatever the case, the larger sense seems to be that the trust that Israel is placing in foreign powers will come back on them (Ewald). The people lack loyalty to YHWH; they have turned away and keep turning to others (Wolff).

Hosea 8

The critique of Israel continues in chapter 8 with a focus on a breach of the covenant that includes idolatrous worship, political apostasy, and foreign policy (Andersen and Freedman; Wacker 2012). Commentators have thus described this chapter as being concerned with 'gods and governments' (Mays: 113) or 'kings and calves' (Calvin: 287). As with previous chapters in the book, the Hebrew of chapter 8 is very difficult and can be hard to interpret, a fact that has been noted throughout history and that has contributed to some of the wide-ranging commentary on the chapter (see Cyril of Alexandria; Luther; Wellhausen).

8:1

The chapter begins in verse 1 with a call to set a ram's horn (*shofar*) to the mouth, an image that resonates with a similar picture in Hos. 5:8 (Landy). The LXX offers a very different reading ('Into their bosom like earth …'), and some church fathers would comment on this translation (Cyril of Alexandria and Theodore of Mopsuestia). However, most interpreters have followed the Hebrew, making note of the *shofar*. The Hebrew does not indicate who is being addressed in relation to the *shofar*; some have suggested an actual horn is to be blown and that perhaps a military officer is here in view (Wolff). However, the majority follow the Targum in suggesting that the prophet is being addressed, and he is to raise an alarm like a horn or trumpet (Vulgate; Jerome; Rashi;

Hosea, Joel, and Obadiah Through the Centuries, First Edition. Bradford A. Anderson.
© 2024 John Wiley & Sons Ltd. Published 2024 by John Wiley & Sons Ltd.

Ibn Ezra; Calvin). For some Christian readers, this is also taken as a reminder that Christian ministers are to be watchmen in the church like the prophets of old (Pusey).

The imagery of a shofar being blown has been influential in both Jewish and Christian contexts. The shofar has long been important in Judaism, including its use on the festival of Rosh Hashanah, the Jewish New Year, where it is sounded 100 times, as well as on Yom Kippur, the Day of Atonement, where its use marks the end of fasting (Eisen 2006). The shofar has also become a symbol of Jewish identity and is often associated with both Judaism and the modern state of Israel. Messianic Jewish Christian groups, keen to retain Jewish rituals and symbols as part of Christianity, also stress the importance of the shofar ('The Great Shofar and Rosh Hashanah' 2023).

The imagery of the shofar is employed elsewhere. *Set the Trumpet to Thy Mouth* is the title of a 1985 book by the New York–based evangelist David Wilkerson, which he takes as a call to preach the Gospel in the contemporary world (Figure 14). The cover of Wilkerson's book indicates a setting of war, with the prophet blowing a shofar as a call to battle. This is in line with the stream of contemporary Christianity with which Wilkerson was aligned and which understands that a spiritual battle is taking place in the world. Christians are called to take part in this spiritual war by spreading the Gospel through evangelism, prayer, and other forms of spiritual warfare.

This alarm is to be raised because one like an eagle (*nesher*; cf. LXX; Targum) or vulture (Wolff; Sweeney) is coming toward the house of YHWH. While occasionally this has been understood as a call to the people to return to the house of the Lord (Rashi), most have interpreted this 'one like an eagle' as an attack from an enemy (Macintosh; Yee 1996), most often read as indicating Assyria (Gill; Pusey; Ewald; Harper). More specifically, contemporary readers have seen this as a likely reference to the events of 733 BCE after Hoshea's submission to Assyria (Mays; Wolff). The 'house of YHWH' has also been a matter of some debate. The Targum renders this as 'sanctuary', which implies the Jerusalem Temple, and others have followed this line of thinking (Jerome; Rashi). Calvin suggests this may refer to the people of Israel (cf. Pusey). A number of twentieth-century scholars have understood this as a reference to the land, which is God's property (Wolff; Mays; Andersen and Freedman).

The reason for this attack is that Israel has broken the covenant (*berit*) and transgressed the law (*torah*). The close connection of covenant and torah in this verse has led some to speculate that this might be a reference to the Sinai traditions or to some aspect of the written law (Macintosh). It is for this reason that Wellhausen assumes this is a later addition, as the written Torah would not emerge until much later in his reconstruction. Others posit that this statement may

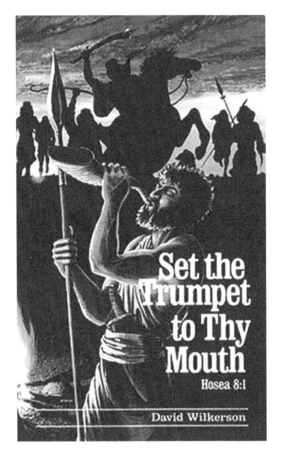

FIGURE 14   *David Wilkerson, Set the Trumpet to Thy Mouth, front cover (1985).*
Whitaker House.

be an authentic message from the prophet but that it refers simply to YHWH's instruction rather than any form of written Torah (Sweeney).

8:2–3

Israel, we are told in 8:2, cries to God, 'We know you!' This calling out to God is juxtaposed with a lack of calling out that was seen in 7:7 and 7:14 (Andersen and Freedman). As Mays notes, 'They break the covenant and say "my God", rebel against the *tōrā* and say, "We know you!'" (116). The Targum expands on this verse, noting that Israel only calls out to God in times of trouble, an idea picked up by subsequent commentators (cf. Rashi; Calvin). Others have offered more specific readings, namely that when the people are in captivity, they will call out to God and will repent (Jerome; Theodore of Mopsuestia; r. Joseph Kara; Gill). Pusey draws comparisons with Jesus's words concerning those who claim to know God in Matt. 7:22, casting out devils in the Lord's name—but who in reality have no real knowledge of him.

In spite of Israel's claim to know God, verse 3 states that they have turned from the good (*tov*). The Targum understands turning from the good as departing from the worship of Yʜwʜ, in line with other themes that occur in this chapter. In a number of rabbinic texts, the good is understood as the Torah, another theme in chapter 8 (y. Roš Haš. 3.8; cf Lam. Rab. 2:1). For some readers, the 'good' here refers to a general sense of justice and righteousness (Calvin) or perhaps the covenant mentioned in 8:1 (May; Wolff). Others suggest the good may in fact refer to God (Radak; Gill; Andersen and Freedman: 'the Good One').

8:4

Beginning in 8:4, the chapter explicitly addresses the political situation, noting that 'They made kings, but not through me; they set up princes, but without my knowledge' (8:4a). Two key issues have vexed interpreters of this verse. First, how should the critique of the kingship be understood in the first part of the verse? And second, how do we make sense of the fact that this action happened without God's knowledge, given his omniscience?

With regard to the critique of the kingship, readers have commonly understood this as a general rejection of the monarchy of the northern kingdom (Cyril of Alexandria; Pusey; Keefe 2016) or as a critique of certain kings in Israel. In relation to the latter, a popular candidate in premodern Jewish and Christian thought was Jeroboam I. Radak notes that Jeroboam was told by Ahijah the Shilonite that he would be king, but the people never consulted God about this (Radak). Jerome hearkens back to Samuel's warnings concerning kings in 1 Samuel 8 and points to the ways in which Jeroboam thus led the people astray (cf. Nicholas of Lyra; Gill; Harper). Others have posited that this refers to the succession of kings and their tumultuous reigns as outlined in 2 Kings 15 (Luther). In the modern period some argued that this rejection of kings and princes may refer to political alliances, where foreign kings become de facto rulers of Israel (Sweeney). Naturally, spiritual and moral readings have also been offered. For some early Christian readers, this verse was a reminder that people should look to God for counsel rather than earthly powers and rulers (John Chrysostom, *Homilies Concerning the Statues* 3.5 [Ferreiro]). Aquinas uses Hos. 8:4 to argue that the people of Israel, rather than God and his law, are to be blamed for the many political- and governance-related inadequacies in Israel's history (*ST* I-II, q. 105, a. 1).

What does it mean that this took place without God's knowledge? This has been a general issue of concern in the interpretive traditions (e.g., Calvin; Pusey). In the Targum, 'without my knowledge' becomes 'against my will' to avoid the perception of God not knowing. Others would expand on the issue of God's will, noting that God allows some things to happen even if it is against his will (Cyril of Alexandria). Some contemporary commentators have understood this as God not acknowledging these rulers rather than God not knowing—thus, the text is not concerned with the divine attribute of knowledge but with recognition and approval (Andersen and Freedman).

The second half of 8:4 comments that idols have been made with their silver and gold. The Targum states that this is gold that was brought back from Egypt. Many readers associate these idols with the calves that are found in the subsequent verses (Ibn Ezra; Gill; Yee 1996). In the contemporary era, it has been noted that the production of cultic idols and private statuettes was common in the eighth century BCE, and this may be a critique of such activities (Mays; Wolff). Wellhausen posits that this polemic against images of the deity in Hosea may be one of the earliest expressions of this idea in the HB (cf. Harper).

8:5–6

In 8:5–6 the text states that Samaria's calf is rejected (LXX: 'Get rid of your bull calf, Samaria'). While the calves of the northern kingdom have been the subject of much attention in archaeology (Mazar 1982), the biblical record does not indicate any calf or bull associated with worship being located in Samaria. Some readers have taken this as a general reference to Jeroboam's calves, linking this to the idols mentioned in 8:4 (Jerome; Theodore of Mopsuestia). If so, the use of the singular 'calf' here is surprising, given that Jeroboam erected calves at both Bethel and Dan. Rashi suggests this must refer to the calf at Bethel, where the kings worshipped (cf. Luther). Some modern readers have agreed, noting that Dan would have fallen to the Assyrians in 733 BCE, and if the text is from this period, there may have been just one bull remaining, that in Bethel (Wolff). Whatever the case, it seems clear that 'the sacred and royal centres are closely linked' (Landy: 104).

Verse 6 states that the calf of Samaria is from Israel itself; it was not made by God but by an artisan. Because of this, it will be destroyed. In spite of all the talk of other nations, this calf is not something borrowed from outsiders—it is of Israel's own making (Luther). Beyond that, it is made of human hands. Radak glosses this with his own question: 'how can the product have more power than its producer?' (219). The god they have created will not help them and will in fact hasten their own destruction (Ewald). While the calf was 'from Israel', its use may have developed over time. Mays and others suggest that the bull was erected as part of the Yʜᴡʜ cult but became associated with Canaan and Baal—thus highlighting both Israel's idolatry and its infidelity (Mays).

While some sort of destruction is in view, the exact end result of the calf is not entirely clear as the Hebrew term that is used is rare (*shvavim*). The Targum says that the calf will be reduced to 'bits and boards'. Jerome suggests that the calf will become like 'spider webs', a reading that he says he has learned from the Jewish tradition—but the provenance of this reading is unclear. Other offerings include 'bits of timber' (Luther) and 'splinters' (Mays).

8:7

In verse 7 we read, 'For they sow the wind, and they shall reap the whirlwind'. This saying seems to indicate that Israel's actions will have consequences greater than what they realize (Calvin). Not only will Israel not benefit, but they will suffer harm (Radak). Early Christian readers found much to ponder in this image. Jerome, for example, notes a point of connection with Gal. 6:8 as those who sow in the flesh reap corruption in the flesh. In the modern period, attention has turned to the sapiential nature of this saying, which highlights Israel's self-deception (Wolff; Macintosh).

This clever turn of phrase regarding the wind and the whirlwind has also been picked up in some unexpected places. This proverb was quoted by the British leader Winston Churchill when he visited Coventry following the city's destruction in 1940. Here the prophet's words are used for rhetorical rather than religious purposes in a threat of what is to come for Germany in retaliation for their actions in the Second World War (Spencer 2016). 'Sow the Wind, Reap the Whirlwind' was also the title of a research article reflecting on Hurricane Katrina fifteen years after the catastrophic event. In this case Hosea's imagery is used in a discussion of natural disasters as a reminder 'that we should anticipate suffering serious consequences as the outcome of our own bad actions or negligence' (Kim-Farley 2020). While the latter does not make any reference to Hosea or the Bible, it is a clear indication of how the imagery of the prophet has become embedded in Western culture.

8:8–9

In 8:8, the prophet depicts Israel as an unclean vessel swallowed up by the nations. While this is most often understood as a reference to Israel's exile at the hands of the Assyrians, some readers have gone further. Pusey takes this in a dangerous direction, suggesting that this is a prophecy concerning the contempt often shown to Judaism throughout history as punishment for their infidelity during the time of Hosea.

'For they have gone up to Assyria', we read in 8:9. Why did they go 'up' to Assyria? While some traditions have understood this as a reference to exile (Targum), most have read this as Israel willingly going to Assyria (Saadia Gaon). This is in line with others who see this as a reference to the visit of the Assyrian king Pul during the reign of Menahem, the latter going from a lower part of Israel 'up' to a higher part to pay tribute to the Assyrian (Radak; Gill). More recent interpreters have seen a possible reference to Hoshea ben Elah's submission to Assyria in 733 BCE (Wolff). Whatever the case, in many of these readings, this going up is not a punishment but a statement of faithlessness (Harper). Macintosh suggests that the use of 'going up' may be sarcastic as this is the language normally reserved for Jerusalem.

Verse 9 continues by calling Ephraim a wild ass who wanders alone, a statement reminiscent of the promise given concerning Ishmael in Gen. 16:12 (Pusey). The medieval Jewish exegete Joseph Kara states that, like a wild donkey, Israel wanders alone and does not listen to anyone, especially the prophets (cf. Luther). Calvin suggests this is indicative of the 'brutish wildness' of the Israelites. More recently, commentators have noted that there may be a wordplay here as 'wild ass' (*para'*) and Ephraim (*'fraim*) are similar in the Hebrew (Macintosh; Yee 1996).

The verse concludes by stating that Ephraim has hired lovers (8:9). Many readers have interpreted this as referring to the tribute that Israel gave to Assyria (Jerome; Radak; Abarbanel; Ewald; Andersen and Freedman). Others have added to this in various ways; Calvin returns to the imagery of the first chapters of the book to suggest that in hiring the nations as lovers, Israel has violated the covenant marriage relationship with God. The direction of the pursuit in this clause has drawn the attention of readers as Israel is said to have gone after lovers. As Pusey notes, 'It is a special and unwonted sin, when woman, forsaking the modesty which God gives her as a defence, becomes the temptress' (84). Mays likewise comments that Israel is a harlot but is desired so little that she must give herself away.

8:10

The theme of 'hiring' lovers (NRSV: 'bargained for') recurs in verse 10: though they hire the nations, God will gather them up. This seemingly innocuous verse became popular in early rabbinic tradition. In PesK (6:3), a collection of homiletical midrashim, the reference to 'gathering them' is said to refer to the exiles who will be gathered on account of study of the Mishnah and oral traditions (cf. Lev. Rab. 7:3). Likewise, in the Babylonian Talmud, this verse is used to suggest that those who repeat Tannaite traditions among the nations will be gathered and may even be exempt from the burden of the king, that is, taxes (b. B. Bat. 8a). However, most readers have understood this 'gathering' as negative, with Israel being gathered and delivered into captivity to the nations they have 'loved' and to whom they have paid tribute (Targum; Radak; Gill; Luther; Pusey; Wellhausen). Some have understood the hiring as paying a 'whore's wages' (Wolff; Yee 1996). In this reading, the prophet seems to be mocking Israel's attempts to bribe or pay off Assyria (Keefe 2016).

The second half of verse 10 states that they will writhe from the burden of kings and princes. Readers have long struggled with how to understand this clause. As noted above, in the Talmud this is used to suggest that some in exile will not have to pay taxes if they are faithful in the study of the oral traditions. Theodore of Mopsuestia takes this to mean that the people will have a reprieve from taxes for a while because they will be in complete servitude (Theodore of Mopsuestia). Following the LXX, Harper suggests this should be understood as Israel no longer anointing their own kings, because of their exile.

8:11

The subject matter shifts in 8:11 to cultic matters. Here we read that 'When Ephraim multiplied altars to expiate sin, they became to him altars for sinning'. As Mays comments, 'the many altars built to deal *with* sin have become a place *to* sin' (122; cf. Macintosh). Radak states that the proliferation of altars points to the fact that Israel worshipped more deities than their ancestors; others have followed this line of thought, suggesting that we see here a reference to 'wholly foreign religions and … customs' in which Israel was taking part (Ewald: 271). A common interpretation sees this as pointing to the time of Jeroboam and the calves at Bethel and Dan (Cyril of Alexandria; Gill). However, it is possible that these altars refer to sacrifices to Assyrian gods, which would link together the religious and political critique (Andersen and Freedman; Sweeney). Not surprisingly, spiritual and rhetorical interpretations have also been put forward: Jerome argues that there is only one altar that brings life, and that is Jesus, while Calvin draws comparisons with Papists, whom he sees as multiplying altars and customs in his own day, only to sin more.

8:12

Verse 12 has led to considerable commentary in both Jewish and Christian traditions, not least because it makes reference to writing: 'Though I write for him the multitude of my instructions,' we read, 'they are regarded as a strange thing'. In the Talmud, there is a debate as to whether this refers to the written or oral Torah (b. Giṭ. 60b). In Numbers Rabbah, we are told that the 'many things' that are written refer to the Mishnah, which would be strange to the Gentiles (14:10). This is perhaps polemic against Christianity, which also claimed the written Torah as Scripture but not the oral Torah (Montefiore and Loewe: 159). Others have suggested that this refers more generally to the many words and teachings from God, including the Torah, but also reminders from the prophets; these were strange to the people, as was the case in the time of Josiah (Radak; see also Nicholas of Lyra; Gill; Pusey). Calvin comments that the 'strangeness' is a lack of understanding: the law was written for the elect people—it is explicitly for them, and because of this they should know better, yet they do not.

Some modern scholars have agreed that this verse points to the existence and knowledge of written traditions by the mid-eighth century BCE (Wolff; Gruber). Others have pushed back against this as a reference to written 'scriptural' texts; this is not pointing to specific religious laws, Wellhausen states, but refers to general knowledge of God. Nevertheless, there is broad agreement that this passage indicates that the people have forgotten about divine teaching and moral instruction and instead are focusing solely on sacrifice and political treaties (Harper; Macintosh; Yee 1996).

8:13–14

God will not accept the sacrifices of the people; instead, their iniquity will be remembered, and they will return to Egypt (8:13). This reference to Egypt has been understood as a reference to Israel going to Egypt to conspire against Assyria (Pusey), or as pointing to the fact that once they have allied themselves with Assyria, those who are against this union will have no choice but to relocate to Egypt (Mays; Wolff). Whatever the case, the threat of Egypt is full of resonance and is not to be taken lightly (Ewald; Sweeney; Moughtin-Mumby 2008).

The chapter concludes in 8:14 by stating that Israel has forgotten its maker and has built temples or palaces, while Judah has built fortified cities. In both cases, these will be destroyed. This verse has been used, among other things, to advocate for using money for charity rather than buildings:

> R. Abun erected two grand gates for the House of Study, and he showed them to R. Mina. The latter Rabbi quoted Hos. VIII, 14, 'Israel builds temples, and forgets his Maker,' and went on to say, 'Had you spend this money more piously, would there not have been many labouring in the Law?' (y. Šeqal. 5:6; Montefiore and Loewe).

More common have been explanations of and elaborations on these temples and fortifications. According to Jerome, Israel built temples and places of worship on all the heights to Baal and other gods, and Judah did not learn from Israel's mistakes. This is proof that Israel and Judah have put their trust in various objects and places rather than in God (cf. Cyril of Alexandria; Luther).

In the modern period, the reference to Judah has been the cause of some deliberation. Macintosh states that this clause could refer to the time of Jeroboam II (and Uzziah), where there was growth and building in both kingdoms. A number of other commentators have noted the resonance with imagery from Amos, which has led to speculation that the second half of 8:14 has been borrowed from the fellow eighth-century prophet (Ewald; Wellhausen; Jeremias 1983). Indeed, such points of contact have led scholars to suggest ways in which this verse may point to the development of the Book of the Four initial Minor Prophets, a precursor to the Book of the Twelve (Werse 2019).

In the Roman Catholic missal, parts of chapter 8 (vv. 4–7, 11–13) are read as part of the liturgy in ordinary time (Year Two, Week Fourteen). Here Hosea is read alongside Psalm 115 and Matt. 9:32–38. The psalm speaks of the worthlessness of idols made of silver and gold and by human hands. The passage in Matthew, meanwhile, ends with Jesus's famous saying that the harvest is plentiful, but the laborers are few. Both of these texts pick up on themes found in Hosea 8, notably the idols of verse 4 and the sowing and reaping of verse 7.

If chapter 8 confronts Israel's reliance on foreign alliances, Hosea 9 critiques religious activity in the homeland. There are two generally agreed-upon sections in the chapter, verses 1–9 and 10–17; however, cutting across both sections are 'bitter tropes of reversal' (Keefe 2016: 830) pointing to the comeuppance that the prophet says Israel will receive for its behavior.

9:1

The first section of chapter 9 offers a critique of religious rituals. In verse 1 the prophet instructs the people to not rejoice or exult like other nations. For some, the command to not rejoice is given because Israel is held to a higher standard than the nations (Amos 3:2; Theodore of Mopsuestia; Rashi; Calvin). Others see the prophet's words as interrupting a festive occasion. This has been understood by some as reference to local Canaanite rituals in which Israelites were taking part (Cyril of Alexandria; Andersen and Freedman). Other readers see here a reference to an Israelite festival, perhaps the autumn celebration of Sukkoth (Tabernacles or Booths), in the years just following the events of 733 BCE (Mays; Yee 1996). In the case of the latter, 'these alleged worshipers of Yahweh are still faithless idolators of Baal; their cultic feasts are heathen activities that must be vigorously destroyed' (Wolff: 154).

Indeed, the prophet continues: 'you have played the whore, departing from your God. You have loved a prostitute's pay on all threshing floors' (v. 1b). The

Hosea, Joel, and Obadiah Through the Centuries, First Edition. Bradford A. Anderson.
© 2024 John Wiley & Sons Ltd. Published 2024 by John Wiley & Sons Ltd.

nature of this 'whoring' has frequently been understood as idolatry and cultic infidelity (Radak; Nicholas of Lyra; Calvin). Modern interpreters have seen here sexual rites associated with Canaanite fertility cultic activities. The infidelity of the Israelites is exemplified in sexual activity on these festive occasions (Andersen and Freedman). Whether prostitution occurred as these rituals is not clear; however, this is the first occurrence of the term 'harlotry' since 6:10. Landy comments, 'Its isolated resurfacing intensifies the reversion to the concerns of a previous part of the book, and makes them emblematic of the political, personal, and prophetic crisis that dominates the latter part' (112). Indeed, while the reference to promiscuity and infidelity draws to mind the events earlier in the book, the gender of the Hebrew term here is masculine, a shift from the way in which the term is used in chapter 2 (Wacker 2012).

The prostitute's pay has been likened by some to the corn which was given to a harlot on the threshing floor in return for services (Gen. Rab. 57.4; Rashi; Gill). Indeed, the reference to the threshing floor has led to reflections on the relationship between Hosea and the book of Ruth (Ruth Rab. 5:15; Sweeney). This prostitute's pay is taken by others to represent the bounty of the harvest, which is being celebrated. Like its pagan neighbors, Israel assumes that the idols or Baal were responsible for the harvest rather than YHWH (Radak). At the very least, they are treating YHWH like Baal (Mays). There is a seeming contradiction here with chapter 8, where we read that Israel hires lovers. Calvin resolves this tension by commenting that Israel has done both: purchased help from Assyria and sold themselves to false gods.

9:2–4

Verse 2 gives us the first of several reversals in this chapter: in spite of the people's rejoicing, they will not find fulfillment in the harvest (Luther). In fact, it is worse, as the people will not remain in the land but will 'return' to Egypt and eat unclean food in Assyria (9:3). There is a play on words here as the people shall not dwell (*yashavu*) in the land but shall return (*shuv*) to Egpyt (Calvin; Yee 1996). Since the people have defiled the land with idols, Radak asserts, they will not be allowed to remain there. Israel will learn the hard way that Canaan is the land of YHWH, and is not Baal's (Wolff). Egypt and Assyria have appeared in close proximity in various parts of the book. While some see the reference to both Egypt and Assyria as speaking of punishment and exile (Pusey), most readers have taken this to mean that Israel will be fugitives in Egypt and later captives in Assyria (Targum; Theodore of Mopsuestia; Luther; Gill). The reference to unclean foods has led some to speculate that Hosea has in mind here purity laws as found in the Torah (Jerome; Nicholas of Lyra).

The cultic imagery continues in verse 4: 'they shall not pour drink offerings of wine to the LORD, and their sacrifices shall not please him'. Readers have understood this either as a critique of current practices, which God will not accept (Rashi; Calvin) or as pointing to the threat of exile, where the people would not be allowed to sacrifice (Gill; Mays). The prominence given here to libations is unusual in the HB, which has caused some to speculate that this refers to Canaanite rituals (Theodore of Mopsuestia; Andersen and Freedman).

The prophet continues in verse 4 by indicating that the sacrifices will be like the bread of mourners, which defiles all who eat it. This image has led to various interpretations through the centuries. Luther suggests that God does not want sad sacrifices, and so the bread in question is defiled by grief and pain, while the Puritan commentator Jeremiah Burroughs uses this verse to describe how the joy of serving God is gone when we are living in sin. More common is the assumption that this relates to bread that was eaten during mourning (Num. 19:14). Mourners were considered unclean, and so the food they came into contact with was defiled (Mays; Pusey). Likewise, the prophet says, the sacrifices of the people will in fact defile them.

9:5–6

Verse 5 begins with a question: 'What will you do on the day of the appointed festival, and on the day of the festival of the LORD?' This seems to relate to the previous verse and the mention of the sacrifices that will not be accepted: when these are taken away, what then will you have left (Calvin)? Some interpreters have understood the appointed day (*yom moʿed*) as referring to coming captivity or devastation (Jerome; Rashi; Nicholas of Lyra). However, most have read the appointed day and festival in parallel (Luther; Harper). Recent commentators have associated these with autumn festivals, perhaps Sukkoth (Wolff; Davies 1992). 1 Kings 12:32 notes that Jeroboam established the Sukkoth festival in the north, and this may be a critique of the northern iteration of the festival (Mays).

'For even if they escape destruction,' the text continues, 'Egypt shall gather them, Memphis shall bury them' (9:6). Some interpret this 'gathering' in a negative manner to mean Israel will be captive in Egypt (Calvin). More common, however, is the understanding that this refers to seeking refuge in Egypt either from the Assyrians (Jerome) or during the time of the Babylonians as recounted in Jer. 43 (Mezudath David; Cyril of Alexandria; Andersen and Freedman). Memphis (*Moph*) was an important city in Egypt, known from Strabo, Pliny, and other sources in antiquity (Gill; Pusey). It was known for its relative proximity to the pyramids (Wolff), as well as massive graveyards; the sense would seem to be that those who go to Egypt will remain there until they die (Mays; Yee 1996). The verse concludes with the prophet declaring that nettles will possess their precious things, and thorns their tents. This again implies the people will be gone for a long period of time, and the land will be overrun (Jerome; Abarbanel; Calvin). Interestingly, this verse was also used by the fourteenth-century Moroccan Muslim 'Abd al-Haqq al-Islami, who had converted from Judaism to Islam. In an attempt to prove that the Hebrew prophets had foretold the coming of the prophet and the emergence of Islam, he transcribed the Hebrew term *mahmad*, 'precious', as the name 'Muhammad' (Wheeler 2021).

9:7

The next several verses are some of the most difficult to interpret in the book of Hosea (Luther). In verse 7, we read that 'the prophet is a fool, the man of the spirit is mad'. It is not clear who 'the prophet' and 'man of the spirit' might be in this clause. Some take these as the words of Hosea spoken about false prophets who are fools (Radar; Calvin; Pusey) or those oracles who pretend to be demented as a show of communicating with the gods (Cyril of Alexandria). Others suggest that this is a saying aimed at the prophets such as Hosea by the Israelites (Jerome; Wellhausen; Harper; Davies 1992). In this reading, the people formerly said the prophet was a fool, but now they know otherwise (Targum). Luther offers a variant of this reading: the foolish prophet refers to Hosea as he is 'compelled to play the fool' because the people will not listen.

Verse 7 ends with a cryptic statement referring to Israel's hostility (*mastema*). Within the HB, this word only occurs in Hosea (cf. v. 8 below); however, the same root would later be used in second Temple literature to refer to the 'tempter' and the figure Mastema (Jubilees 10.8; 1QM 13:11; Wolff). Some traditions render this use in Hos. 9:7 as 'a great hatred', which is the title of Maurice Samuel's 1940 study of anti-Semitism, *The Great Hatred* (cf. Gruber).

9:8–9

The Hebrew of verse 8 is often thought to be 'hopelessly confused' (Dobbie 1955; Harper; on emendations, see Macintosh). The NRSV renders the first part of this verse as 'The prophet is a sentinel for my God over Ephraim, yet a fowler's snare is on all his ways'. A sentinel or lookout was a designation used for leaders (Ezek. 3:17). However, it is unclear who the sentinel might be in this context and how they relate to God. The Targum interprets the snares as referring to Israel's worship of idols, which are traps that they lay for their prophets (cf. Rashi). Another interpretation is that Ephraim was meant to be a sentinel set by God to look after the truth, but Israel has instead turned the people away like a false prophet (so the ninth-century theologian of the eastern church Isho'dad of Merv). Jerome offers a similar reading but focuses on the princes and leaders who should be watching out for their people yet do not (cf. Calvin). Modern readers have tended to see this as referring to the true prophets, who, even though serving as watchmen for God, are persecuted and tripped up (Harper; Wolff). The verse ends with a reference to 'hostility in the house of his God'. Rashi takes this as a reference to the Temple and the assassination of Zechariah there as outlined in 2 Chron. 24:21. Radak disagrees, indicating that this relates to false prophets in Ephraim who generally create enmity and hostility. A number of other commentators take this to refer to hostility at Bethel, which means 'house of God' (Jerome; Calvin; Gill).

'They have deeply corrupted themselves,' we read in verse 9, 'as in the days of Gibeah'. The reference to Gibeah is most often associated with Gibeah of Benjamin and the rape of the Levite's concubine as outlined in Judges 19 (Cyril of Alexandria; Nicholas of Lyra; Luther; Ewald; Wolff). Given the critique of leaders in the book, others see this as a reference to the people asking for a king, and the choosing of Saul, which is connected with Gibeah in 1 Samuel 10 and 15 (Rashi; Gill; Arnold 1989; Yee 1996). As Gibeah is also mentioned in Hos. 10:9, Harper suggests this reference is out of place and may be a gloss.

9:10

Verse 10 begins a new section. Among other things, we begin to see references and allusions to Israel's history, an aspect not found in the first part of the book (Davies 1992). Wolff thinks this points to a particular audience, in this case those who transmitted Hosea's sayings and were familiar with Israel's traditions (cf. Holt 1995). Ben Zvi (2005) suggests a much different audience is in mind: the literati of post-exilic Yehud.

The prophet begins this section speaking for God: 'Like grapes in the wilderness, I found Israel. Like the first fruit on the fig tree in its first season, I saw your ancestors' (9:10a). The reference to the wilderness and the ancestors has led commentators to see here an allusion to both the patriarchs and early Israel in the wilderness after the exodus (Nicholas of Lyra; Wolff). The verse is seen by many as referring to the election of Israel, the 'great and unmerited love of God to his people' (Gill; cf. Gen. Rab. 1:4). A number of commentators take pains to note that the comparison with grapes is not because of any inherent goodness in Israel but simply to highlight God's affection and pleasure (Deut. 7:6; Gill). Mays sees here a sense of nostalgia on the part of God, longing for the beginning of his time with Israel.

The verse continues by noting that 'they came to Baal-Peor, and consecrated themselves to a thing of shame, and became detestable like the thing they loved'. The mention of Baal-Peor has led to various readings. Given the reference to the wilderness earlier in the verse, many readers see here an allusion to the events of Num. 25, one of the first examples of Israel's infidelity before they had even entered the land of promise. In rabbinic tradition, this connection with Num. 25 is assumed, and it is further elaborated that the Israelites were enticed by women who encouraged them to separate themselves from the Torah (Sifre Num. 131:2). This connection with Num. 25 was also common in Christian tradition, where it was thought to reference idolatry (Theodore of Mopsuestia; Nicholas of Lyra; Gill), along with sexual activity and rituals (Calvin; Mays). For the prophet, the sin of Baal-Peor is not just historical: the underlying issues of faithlessness continue into Hosea's day (Wellhausen; Harper).

The designation 'Baal-Peor' has been variously understood. Some readers understand this as a general name for one of the Baals (Radak; Rashi), while others offer more specific descriptions: based on the events in Num. 25, several commentators take this to be a god of Moab and Ammon (Nicholas of Lyra), the name of a god worshipped at Mount Peor (Gill; Wolff; Yee 1996) or more broadly a place associated with a particular god (Andersen and Freedman; Davies 1992).

Whatever the case, the prophet says that the people became detestable, like that which they loved. Rashi takes this to mean that when the people loved the daughters of Moab (Num. 25), they became detestable like their neighbors. This statement also became a point of reflection for Aquinas in his discussion of whether love is a passion that can wound the lover. He notes:

> Consequently love of a suitable good perfects and betters the lover; but love of a good which is unsuitable to the lover, wounds and worsens him. Wherefore man is perfected and bettered chiefly by the love of God: but is wounded and worsened by the love of sin, according to Osee 9:10: 'They became abominable, as those things which they loved.' (*ST* I-II, q. 28, a. 5)

9:11–14

The next several verses (9:11–14) speak to the removal of Israel's glory, illustrated by the lack of fertility in its future: 'no birth, no pregnancy, no conception!' (v. 11). A number of readers note the connection between honor and children elsewhere in Scripture (e.g., Prov. 17.6; Theodore of Mopsuestia; Rashi; Wolff). Indeed, even if they bear children, death will follow them, and their youths will not survive to adulthood (v. 12). Calvin notes that this does not just refer to offspring: the part speaks for the whole, and Israel has no future. Wacker (2012) points out that this is the first time that the women of Ephraim are mentioned in the text; however, it is only in relation to their reproductive capabilities – or in this case, the lack thereof.

The Hebrew of 9:13 is difficult; in the NRSV the verse begins, 'Once I saw Ephraim as a young palm planted in a lovely meadow'. However, some traditions render 'Tyre' where the NRSV has 'young palm' (see Targum; Calvin; Gill). The reading of Tyre may be substantiated by Josephus, who notes Tyre's revolt against Assyria and subsequent siege (*Ant.* IX 277–87; Kuan 1991). Verse 13 ends by asserting that the children of Ephraim must be led out to slaughter. Some early traditions took this to mean children would be slaughtered in worship of idols (Rashi; Targum), while others read this as a reference to a looming enemy, like the Assyrians, to whom even children would fall in battle (Radak).

The theme of infertility continues in verse 14 with a rhetorical question from the prophet: 'Give them, O LORD—what will you give?' This is followed by a call to give them miscarrying wombs and dry breasts. According to some, this should be understood as an intercession; it is better to not have children than to watch them die (Mays; Jerome). Others, however, see this as a further imprecation, yet another judgment on the people (Rashi; Yee 1996). The lack of fertility here is juxtaposed with the rites in which Israel took part, celebrating Baal's bounty (Sweeney). In this sense, the actions of the 'fathers' have implications for wives and children, and their collective relationship to God (Wacker 2012).

9:15–17

The prophet continues by stating that 'Every evil of theirs began at Gilgal; there I came to hate them' (9:15). As with the other historical references in the chapter, the mention of Gilgal has garnered significant attention. Some readers observe that Gilgal was a site of significant idol worship and Baal cultic activity in antiquity (the twelfth–thirteenth-century Talmudist Isaiah da Trani; Rashi; Cyril of Alexandria; Harper). Another perspective points out that Gilgal may refer to its connection with the people's request for a king and the reign of Saul (1 Samuel 11; Radak; Jerome; Luther; Mays). Yet another interpretation is that Gilgal was the site where the Israelites camped after crossing the Jordan; if Baal-Peor is the paradigmatic sin before entering the land, Gilgal is a reference to their continued state of sinfulness even in the land, just across the Jordan (Ibn Ezra; Landy).

Because of their wickedness, God states, 'I will drive them out of my house' (v. 15). 'My house' has been interpreted by some as the holy land (Gill; Jerome). Another approach sees this as divorce language, reminiscent of Hosea 2 and Deut. 24:1–4: God will cast Israel out of his house as if they are divorced (Davies 1992). Jerome offers a spiritual reading: casting out of the house refers to heretics, and here he specifically names Marcion and Valentinus. For Jerome, this also foreshadows Jesus's cleansing of the Temple in John 2.

The chapter concludes with a reminder that the people have not listened to God, and so he will reject them; indeed, 'they shall become wanderers among the nations' (9:17). This 'wandering' has frequently been understood as captivity and exile (Theodore of Mopsuestia; Luther; Gill). Calvin elaborates on this idea, stating that the people would be restless among the nations, which is the opposite of the rest they were supposed to experience in the land of promise. This image has also been used by Christian interpreters in an essentialist manner to suggest 'an abiding condition' of Jewish wandering (Pusey). Such readings have contributed to anti-Jewish tropes of the eternally Wandering Jew, a trope that emerged in thirteenth-century Europe (Ben Zvi 2005). The Wandering Jew was a Christian legend concerning a Jewish man who taunted Jesus when he was crucified and was thus cursed with wandering the earth until Christ's return. This legend would gain popularity at various points in history and in diverse cultural contexts, including Percy Shelley's 1831 extended poem, 'The Wandering Jew', and in works of art such as Gustav Doré's well-known depictions (see Figure 15).

In time, imagery of the wandering or eternal Jew would be used in anti-Semitic propaganda by the Nazi regime. While wandering and traveling are key elements of the story of the Israelites in the Bible, including the imagery found in Hos. 9:17, this particular legend 'is an anti-Jewish legend that takes old Jewish ideas and ways of self-knowing and twists them into a freakish specter' (Secunda 2022).

FIGURE 15   Gustav Doré, The Wandering Jew (1856).

Credit: Victoria and Albert Museum, Department of Engraving, Illustration and Design, and Department of Paintings. Archivist/Adobe Stock.

Hosea 10

Chapter 10 returns to a number of themes that were introduced in Hosea 8–9, including critiques of both the monarchy and religious traditions (Ben Zvi 2005). Further, as was the case in chapter 9, memory continues to play a key role in this chapter as the text draws on the past to illuminate the present (Yee 1996). As with much of the book, Hosea 10 is not always easy to interpret. As Luther notes, even when the words are clear, 'the meaning is obscure' (53). This complexity has led to wide-ranging commentary through the years on a number of issues outlined below.

10:1–2

Chapter 10 begins with an attack on both king and cult (Davies 1992; Landy). While early interpreters were not overly concerned with a specific historical setting for these verses, modern readers have put forward a number of options. Wolff suggests that this oracle dates to the period just after 733 BCE, when life was returning to normal after the tumultuous events during the reign of Hoshea. Others have suggested the festival of Sukkot as a general backdrop for these verses, drawing on the imagery of vineyards, wine, and the autumn harvest to illustrate Israel's apostasy (Sweeney; Yee 1996).

In 10:1, Israel is compared to a vine. How this comparison should be understood, however, is unclear; the Hebrew term that is used to describe the vine (*boqeq*) can be interpreted in a positive or negative manner. The NRSV translates

Hosea, Joel, and Obadiah Through the Centuries, First Edition. Bradford A. Anderson.
© 2024 John Wiley & Sons Ltd. Published 2024 by John Wiley & Sons Ltd.

this as a 'luxuriant vine', drawing on the positive reading found in earlier traditions (LXX; Vulgate). In this reading, Israel was once full and fruitful when it followed the law and kept the covenant (Cyril of Alexandria). However, this term frequently has a negative connotation, and the Targum renders this as a 'ravaged vine' (cf. Rashi; Calvin; Macintosh). Julian of Eclanum, the fourth–fifth-century bishop and leader of the Pelagian movement, drawing on the imagery from chapter 9, comments that the 'vine that had been planted from the stock of the chosen fathers was converted into a cluster of bitter grapes and a vine of Sodom' (169). The ambiguity of the term *boqeq* has led others to suggest that the use of this term is intentional: this is a vine that is 'splendid but useless' (Luther), luxurious but without fruit (Pusey; Moughtin-Mumby 2008).

Verse 1 goes on to state that 'the more his fruit increased, the more altars he built; as his country improved, he improved his pillars', and the imager of altars and pillars recurs in verse 2. The sense of verse 1b is frequently understood as saying that the more God provided for his people, the more their altars proliferated, and with this their idolatrous worship (Jerome; Rashi; Ewald). Theodore of Mopsuestia comments: 'the abundance in which they found themselves owing to God's blessing they repaid with a great extension of impiety, erecting altars in honor of the idols to match their own numbers' (81; cf. Nicholas of Lyra). Later readers gave more specific attention to the altars and pillars (Heb. *mizbehot* and *matsebot*), which function as a pair (Gruber). Some suggest that these may be related to the Baal cult or fertility rites, perhaps during the time of abundance in the reign of Jeroboam II (Harper; Wolff). It is noteworthy that during the reforms of Josiah, the same terminology appears as the pillars and altars are torn down as part of the Judahite king's reforms (2 Kgs 23:14–15; Yee 1996). In verse 2 we read that because their heart is false, God will break down and destroy their altars and pillars. The Hebrew term that denotes Israel's 'false' heart, *chalaq*, is also used for Jacob in Gen. 27:11, where he is described as either smooth or duplicitous; in this sense, 'Israel's future behavior can already be discerned in Jacob' (Ben Zvi 2005: 209).

10:3–4

The prophet continues by speaking in the voice of the people in verse 3: 'For now they will say: "We have no king, for we do not fear the LORD . . ."' Some see parallelism in this verse, with the reference to having no king as indicating God: YHWH is not their king, and they do not fear him (Yee 1996). Another reading suggests that this is a taunt from the people, suggesting that they do not need a king (Mays; Sweeney). Finally, some understand this as a future statement of repentance from Israel when in exile, acknowledging their guilt; at a future point they will realize their kings have failed them, and indeed they will no longer have a king (Jerome; Radak; Pusey; Macintosh). The latter reading is influenced by the subsequent verse, where the people are accused of uttering mere words and making contracts with empty oaths (10:4). This critique of 'mere words' and 'empty oaths' is often understood as pointing to political agreements and treaties, either in the past (Radak) or presently, with the Assyrians (Andersen and Freedman).

10:5–6

The prophet's critique of Israel's religious practices continues in verses 5–6. Verse 5 begins by stating that 'the inhabitants of Samaria tremble for the calf of Beth-aven'. *Beth-aven* ('house of iniquity') is used elsewhere as a derogatory term for Bethel, 'house of God' (Gen. Rab. 39:15; Mays). In the Babylonian Talmud, Rav Nahmen uses this example as proof that mockery is forbidden except when it is aimed at idolatry (b. Sanh. 63b). Why do the people tremble? Some understand this as fear because of retribution that will come on Bethel or the people themselves because of the calf (Rashi; Radak). Others suggest that the people are fearful that the calf will be taken away (Nicholas of Lyra; Luther). Yet another tradition reads this 'trembling' as fearful worship (Vulgate; Wolff). While the NRSV renders the object of this trembling in the singular (calf), in the MT we find plural 'calves'. Although there was only one calf at Bethel, the plural may refer to a general abstraction, what Landy refers to as 'calfishness' (127). Further, the calves are referred to here as heifers, or cow calves, which many interpreters see as mocking such worship (Calvin; Pusey; Ben Zvi 2005).

Verse 5 continues by noting that the people will mourn for the calf, and the priests will wail over it because 'its glory has departed from it'. Jerome understands the people and priests as having different reactions: while the people mourned, the leaders rejoiced. This he relates to a Hebrew tradition which says that the priests and leaders had substituted the calves with bronze versions, and so the people unknowingly mourned the replacement calves, which were carried off (Jerome; cf. Julian of Eclanum). The term used for priests here is *komer*, a word that normally refers to pagan priests (Mays; Gruber). Modern scholars have suggested that the mourning in verse 5 may thus point to Canaanite rituals that mourn the god Baal who is symbolically dead and rises to life with the autumn rains (Sweeney).

In verse 6 we read that 'The thing itself shall be carried to Assyria as tribute to the great king.' Jewish and Christian readers understood 'carrying to Assyria' as referring to the exile of the northern kingdom, suggesting that at this time Bethel's calf was taken to Assyria (Jerome; Rashi; Targum). Wolff suggests the calf of Bethel was surrendered as tribute in the time of Hoshea, which brought further shame to the kingdom. What the NRSV translates as the 'great' (*yareb*) king has been interpreted variously as the term in question is not self-evidently clear. Like the NRSV, some take this as an adjective meaning 'great', thus pointing to one of the significant Assyrian kings (Rashi; Wolff). Others understand this term as an avenging and contentious king who does harm to Israel (Cyril of Alexandria; Landy). Still others see Jareb as the proper name of an unknown Assyrian king (Radak; Luther; Calvin). Whatever the case, the calf is given as a tribute or gift (*minha*) to this king, a term that carries connotations of offerings and appeasement (Landy). A number of early Christian interpreters read this reference typologically concerning Pilate handing over Jesus as a gift to King Herod in Luke 23:7 (Justin Martyr, *Dialogue with Trypho* 103; cf. Tertullian, *Against Marcion* 4.42 [Ferreiro]).

10:7–8

In verses 7–8, the prophet declares that Samaria's king will perish, and the high places of Aven will be destroyed. While a few modern interpreters have understood this reference to Samaria's king as pointing to Baal (Nyberg 1935), most readers have interpreted this as concerning the ultimate end of the monarchy in the northern kingdom (Gill). The reference to the high places of Aven points back to verse 5 and the indictment of Bethel as Beth-aven (Targum; Rashi). The 'high places' (*bamot*) are often understood as places of impiety and idolatry (Calvin); while there was some room for worship at these high places in the stories concerning Israel's ancestors, they are increasingly associated with foreign worship as the story of the Hebrew Bible unfolds (Wolff).

Verse 8 ends with the following: 'They shall say to the mountains, Cover us, and to the hills, Fall on us.' Interestingly, the sentiment is quoted twice in the New Testament, in Luke 23:30 and Rev. 6:16. Both passages speak of warnings concerning those hiding from impending doom. The passage in Luke occurs when Jesus has been arrested and is being taken to his crucifixion. Jesus quotes this passage in his warning to those who are mourning for him, telling them that they should instead weep for themselves and their children. The reference in Revelation occurs at the opening of the sixth seal; here the powerful ones are said to seek refuge from the wrath of the lamb who is seated on the throne. Luther notes this usage in the New Testament, commenting that this saying gets applied to future misfortune or devastation (cf. Pusey; Wolff).

10:9–10

The chastisement of Israel continues in the second half of the chapter, with the focus shifting to the lack of righteousness and justice. This begins in verse 9 with a reference to Gibeah, which was previously mentioned in 9:9. In 10:9, the prophet says, 'Since the days of Gibeah you have sinned, O Israel; there they have continued', indicating that past sins have continued into the present (Rashi). The LXX offers a substantially different reading, suggesting that Israel has sinned 'since the hills'. This reading was followed by a number of early Christian interpreters, who understood this to mean that Israel had been sinning for a very long time before the idolatrous heifers were even on the scene (Cyril of Alexandria). For those following the Hebrew text, the mention of sinning at Gibeah in verse 10 has been interpreted in various ways (similarly to the approaches to understanding Gibeah in 9:9; see Harper). Some see this as referring to the people asking for the crowning of Saul (Targum). Most often, however, this has been linked to the episode of the Levite's concubine and the subsequent war as outlined in Judges 19 (Julian of Eclanum; Rashi; Calvin; Gill; Wellhausen; Andersen and Freedman).

Verse 10 reiterates that God will come against the people, and they will be punished for their 'double iniquity'. The reference to 'double iniquity' has puzzled readers for centuries and has featured prominently in the traditions. While Ibn Ezra understands this as pointing to both Judah and Israel being subjugated and exiled, most end up suggesting that the Israelites will be gathered for exile because of two iniquities (Abarbanel). Some see the double iniquity as the two calves at Dan and Bethel (Jerome; Luther). Others posit that this refers to the (unspecified) historical and present sin in Gibeah noted in verse 9 (Wolff; Davies 1992).

10:11–12

The imagery of a heifer recurs in verse 11. However, it is used here in a different way as Ephraim is compared to 'a trained heifer that loved to thresh, and I spared her fair neck'. As far back as Jerome it was noted that this verse is difficult to interpret. One difficulty is how to understand the description of the heifer. Some traditions render this as a 'goaded heifer', one which is wounded and humbled because it did not follow Torah (Rashi). However, the dominant reading is that this speaks of a 'trained' heifer whom God has instructed (Jerome; Radak). Indeed, this imagery became popular in rabbinic tradition to advocate for the utility of studying the Torah in one's youth (as seen in the collection of rabbinic teaching found in Fathers According to Rabbi Nathan 23.4 [Neusner]). What does it mean that the heifer 'loved to thresh'? Citing Deut. 25:4, Harper comments, 'Israel, in her past history, is compared to a young heifer to whom is assigned the easy task of walking round and round the threshing-floor, an occupation that carries with it the privilege of eating freely, for no muzzle was allowed' (Harper: 353). Others have interpreted this as relating to the traditions concerning Israel's election and in particular the idea that election is for service (Wolff). In this reading, over time Israel came to disdain the hard work involved in maintaining their covenant with God for which it had been called (Calvin; Mays). A further complexity in verse 11 is the prophet's statement that the heifer's fair neck was spared. While some interpret this as God giving Israel a light yoke with the Torah (Radak), others suggest that this implies an attempt to train through hardships and afflictions (Pusey).

Verse 11 concludes with agricultural imagery of breaking the ground and plowing, and this motif continues in verse 12, where the people are told to 'Sow for yourself righteousness, reap steadfast love'. The image of sowing righteousness and reaping loving kindness was picked up in rabbinic tradition to suggest that while almsgiving was greater than sacrifice, loving deeds were greater than almsgiving (Rabbi Eleazar, b. Sukkah 49b). This imagery was also popular with early Christian commentators in relation to bearing fruit (Origen, *Homilies on Leviticus* 6.4.4; Basil the Great, *On Baptism* 2.9 [Ferreiro]). Christian readers have also noted that a similar sentiment is found in Gal. 6:7, where Paul states that you reap what you sow (Cyril of Alexandria; Luther; cf. 2 Cor. 9:20). Ben Zvi sees here an 'intellectual setting in which there was a general, implied, positive approach to the world of what we may call "nature", and which is for the most part centered around the cultivated land' (2005: 220–21).

Verse 12 ends by reminding the people that it is time to seek the LORD, 'that he may come and rain righteousness upon you' (10:12). The word 'rain' (*yoreh*) can also be translated as 'teach', giving the sense that God will teach righteousness. Some have suggested that this imagery may have contributed to the later development of the 'teacher of righteousness', a title well known in the texts from Qumran (CD 6.11; Davies 1992).

10:13–15

The farming metaphor continues in verse 13 as the prophet reprimands Israel for not living up to this command of seeking God: indeed, they have done the opposite, plowing wickedness and reaping injustice. Jewish and Christian commentators would make note of the fact that wickedness leads to injustice (Jerome; Rashi). The result of this, the prophet declares, is that Israel will suffer the unpleasant effects of war because it has trusted in its power and its warriors (vv. 13–14). Here military strength is depicted as part of Israel's false trust, which leads to the desolation of the land (Wolff). Overall, the prophet seems to offer a harsh and negative depiction of war and military endeavors, as well as the consequences of such (Keefe 2016).

Indeed, the prophet continues, Israel will face destruction 'as Shalman destroyed Beth-arbel when mothers were dashed in pieces with their children' (v. 14). This cryptic statement has led to considerable speculation (see discussion in Harper). To begin with, Shalman has been understood in various ways. Some understand this as a shortened version of the Assyrian name Shalmaneser (Calvin; Ibn Ezra; Pusey). This has been identified with either Shalmaneser III (858–24; Tammuz 2016) or Shalmaneser V (727–22). A number of early Christian readers, following the LXX, understood this as referring to Zalmunna, a character mentioned in Judges 7–8, a story where mothers and children were also dashed to the ground (Jerome; Cyril of Alexandria; Julian of Eclanum; Nicholas of Lyra). More recently, it has been suggested that this is a possible reference to Salamanu, an eighth-century king of Moab (Lemaire 2005; Macintosh). However, many readers have been unwilling to offer a specific historical reference; a common interpretation is that this refers to a well-known story from the prophet's day that is otherwise unknown, perhaps indicating an unknown Assyrian king of this name (Theodore of Mopsuestia; Radak; Luther; Wolff).

Similar uncertainty revolves around Beth-arbel. While some have understood this as a person that was destroyed by Shalman (Radak), most see this as pointing to a place where the destruction happened. One possibility comes from Josephus, who indicated that Arbel was in Galilee, a location with fortified caverns (*Ant.* 12, 11, 1). Others have equated Arbel with the mound of Irbid in Gilead, which the Greeks referred to as 'Arbela' (Gill; Mays). Ewald, meanwhile, posits that this refers to a well-known city on the Tigris.

Whatever the case, the text paints a bleak picture, as mothers are dashed to pieces with their children. This imagery was picked up in several places by the Sages. In the Talmud, this passage is understood as referring to a time when the people will flee, and the mothers and children will be abandoned and left to the enemy (b. B. Meṣ. 39a; Radak). In Lev. Rab. (27:11), this verse is used as a description of the cruelty of Sennacherib (Neusner).

The chapter concludes with another declaration that Bethel will face consequences because of its wickedness. Indeed, 'At dawn the king of Israel shall be utterly cut off' (v. 15). Again, the prophet highlights that there are political implications for Israel's actions (Rashi). While dawn often signifies hope and salvation, here the picture points to coming loss and destruction (Landy).

Chapter 10 is found as an Ordinary Time lectionary reading in the Catholic missal (Hos. 10:1–3, 7–8, 12; Year Two, Ordinary Time, Week Fourteen, Wednesday). Here it is read alongside Ps. 105:2–7, which speaks of seeking God, and Matt. 10:1–7, which sees Jesus calling the twelve and sending them out 'to the lost sheep of the house of Israel' (Matt. 10:6).

Hosea 11

In Hosea 11, the focus returns to God's 'consistent love' for Israel, as well as Israel's 'consistent ingratitude' (Macintosh: 436). Rather than the love of a spouse, as seen earlier in the book, here God's love is portrayed in terms of parental love. The chapter includes historical references, particularly in the opening verses; however, the chapter also speaks to Israel's present and future situation as the chapter unfolds (Yee 1996).

(This commentary follows the English versification of chapter 11, which includes twelve verses. In the Hebrew traditions, the chapter concludes at verse 11, with the following verse serving as verse 1 of chapter 12.)

11:1

The chapter begins with one of the more well-known sayings in Hosea: 'When Israel was a child, I loved him, and out of Egypt I called my son' (11:1). In early rabbinic tradition, this statement was understood as a paradigmatic text illustrating Israel's elect status as the chosen people (see the late antique midrash Deut. Rab. 5.7; Montefiore and Loewe). However, this verse would take on particular significance in Christian tradition because the New Testament book of Matthew quotes Hos. 11:1 in reference to the holy family's flight to Egypt to escape Herod (Matt. 2:15). Some Church Fathers understood this as a prediction that Jesus and his family would go to Egypt (Chrysostom, *Demonstration against the Pagans* 3.7; Ephrem, *Commentary of Tatian's Diatessaron* 3.8–9

Hosea, Joel, and Obadiah Through the Centuries, First Edition. Bradford A. Anderson.
© 2024 John Wiley & Sons Ltd. Published 2024 by John Wiley & Sons Ltd.

[Ferreiro]). Others read this typologically: Christ is the fulfillment of the type set out in Hosea (Jerome; Julian of Eclanum).

This quotation from Matthew would continue to interest Christian interpreters through the centuries as readers grappled with how to understand this use of the Old Testament in the New. Continuing the language of the story of Jesus, Calvin remarks that 'The nativity of the people was their coming out of Egypt' (386). Matthew offers here a comparison, Calvin notes, but it is more than that, as both stories point to God as the redeemer of his people. Others were less circumspect. Normally more judicious in his commentary, John Gill states that this reference is neither allusion nor typology; rather, this refers explicitly to Christ. This is 'the first and only sense of the words'. Most common have been readings that see this as typology. The chosen and loved Israel paves the way for the 'true Son' (Pusey).

In the modern period, attention has turned to other matters in 11:1. A number of commentators have focused on God's love for Israel and the related theme of Israel's election (Andersen and Freedman; Wolff). Mays suggested that Hosea was the first to frame YHWH's relationship with Israel in terms of love. Others have focused on the image of Israel as a child. The term used for a child (*na'ar*) more properly means 'youth', and so the age of the child can be understood broadly from an infant to a young man (Sweeney). This has led some to suggest that the imagery in verse 1 points to an adopted son, particularly the use of the term *called* (Ben Zvi 2005). Whatever the case, the focus on the child brings to mind the final child born to Gomer in chapter 1. While previously the reference is to Lo-Ammi, 'Not my people', God nonetheless remembers calling and loving Israel from their youth (Yee 1996).

The phrase 'Out of Egypt' can be found in various social and cultural contexts. The first installment of Anne Rice's retelling of the story of Jesus is entitled *Christ the Lord: Out of Egypt* (Knopf 2005). *Out of Egypt* is also the title of Andre Aciman's memoir of a Jewish family's life in Egypt (Picador 1994) and is the name of a 2009 television show on the Discovery Channel, exploring aspects of ancient Egypt. Hosea 11:1 is also portrayed in Duccio di Buoninsegna's fourteenth-century depiction of Hosea, where the prophet is seen holding a scroll with these famous words (Figure 16). Duccio's quotation from Hosea is not surprising given that it is part of the fourteenth-century Maesta Altarpiece from Siena, which depicts the Madonna with the child Jesus, surrounded by angels and saints. Hosea's words, picked up by the evangelist to describe the holy family's flight to Egypt, provide a fitting connection with the larger tableau offered in this visually stunning piece.

FIGURE 16   *Duccio di Buoninsegna, Hosea, part of the Maestà altarpiece (ca 1308–11). Currently housed in Museo dell'Opera del Duomo (Siena).*

Web Gallery of Art/Wikimedia Commons/Public Domain.

11:2–3

The prophet continues in the voice of God in verse 2. The more the people were called, the more they turned to Baals and idols. How were the people called? This has most often been understood as pointing to the prophets who had called the people back to God (Targum; Rashi; Nicholas of Lyra; Calvin). However, the LXX renders this as 'I called', implying that God has called his people, and this is followed in some contemporary readings (NRSV; cf. Davies 1992). Some thus understand this as indicating that the people immediately turned from God and toward Baals and idols after he saved them from Egypt (Theodore of Mopsuestia; Wolff).

The parental imagery carries on into verse 3, as does God's speech. God reminds the people that it was he who taught Ephraim to walk (LXX: 'bound the feet of Ephraim'). The verse continues: 'I took them up in my arms; but they did not know that I healed them' (11:3). Rashi sees the first part of the verse referring to Moses, who trained the people and took them in his arms (Num. 11:2). However, Ibn Ezra stresses that this is about God, who helped Israel walk on its feet, strengthening them as a parent would a child. Most readers have followed the latter reading, seeing here a depiction of God as a caring parent (Cyril of Alexandria; Calvin). The people have turned away in spite of God's fatherly care (Mays). The eighteenth-century Baptist John Gill noted that the imagery in this verse is maternal, with God depicted as a mother helping her child. This interpretation would find new life in the late twentieth century, with several scholars suggesting that this verse depicts a mother caring for her son, not allowing him to be put to death as was permitted in Deuteronomic law (Schügel-Straumann 1995; Wacker 2012). Reading from the perspective of queer theory, Macwilliam has also noted the 'gender slippage' in these verses, observing what he describes as a feminine and maternal portrayal of God. This perspective complicates the depiction of God as simply an angry husband found in the early chapters of the book (Macwilliam 2011).

11:4

The imagery of verse 4 has provided fertile ground for interpreters. The first half of the verse states, 'I led them with cords of human kindness, with bands of love.' In the Jewish midrash *Genesis Rabbah*, these 'cords of kindness' are connected with the story of Joseph, who was bound and taken to Egypt. Thus, even during adversity, God guides and takes care of his people

(Gen. Rab. 86:1 [Neusner]). Similarly, Jerome draws a comparison with John 6:44, noting that God draws people to himself. Another stream of interpretation notes the resonance with the imagery of the heifer from Hos. 4:16 and 10:11. While Israel has previously been compared to a heifer, God does not in fact treat Israel in this way. Instead, he draws them with the cords of a man, not of a beast (Pusey; Radak). Similarly, others have suggested that the bands of love are indicative of a light yoke (Matt. 11:30; Gill; Luther). Modern readers have made further contributions. The term *cord* (*hebel*) can also be interpreted as labor pains, and so some translate the phrase as 'with labor pains, I drew them out', highlighting the maternal aspect of God's involvement (Sweeney: 114).

This imagery can also be found in visual representations, such as the seventeenth-century image below entitled 'The Binding of the Heart with the Cords of Christ' (Figure 17). Here an angelic figure uses a cord—depicted as the cords of Christ—to pull a person along via their heart.

The second half of verse 4 is difficult and has challenged commentators. The NRSV reads, 'I was to them like those who lift infants to their cheeks. I bent down to them and fed them,' which gives a positive portrayal. Others have understood this as not related to cheeks but to lifting the yoke on the bridles, lightening the load for cattle to give them rest (Targum; Rashi; Calvin). The final clause is more straightforward, indicating that God has fed his people. Because of the earlier mention of Egypt, a number of traditions understand the reference to feeding as an allusion to the wilderness and perhaps to the provision of manna (Jerome; Targum; Mays). Jerome adds a Christological reading; like in the incarnation, God came near but also gave himself: 'I gave them my body as food; I was both food and table companion' (236).

11:5-7

The pairing of Egypt and Assyria, which we have seen elsewhere in Hosea (7:11), recurs in verse 5. The NRSV translates this verse with the following: 'They shall return to the land of Egypt, and Assyria shall be their king, because they have refused to return to me' (11:5). There is disagreement, however, as to how the first clause should be understood: the first word in the Hebrew is *lo*, a term that can be translated as the negative particle ('They shall not return …') or as a note of exclamation ('Lo! They shall return …'). Readers who follow the former reading understand this as an indication that the people will not have a safe return to Egypt for assistance but will instead go to Assyria as exiles (Rashi; Luther; Macintosh). Modern commentators have posited specific

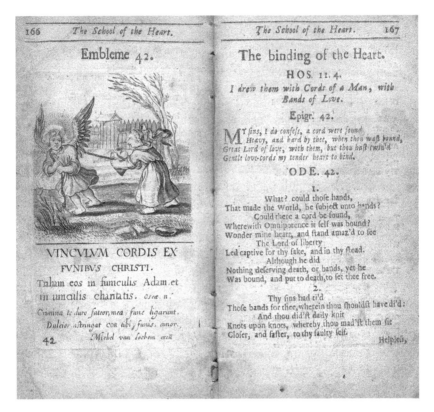

FIGURE 17   The Binding of the Heart with the Cords of Christ. Emblem from the book, depicting an angel leading a woman with a cord. Accompanied by text of Hos. 11:4. Published anonymously and adapted from Benedictine writer Benedict van Haeften's Schola Cordis (1629).

Courtesy of Pitts Library Digital Archive/ Emory University.

settings for this, such as Israel's attempt to pull free from Assyrian influence after the death of Tiglath-Pileser (Wolff). However, as noted above in the NRSV, most modern translations and interpreters have followed the LXX in rendering this clause as a note of exclamation and so suggest that Israel will indeed go to Egypt. In this reading, both Egypt and Assyria are understood as places of exile and punishment (Harper). There is likely a play on words here with the recurring use of the key term *shuv*, 'return' (Calvin; Ewald; Gruber). More clearly evident is the fact that it is the people's unwillingness to return to YHWH that leads to their banishment to Assyria. Indeed, the culmination of this is seen in verse 6 as the prophet states that the sword will rage in their cities, perhaps pointing to the Assyrian occupation of the land (Macintosh).

Verse 7 is difficult to interpret, as is often noted by commentators (Cyril of Alexandria; Rashi; Luther; Wellhausen; Harper). Most readers have understood this verse as an indictment of the people's propensity to turn away from God even if they call out to God from time to time (Radak; Gill). Again, we find the key root *shuv* used here to refer to the people turning or 'backsliding' from God (Calvin). As challenging as this verse is, it is nevertheless the beginning of a *haftarah* reading for the story of Jacob in Genesis in Jewish tradition (see below). This verse also states that Israel calls *'el 'al*, often rendered as 'to the most High' (NRSV). Taken literally, the phrase means 'to above' and is the name of the state airline of modern Israel, El Al (Gruber).

11:8–9

Verse 8 represents what many interpreters see as a pivot or turning point in the book as a whole (Davies 1992; Keefe 2016). The NRSV reads: 'How can I give you up, Ephraim? How can I hand you over, O Israel? How can I make you like Admah? How can I treat you like Zeboiim? My heart recoils within me; my compassion grows warm and tender' (11:8). In spite of the continual turning away from God, God cannot give up on his people. Some have suggested that the language of 'handing over' may reflect the law from Deuteronomy 21, which allowed parents to hand over a rebellious child for stoning (Yee 1996). Admah and Zeboiim were cities in the vicinity of Sodom and Gomorrah, as noted in Gen. 14:2 and Deut. 29:22–23, where they are explicitly linked with the destruction of their neighbors (Jerome; Radak; Wolff). 'To be like Admah and Zeboiim,' Mays notes, 'is to exist only as a memory of swift and final calamity' (157). The words of the prophet here indicate that Israel will not suffer the same fate.

The second half of verse 8 has interested readers, not least because it speaks of God's change of mind (*niham*; NRSV: 'my heart recoils'; Rashi: 'my remorse has been kindled'). Some downplay this imagery, suggesting that it uses human terms to help people understand divine mercy (Calvin). Many, however, see here a struggle within the divine will between justice and mercy, even if it is inclined toward mercy in the end (Cyril of Alexandria; Gill; Pusey). There is a divine capacity to change and to choose redemption over destruction—as demonstrated in verse 8 (Keefe 2016; cf. the studies of Jeremias 1997; Fretheim1984).

The inclination toward mercy continues in verse 9 as God declares that he will not execute his fierce anger or again destroy Ephraim. In Lev. Rab. 6:1, God's promise to not execute his wrath is used as an example of how God comes to the defense of sinners (Neusner). In Christian tradition, too, this verse has been seen as 'a wonderful promise of the mercy of God' (Luther: 61; Jerome). The second part of verse 9 gives the reason for this forbearance as God declares that 'I am God and no mortal (*ish*), the Holy One in your midst'. What does it mean that God is not mortal? In recent decades, some feminist scholars have suggested that this statement might indicate that God is not male, and so is 'a renunciation of male behaviour' (Wacker 2012). More common, however, is the notion that it is divine faithfulness and mercy which sets God apart from humanity (Davies 1992). Thus, in Jewish tradition, this is understood as a reference to God keeping his word (Rashi) or to the fact that God is long-suffering and patient, unlike humanity (Radak). This statement can also serve as a reminder regarding the incomplete and insufficient nature of the various metaphors and anthropomorphisms found throughout the book (Mays).

The final clause of verse 9 is difficult. The early translations understood the last word in the verse as 'city'. The LXX renders this cryptically as 'I will never enter the city ...' (cf. Jerome; Rashi), while the Targum states that God will never exchange Jerusalem for another city (cf. Radak). More recent translations and commentators understand this term as a homonym meaning 'wrath', indicating that God will not come to destroy, matching the first part of the verse (Davies 1992; NRSV).

11:10–11

If the previous verses have pointed to God's love and restraint in the past and in the present, verses 10–11 paint a picture of the future. A change of tone here has been noted since antiquity (Theodore of Mopsuestia), with many modern commentators suggesting that these verses are secondary additions (Davies 1992). The prophet begins in verse 10 by stating that 'They shall go after the LORD, who roars like a lion; when he roars, his children shall come trembling from the west'. The imagery of God as a roaring lion is found elsewhere in Scripture (Amos 1:2; Jerome). The use of this picture in verse 10 has been taken up in diverse ways. In the Babylonian Talmud, this statement is used to urge people to make haste, take up the law, and go to the synagogue: God roars like a lion, and his children should hurry to him (b. Ber. 6b). In Christian tradition, Christological connections are common, including associations with Jesus as the 'lion of Judah' (Gill; Pusey). Indeed, the fact that the people follow the LORD after he roars suggests to some readers that this refers to the preaching of the Gospel (Luther). The verse ends by noting that children will come trembling from the west (*mayam*). As Egypt and Assyria are mentioned again in verse 11, several traditions have understood this as a reference to the return of exiles (Targum; Theodore of Mopsuestia; Rashi; Harper). The final word, *mayam*, can refer to the west or the sea. Thus, some interpreters take this to mean not exiles but the in-gathering of the children of the sea, that is, hostile nations (Julian of Eclanum; Luther).

In verse 11 the theme of return continues, as the prophet declares, 'They shall come trembling like birds from Egypt, and like doves from the land of Assyria; and I will return them to their homes, says the LORD.' The mention of birds and doves in this verse has led to a number of intertextual discussions. Some have suggested that this imagery reverses the picture of the foolish dove, which is found in chapter 7 (Ibn Ezra; Macintosh; Yee 1996). Others have pointed out a connection with similar imagery in Song of Songs, suggesting that both texts highlight God's care for his people (Cant. Rab. 15.1; Neusner). The final clause has a further use of the keyword *shuv*, as God promises to 'return' the people to their houses. While some Christian readers take this to mean gathering the people into the church (Luther), most understand the reference to houses as indicating a safe and stable return to the homeland following exile (Radak; Gill).

11:12

English translations include a twelfth verse in chapter 11, while in the traditions that follow the Hebrew, this verse is the first of chapter 12. Ephraim, we are told, has surrounded 'me' with lies and the house of Israel with deceit. Judah, however, continues to walk with God. The speaking voice of this verse is unclear as it can be understood as either the prophet or God (Wolff). While the LXX includes Judah in the negative portrayal, most premodern readers took this to mean that while Israel was turning away from God, Judah and its rulers re-mained faithful (Jerome; Rashi). In the modern era, the positive reference to Judah has often been seen as a later addition from the hand of Judean redactors (Emmerson 1984; Wellhausen; Harper; Emmerson 1984). The verse ends by noting that Judah is faithful to the *qedoshim*, a plural form of the root 'holy'. Some suggest that this term refers to the divine council (Wolff), or to angels, in keeping with the broader connection with the Jacob traditions (Gruber). More common, however, is to see this as a 'plural of majesty' and thus referring to God, the Holy One (NRSV; Nicholas of Lyra; Luther; Sweeney).

Hosea 11 is a significant text in the liturgical traditions of both Judaism and Christianity. In Judaism, Hos. 11:7–12:12 is the *haftarah* reading for the Torah reading Vayeitzei (Gen. 28:10–32:3) in Sephardic tradition and for Vayishlach (Gen. 32:4–36:43) in Ashkenazic tradition. Both Torah readings are part of the cycle of stories concerning the patriarch Jacob, who is also mentioned in Hosea 12 (see commentary on chapter 12 for more on these connections). The sins and misdeeds of Ephraim are read in light of Jacob as both are loved and chosen in spite of their shortcomings (Fishbane 2002).

Chapter 11 also plays an important role in Christian liturgy. In the Revised Common Lectionary, Hos. 11:1–11 is the first reading on the eighth Sunday after Pentecost (Year C, Proper 13 [Proper 18 in the Roman Catholic Church]). Here the prophet's message is read alongside Ps. 107:1–9, 43; Col. 3:1–11; and Luke 12:13–21, readings that touch on God's steadfast love as well as the importance of focusing on the things of God (and turning from sin). Hosea 11 also features elsewhere in Roman Catholic liturgy—twice, in fact. Most notably, Hos. 11:1, 3–4, 8–9 is the Old Testament reading on the Friday after the second Sunday after Pentecost, where it is read alongside John 19:31–37, which outlines the piercing of Jesus's side while on the cross. Over time this has become part of the Solemnity of the Most Sacred Heart of Jesus, a remembrance that originally focused on the wound in his side but shifted over time to focus on the heart of Jesus (Solemnity of the Most Sacred Heart 2006). The connection with Hosea 11 is not immediately clear; perhaps the love of God for his children and the sacrifice of Jesus are equated. Hosea 11: 1–4, 8–9 is also read on the Thursday of Week Fourteen in Ordinary Time (Year 2) in Roman Catholic tradition. Here Hosea is read with Matt. 10:7–15, which, among other things, mentions Sodom and Gomorrah in Jesus's instructions to his disciples as he sends them on their first mission—perhaps alluding to the reference to Admah and Zeboiim in 11:8 (a resonance also noted by Jerome).

Hosea 12

Chapter 12 is often viewed as the beginning of a new section within the book of Hosea, distinct from chapters 4–11 (Wolff; Ben Zvi 2005). Even so, chapter 12 elaborates on a number of themes found elsewhere in Hosea, including the propensity to draw on Israel's past history when describing its current situation (Holt 1995). This is most obvious in Hosea's use of the patriarch Jacob in chapter 12 (for a sample of literature on Hosea and Jacob, see Vriezen 1941; Ackroyd 1963; McKenzie 1986). At least six elements from the story of Jacob are found in this chapter, though not recounted in the same sequence as found in Genesis. Further, the references to Jacob are ambiguous—it is not clear whether they should be understood positively, negatively, or a mixture of both. Along with the complicated employment of the Jacob traditions, critical scholarship has focused on several other issues, including potential historical settings for this text in the eighth century BCE (Davies 1992), as well as the extensive editorial history of the chapter (Yee 1987).

(A note on versification: Hebrew versions begin chapter 12 with what is 11:12 in English translations and so attribute fifteen verses to chapter 12. Thus, 12:1 in English Bibles is 12:2 in Hebrew texts, and so on. This commentary follows the versification of English translations, where chapter 12 has fourteen verses.)

Hosea, Joel, and Obadiah Through the Centuries, First Edition. Bradford A. Anderson.
© 2024 John Wiley & Sons Ltd. Published 2024 by John Wiley & Sons Ltd.

12:1

The prophet begins chapter 12 by noting that 'Ephraim herds the wind (*ruah*), and pursues the east wind all day long; they multiply falsehood and violence' (12:1). The Greek LXX draws on the elasticity of the Hebrew term *ruah* ('wind, breath, spirit') and translates that Ephraim is an 'evil spirit' (cf. Cyril of Alexandria). Most traditions, however, see this as a reference to wind. Indeed, the Aramaic Targum revisits the language of 8:7, suggesting that Ephraim again 'sows the wind and reaps the whirlwind'. The majority of commentators understand Ephraim's 'herding the wind' as the pursuit of those things that do not last, exemplifying vain hope (Jerome; Theodore of Mopsuestia; Radak; Calvin). The 'east wind', meanwhile, is often associated with the strong winds that brought damage in Israel (Luther; Sweeney). In this sense, there was both self-deception and self-destruction in Israel's actions (Macintosh).

Verse 1 goes on to clarify what is meant by Ephraim 'pursuing the wind': a treaty is made with Assyria, and oil is given to Egypt. The pairing of Assyria and Egypt is found several times in Hosea (7:11; 9:3; 11:5). Here the prophet indicates that Ephraim's political dalliances with Egypt and Assyria are yet further examples of Israel's vain hope in the nations rather than Yhwh. The reference to oil is understood as a tribute given to Egypt (Targum; Rashi), and oil may have been a part of treaty negotiations in antiquity (Gruber). Jerome suggests that this refers to the reign of King Menahem (2 Kgs 15:19), while modern commentators tend to associate this with the reign of Hoshea ben Elah, whose allegiance vacillated between Assyria and Egypt (2 Kings 17; Wolff).

12:2

The prophet continues in verse 2: 'The Lord has an indictment against Judah, and will punish Jacob according to his ways'. The use of the Hebrew term *rib* ('indictment, suit') has led some to suggest that this is an announcement of a legal suit by Yhwh and that a court scene is envisioned (Mays). Why, though, is there an indictment against Judah? Rashi suggests that God was explaining to Judah his contention with Israel. Radak disagrees, noting that while Judah had followed God (cf. 11:12), their loyalty had also deteriorated (cf. Jerome; Julian of Eclanum). For Calvin and others, this reference to Judah was meant to arouse fear in the Israelites—even faithful Judah will not escape punishment if they do not remain true. In the modern era, scholars began to argue that the use of Judah in 12:2 is a later interpolation, where it had replaced a reference to Israel, a more natural fit (Harper; Harper; Wolff; Macintosh). However, others have pointed out that Judah and Jacob are also paired in 10:11 (Landy).

The second half of verse 2 offers us the first reference to Jacob in the chapter. While the NRSV states that Jacob will be punished, readers have noted that the verb *pqd* can be understood both positively and negatively (e.g., 'visit' or 'punish'; cf. Gill). Thus, the reference to Jacob in chapter 12 is ambiguous from the start. Nevertheless, most interpret this clause as a critique of Jacob (and in turn Israel). Jacob traditions are closely associated with the northern kingdom, and so it is not surprising that this patriarch is used when discussing Ephraim. Mays speaks for many when he says concerning Israel, 'They are chips off the old block, and in their pervasive deceitfulness . . . are living up to their heritage' (Mays: 162).

12:3–4

In verses 3–4, the prophet provides a fuller account of Jacob: 'In the womb he tried to supplant his brother, and in his manhood he strove with God. He strove with the angel and prevailed, he wept and sought his favour; he met him at Bethel, and there he spoke with him' (12:3–4). Verse 3 reflects traditions that are also found in Gen. 25:26 and 32:22–32: the former recounting Jacob struggling in the womb with his brother Esau, the latter his night struggle at the Jabbok. The references in verse 4 also point to events in Jacob's life. The penultimate clause notes that 'he wept and sought his favour'. While many readers see this as a continuation of the previous allusion to Jacob's experience at the Jabbok, others see here a reference to the reunion of Jacob and Esau in Gen. 33:4–14, where there is both weeping and the seeking of favor. The final reference to Bethel reflects traditions found in Gen. 28:10–22 when Jacob encounters God as he flees his homeland. These verses have intrigued and vexed interpreters through the centuries—both in terms of the order in which the material is presented, as well as how it should be understood.

In relation to the order of the material, most premodern readers assumed Genesis was the earlier text and that Hosea was borrowing material from Genesis and presenting it in his own manner for his own rhetorical purposes. A number of modern readers agree, and various attempts have been made to reorganize the material in order to reflect the sequence found in Genesis (Wellhausen; see Macintosh for such proposals). However, there are sticking points, including the fact that the text can be read to indicate that Jacob wept during the struggle at the Jabbok, a point that is not recounted in Genesis (Calvin). E. B. Pusey makes note of this and suggests that 'Hosea then knew more than Moses related', though adding that this is 'in harmony' with Moses (Pusey: 118). Others argue that Hosea draws on the Genesis traditions but is creative in his engagement with presenting it (Wolff). Further possibilities have also been put forward, including that Hosea's material reflects an alternative source—or a common source that predates the Genesis material (Whitt 1991). Whatever way the relationship between Hosea and Genesis is understood, it is clear that there are a number of overlaps between the traditions that need to be accounted for. Not only do we find the broad contours of major events in Jacob's life in Hosea, but the text also seems to reflect traditions concerning the etymology of the names 'Jacob' and 'Israel' that are also found in Genesis (Mays; Macintosh).

Further attention has been paid to the issue of how these references to Jacob should be interpreted. In antiquity, a few readers saw these references as a condemnation of Jacob (Theodore of Mopsuestia). This, however, was a minority reading; instead, most premodern readers understood these as reflecting positively on Jacob, in line with a broader tendency to avoid negative portrayals of the patriarchs. Thus, the Targum points to the oracle given to Rebekah before the twins were born, indicating that Jacob would be greater than Esau. Others see Jacob's 'heel grabbing' in the womb as an indication of his elect status: all of this was done with the help of God because he was the chosen son (Cyril of Alexandria; Rashi; Radak; Luther). For many of these interpreters, the people of Israel have not lived up to the example set by the patriarch even if they carry his name (Jerome; Calvin). Cyril writes, 'Whereas Jacob was a supplanter from the womb, therefore, you for your part are always supplanted instead of supplanting sin' (226). This assumption that the text is positively disposed toward Jacob can be seen in later interpretations as well (Pusey; Ackroyd).

However, there is less unanimity on this among contemporary readers than there was in antiquity. Many modern commentators have suggested that verse 3 in particular points to Jacob's deceitful character, going back even before his birth (Andersen and Freedman). Such readings often see verse 4 as more positive, representing a development in Jacob's character, which Israel is to emulate (Harper). Jacob began as deceitful and struggling with God but would go on to weep, supplicate, and repent—and so should Israel (Wolff). Jacob's story becomes 'appeal and warning . . . tears and entreaty are their only future' (Mays: 164). An influential reading in this vein is offered by Holladay (1966), who sees Jacob as the subject of each clause in these verses (with the reference to weeping pointing to the events with Esau in Gen. 33). In this reading we see the development of Jacob's character, and he becomes the paradigm for repentance and change (cf. Yee 1996). However these verses are understood, the presentation of Jacob is deeply ambiguous, and readers do not have straightforward solutions (Wacker 2012). And yet, in a sense, this is fitting: 'If Jacob has transmitted anything to his descendants, it is this complexity' (Landy: 145).

Several other issues in verses 3–4 have also been the subject of considerable attention. One such issue relates to the scene at the Jabbok as verse 3 ends by noting that 'in his manhood he strove with God', while v. 4 continues this with, 'He strove with the angel and prevailed'. Why does verse 3 mention God (*elohim*), while verse 4 mentions an angel (*el-malak*)? This issue has been of particular interest in Judaism. The Targum clarifies this by using 'angel' in both instances. This is in line with parts of Jewish tradition, where Jacob's foe is often understood as Esau's guardian angel (as seen in the midrashic text Gen. Rab. 77:3). Hosea's portrayal of the foe as an angel has had a considerable impact on the visual reception of the story of Jacob. Many artists, including Rembrandt (Figure 18), depict the scene of Jacob's struggle at the Jabbok as an encounter with an angelic being. Who then prevailed? While Ibn Ezra suggests that the

FIGURE 18   *Rembrandt, Jacob wrestling with the angel (1659).*
Gemäldegalerie/Wikimedia Commons/Public Domain.

angel prevailed, Rashi says that the angel wept and beseeched Jacob because the patriarch prevailed (cf. Sweeney).

In the Christian tradition, it is most often understood that Jacob's foe is indeed God, drawing on Genesis 28. How, then, do we account for Jacob prevailing over him? Here one finds the utility of spiritual readings: God makes himself an antagonist in trying and testing our faith, Calvin suggests; when we overcome those trials, it is God who is strengthening us.

Another issue arises in verse 4b. The NRSV suggests that at Bethel God spoke with 'him', indicating Jacob (cf. LXX). However, the MT has a plural suffix 'us', and this is followed by a number of traditions (Targum; Gen. Rab. 78:2). This plural form is often understood as incorporating Israel: God spoke to Jacob, but the message is intended for the whole people (Calvin; Gill; Pusey). Indeed, interpreters have long noted the significance of Bethel in both Genesis and Hosea. At Bethel, the current place of idolatry (10:5), Jacob had once encountered God, and God could speak there again (Ewald).

12:5–6

In verse 5, the prophet declares, 'The LORD the God of hosts, the LORD is his name!' It is unclear on an initial reading how this might relate to the preceding verses regarding Jacob. Some modern commentators have argued that this is a doxology inserted into the passage (Wolff). However, throughout history, readers have been keen to note connections with the surrounding context. The Targum addresses the issue by inserting a reference to both the patriarchs and Moses, with the resultant resonance with Exod. 3:15 (cf. Rashi). John Calvin, meanwhile, says that this verse clarifies the previous verse: it was indeed God who Jacob struggled with even if he appeared as an angel (cf. Macintosh).

Verse 6 delivers a set of directives: return to your God, hold fast to love and justice, and wait continually on God. As with verse 5, this verse has been understood variously in terms of its relation to the surrounding context. Some have taken this as general moral and ethical teaching. We should combine justice and mercy; Basil the Great comments, 'spending in mercy what you possess with justice' and not taking advantage because you have the power to do so (Basil the Great, *Homily on Mercy and Justice* [Ferreiro]). Calvin suggests that this is a general call to repentance, a 'reformation of the whole life' (432). More recently, commentators have focused on the significance of the use of 'return' (*shuv*) and the points of contact with the promise to bring Jacob back to the land of promise in Gen. 28:15 (Davies 1992). Thus, this verse may indeed be related to Jacob's return to the land while also pointing to what Israel needs to do in its own return to God (Macintosh; Sweeney).

12:7–8

The theme of (in)justice continues in verse 7. Here we are told that a merchant, with false balances, loves to oppress. The Hebrew term rendered here as *merchant* is also the proper name 'Canaan'. Over time, this term came to be used in various ways, including as a reference to traders or merchants. When read in this way, Hosea is offering a rebuke to merchants with lying scales (Targum; Rashi; Luther). Circling back to the story of Jacob, Sweeney suggests that this may be a reference to Jacob and Laban, and Jacob's acquisition of wealth and protestations of innocence (Gen. 31:22–42). Conversely, a number of traditions retain the proper noun and understand this as explicitly referencing Canaan (LXX; Jerome; Cyril of Alexandria). Here the name is used pejoratively: they are 'no better than the Canaanites' (Theodore of Mopsuestia; Nicholas of Lyra; Calvin; Harper 91). Ben Zvi (2005) notes that, if read in this way, this is the first mention of Canaan in the book, and here it refers not to cultic rites as one might expect but to socioeconomic issues.

The text of verse 8 is difficult. In the first part of the verse, Ephraim states that 'I am rich', and this wealth, the people indicate, is their own doing. The second half of the verse has been understood by some as a critique of Ephraim's wealth: in spite of their prosperity, none of the fruits of their labor will be available to them (LXX; Targum). While the people thought they were safe because of their success, it turns out that riches will not protect them from their sins (Jerome; Julian of Eclanum; Calvin). Others interpret the second half of the verse as a continuation of Ephraim's speech and the theme of Israel's self-deception: we are wealthy, which is a sign of divine approval; no harm will come to us, they say, because there is no sin to be punished (Wolff). Here a comparison with Jacob can also be made: 'the nation's preoccupation with the vigorous acquisition of wealth derives from a moral fault comparable with that of their eponymous ancestor and that, like it, it stands indicted by the God of the nation and its ancestor' (Macintosh: 498).

12:9–10

The voice is again God's in verse 9: 'I am the LORD your God, from the land of Egypt'. Early traditions were quick to clarify that this meant that God had brought his people out of Egypt rather than indicating that Israel's God was actually from Egypt (Targum; Jerome). Readers have also connected this declaration to the statements concerning Ephraim in verse 8: the self-assertion 'I am rich' is followed by God's assertion, 'I am YHWH' (Wolff).

The voice of God continues in the second half of verse 9: 'I will make you live in tents again, as in the days of the appointed festival.' This reference to 'tents' has led to various interpretations. Some Jewish traditions drew on midrashic texts that indicated that Jacob studied the Torah in tents. Thus, Rashi sees this as an instruction to set up students among you who are engaging in Torah study, as Jacob did (drawing on Gen. Rab.). Others took this as pointing to a new deliverance: since Egypt your ancestors knew me, and I will deliver you again as I did then, dwelling in tents on your journey back to the land (Ibn Ezra).

This latter reading would prove popular, with many suggesting that the references to 'tents' and the 'appointed festival' are allusions to Sukkot (or the Feast of Tabernacles), which serves as a reminder of God's deliverance and provision in the wilderness period (Jerome; Cyril of Alexandria; Yee 1996). The people have forgotten God's redemption, and the reference to tents indicates that a new redemption is needed (Calvin; Harper; Andersen and Freedman). Others see in 'tents' a threat to a return to nomadic life like the ancestors (Wolff; Davies 1992). A mediating position brings together threat and promise; in these readings, the tents point to both punishment and redemption (Macintosh).

In verse 10 God states, 'I spoke to the prophets; it was I who multiplied visions.' What does it mean that God multiplied visions? In the rabbinic text *Leviticus Rabbah*, this is seen as a comment on the primacy of Moses as the paradigmatic prophet and in condemnation of the other prophets: while other prophets all saw through a 'dirty lens' and needed many visions, Moses's vision was clear, and he only needed one revelation (Lev. Rab. 1:14). More often, however, this 'multiplying visions' has been understood as a positive statement of God's self-disclosure. Irenaeus relates this to Paul's exhortations regarding the spirit in 1 Cor. 12:4–11, as the spirit is working in diverse ways (*Against Heresies* 4.20.6 [Ferreiro]). Others have noted similarities with Joel 2:28, where we read that sons and daughters will prophesy, old men will dream dreams, and young men will see visions (Pusey).

Verse 10 ends with God saying that 'through the prophets I will bring destruction'. Like the NRSV, Rashi understands the final term (*adameh*) as relating to coming punishment. However, this word can also be interpreted as 'parables', and Christian readers in particular have understood it in this way (LXX). Parables are an example of how God gradually reveals himself to us and indeed accommodates himself to humanity (as noted by the early church preacher John Chrysostom, *Homilies on John* 15; Calvin). In his *Summa*, Thomas Aquinas uses this as part of an argument that it is good and fitting that scripture uses metaphors: 'God provides for everything according to the capacity of its nature' (*ST* I-I, q. 1, a. 9).

12:11–12

The subject changes in verse 11, returning to a critique of Gilead and Gilgal—the former cited for its iniquity, the latter for its sacrificial practices and altars (b. Sanh. 102b). While both are mentioned earlier in the book (Hos. 6:8; 9:15), here they are used in parallel, and many readers have understood this as a chastisement of false worship in both locations (Theodore of Mopsuestia; Calvin). The verse concludes by noting that Gilgal's 'altars shall be like stone heaps on the furrows of the field'. Ibn Ezra says that the altars of Gilgal were numerous and widely known. While they started off in secret, the Israelites grew in brazenness in multiplying their altars. As recompense for their apostasy, these altars will be overturned and piled up like furrows in the field (cf. Luther).

In verse 12, the prophet returns to the patriarch of Genesis: 'Jacob fled to the land of Aram, there Israel served for a wife, and for a wife he guarded sheep.' Readers have long noted the odd placement of this verse, given that most of the Jacob material occurs earlier in the chapter (Jerome; Rashi). Julian of Eclanum explains this by suggesting that Hosea's 'sermon proceeds like waves', which accounts for the recurrence of these themes. In the modern period, a number of different attempts have been made to rearrange the order of the verses within the chapter to offer a more coherent reading (see Macintosh).

This vignette corresponds with the events recounted in Genesis 29, when Jacob flees to Paddan-Aram and takes Leah and Rachel for his wives. But how should Hosea's depiction be understood? The majority of interpretations understand this as a positive portrayal of Jacob. One midrashic tradition uses this verse to argue that danger to one's life annuls the Sabbath restrictions, and one can flee if one's life is in danger, as Jacob was forced to do (Tanhuma A, Masse'e 81a; Montefiore and Loewe). Rashi similarly understands this as God guarding Jacob when he had to flee. Meanwhile, in the Christian tradition, Luther takes this verse to mean that Jacob toiled in adverse circumstances, while the Israelites cannot even serve God in their own land and abundance. For Pusey, this relates to Jacob's integrity: 'Jacob chose poverty and servitude rather than marry an idolatress of Canaan' (124). Contemporary readers have tended to agree; Macintosh sees here unselfish devotion on Jacob's part, which is an element of his redemption. If the ancestor could change and serve others, so can Israel (cf. Sweeney). An alternative view suggests that this is a negative portrayal of the patriarch, with Aram referring to foreign powers. Jacob's serving for a wife might be a reference to sex rites in the cult, hearkening back to the form-critical readings found earlier in the book: 'the patriarch of Israel had begun his disgraceful association with the foreign woman in Aram and thus became the prototype of the condemned priesthood' (Wolff: 216; cf. Mays).

12:13–14

The context switches to the exodus in verse 13 as God reminds the people of their origins: 'By a prophet the LORD brought Israel up from Egypt, and by a prophet he was guarded.' The natural identification of this prophet is Moses (Radak), though some see different prophets in view in the two halves of the verse—perhaps Moses and Samuel—matching the two wives of Jacob in the previous verse (Andersen and Freedman). Wolff posits that historically this may be the first reference to Moses as a prophet, a theme that is picked up again in Deuteronomy (18:15).

A number of interpreters have noted a play on words in verses 12 and 13, as both use the term *shamar*, 'to guard': Jacob guarded sheep for a wife, and the people were guarded by a prophet. If the two verses are indeed to be read in light of one another, is the correlation to be understood as positive or negative? Some see these as scenes that are juxtaposed: Israel is encouraged to look to the exodus rather than Jacob to find their identity (Mays). Ben Zvi (2005) states that this may be a comparison between Israel's future through women (progeny) or through the prophets (divine word)—and Israel needs to choose wisely. In both of these cases, Jacob is understood negatively, still living up to his reputation. On the other hand, Landy posits that Jacob is presented here as a prototype of Moses and God's deliverance of Israel. Yee concurs: 'Just as Jacob moved to a foreign country to take a wife and bring her back, so also God travels to a foreign country to take a wife and bring her back' (Yee 1996: 286; cf. Coote 1971). However we understand these connections, we can nevertheless recognize that these and previous verses offer a complex interweaving of traditions, including ancestors, exodus, wilderness, and prophets (Yee 1996).

The chapter concludes by returning to Ephraim, who has given 'bitter offense'; because of this, his blood will be returned on him, and he will be repaid (12:14). God will bring the reproach of the people back on them (Luther). The reference to blood has led some modern scholars to suggest this is a cultic legal formula related to bloodguilt (Wolff).

———

As noted in chapter 11, Hosea 11–12 together are an important part of Jewish liturgical traditions. Hosea 11:7–12:12 is the *haftarah* for the Torah reading Vayeitzei (Gen. 28:10–32:3) in Sephardic tradition and for Vayishlach (Gen. 32:4–36:43) in Ashkenazic tradition (Fishbane 2002; cf. Mann 1940). (Further, Hos. 12:13–14:10 is the *haftarah* for Vayeitzei in the Ashkenazic tradition.) Both Torah readings are part of the cycle of stories concerning the patriarch Jacob in Genesis. The patriarch and the people of Israel are brought together in these readings, with all of the complexities and ambiguities noted above. Whether Jacob is to serve as a warning or as a model (or both!), the invocation of the patriarch alongside the message of Hosea is a reminder that the people have been called, chosen, and delivered by God.

Hosea 13

The penultimate chapter in Hosea is particularly harsh and full of threats, though the most famous verse, verse 14, is ambiguous and, for some readers, offers a glimmer of hope amid the accusations. For those predisposed to situating the chapter historically, it is generally assumed that this chapter is later than previous ones, perhaps 725–24 BCE (Pusey; Wolff; Davies 1992).

(Chapter 13 has sixteen verses in English translations, though only fifteen in Hebrew versions. This commentary follows the English versification.)

13:1

The end of chapter 12 focuses on Ephraim's guilt and 13:1 picks up this theme. 'When Ephraim spoke', the prophet declares, 'there was trembling; he was exalted in Israel; but he incurred guilt through Baal and died'. Many readers through the centuries have understood this verse as moving from a positive portrayal of Ephraim to a negative one. However, regarding the particulars in the verse, there has been significant variation (see Harper). A number of traditions suggest that the exaltation of Ephraim mentioned in the first half of the verse relates to Jeroboam, who was from the tribe of Ephraim (Lev. Rab. 12.5 [Neusner]; Jerome; Rashi; Gill). Another interpretation is that this relates to the tribe of Ephraim (and perhaps their eponymous ancestor; see Gen. 48:8–20), which at points was particularly strong among the tribes (Calvin; Sweeney). Still others suggest that all Israel is here in view; Israel was exalted because they

Hosea, Joel, and Obadiah Through the Centuries, First Edition. Bradford A. Anderson.
© 2024 John Wiley & Sons Ltd. Published 2024 by John Wiley & Sons Ltd.

had received the law from Moses—but they rejected this and turned to Baal (Targum; Cyril of Alexandria; Theodore of Mopsuestia).

The guilt incurred through Baal has been understood by many as idolatry (Targum; Nicholas of Lyra; Wellhausen). Some modern form critics, meanwhile, take this as a reference to the Canaanite fertility cult associated with Baal (Mays). The Hebrew uses the preposition *bet* before Baal, which can be translated as 'in' or 'at'. Thus, some interpret this literally as 'at Baal'—referring to a specific place at which guilt was incurred, such as Baal-Peor (Numbers 25; Yee 1996). What does the mention of 'death' refer to at the end of the verse? Rashi suggests that this points to the termination of Jeroboam's dynasty. Others understand this as the death of Israel, perhaps at the hands of the Assyrians (Jerome; Wolff). For Luther and others, this rejection of God leads to spiritual death (Luther; Pusey). However one understands this death, its occurrence in verse 1 introduces one of the main themes of the chapter (Landy).

13:2–3

If verse 1 points to the past, verse 2 looks to the present: 'And now they keep on sinning.' This, we are told, includes making images as well as idols of silver. Some readers have understood this as a reference to the golden calves; why then are they made with silver? Radak posits that the calves were made of gold, but the people bought the gold with their silver currency. Others understand this more broadly as idol worship. In the Talmud, for example, we read that each person made an image of their god and put it in their pocket (b. Sanh. 63b). Modern commentators have likewise suggested that a national cult devoted to these man-made idols may have emerged during this period (Mays; Wolff).

Verse 2 concludes with a cryptic reference to sacrifices and kissing calves. The difficulty with this clause is whether it speaks of human's offering sacrifices or of the sacrifice of humans (i.e., child sacrifice). The NRSV follows the former understanding, taking this to mean general sacrificial offerings, and a number of readers throughout history have also understood the text in this way (e.g., Gill; Pusey). However, more common is the assumption that the prophet speaks here of human sacrifice (see NIV). This reading is found in the LXX, as well as in the Babylonian Talmud: 'Whenever anyone sacrifices his son to an object of idol worship, the priest says to him: "The Master has sacrificed a great gift to the idol; therefore, he has the right to come and kiss it"' (b. Sanh. 63b). Commentators from Jerome, to Ibn Ezra, to Calvin have suggested likewise, as have modern readers (Andersen and Freedman).

In verse 3 we move to the future, and we are told the result of this apostasy: Israel will be destroyed quickly (Radak). The prophet uses four images that all suggest something that is temporary and passing quickly: morning mist, dew, chaff, and smoke. These things are 'visible for a time', Cyril of Alexandria notes, 'but proceeding to ruination and ending in nothingness'.

13:4–6

In verses 4–6, the speaker is again God, and the text returns to the theme of salvation history, particularly Israel's deliverance from Egypt and their time in the wilderness (Theodore of Mopsuestia). Verse 4 begins with a reminder that YHWH has been their God since the land of Egypt, a period in Israel's history already noted in Hos. 12:12–13 (Jerome; Calvin). Cyril of Alexandria suggests this statement counters Jeroboam's words in 1 Kgs 12:28 that it was the calves that brought the people out of Egypt. The verse ends by noting that 'you know no God but me, and besides me there is no saviour' (13:4). These statements have some resonance with the first part of the Decalogue, which has led to some discussion concerning the relative dating of the Decalogue and Hosea (see Gruber). The final word is the Hebrew term *moshia'*, often translated 'savior'. Because of the weight of this term, particularly in Christianity, some Jewish translations render this as 'helper' (JPS).

The voice of God continues in verse 5 by noting that it was he who 'knew' them in the wilderness. The LXX renders 'knew' as 'shepherded', while the Targum states that God provided for their needs (cf. Rashi). A number of commentators take this to mean the provision of manna and other food in the wilderness following Egypt (Jerome; Nicholas of Lyra). Ibn Rabban, the ninth-century Muslim scholar, argued that this verse in fact relates to Muhammad, as God raised him up and tended to him in the desert (Wheeler 2021).

When God led them to pasture, verse 6 informs us, they were satisfied. This led to a proud heart, and 'therefore they forgot me' (13:6). The Talmud indicates that this refers to when the people entered the holy land (b. Ber. 32a; cf. Ibn Ezra; Gill). The fact that people turn from God when they feel secure and prosperous is highlighted by a number of readers, many of whom point to a similar assertion made in Deut. 8:12–14 (Jerome; Radak; Calvin; Harper). As Cyril of Alexandria notes, 'Luxurious living is therefore risky and difficult to manage, and is, as it were, a slippery path to apostasy from God; far better is moderate tribulation' (241). In the Babylonian Talmud, this verse is also used in a discussion of sexual moderation (b. Sukkah 52b).

13:7–8

While God had previously 'pastured' the flock (v. 6), in verses 7–8 he seems to become the animals that would threaten that very flock: lion, leopard, and bear will tear, devour, and mangle the people (Moughtin-Mumby 2008). Some see here a reference to the Assyrians, who will devour Israel (LXX: Cyril of Alexandria; Radak); others maintain that it is God's depth of feeling and his own action that is envisaged (Calvin). The latter notion seems clear in verse 8, where God says, 'I will fall upon them like a bear robbed of her cubs, and will tear open the covering of their heart'. Readers have frequently noted that a bear bereaved of her cubs is the most ferocious of all animals (Cyril of Alexandria; Rashi; Pusey). However, the image of God as a raging mother bear also 'deflates overly romantic-bourgeois images of mothers' and complicates the depiction of gender in Hosea (Wacker 2012: 382; cf. Sherwood 1996).

An eighteenth-century illustrated Bible for children offers a provocative depiction of this verse (see Figure 19). Along with parts of the text of verse 8, we have images of a bear chasing a person and a feeding lion. It is interesting that the illustrators decided to focus on this verse; perhaps it is because of the animals, which it is assumed will appeal to children. And yet there is dissonance between the text and the imagery in this case, as a text with violent rhetoric is envisioned in an amusing way for children.

The theme of Israel's destruction continues in verse 9, though the text can be understood either to indicate that God will destroy Israel (Harper; Wolff; NRSV) or that Israel has destroyed itself (Jerome; Rashi). Aquinas follows the latter reading when he uses this verse in a discussion of whether grace is given only to those who prepare for it: 'The first cause of the defect of grace is on our part; but the first cause of the bestowal of grace is on God's according to Osee 13:9: "Destruction is thy own, O Israel; thy help is only in Me"' (*ST* I-II, q. 112, a. 3).

13:10–11

Verses 10–11 turn to the issue of the monarchy. While some readers suggest that in verse 10 God says, 'I am your King' (Gruber), most interpreters and translators understand this as an interrogative: 'Where now is your king, that he may save you?' (NRSV; cf. Rashi). The text continues by asking where Israel's rulers are, 'of whom you said, "Give me a king and rulers"'. Interpreters often see here an allusion to the events of 1 Samuel 8, where the people ask for a king,

FIGURE 19   Image Depicting Hos. 13:8 from 'A New Hieroglyphical Bible for the Amusement & Instruction of Children' (1796).

Courtesy of Pitts Library Digital Archive/Emory University.

and God acquiesces (Jerome; Radak). If the people had looked to God he would have delivered them; now, they will bear the brunt of their own folly (Theodore of Mopsuestia; Aquinas; Calvin).

The result of this is laid out in verse 11: 'I gave you a king in my anger, and I took him away in my wrath.' Because of the points of contact with 1 Samuel 8, it is common to interpret this as pointing to Saul (Cyril of Alexandria;

Ibn Ezra; Gill). However, others have understood the 'king given' as Jeroboam, and Hoshea ben Elah, the final king of the northern kingdom, as that which was taken away in wrath (Jerome). Modern readers have suggested that this is a general critique of the monarchy and that all the kings from Saul to Hoshea are in view (Wolff; Davies 1992).

13:12–13

God has not forgotten Ephraim's iniquity, we read in verse 12; rather, their sin has been bundled up and stored for remembrance (Rashi; Holtz 2012). This seems to be related to the following verse, which speaks of coming judgment described in terms of childbirth: 'The pangs of childbirth come for him, but he is an unwise son; for at the proper time he does not present himself at the mouth of the womb' (13:13). The 'unwise son' has been understood in various ways. Jerome compares this to the senseless dove noted in 7:11, while for Macintosh this brings to mind the son whom God called in 11:1–14. Radak, meanwhile, states that this relates to the generations who did not learn from the distress of their fathers.

What is the meaning of this imagery? One interpretation is that instead of learning from judgment (pangs) and turning it into a time for new life (birth), Israel is continuing in their obstinate and wrongheaded ways, unwilling to learn (Wolff). The unwise son is one who is not birthed: he does not do what comes naturally and at the right time (Eccl. 8:5), and so instead of joy, there is further sorrow (Harper; Yee 1996). These are 'labour pains doomed to failure' (Macintosh: 544) and may reflect the imagery of the womb as tomb (Wacker 2012). The imagery used here is unusual and again complicates the figurative use of gender in the book: 'The metaphor of son giving birth to itself allows a transfer from male to female personae. As well as son, Ephraim is travailing mother' (Landy: 264).

13:14

Verse 14 is one of the more well-known verses in Hosea but also one of the more disputed (Yee 1996). The verse speaks of Sheol and Death, though it is unclear how these references should be understood. While there are numerous different ways in which the verse can be translated, there are essentially two main directions of interpretation (Ben Zvi 2005). In one reading, this verse can be understood as offering a promise of mercy in the midst of a series of threats, pointing to God's mercy as he overcomes death and rescues his people. This is the approach taken in the NIV, which reads: 'I will deliver this people from the power of the grave; I will redeem them from death. Where, O death, are your plagues? Where, O grave, is your destruction?' (13:14, NIV).

This is the more well-known reading; while found in some Jewish traditions (including the Talmud, b. Pesah.), it is most famous because it is quoted by Paul in 1 Cor. 15:55 as part of a larger discussion of resurrection (Barrett 1968). Paul draws on the LXX's rendering of the verse, which translates the first part of the verse as statements and the second half as questions. Not surprisingly, Christian readers through the centuries have been quick to draw on Paul's usage—and some felt they had no choice but to follow the apostle's reading, even if they had questions about it (Jerome). For many of these early Christian readers, it was clear that death and hades were overcome through Christ and that this victory was both spiritual and physical (Augustine, *Sermon 128*; Cyril of Alexandria). Medieval and Reformation era readers likewise read this as pointing to the work of Christ (Aquinas; Nicholas of Lyra)—with many suggesting that the prophet actually had Christ in mind (Luther; Gill). Calvin agrees that this is indeed about redemption: God is 'the ruin of death, and the excision of the grave' (476). However, Calvin notes that the apostles do not always take a passage in context when quoting but take hold of a word or idea and expand upon it—thus, Paul uses Hosea to speak of the power of God over death, using the prophet as an example of this, even if the prophet does not himself speak of Christ.

Calvin's warning about how the apostles use Scripture is appropriate, as this verse can be understood as saying the opposite of Paul's understanding: if the initial clauses are read as questions, God is seen as choosing *not* to save his people from death (Harper). This interpretation is found in the NRSV's translation: 'Shall I ransom them from the power of Sheol? Shall I redeem them from Death? O Death, where are your plagues? O Sheol, where is your destruction? Compassion is hidden from my eyes' (13:14, NRSV). This understanding can be seen in various traditions and commentators (Targum; Rashi; Wolff; Ben Zvi 2005). As a number of interpreters have noted, this reading fits much better with the tone and context of chapter 13, as the verses preceding and following this are both statements of coming judgment (Davies 1992; Mays). Read in this way, the temptation to rescue the people is real for Israel's God, but in the end it is excluded (Macintosh). If this reading is correct, then Paul takes what was a call to death for Israel and puts it to use as a mockery of death (Wolff). Yee suggests that we retain the multivalence of these images 'since all these possibilities are in some way true and deeply imbedded in the theological drama' (Yee 1996: 292).

The mention of death and Sheol (or Hades/Hell) has also captured the attention of readers (Landy). Jerome posits that Hosea is drawing a distinction between death and hell, which he explains at great length (cf. Luther; for a strong rebuttal, see Calvin). Julian of Eclanum, meanwhile, suggests that these are different names for the Assyrians, whom God will overcome. Several contemporary commentators have suggested that these might refer to other gods—Mot and Sheol—in which case the text speaks of the ability of Israel's God to overcome these other deities or even to take on their attributes (Andersen and Freedman; Gruber).

Paul's citation has meant that Hosea's imagery in verse 14 has appeared in various cultural and religious contexts, including music. One example is the use of the prophet's words in George Frideric Handel's famous work *Messiah* (1741), where the refrain 'O death where is thy sting? O grave where is thy victory?' is repeated (Part 3; SATB) (see Figure 20). Hosea's imagery is also found in Charles Wesley's hymn, 'Christ the Lord is Risen Today' (1739). Verse 3 has the following lyrics:

> Lives again our glorious King, Alleluia!
> Where, O death, is now thy sting? Alleluia!
> Once he died our souls to save, Alleluia!
> Where's thy victory, boasting grave? Alleluia!

Both Handel and Wesley follow Paul's positive interpretation of these words and envision these interrogatory statements as mocking death and the grave.

13:15–16

The condemnation of Ephraim continues in verse 15. This verse begins with a reference to Ephraim's flourishing either among the rushes (NRSV; Rashi) or among brothers (LXX; Targum; Cyril of Alexandria; Sweeney). The latter reading—a reference to brothers—has been understood as a reference to Israel's occasional ascendancy over Judah (Theodore of Mopsuestia; Calvin). In spite of this flourishing, an east wind is coming from the wilderness, and 'his fountain shall dry up, his spring shall be parched' (13:15, NRSV). The Targum amends this to read that a king as strong as the east wind will come upon Israel (Rashi). A similar politically focused reading sees the wind as referring to the

FIGURE 20   *George Frideric Handel, Messiah, Part 3. Duet: 'O death, where is thy sting?'*
Copyists manuscript, 1743–46, p. 28.

Credit: The Morgan Library & Museum/Cary 40.

Assyrians (Gill; Harper; Macintosh). Spiritual interpretations have also been offered, including Luther's suggestion that this refers to the Holy Spirit, who comes to 'dry up' sin. The fountain and spring drying up can also be understood as referring to sterility—and offer a juxtaposition to Ephraim's flourishing and 'fruitfulness' (Moughtin-Mumby 2008).

The chapter comes to a close with a final threat, this time concerning Samaria, who, we are told, will bear her guilt because of her rebellion against God. The result is that they will fall by the sword, 'their little ones shall be dashed in pieces, and their pregnant women ripped open' (13:16 [Heb. 14:1]). Samaria is given special mention here because it was the capital of Ephraim, and thus the threats to Ephraim and Samaria bookend the chapter (Jerome; Radak; Wellhausen).

The seventeenth-century Puritan Jeremiah Burroughs compared this verse to the situation of England in his own day and has no issue with the violent language, which he sees as appropriate: the English are barren and lifeless because of rebellion against God. As the Israelites were idolatrous and suffered consequences, so too will England be punished, Burroughs notes, for its various sins, ranging from self-seeking to anarchy to atheism (1863: 606–10). However, other commentators would note the violent language of this verse with some unease. A rabbinic text notes that while verse 16 is a harsh statement, the subsequent verse (14:1) calls for repentance and return. This juxtaposition proves Rabbi Aqiba's axiom that 'every passage contiguous to another provides an appropriate occasion for a lesson to be derived therefrom' (*Sifre Num.* 131.1; Neusner). Cyril of Alexandria, meanwhile, comments that opposition to God is a difficult and harsh reality, and Calvin notes that while the images are abhorrent, we cannot question God's justice and judgment; further, the words of the prophet are clearly a warning to avert such disaster. The feminine personification of Samaria, along with the reference to mothers and babies, has been highlighted by contemporary commentators (Yee 1996). Wacker (2012) points out that Samaria is presented as a mother that cannot protect her children, while O'Brien (2008) reminds us that we see here yet another example of women as the recipients of violence and abuse.

Hosea 13 is part of Jewish liturgical tradition, standing in the middle of Hos. 12:13–14:10, which is the *haftarah* reading for Vayeitzei (Gen. 28:10–32:3) in Ashkenazic tradition (Fishbane 2002). This liturgical reading is discussed further in the commentary on Hosea 14.

Hosea 14

Chapter 14 brings us to 'the prophet's farewell' (Luther: 74). The focus of this chapter is a call to repentance and return to Yhwh, as well as God's care for his people. These verses provide a positive conclusion to the book that reverses and transforms the previous threats of destruction into a statement of hope (Andersen and Freedman; Ben Zvi 2005). Many commentators have been moved by the rhetoric of the chapter: Ewald notes that this chapter announces 'what rests beyond these storms in the eternal bosom of divine love' (300). Pusey, meanwhile, comments that while 'billow upon billow have rolled over Ephraim', here 'every word is full of mercy' (135). However, not everyone is sold on this transformation. Landy counters that this chapter is 'a poetic wish-fulfilment; the corpse rises and lives happily ever after' (169). Wacker notes that if women can appropriate this chapter in any way after all that has come before, it must be as 'resistance readers' (2012: 384).

Although most premodern readers assumed this chapter reflected the prophet's words, modern readers have varied, with proposals including that it came later in the prophet's career near the fall of Samaria (Wolff; Davies 1992), that it was added by a redactor or the prophet's disciples at a later time (Harper; Jeremias 1983), or that it was the intentional work of a later author (Ben Zvi 2005).

(Chapter 14 has nine verses in English translations and ten verses in Hebrew versions. This commentary follows the English versification of 14:1–9.)

Hosea, Joel, and Obadiah Through the Centuries, First Edition. Bradford A. Anderson.
© 2024 John Wiley & Sons Ltd. Published 2024 by John Wiley & Sons Ltd.

14:1

The chapter commences with a prophetic summons to repentance in verses 1–3 (Wolff). The prophet begins with a call that epitomizes the entire book: 'Return, O Israel, to the Lord your God, for you have stumbled because of your iniquity' (14:1). Drawing on the key term *shuv* ('return'), this verse has long been noted for highlighting the significance of repentance (Gen. Rab. 84:19). One stream of rabbinic tradition notes that the different names for God are used here to stress the importance of repentance: Israel should return while the Lord is Yhwh, that is, merciful, or they will be judged by Elohim in his justice (PesK 164a; Montefiore and Loewe; cf. Rashi). Is there a contradiction in this call to return as previously God has threatened annihilation? No, Calvin argues, as previous messages were to the whole people, but this is aimed at the faithful remnant.

The call to 'return' plays an important role in Jewish tradition as chapter 14 serves as the reading for Shabbat Shuvah, the Sabbath of Return at the start of the Jewish year. This is the Sabbath between Rosh Hashanah and Yom Kippur, where there is a strong focus on atonement, highlighting the significance of prayer in repentance. The phrase 'Return O Israel' is also a popular name for sermons exploring Hosea 14 and is the name of a controversial Christian group that advocates for the return of Jews to the land of Israel (https://www.returnoisrael.org/).

14:2

The prophet continues in verse 2: 'Take words with you and return to the Lord; say to him, Take away all guilt . . .' The command to 'take words' has led to considerable discussion through the centuries. Many readers have understood this as the prophet providing the people with a formulaic prayer of repentance (Jerome; Gruber). One rabbinic midrash states that if you are poor and have no sacrifices to bring, God says, 'I need only words' (Exod. Rab. 38.4; Montefiore and Loewe). Similar sentiments are found throughout the history of interpretation: God does not desire silver, gold, or burnt offerings but repentance (Radak; Ibn Ezra; Nicholas of Lyra). This is a call to return to God through the 'gift of words', the cheapest of gifts (Cyril of Alexandria; Pusey).

The final clause of verse 2 is difficult and much depends on how one understands the Hebrew term *pari'm*. This word is most frequently understood as meaning 'bulls' (cf. Targum). In this reading, the sense seems to be that the offering of lips is like a bull offering and takes the place of sacrifice (Calvin;

Macintosh). However, the LXX translates the Hebrew term *pari'm* as 'fruit' (cf. Vulgate; Rashi). This reading has generally been followed by modern commentators and translations, including the NRSV, which renders this as 'we will offer the fruit of our lips' (cf. Wellhausen; Harper; Wolff). The notion of the 'fruit of our lips' has resonance with the 'sacrifice of praise' found in Ps. 50:14 (Julian of Eclanum; Gill). The imagery of the 'fruit of our lips' would become popular in later Jewish and Christian texts (1QH 1:28–29; Heb. 13:15; see Davies 1992). Andersen and Freedman comment that while the verse can naturally be read as referring to 'fruit', there may well be a 'bovine pun in a bit of bet-hedging' (645). However one renders this term, this clause seems to echo the first part of verse 2, pointing to the fact that repentance is desired over sacrifice (Jerome; Radak).

14:3

The confession continues in verse 3; after their repentance, the people are to promise not to revert to their former ways as outlined elsewhere in the book (Pusey). To begin, the people are to declare that 'Assyria shall not save us; we will not ride upon horses'. Here the prophet again challenges the false confidence in political alliances (Calvin). Alongside the mention of Assyria, the reference to horses has led some to suggest that this is an allusion to Egypt (Rashi; Ibn Ezra; Harper) or to traveling and looking for aid from others (Calvin). While some see a disaster, such as the fall of Samaria, as already having taken place (Wolff), Sweeney feels that an alliance is still possible, which is why the people need to swear off further pursuits.

The people next pledge to no longer call the work of their hands 'Our God', a clear reference to idolatry. Some understand this to refer to the calves at Dan and Bethel (Jerome; Gill), while others see it as referring more broadly to Israel's idolatrous behavior (Calvin). Verse 3 ends by noting that 'in you the orphan finds mercy'. According to the Targum, this refers to the mercy shown to Israel's fathers, who were like orphans in Egypt (cf. Jerome; Radak). This reference to mercy also reverses the threat implicit in the naming of the daughter in 1:6 (Lo-Ruhamah, 'no mercy'; Yee 1996).

14:4–5

Beginning in verse 4, the voice switches to that of God, who notes that 'I will heal their disloyalty; I will love them freely, for my anger has turned from them'. Yhwh's change from anger to mercy has been referenced by readers throughout the centuries, with many understanding this as an example of God's abounding love (Jerome). However, the mention of anger also brings to mind previous references to anger in chapter 2, as well as in 3:1 and 11:3 (Landy). As Yee notes, 'The reader vividly recalls descriptions of God/husband taking out his wrath on the wife (Hosea 2). Remembering the physical price the wife had to pay to regain her husband's favor, one becomes uncertain about the beautiful metaphors of the wife's abundant fertility. They are built on a series of images that are all too real and painful for many women' (1996: 297).

God's speech continues in verse 5 in a series of similes that describe 'the sweetness of deliverance' (Julian of Eclanum: 192). God will be like the dew to Israel, an image that, as Jerome notes, has resonance elsewhere in the HB (Gen. 27:28; Deut. 32:2). Indeed, dew was used previously in Hosea to speak of Israel's fleeting loyalty to God; now it is a symbol of sustenance and life in God (Macintosh). In contrast to 13:15, where Israel was told that their springs would dry up, here the imagery suggests that God's goodness will not in the end be withheld (Radak; Pusey). With this provision from YHWH, Israel will blossom like a lily and will 'strike root like the forests of Lebanon' (14:5). The Hebrew text refers simply to Lebanon, with many interpreters and translations supplying the reference to Lebanon's famous forests and trees (Targum; Macintosh). Calvin suggests the twofold image of lily and roots is intentional: Israel's restoration will be quick, like a lily in bloom, and enduring, like the roots of the famous trees of Lebanon (cf. Pusey).

14:6

The arboreal imagery continues in verse 6, where we read that Israel's shoots will spread out, and his beauty will be like the olive tree. The Targum renders 'shoots' as 'sons and daughters', implying that Israel's blossoming refers to its descendants (cf. Theodore of Mopsuestia). The connection between beauty and the olive tree, meanwhile, has led to various interpretations, particularly in Jewish tradition. According to the Targum, this refers to a candelabrum, likely drawing on the reference to the olive tree and its connection to oil. Rashi takes this imagery further: their beauty, he writes, is like the menorah in the Temple. The final clause of verse 6 returns to Lebanon: 'his fragrance is like that of Lebanon', and many traditions again supply 'cedars' in this clause. Rashi again draws a connection to the Temple: the fragrance of Lebanon may be a reference to the sanctuary because of the use of the cedars of Lebanon. For Luther, this has resonance with 2 Cor. 2:15 as the people of God are to be the 'aroma of Christ'.

14:7

Natural imagery is also the theme of verse 7. The first clause again employs the Hebrew term *shuv* with the sense that the people will return and dwell beneath God's shade. The concept of 'return' has led some to assume that this is a reference to an ingathering of those in exile (Targum; Rashi; Radak). Another rabbinic tradition holds that this relates to proselytes who take refuge in Israel's God (Lev. Rab. 1.2; Montefiore and Loewe). For others, the use of 'return' points again to repentance and a return to God's ways; in this sense, a return to the land is dependent on a return to YHWH (Cyril of Alexandria; Yee 1996). The imagery of God's shade has also been generative. In the Targum, this is rendered as the 'shade of the anointed One' with potentially messianic overtones (see Cathcart and Gordon). Others have pointed out this image's resonance with Song of Songs 2:3 and have suggested that dwelling in the shade may be invoking the imagery of lovers, hearkening back to the marriage imagery from earlier in the book (Ben Zvi 2005).

Verse 7 continues by comparing Israel to flourishing grain, a blossoming vine, and the fragrance of the wine of Lebanon. The latter point has led to some speculation on the part of interpreters. While the Targum offers a significant expansion, which refers to matured wine poured out in the sanctuary, a common refrain among commentators is that the wine of Lebanon was famous in antiquity, noted by Pliny and others for its exceptional quality (Jerome). Radak comments that the wine of Lebanon had 'an exceptional bouquet' that was well known. Israel's reputation (fragrance) in the future would thus be like that of Lebanon's wine (Radak).

The combination of grain, oil, and wine in these verses has not escaped the attention of readers, even if interpreted in diverse ways. Luther points out that some in his day understood the reference to grain and wine as an allusion to the bread and wine of communion. For others, the use of grain, oil, and wine brings to mind the critique of chapter 2 and may be one last denunciation of the Canaanite fertility cult—a final reiteration that YHWH is the true source of Israel's sustenance (Andersen and Freedman; Macintosh).

As noted earlier, a number of images found in verses 5–7 are strikingly similar to those found in the Song of Songs (Landy; Wolff). Some see this as indicating a return to the marital metaphor of the early chapters of Hosea (Yee 1996). This love language may be seen as an attempt to redeem the earlier language of fornication and infidelity. Even if this is the case, however, the reversal so often noted may not be as clear and straightforward for some readers, particularly women (Moughtin-Mumby 2008; Wacker 2012).

14:8

Verse 8 begins with one final renunciation of idols on the part of either God (MT; NRSV) or Ephraim (LXX; Rashi; Calvin). Rather than idols, God declares, 'I will answer you and look after you.' Wellhausen famously amends the text here to read 'I am his Anat and his Asherah', referring to the Canaanite goddesses, though this reading has not gained wide acceptance (see Harper). However, Wellhausen's suggestion is interesting in light of the subsequent clause, which reads, 'I am like an evergreen cypress, your fruit comes from me' (NRSV). This is the only place in the HB where YHWH is compared to a tree (Wolff). In what way is God like a cypress? In one rabbinic text, God is likened to a cypress because he bows down to uproot the desire for idolatry in Israel (Cant. Rab. 17.1; Neusner). Another tradition suggests that, like a tree bent down close to the ground, God is accessible to humanity (Rashi). Others have posited that God is like a tree that offers protection and shade (Calvin; Cyril of Alexandria). More recently, scholars have suggested that the tree and shade imagery may refer to a tree goddess (such as Asherah), with God himself taking on this role for his people (Moughtin-Mumby 2008; Wacker 2012). Whatever the case, the extensive use of the natural world in these verses is striking. Von Rad comments, 'It is a remarkable fact that the same prophet who thinks so emphatically in terms of saving history can at the same time move Yahweh's relationship to Israel over into the horizons of an almost plant-like natural growth and blossoming, where all the drama of the saving history ebbs out as if in a profound quiet' (1968: 117).

14:9

The book of Hosea concludes with a verse that appears to be a commentary on the interpretation of the prophet's words: 'Those who are wise understand these things; those who are discerning know them. For the ways of the LORD are right, and the upright walk in them, but transgressors stumble in them' (14:9). Philo would make reference to this verse in several places, noting that esoteric things should only be shared with those who can appreciate and understand these messages (III Plant. 138; V Mut. 137–39; see Cohen 2007). In the Babylonian Talmud, this verse is seen as highlighting the importance of the intentions of those who claim to follow God (b. Hor. 10b; Montefiore and Loewe). Radak, meanwhile, suggests this is a statement from the prophet calling on those who are wise to understand his message and admonition. Christian readers likewise found much to say about this verse. While Origen sees this as an invitation to understand scripture figuratively (*Homilies on Jeremiah* 28.5; Ferriero), Jerome says that the prophet's words in this verse point to the 'obscurity of this book and the difficulty of explanation' (261). This closing statement, Pusey states, is a call to reflect not on the prophet's words but on their substance.

Readers have long noted the presence of wisdom in this verse; Nicholas of Lyra pointed out that this call to wisdom is similar to that in the NT in Jas. 3:13. Modern interpreters have given further attention to the connection with wisdom literature and wisdom themes found elsewhere in the HB and beyond (Sheppard 1980; Seow 1982). The incorporation of wisdom, along with the fact that the verse is interested in 'interpretation and actualization', suggests to some that this verse is a postscript that comes from a later period, even if it carefully integrates themes and terminology from elsewhere in the book (Harper; Wolff; Macintosh). While uncomfortable with the nature of the 'reversal' of chapter 14 that returns to a portrait of a loving God, Yee highlights the potential that wisdom offers readers in terms of presenting another perspective from which to view the end of the book. She notes that wisdom is often given a female personification (lady wisdom) and is also described as a life-giving tree (Prov. 3:18). In this reading, God as husband is replaced with the Wisdom of God, who is the tree of life (Yee 1996).

In light of this connection of Hosea and (lady) wisdom, the placement together of Hosea and the Delphic Sibyl by Pinturicchio in the Vatican's Hall of Sibyls is interesting (Figure 21). Known as an oracle (or perhaps the sister) of Apollo, the Delphic Sibyl was one of several well-known sibyls or prophetesses, and her final prediction was said by Christians to be of the coming of Christ. As Hosea is holding his own words from Hos. 11:1 ('Out of Egypt I called my son'), with its implicit reference to the coming of Christ, both Hosea and the Delphic Sibyl are likely understood to be foretelling the coming of Christ. Indeed, the Sibyl's placement here alongside Hosea may be meant to signify that Christ's coming would be for the benefit of the entire world, even pagans. However, the connection of the prophet with a female sibyl is also a reminder of the complex role of gender in the book of Hosea—even if it is not Gomer, who remains voiceless to the end.

———

Hosea 14 plays a significant role in both Jewish and Christian liturgy. In Judaism, Hos. 12:13–14:9 is the *haftarah* for the Torah reading Gen. 28:10–32:3 (Vayeitzei) in Ashkenazic tradition (see Fishbane 2002). As with previous

FIGURE 21   *Bernardino di Betto (Pinturicchio), the Prophet Hosea and the Delphic Sibyl Fresco, Borgia Apartments, Hall of the Sibyls, Vatican (1492–94).*
Unknown/Wikimedia Commons/Public Domain.

readings from Hosea paired with Genesis, this reading makes connections with Jacob's life, particularly his time away from the promised land with Laban's family. However, along with the threats of Hos. 12–13, this reading also includes the more positive outlook of chapter 14. As Fishbane points out, this pairing

> does not wish to end with denunciation and doom. Rather, its intent is to prod its listeners to a new religious consciousness—to a confession of sins and a whole-hearted return to God. For Hosea, this means a renunciation of idolatrous artifacts and the promise of political power. Renewal of Israel's being is a renewal of her awareness that God alone is the source of all—in nature as in history.
>
> (2002: 33)

Hosea 14:1–9 is also a reading for the first Sabbath of the Jewish year called Shabbat Shuvah (Sabbath of Return), named after the call to return in Hos. 14:1. This is the Sabbath that takes place between Rosh Hashanah and Yom Kippur, that is, the Jewish New Year and the Day of Atonement. Here Hosea 14 is read alongside Mic. 7:18–20 (Sephardim) and Joel 2:15–27 (Ashkenazim), and Hosea serves as a key text, which highlights the themes of repentance and reconciliation. Chapter 14 is found elsewhere in Jewish liturgical traditions: the chapter serves as the *haftarah* for Deut. 31:1–30 (Vayalekh) and in Sephardic tradition is one of the afternoon readings on Tish'ah B'av (the fast of the 9th of Av), which commemorates a number of tragedies in Jewish history, including the destruction of the first and second temples.

The final chapter of Hosea also has a place in Christian liturgy. In particular, Hosea 14 is read during Lent, on the Friday of Week Three. Here the prophet's words are read alongside readings from Ps. 81:8–14 and Mark 12:28–34. In the Gospel reading from Mark, Jesus replies to a question from the Scribes by quoting the Shema as the most important commandment. One scribe replies by noting that the love of God is more important than burnt sacrifices, a statement that has a strong resonance with the themes found in Hos. 14:1–2.

Joel: Introduction and Overview

Although one of the shorter books in the Hebrew Bible, the book of Joel has a considerable and wide-ranging history of reception. This is due in part to the book's vivid imagery, as well as to the prominent use of Joel in the New Testament. This chapter offers a broad overview of the reception of Joel, including (1) a brief history of interpretation, including broad trajectories in the reception of the book; (2) key historical and literary issues in the book's interpretation; (3) important theological, thematic, and rhetorical issues that have shaped the use and impact of the book; and (4) liturgical and cultural reception of the prophet and the book. These issues are explored further throughout the commentary.

A note on the numbering of chapters and verses that were assigned to the text over time: modern English Bibles tend to divide the text into three chapters, following some Greek and Latin traditions. The MT and others, which follow Hebrew traditions, divide the book into four chapters. This commentary follows the convention of three chapters, which is common in English translations.

English versification	Hebrew versification
Joel 1	Joel 1
Joel 2:1–27	Joel 2
Joel 2:28–32	Joel 3
Joel 3	Joel 4

Hosea, Joel, and Obadiah Through the Centuries, First Edition. Bradford A. Anderson.
© 2024 John Wiley & Sons Ltd. Published 2024 by John Wiley & Sons Ltd.

A Brief History of Interpretation

As noted in the opening chapter exploring Hosea, Joel, and Obadiah as part of the Book of the Twelve, Joel occupies different places in the Hebrew and Greek orderings of the canon, an issue highlighted as far back as Jerome. In the Hebrew MT, Joel is the second of the Twelve, coming after Hosea and before Amos. However, in the Greek LXX, Joel is the fourth book in this collection, following Hosea, Amos, and Micah, and is grouped with Obadiah and Jonah, two other books that are more difficult to date. Meanwhile, the earliest translations of Joel reflect the tendencies seen in other Minor Prophets. While the LXX offers a translation that is for the most part quite literal and which adheres closely to the MT, the Aramaic Targum is much more expansive and takes significant license in attempting to clarify the text.

Early Jewish and rabbinic engagement with Joel is varied. While there are numerous examples from the Talmud and Midrash where Joel is used as a proof text or where it is employed as a philological example, we also find uses of Joel that focus on theological and thematic issues, notably restoration and deliverance from calamity (Gen. Rab., PesK, b. Ketub.). We also find canonical and intertextual links that put Joel into conversation with other parts of the Hebrew Bible (see Ruth Rab., and b. Sukkah, the latter in relation to the notion of the 'evil inclination'; see commentary on 2:20). Another interesting element that can be found in rabbinic engagement with Joel is the focus on issues of ecology and the land. For example in the Palestinian Talmud (y. Ta'an.), Joel is used in a discussion of the fate of animals in a time of drought, while Lam. Rab. discusses the weeping of the sun and moon for Israel, and b. Šabb. uses Joel to connect the sin of robbery to the coming of famine. Thus, the vivid imagery of Joel, including that related to nature, was not overlooked by the Sages.

In the medieval Jewish commentary tradition, Rashi exhibits a strong move toward the *peshat* and literal interpretation with philological observations and attention to historical context. By way of example, Rashi suggests that the references to locusts in chapter 1 are literal, a theme that follows throughout his comments on the book. Rashi does make note of the Targum, as well as references in the Talmud. However, these are often given among interpretive options, and rarely does he use them to espouse solely figurative readings. Other interpreters from this era, including Radak and Ibn Ezra, continue this trajectory with an even greater focus on philology and the plain sense of the text.

Joel's influence on the New Testament and early Christianity is far greater than the book's size would suggest. Most notably, Peter's sermon at Pentecost in Acts 2:17–20 draws on Joel 2:28–32, using the rhetoric of the coming of the spirit and the imagery of a new era to describe the contemporary event, an association that has proved very popular throughout Christian history. Romans 10:13 would also use part of Joel 2, confirming with Joel that 'all who call on the name of the Lord will be saved'. Revelation 9 employs some of the imagery from Joel, notably attacking locusts (Rev. 9:3–9; Joel 1:4) with the appearance of horses (Rev. 9:7; Joel 2:4–5), employing Joel's vivid imagery in this more overtly apocalyptic work. These are discussed in further detail in the commentary.

The Church Fathers would make frequent use of Joel with notable commentaries from Jerome, Cyril of Alexandria, Theodore of Mopsuestia, Julian of Eclanum, and Isho'dad of Merv. Among other issues, these readers offer comments on pastoral concerns such as faith, sobriety, pride, and fasting (Cyril of Alexandria; Jerome). Also frequent, however, are figurative readings that connect the book to Christ, the day of the LORD or final judgment, and the coming of the Holy Spirit at Pentecost (Ambrose; Basil; Jerome; Justin Martyr; Tertullian; see Ferreiro). While by no means limited to the use of Joel in the NT, this usage did elicit extensive reflection from the fathers and seems to have given these early Christian commentators an explicit example of the continuity between the Old and New Testaments, fueling their own exercise of making such connections (Origen).

The Reformation-era comments from the German Martin Luther and the Frenchman John Calvin exhibit tendencies found elsewhere in their work, notably a concern for literal reading and theological concerns. Both Luther and Calvin note that the historical context of Joel is unclear; Luther, following 'the ancients', suggests that Joel was a contemporary of Hosea and Amos. Calvin, meanwhile, lays out several options and in the end declares that the historical context is not of utmost importance for understanding this prophet (similar to his reflections on Obadiah). Both Luther and Calvin begin their commentaries with a focus on the plain sense of the text and historical issues; Calvin sees both literal locusts and war in the first chapters, while Luther sees the Assyrians as the main focus of the imagery. However, as the book progresses they both move toward figural and Christological interpretation, particularly in relation to the coming of the Spirit and the final judgment. This is especially evident in Luther's reading. While proposing that the prophet is recounting a present-day event in chapter 1, Luther nonetheless asserts that the true meaning of the prophet's message is Christological:

> All the prophets have one and the same message, for this is their one aim: they are all looking toward the coming of Christ or to the coming kingdom of Christ. All their prophecies look to this, and we must relate them to nothing else. Although they may mix in various accounts of things present or of things to come, yet all

pertain to this point, that they are declaring the coming kingdom of Christ ... One may seem the same thing here in the prophet Joel, who is the first to treat the most destructive pest brought upon the people of Judah. He took up this subject to terrify the Jews and to call back to repentance those whom he had frightened, so that they might thus wait for the coming of Christ (79).

With the rise of critical biblical studies in the modern period, several issues would take precedence in the study of Joel. The first is the unity of the book, as chapters 1–2 seem to describe disaster while chapter 3 seems to predict restoration. Some hold that the book contains a unified message, which can be traced to a prophetic figure (Ahlström 1971; Wolff), while others argue that these parts are too different to be unified and so posit distinct origins for these sections, often with further subsections (Duhm 1911; Hiebert 1992; Barton). Another significant issue in the critical study of Joel has been the date and setting of the book, with suggested settings ranging between the ninth and second centuries BCE (more on these issues below).

The modern era also witnessed a growing interest in the possible relationship of Joel to apocalyptic perspectives and the rise of apocalypticism in Hebrew prophecy (Plöger 1968; Wolff). Further, contemporary interpreters have focused on the theme of the Day of the LORD, which is found throughout the book; while not the focus of significant attention in premodern interpretation, modern readers have noted the importance of this theme in Joel and the broader prophetic tradition (von Rad 1968; Simkins 1991; Rendtorff 1998). Contemporary interpreters have also explored the place of Joel in the Book of the Twelve and potential redactional histories of the book and the collection (Nogalski 1993). Finally, the recurring environmental and creational issues in Joel have proved useful for those who wish to read the book in light of ecological and environmental concerns, issues of increasing importance for contemporary readers (Braaten 2006; Marlow 2009).

Historical and Literary Issues in Reading Joel

Historical questions in the reception of Joel have tended to center on how best to locate the prophet historically and how to contextualize the vivid imagery within the book. As noted earlier, questions of unity, authorship, and dating are complex in relation to Joel, in large part because the book offers little by way of definitive evidence. Premodern interpreters broadly assumed Joel was an early, pre-exilic prophet. Making an intertextual link, the midrashic text Ruth Rabbah equates Joel with Samuel's son of the same name (1 Sam. 8:2), which would place Joel near the rise of the monarchy (cf. Rashi). The link to a drought led some to place the book near the time of Jehoram in the ninth century BCE, while others suggested the seventh century during the time of Josiah. More common, however, was the assumption that Joel should be located among the eighth-century BCE prophets, most likely because of its placement in the Hebrew ordering of the Twelve near Hosea and Amos (Cyril of Alexandria; Luther). There are premodern exceptions; the rabbinic text PesK 16.8 indicates that Joel comes after the destruction of the first temple and locates Joel among the postexilic prophets, while the eastern theologian Isho'dad of Merv equates the events in Joel with various invading empires. While some say that the date cannot be determined, and that it is not overly important for understanding the message of the book (Ibn Ezra; Calvin), premodern interpreters by and large assume that Joel's context is pre-exilic.

Some modern commentators have continued to advocate for a pre-exilic setting for Joel (Bič 1960). There are, however, a number of elements in Joel that suggest a later date, including references to priests and cult but not to a king, mention of exile, and reference to Greeks. Coupled with the many references to other biblical texts found in Joel, scholars have increasingly come to view the book as a postexilic creation (Vatke 1835; Bewer; Ahlström 1971; Crenshaw; Barton; Collins; Achtemeier). This, in turn, has led to reflection on the life setting of the prophet. The various calls to lament found in the book have led some to suggest that Joel may have been a cult prophet, leading the people in lamentation during a time of crisis (Wolff). Others have focused on the proto-apocalyptic nature of the book, arguing that the prophet should be understood in that emerging stream, which envisioned a complete reordering of the current situation (Plöger 1968).

Along with these concerns about the authorship and origins of Joel, other elements in the text have also been the subject of historical speculation. Chief among these is the reference to an invasion of locusts in Joel 1 (and possibly chapter 2). While locating such an invasion in a precise historical context has proven difficult, from antiquity readers have given evidence to suggest that such a locust infestation was possible and accurate in its description (Jerome; Pusey; Ewald). A number of visual depictions of Joel portray the prophet along with encroaching locusts—even if the prophet himself is not located within the narrative of the book. An example is a 1704 woodcut by J. Sturt in a history of the Old Testament presented in verse. Here the prophet stands next to a tree delivering his message, with attacking locusts in the background (Figure 22).

Readers have also spent considerable energy on the relationship of the disasters in chapters 1–2: whether these refer to the same or separate locust

FIGURE 22   Joel surrounded by locusts; woodcut by J. Sturt, in Samuel Wesley, the History of the Old Testament in verse (1704).
Courtesy of Pitts Library Digital Archive/ Emory University.

attacks or if one (or both) refers to military incursions (see Hadjiev 2020, as well as the commentary below).

These historical questions have also shaped how readers have understood literary elements in the book. Although premodern readers read the book as a unified whole, from antiquity there were questions concerning how the book coheres in terms of its themes and content. Readers have queried how to hold together the description of a locust invasion with the seeming reference to military battle as well as a restoration that includes the defeat of 'the nations' in the final parts of the book. Beginning in the nineteenth century, scholars began to suggest a more complex history of the book. Ewald asserted that there were two separate addresses from the prophet that were brought together at a later time, while Maurice Vernes (1872) was an early proponent of the idea that the latter portions of the book did not come from the prophet Joel but were later additions (cf. Duhm 1911). In the early twentieth century, Julius Bewer argued that chapter 3 in particular not only has different themes but is stylistically inferior to chapters 1–2. While some contemporary commentators continue to follow this approach, suggesting that the book is a composite literary work (Barton; Jeremias 2007; Hadjiev 2020), others advocate for understanding the book as a unified text, even if allowing for some later additions in the work in its final shape (Crenshaw; Prinsloo 1985).

Another key literary aspect in Joel is the significant overlap with other texts from the HB, including Isaiah, Amos, Ezekiel, and Obadiah. While some readers have suggested that Joel was a source for these other texts, most commentators now believe that Joel is drawing on these other biblical texts and traditions (Bergler 1988; Strazicich 2007; Wolff; Crenshaw). This use of other biblical themes is woven into a rich tapestry in the book, with some referring to Joel as a 'learned prophet'—even if these themes and imagery are taken up in diverse ways, such as Joel's reframing of Isaiah 2 and Micah 6 as a call to arms in Joel 3:10. These and other intertextual links are discussed in the following commentary.

Theological, Thematic, and Rhetorical Issues in Interpreting Joel

Engagement with the thematic and theological elements of Joel has also been wide-ranging and varied. The theological and ideological questions that have motivated reflection on Joel have often been closely tied to the imagery in the text, revolving around the interplay of judgment and restoration, ecological/environmental concerns, and the related apocalyptic perspectives found in the book. The Christian usage of this book, particularly with reference to the pouring out of the spirit, is in fact closely related to the perspective that the book envisions concerning an utterly changed world and the ushering in of a new dispensation.

Jewish and Christian readings of this prophet have not been uniform, yet both traditions have read the book constructively and with an eye toward their own contexts. As highlighted earlier, we find Jewish readings focusing on issues such as restoration and deliverance (as can be seen, for example, in rabbinic texts such as Gen. Rab.; PesK; b. Ketub). Early Christian readers focused on pastoral concerns such as fasting and repentance (Cyril of Alexandria; Gregory the Great), along with figurative readings that gave special attention to

Christological, eschatological, and pneumatological concerns, particularly in light of NT usages of Joel 2 (Ambrose; Basil; Jerome; Justin Martyr). The medieval theologian Thomas Aquinas, while making occasional Christological or pneumatological connections, primarily uses Joel in discussing issues of doctrine and morality, including fasting, penance, true worship, and the last judgment.

The Reformation-era comments from Luther and Calvin converge and diverge in significant (and sometimes curious) ways. To begin with, Luther comments that Joel is 'a kindly and gentle man', lacking the denunciation so common in other prophets. Peter's use of Joel in Acts means that Joel provides 'the first sermon that was preached in the Christian Church'. Calvin, meanwhile, sees Joel as a book full of calamitous warnings and at several points speaks harshly of the recipients, noting their stupidity and ignorance. As noted earlier, as the book progresses both Luther and Calvin move toward spiritual and Christological interpretation, particularly in relation to the coming of the spirit and the final judgment. Again, however, the tenor of the two works diverges as they conclude: Luther sees the judgment as the summoning of the nations to the Church; Calvin's more ominous perspective remains as the judgment in Joel's finale is seen as a judgment on the nations who have wronged the Church, even if there is some hope of mercy in the end.

Joel's contention that the spirit of God would be poured out on 'all flesh' (2:28–29), with both sons and daughters prophesying and the spirit promised to both male and female slaves, has meant that Joel has been the subject of significant attention from those seeking a more equal and prominent role for women in communities of faith. Groups ranging from the second-century Montanists to the early modern Anabaptists have employed Joel in this way. Meanwhile, the focus on dreams and prophecy in these verses has led to attention from those seeking more ecstatic and mystical elements of religious practice, notably within Christianity. Such use of Joel can be seen in some early German Pietists and later in Pentecostal and Charismatic Christians in the twentieth century and down to the present. A movement within Pentecostalism that took shape in the twentieth century, known as the Latter Rain movement, took its name from Joel 2:23, and those who would exhibit the fullness of the spirit of God were even known as 'Joel's army'.

More recent critical engagement with the thematic and theological elements of Joel can be seen in several interpretive trajectories. First, the increasing interest in apocalypticism and possible apocalyptic perspectives in Joel has led to reflection on these elements of the text, including a critique of the worldview that the book exhibits. As Hiebert notes,

> the apocalyptic mentality which dominates Joel 3–4 (Eng 2:28–3:21) has been faulted for its otherworldly orientation, its violent resolution to the predicament of postexilic Israel, and its exclusiveness which reserves salvation only to the community on Mount Zion. Indeed, when the author of 4:10 (Eng 3:10) calls for the nations to beat their plowshares into swords, he reverses a traditional prophetic image (Isa 2:4, Micah 4:3) which anticipated the resolution of Israel's relations with the nations in more peaceful and inclusive terms.
>
> (Hiebert 1992: 877)

Some have said this needs to be counterbalanced with an understanding of apocalypticism and particularly of subjugated peoples dealing with oppressive power structures and those who have experienced trauma (Claassens 2014a). Nevertheless, the language and imagery of Joel have led to discomfort for some contemporary readers (Wacker 2012).

Second, because of the book's use of natural imagery, Joel has received increasing attention in recent years in light of ecological concerns (Simkins 1991; Horrell 2010; Braaten 2006). The book uses imagery such as drought, locusts, fire, and the darkening of the sun, moon, and stars but also green pastures, rain, and lush produce. Here focus is placed on the interrelatedness of God, humanity, and the world; exploring issues such as covenant and divine-human engagement, Joel is used as an example of the indelible link between humanity and the wider creation (Marlow 2009).

Liturgical and Cultural Engagement with Joel

The prophet Joel has been utilized in both Jewish and Christian liturgical traditions. In Judaism, Joel 2:15–27 is the *haftarah* for the Sabbath preceding Yom Kippur, along with Hos. 14:2–10 and Mic. 7:18–20. In the Roman Catholic tradition, Joel 2:28–32 is an optional reading at the Vigil Mass on Pentecost Sunday. The prominence of Joel in Peter's Pentecost sermon has meant that Joel has been a popular text in Christian liturgical and worship music (Dowling Long 2017). Joel is commemorated on 19 October in the Eastern Orthodox Church (see Figure 23).

FIGURE 23   Russian icon of the prophet Joel, eighteenth-century iconostasis of Kizhi Monastery, Russia.

Iconostasis of Kizhi monastery/Wikimedia Commons/Public Domain.

Visual depictions of the prophet Joel have focused on the prophet and his message. Perhaps most famous is Michelangelo's portrayal of Joel in the Sistine Chapel, a representation that is known for its intense and thoughtful depiction of the prophet, who is holding a scroll (Figure 24). Others, which focus on the message of the book, depict the prophet with natural features noted in the text, such as locusts, a vine, or moon and stars (as in the portrayals on Amiens Cathedral as well as several Reformation and early modern wood carvings). Finally, a good deal of artwork in the Christian tradition has depicted Joel in relation to the events of Pentecost. This includes portrayals of Joel where time is collapsed, and Joel's message is brought into line with the events of Acts 2. The latter approach was common in the Reformation era; an example is Brosamer's portrayal, which has Joel preaching in the foreground, the spirit represented as

FIGURE 24   Michaelangelo, prophet Joel. Sistine Chapel ceiling (1508–12).
Self-scanned/Wikimedia Commons/Public Domain.

a dove, and Peter delivering his own message in the background. (See commentary for these and other examples.)

Imagery and turns of phrase from Joel have also been employed in literature. The reference to 'what the locust has eaten' (2:25) has been used in a variety of contexts, including Annie Holdsworth's *The Years that the Locust Hath Eaten* (1897). The language related to dreaming dreams and prophesying from 2:28–29 has also been used in diverse contexts, often as literary turns of phrase rather than linked in any way to the book of Joel. Such references can be found in Shakespeare's *Troilus and Cressida*, George Bernard Shaw's

Man and Superman, and Washington Irving's short story 'The Legend of the Sleepy Hollow' (see Tiemeyer 2017).

We have already noted the use of Joel in liturgical settings. Elsewhere, the invocation to 'blow the trumpet in Zion' (Joel 2:1) has inspired much in the world of music from liturgical pieces dating from the sixteenth century to contemporary pieces, both choral and instrumental (see Dowling Long 2017). The call to 'rend your hearts' (2:13) has also proved inspirational, used in works such as Mendelssohn's *Elijah*, while the reference to the coming of the spirit in 2:28 has been put to use by Edward Elgar in the oratorio *The Kingdom* (1901–06).

For further explorations of the reception of Joel, see Merx (1879) and Troxel (2015). Helpful overviews of the themes and contemporary issues in the study of Joel can be found in Mason (1994), Hadjiev (2020), and Hagedorn (2021), while theological issues are explored in Prinsloo (1985).

Joel 1

The book of Joel begins by briefly introducing the prophet before moving to the first prophetic message concerning a devastating event that includes an attack of locusts. We also encounter in this chapter the first use of the 'day of YHWH', a theme that recurs throughout the book. A number of readers venture that chapter 1 is dealing with a contemporary situation or the recent past, while chapter 2 speaks about a future threat (Calvin; Ewald; Wolff).

1:1

The book begins by stating that the word of the LORD came to Joel, son of Pethuel. Christian readers have commented that this 'word of the LORD' guarantees to the listener that what is said is true and will come to pass (Cyril of Alexandria) and that Joel brings only God's word, not his own (Calvin; Pusey). The text gives us very little information about the prophet. The name Joel (*yo'el*) is most often understood to mean 'YHWH is God' (Wesley; Bewer), though Jerome suggests 'God is . . .' as an alternative. The name of Joel's father, Pethuel, is otherwise unattested in the HB. The LXX renders this as Bethuel, matching the name of Rebekah's father in Gen. 22:23. Abarbanel draws on Talmudic tradition and states that since his father's name was mentioned, Joel was the son of a prophet (see commentary on Hos. 1:1 for more on this tradition). The book of Joel has few geographical details, so attempts to situate the prophet have varied widely. In the ancient collection known as the *Lives of the Prophets*, Joel

Hosea, Joel, and Obadiah Through the Centuries, First Edition. Bradford A. Anderson.
© 2024 John Wiley & Sons Ltd. Published 2024 by John Wiley & Sons Ltd.

is said to come from the tribe of Reuben (Hare 1985). However, the focus on Jerusalem leads most to assume that the prophet is based in Judah and that his message is directed there as well (Calvin; Bewer).

Most premodern readers assumed Joel was one of the earliest prophets. Some attempts were made to identify the prophet with other characters named Joel in the HB, though these have not gained much traction in the history of interpretation. Rashi, for example, says that this prophet is the son of Samuel named Joel, who is noted in 1 Sam. 8:2 (cf. Num. Rab. 10:5). While Samuel's sons did not walk in God's ways, Rashi follows the Sages, who indicate that over time the sons changed their ways and repented. Though hard to square with his assertion that Joel is the son of Samuel, Rashi also suggests that the events that are described in the book refer to the seven years of famine which Elisha decreed during the reign of Jehoram. Radak, meanwhile, says that Joel was from the time of Manasseh, king of Judah.

Premodern Christian readers tended to locate Joel more generally during the time of Hosea (Jerome; Cyril of Alexandria; Theodore of Mopsuestia; Julian of Eclanum; Nicholas of Lyra) or even earlier (Luther). This is in part because of the book's location in the Hebrew ordering of the Book of the Twelve, where it comes between Hosea and Amos. Calvin notes that the date of Joel is difficult to pinpoint, and 'as there is no certainty, it is better to leave the time in which he taught undecided; and, as we shall see, this is of no great importance. Not to know the time of Hosea would be to readers a great loss . . . but as to Joel, there is, as I have said, less need of this' (xv). Early modern readers likewise noted the difficulty in dating Joel but still hedged toward an early setting (Wesley; Credner 1831). Many of these point to the similarities between Joel and other prophetic texts and assume that the others (such as Amos) draw on Joel's words (Ewald; Pusey).

Some recent commentators have suggested dates in the eighth–sixth centuries BCE for the book (Bič 1960; Assis 2013). However, beginning in the nineteenth century, it became common for scholars to assign Joel to the postexilic period (Vatke 1835; Achtemeier). This understanding is based on several factors, including the fact that the text seems to assume the exile is in the past, there is no reference to the monarchy, the Temple is rebuilt and sacrifices are still in effect, and the name Joel is particularly common in the postexilic period, as seen in Chronicles. A fifth-century BCE date for Joel is commonly put forward (Wolff; Crenshaw; Watts; Barton).

Can anything more specific be said about the prophet? As discussed below, the text of Joel 1 has much in common with communal lamentations and liturgical settings. Thus, some have suggested that Joel is a cult prophet located in Jerusalem (Watts; Wolff), or even perhaps a priest (Ewald). Others claim that while Joel draws on liturgical traditions, this does not mean that he created a liturgy for the people himself. Instead, Joel has more recently been depicted as a learned prophet, engaging with and reworking other traditions from Israel (Barton).

Because we are told so little about the prophet himself, visual depictions of the prophet use various strategies when attempting to portray Joel. A number of Latin manuscripts offer illuminations of the text, including Joel 1, with broadly generic depictions of the prophet. A thirteenth-century Latin manuscript from Italy offers a vibrant depiction of Joel holding in one hand a scroll—presumably the prophet's own message—while the other hand is raised as he speaks to an unseen audience (see Figure 25).

Other depictions tend to portray the prophet in light of elements within the book, such as locusts (see Figure 22), or with interpretive depictions that attempt to capture the tone and demeanor of the prophet. A good example of the latter is James Tissot's portrayal of Joel (Figure 26). Tissot's painting situates Joel in a garden surrounded by growth and vegetation. And yet the prophet is depicted in a dark robe with crossed arms and a downward gaze, giving a sense of foreboding, perhaps in relation to the attack from the locusts and/or army that is to come, and the devastation that this will bring.

For most of history, readers assumed the prophet was responsible for the entirety of the book bearing his name. However, diverse themes and sections within the book have long been noted. Radak, for example, notes that Joel first prophesied about a locust plague and then about the messianic era (cf. Calvin). This comment foreshadows the work of early critical scholars, who questioned the unity of the book (Vernes 1872; Duhm 1911; Barton). Some posited that the prophet may have written the first two chapters (with some later additions) but that the latter parts of the book in particular came from a later period (Bewer). In recent years, a number of scholars have again stressed the literary unity of the book (Rudolph 1971; Wolff). (See 'Joel: Overview and Introduction' for further discussion on these issues.)

1:2–3

Following the superscription, the prophet's message begins with a call to 'hear', directed at the elders and all the inhabitants of the land. Calvin suggests that the 'elders' are singled out here because 'He who has passed his fiftieth or sixtieth year, and sees something new happening, which he had never thought of, doubtless acknowledges it as the unusual work of God' (21). While Wolff

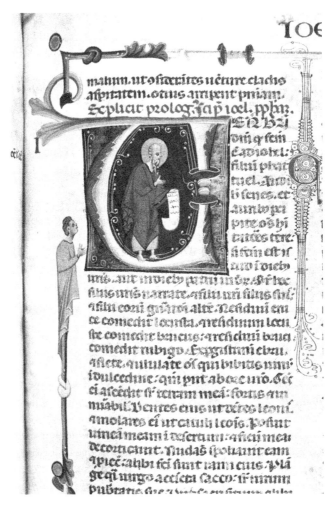

FIGURE 25   *Detail of Joel 1. Oxford, Bodleian Library MS. Canon. Bibl. Lat. 57 (thirteenth century, Italy).*

© Bodleian Libraries/University of Oxford.

speculates that this may refer to a leadership class in the postexilic period, others disagree and think that this merely refers to 'old timers' rather than a distinct authoritative group (Achtemeier; Crenshaw).

What follows in the book is unprecedented, we read in verse 2—it has not happened in the hearers' own time, nor in the days of the ancestors. Because of this, they are to tell their children, who will tell their children, and so on (1:3).

FIGURE 26 James Tissot, Joel (1896–1902).
GRACE COMMUNION INTERNATIONAL / Wikimedia Commons/Public Domain.

Why does the book begin in this way? The thrust of these verses is that events are coming that are so great that they need to be relayed to the next generation in order that those in the future might come to their senses (Theodore of Mopsuestia). It is not only the mountain-top experiences that should be passed on, but calamities and sufferings also need to be told to the next generation, as these serve as warnings (Cyril of Alexandria).

In Sifre to Deuteronomy (342.1), Joel 1:2–4 is read alongside the hopeful message of Joel 2:25 as an example of how the prophets begin with a word of warning and rebuke before bringing words of mercy and salvation (cf. Theodore of Mopsuestia). The reference to the ancestors and the subsequent mention of locusts led some to draw connections with the Egyptian plague: while in the event recounted in Exodus there was only one kind of locust, here

Joel outlines four, signifying that this is much worse (Radak). The call to tell children what God has done is also seen as having resonance with the exodus traditions (e.g., Exod. 12, 13; Deut. 6; see Sweeney).

1:4

In verse 4, we see why the prophet is offering this call to attention: 'What the cutting locust (*gazam*) left, the swarming locust (*arbeh*) has eaten. What the swarming locust left, the hopping locust (*yalek*) has eaten, and what the hopping locust left, the destroying locust (*hasil*) has eaten' (NRSV). Issues in the interpretation of this verse revolve around how to translate the terms used, as well as how to understand the nature of the events described (Andiñach 1992).

The ancient versions struggled with how to render these terms describing the insects in this verse. The LXX suggests caterpillar, grasshopper, locust, and rust, the Targum proffers crawling locust, locust swarm, winged locust, and creeping locust, while in the Vulgate we find palmerworm, locust, bruchus, and mildew. Modern translations tend to translate these as either descriptors of different types of locusts or functions related to locusts (see NRSV, above). In his translation, Crenshaw offers the chewer, the locust, the jumper, and the finisher.

Closely related to the question of translation is how this verse should be understood more broadly. While some medieval Jewish commentators interpreted these as four types of locusts that ravaged the land (Radak; Rashi), others read them allegorically as four kingdoms that would impact Israel: Babylon, Persia, Greece, and Rome (Abarbanel). In Christian tradition, we again find significant diversity on this issue. According to Julian of Eclanum, this refers to actual locusts that led to a famine. However, most church fathers read this verse figuratively. Theodore of Mopsuestia understands this as a reference to coming trouble from foreign nations, notably Assyria and Babylonia, and sees here allusion to the rulers Tiglath-Pileser, Shalmaneser, Sennacherib, and Nebuchadnezzar (cf. Ephrem; Ishoʻdad of Merv). Jerome points out a potential connection with the four horns noted in Zech. 1:19; he also draws on philosophy to emphasize the significance of 'four', particularly the four disturbances of the soul: grief, joy, fear, and hope (cf. Gregory the Great, *Morals on the Book of Job* 6.33.65 [Ferreiro]). Cyril of Alexandria offers a mediating position. He proposes that the obscure and difficult imagery of the prophets is purposeful, making it more palatable for listeners. While there may have been locust invasions, this more likely refers indirectly to Israel's enemies and subsequent captivities. These various approaches can be seen in the medieval period as well (see Nicholas of Lyra and the *Glossa Ordinaria*).

In the late medieval and early modern periods, literal readings of the locusts would become more common (Rashi; Radak). One recurring interpretation is that this verse recounts a historical infestation that led to plague and drought and which was meant to point the people back to God (Luther; Wesley; Darby). Others would offer more specificity, seeing here a description of successive infestations by four distinct species of locusts that were well known (Calvin; Gill; Ewald). This is the basis of why the prophet's message came about: 'an unusually violent plague of locusts had for successive years laid the land waste (i.4; ii.25), and we have here a most accurate and vivid description of it, so much so that all descriptions of modern travellers confirm it in every particular' (Ewald: 107). Thus, according to Ewald, the prophet must have been an eyewitness of this event.

While literal interpretations were more common, figurative readings did continue into the modern period, and some readers saw both a locust invasion and a metaphorical scene being described in chapter 1 (see Merx 1879). Although offering an extensive discussion of locusts, Pusey stressed that the imagery does not make sense if speaking only of locusts; it must also refer to other invaders, particularly the Assyrians (cf. Assis 2013, though he sees the focus as the Babylonians). Childs (1959), meanwhile, suggests that the imagery is a stand-in for divine judgment, while Bourke (1959) sees the locusts as a foretaste of the coming day of Yʜᴡʜ, which is discussed later in the chapter (v. 15).

Nevertheless, modern scholars increasingly interpreted this as referring to real devastation brought on by an invasion of locusts (Wolff; Crenshaw; Watts; Sweeney). An influential contribution came from Credner (1831), who speculated that the four names refer to different stages of the desert locust's development (cf. Thompson 1955). Bewer comments that allegorical understandings are understandable, but 'the arguments for interpreting the locusts literally are so strong that they cannot be resisted' (66). It became common to pass on accounts of travelers who had witnessed the effect of locust infestations that matched very well the depiction of events in Joel 1 (Pusey; Bewer). The recurring threat of locusts in the ancient world was also pointed out by scholars who highlighted that in other texts from the ANE, locusts were also compared with invading armies (Thompson 1955). While agreeing that a historical infestation is likely in view, some readers, following Wellhausen, have suggested that the four names are clustered here only to give a sense of the overwhelming nature of the incursion rather than specific details of the locusts themselves. As Barton notes, 'by heaping up names for the locusts, the prophet emphasizes the totality of the destruction they wreak' (42; cf. Simkins 1991; Hagedorn 2021).

The imagery of locusts recurs in the New Testament in Rev. 9:1–11, where they are portrayed as an attacking army at the fifth trumpet blast, though the Apocalypse may draw more on the depiction in Joel 2 than the imagery found in chapter 1. Nevertheless, the use of this imagery in Revelation points to the way in which Joel could easily be adopted for apocalyptic purposes in subsequent generations. The theme and imagery of locusts are also common in literature and artistic portrayals of Joel, such as the twelfth-century Admont Giant Bible, which depicts the prophet receiving a divine message while trying to save a tree from attacking locusts (Figure 27). Though the prophet is not present as a character in the text of the book, a common artistic approach is to visualize the prophet in such a way, placing him within textual elements of the book bearing his name. For further examples of the use of Joel's locust imagery, see the commentary on Joel 2.

1:5

In verse 5, the prophet addresses the drunkards and wine drinkers because the 'sweet wine' is cut off from them. While some Jewish readers understood this as referring to actual wine (Radak), Christian interpreters often made other connections. Thus, the wine is seen as referring to vices (Jerome), to those things that 'inebriate the heart' such as luxury and pleasure (Cyril of Alexandria), to luxurious lives and abundance (Luther), or generally to sin (Pusey). In all of these cases, this is understood as a call to repent while there is still time. Modern commentators have noted the importance of grapes and wine; as these were staples of the produce in Judah, any impact by a locust invasion would have serious implications on the economy as well as for individuals (Sweeney). Indeed, Thompson (1955) notes that after a locust plague in 1915, wine doubled in price. Some modern scholars see the cutting off of wine as the beginning of a call to communal lamentation, a liturgical form used to appeal to YHWH (Wolff; Sweeney).

The rabbis noted that this verse seems to contradict 3:18, which says the mountains will drip sweet wine; how do we account for this discrepancy? According to PesK 16:8, this is evidence that the prophet could not offer comfort and hope until God himself intervened, which happens later in the text (see Neusner).

1:6

Verse 6 states that 'a nation has invaded my land, powerful and innumerable; its teeth are lions' teeth, and it has the fangs of a lioness'. The image of 'teeth as lion's

FIGURE 27   *The vision of locusts. Admont Giant Bible, middle of the twelfth century.*
Courtesy of Österreichische Nationalbibliothek.

teeth' in 1:6 may be used in Sirach 21:2, which uses very similar imagery when speaking of sin (Lange and Weigold 2011), and the locusts described in Rev. 9:7 are also said to have teeth like lion's teeth. Readers have long wondered how this verse relates to the insects of verse 4. The ancient translations all retain the reference to a 'nation' (LXX; Targum; Vulgate). Rashi and Radak interpret this to mean that the locusts are called a nation, a literary device found elsewhere in Scripture (e.g., Prov. 30:24ff). Abarbanel, on the other hand, understands this to mean a literal nation is coming to invade the land. Similar disagreements are found in Christian tradition. Jerome suggests this should be read as describing the arrival of the Assyrians and Babylonians, Julian of Eclanum considers this to be a 'battle line' of locusts, and Cyril of Alexandria asserts that it may refer to locusts or a foreign invader. Reformation readers would offer similar diversity: while Luther proposes that this refers to an army of locusts, Calvin claims that judgment has already come in the form of invasion and war with enemies. Over time, consensus began to shift that this refers to locusts, presented as a nation or army (Gill; Wesley; Wellhausen; Wolff; Crenshaw; Simkins 1993). This is a theme we find elsewhere in the HB and in other texts from the ANE (Thompson 1955; Simkins 1991). However, many commentators note that even if the locusts are literal, the imagery is hard to disentangle, and it may be used as a metaphor pointing to the threat of enemy nations (Bergler 1988; Sweeney).

1:7–8

The imagery turns to that of the land in verse 7: we read that 'my' vines are laid waste and 'my' fig trees are splintered; bark is stripped off, and the branches have turned white. There is some debate as to who is speaking in this verse. The Targum changes the wording, indicating that the vines and figs are 'of the people', and Radak concurs, proposing that it is the people speaking here (cf. Luther). Others have suggested that it is God whose vines and figs are destroyed, referring to the land in general, which God has tended (Theodore of Mopsuestia; Pusey). Regardless of who might be speaking, most readers understand these verses as referring to the vines and trees that have been destroyed by the aforementioned invading locusts (Luther; Gill).

The prophet continues with a call to lament like a virgin mourning the husband of her youth (v. 8). While some have suggested that the land (Wellhausen) or Jerusalem (Achtemeier) is called to lament, most interpret this as a call to all the people, or at least a godly remnant, that is called to lament (Targum; Gill). How can a virgin (*betulah*) lament her husband? The LXX addresses this issue by changing the subject to a bride. Others have suggested this might refer to a betrothed woman, not yet taken home as a wife (Wolff; Sweeney). More common is the notion that this points to the early years of marriage, when the husband has died while still young (Theodore of Mopsuestia; Radak; Crenshaw). Some attempts have been made to identify the bride and groom more specifically. Jerome proposed that God is the intended husband and that he is taken away from his people. Cyril of Alexandria would offer a similar reading, though far more sinister in its supersessionism: the synagogue of the Jews, he notes, has not lamented the bridegroom of heaven, Christ; a new bride, the church, has taken her place. In the modern era, some suggested that this lamenting refers to the myth of 'Anat and the annual ritual of mourning her husband Baal (Hvidberg 1962), though like Jerome's reading, this has not garnered a significant following.

1:9

In verses 9–12, the text returns to the theme of the land and its inhabitants. Verse 9 begins by noting that 'the grain-offering and drink-offering are cut off from the house of the LORD'. Because of this, we are told, the priests and ministers of the LORD mourn. This verse seems to refer to the offerings in the Temple, and the Targum removes any ambiguity by translating 'house' as the LORD's 'sanctuary'. Some readers have inferred that the cutting off of sacrifices is a reference to the Babylonian destruction of the Temple (Theodore of Mopsuestia). More common is a correlation with the previous verses: the locusts have ruined the harvest, and if the corn and wine are cut off, there is nothing to be offered in the Temple (Radak). A number of commentators note that these daily offerings were considered very important, and their cessation would have been a humiliation (Calvin; Luther; Wellhausen). The priests mourn because the cutting off of the offering means that they have no work to do, and nothing to live on, as their provisions were taken from sacrifices made in the Temple (Jerome; Gill; Barton). Achtemeier points out that the key phrase 'cut off' recurs again here in verse 9: the cutting locust (v. 4) led to the sweet wine being cut off (v. 5), and so the temple offerings are also cut off. For some, this mention of priests and sacrifices being offered in the Temple is a sign of the book's antiquity, as it must have predated the Babylonian conquest (Ewald). Others have noted that the pairing of meal offerings and libations only occurs in later texts, which points to a postexilic setting after the rebuilding of the Temple (Wolff).

1:10–12

In verse 10, the focus shifts to the land and its produce. The fields are devastated, and the ground mourns; the grain, wine, and oil all fail. The imagery here seems to be moving from plague to drought (Wolff; Crenshaw). Some have suggested that locust plagues and drought do not go together, as the locusts themselves cannot survive in drought; others have argued that the drought imagery may be the after-effects of the locusts, along with the normal heat of summer (Simkins 2016). The focus on the land has long captured the attention of commentators. Theodoret of Cyr wrote that the prophet instructs the produce and land to lament 'not as ratio-nale creatures but in his attempt to rouse those endowed with reason through the inanimate creatures' (*Commentary on Joel* 1.11–12 [Ferreiro]). In recent years, readers have begun reading Joel in light of ecological concerns (Horrell 2010). Thus, not only do the people lament, but (contra Theodoret) the ground itself mourns, and the earth suffers as part of humanity's suffering (Claassens 2014a; Marlow 2009). Indeed, Braaten (2006) calls for a geocentric perspective when reading these first chapters of Joel, as the earth is the main participant.

Verses 11–12 address the farmers and vine-dressers, who are to lament over the failing crops: wheat, barley, and vines are all ruined, as are the fig, pome-granate, palm, and apple trees. Because of this, the people's joy withers away, just like their produce. Several of the church fathers read these verses figura-tively; Cyril of Alexandria states that the vines and trees can be understood as virtues if reading this spiritually. However, most readers have understood this literally, pointing to the termination of the land's produce. The bounty of the land, which was a gift from God, has been taken away (Rashi; Achtemeier). For Calvin, 'all this sterility was a clear sign of God's wrath' (32).

One of the depictions of Joel on Amiens Cathedral portrays the prophet looking mournfully at a withered vine and fig tree (Figure 28). As noted earlier, placing the prophet alongside imagery from the book bearing his name is one way in which artists attempt to visualize the prophet when he is not actually present as a character within the text of the book itself.

1:13–14

Beginning in verse 13, the chapter offers further instructions and reasons for lamentation, what Wolff calls the climax of the call to lament. This section begins with a call to 'gird and lament, you priests'. The priests and ministers of

FIGURE 28   *Joel sees withered vine and fig tree; Amiens Cathedral, France.*
Used with permission from Stuart Whatling.

the altar are to 'pass the night in sackcloth', in part because the grain and drink offerings have been cut off (1:13). Calvin notes that the prophet begins with the priests and leaders in calling all the people to lament, pointing to the importance of leadership in such times (cf. Gill; Wolff).

The instructions continue in verse 14, as the leaders are told to 'sanctify a fast, call a solemn assembly'. The elders and all inhabitants of the land are to be gathered at the house of the LORD, and are to cry out to him. The introduction of fasting has drawn considerable commentary through the years. In the Talmud, the combination of fasting and a solemn assembly in this verse is used as part of a discussion as to why acts of labor are forbidden on days of fasting (see b. Ta'an. 12b; cf. Ibn Ezra). Radak draws on this, noting that the people are to stop working, assemble in the Temple, and pray to God for mercy. Early Christian readers were interested in what it means to 'sanctify' a fast. Not all fasting is acceptable (Isa. 58:5; Matt. 6:16), and indeed heretics such as Manichaeus also fast. Thus, what is in mind here is a fast that is set apart and made holy for this purpose (Jerome; Theodore of Mopsuestia). Calvin likewise notes that while there are many reasons for fasting, this one obviously relates to repentance. Not everyone agrees that this is about repentance, as there is no mention of sin or wrongdoing (Sweeney). Whatever the case, this solemn assembly is the first sign of a remedy offered by the prophet (Bewer).

1:15

Verse 15 introduces another key theme in the book, that of the day of the LORD: 'Alas for the day! For the day of the LORD is near'. The day of the LORD is a common theme in the Book of the Twelve (see Rendtorff 1998), and the phrase also occurs in various parts of the NT, including Acts 2:20 and 2 Pet. 3:10 (cf. the commentary on Joel 2:31).

While this phrase is noted by virtually all contemporary interpreters as significant, neither rabbinic nor Christian readers would see the day of YHWH as particularly important as a formulaic saying. The Targum interprets this clause as 'near is the day that will come from before the Lord' (66). Abarbanel combines this verse with the fast in the previous one to suggest that the 'day' mentioned here is the ninth of Av, a day of mourning for the destruction of the Temple. Jerome, meanwhile, says that this is a day of judgment and retribution for all sins but may also be related to captivity under the Assyrians and Babylonians.

More attention would be given to this phrase beginning in the Reformation period. Luther, Calvin, and Gill all comment on this clause and argue that it points toward a more severe judgment coming in the future. Calvin calls this a day when God will rise up and show himself as judge of the world. In all of these readings, the Day of YHWH begins to take on eschatological significance. This idea would be continued in the early modern period. Both Wesley and Darby see the Day of YHWH as a day of great trouble coming in the future. Ewald likewise points to the significance of this trope and suggests that this is the earliest and simplest form of the 'day' motif as one of coming judgment (cf. Pusey).

The Day of YHWH has been the subject of considerable attention in critical scholarship (see von Rad; Everson 1974; Cathcart 1992; Rendtorff 1998). While Mowinckel (1958) suggested that this idea may have originated in a cultic feast day, more common is the assumption that the origins lie in God's battle against enemies (von Rad). In this reading, the day of YHWH is a day of God's intervention on behalf of his people. Over time, it became a way to interpret important events, including God's potential judgment on Israel (Amos 5:18) (Achtemeier; Everson 1974). It is in this context that commentators have generally understood Joel's first use of the Day of YHWH in 1:15: the locusts are harbingers of the Day of YHWH (Wellhausen; Bourke 1959; Wolff; Barton). This connection of the locusts and the coming Day of YHWH suggests to some readers that we see here the beginning of the apocalyptic and eschatological use of the Day of the LORD (Crenshaw). Whatever the case, as Wolff points out, Joel offers the most detailed and sustained use of the Day of YHWH theme in the HB.

Verse 15 ends by noting that destruction will come from the Almighty (*shaddai*). The LXX translates this as destruction coming 'like misery from misery'. Following the Targum ('like plunder'), Rashi suggests this destruction will come unexpectedly, like brigands plundering. Christian readers have pointed out the rare use of the name Shaddai for God in this instance. Jerome renders this as 'the mighty', while Calvin prefers 'conqueror' or 'destroyer'.

1:16–18

The prophet returns to the impact on the land and animals in verses 16–18. In verse 16 we read that the food is cut off, and so joy and gladness are likewise removed from the 'house of our God'. What would normally have been a joyous occasion of bringing sacrifices for the harvest festival becomes a time of mourning, and the people themselves bear witness to this ruination (Bewer; Radak).

Verse 17 draws again on the imagery of farming: seeds shrivel, storehouses are desolate, grain fails, and so the granaries are ruined. The first clause of verse 17 is difficult in the Hebrew. The LXX translates this as referring to heifers jumping at their mangers, giving the idea that the animals are going mad (cf. 4QXIIc; Peshitta; Jerome; Theodore of Mopsuestia). The Targum, meanwhile, renders this as 'bottles of wine are decaying under their seals' (cf. Rashi; Radak). Over time, a different consensus would emerge: that this refers to seeds shriveling under their clods, which seems to match the parallelism of the next line and its reference to desolate storehouses (Ibn Ezra; Luther; Calvin). Readers throughout history have seen here a depiction of drought that followed on from either the plague or warfare (Jerome; Ewald; Wellhausen; Wolff).

Verse 18 turns to the effects on animals. The animals groan; cattle wander about and sheep are dazed because they have no food in the pasture. The animals are confused and no longer know what to do because of the devastation that has come (Radak). Like their human counterparts and the land itself, the animals sigh or groan, indicating that they are joining the lamentation and mourning (Claassens 2014a). Indeed, the interrelationship of humanity, animals, and the physical environment as depicted in these verses has gained increasing attention in recent years (Simkins 1993).

1:19–20

Verse 19 begins with a further lamentation: 'To you, O Lord, I cry'. While the speaker is not identified, many assume this to be the cry of the prophet (Ibn Ezra; Calvin; Wolff). Here it is fire that is lamented, as it has 'devoured the pastures of the wilderness' and its flames have 'burned all the trees of the field'. The phrase 'pastures of the wilderness' has been understood variously. Following the Targum, Rashi sees this as dwellings of the wilderness, perhaps referring to the tents of shepherds. Jerome interprets this as blossoming meadows, while Luther opts for 'habitations' of the wilderness. However this imagery is understood, the introduction of fire brings a new threat, and the depiction of the devastation increases: from locusts to drought to fire (Barton).

Chapter 1 concludes in verse 20 by noting that 'even the wild animals cry to you' as the watercourses have dried and the fire has devoured the wilderness. Most commentators have pointed out the continuity here with the previous verses. Even the brute animals will suffer, and these will show the people how they should respond: 'If I and the other Prophets have lost all our labour . . . let the very oxen at least be your teachers' (Calvin: 42). And yet there is still no mention of sin or wrongdoing—rather, this can be seen as a cry for God to act and intervene in a time of crisis (Barton). Indeed, the imagery of chapter 1 brings to mind contemporary issues, such as food shortages and natural disasters, issues that have an inordinate impact on the poor and those in the developing world, often through little fault of their own. In this sense, Joel has been understood as an example of theology done in response to (or during) collective hardship or trauma (Claassens 2014a).

Joel 2

Chapter 2 continues themes found in chapter 1, namely devastation in the land, as well as calls to lamentation. However, the present chapter is most often understood as pointing to a danger that is still yet to come as opposed to the devastation that many assume has already passed in Joel 1. Many readers see chapter 2 moving from a warning of coming danger, to a call to lament and return to God, to a promise of future deliverance. Joel 2 has had a significant impact on Christianity, in part because it is used extensively in the New Testament, including an extended quotation from Peter at Pentecost in Acts 2.

Readers have long noted issues with the chapter divisions in Joel; Calvin speaks for many when he asserts that the chapters have been 'absurdly and fool-ishly divided' (xvi). The Hebrew text of Joel is divided into four chapters—chapter 2 ends at verse 27, and chapter 3 has five verses. In English translations, the book has three chapters, and chapter 2 has thirty-two verses (including all those that are part of chapter 3 in the Hebrew tradition). Thus, 2:28 in ET is 3:1 in HB, and so on. This commentary follows the English versification. For more on the chapter and verse divisions, see Wolff and Crenshaw.

2:1

The chapter begins with a command to blow the shofar in Zion and sound an alarm on the holy mountain (2:1). Some understand the blowing of the shofar as a call to the people to repent (Rashi), and the reference to Zion leads some

Hosea, Joel, and Obadiah Through the Centuries, First Edition. Bradford A. Anderson.
© 2024 John Wiley & Sons Ltd. Published 2024 by John Wiley & Sons Ltd.

to suggest that this is addressed to the priests, who are to assemble the people (Calvin; Gill; Wesley; Bewer). Others note that it might also be a war trumpet, sounding the alarm for a coming attack as in Num. 10:9 (Jerome; Darby; Achtemeier). In the Hebrew, verse 1 concludes by stating that the inhabitants of the land are to tremble because the day of the LORD is coming and is near. Both the LXX and the Targum indicate that the day of the LORD has come, a small change that nonetheless may be an attempt to connect the events of chapter 1 with chapter 2. The day of the LORD is not just about final judgment, Luther notes. Rather, this can also be used to describe a day of visitation, of God visiting his people 'in grace or in anger' (90). Barton observes that the use of the day of YHWH here is clearly referring to judgment; however, as the chapter makes clear, beyond this judgment stands the possibility of restoration.

The shofar has taken on symbolic significance in both Jewish and Christian traditions (see also the commentary on Hos. 8:1). In Judaism, the shofar is blown 100 times on Rosh Hashanah, the Jewish new year, and on Yom Kippur it is used to note the end of the period of fasting (Eisen 2006). The shofar has also become part of the visual iconography of Jewish identity in historical and contemporary contexts and is often associated with both Judaism and the state of Israel. This can be seen in early modern Christian depictions of Jewish practices, where blowing the shofar is depicted as one of the distinctive Jewish religious practices alongside the use of tefillin or phylacteries, mezuzah, and the Torah scroll (see Figure 29, lower left quartile).

The imagery of blowing the trumpet in Zion has been generative for musical artists. This verse was particularly popular in medieval and early modern liturgical pieces (Dowling Long 2017). One early modern example is the piece 'Blow up the Trumpet in Sion', a 1679 anthem written by Henry Purcell, a seventeenth-century English composer. This song, written for seven soloists and an eight-part chorus, was used as a penitential text during Lent. Along with the trumpet blast of verse 1, the song also draws on verses 15–17 and the call to assemble the people and seek God's mercy (Dowling Long and Sawyer 2015). The imagery of verse 1 is also used in the popular 1983 Christian praise and worship song 'Blow the Trumpet in Zion' by Craig Terndrup (Sounds of Vision/Integrity's Hosanna! Music). Terndrup recalls that he was inspired by the book of Joel and its promise of the coming of the spirit (Terndrup 2011). His song is an interesting interweaving of various themes in the book. It begins with the proclamation:

> They rush on the city; they run on the wall.
> Great is the army that carries out His Word.
> The Lord utters his voice before his army.

Here the locusts or army described in Joel 2:9 is reenvisioned as the people carrying out God's word rather than as an attacking enemy, drawing on the

FIGURE 29   *Johannes Leusden, image of Jewish objects and ritual uses, in Philologus Hebraeo-mixtu; seventeenth century.*

Courtesy of Pitts Library Digital Archive/Emory University.

ambiguity of verse 11, which describes God as the head of his army. The chorus then instructs the singers to

> Blow the trumpet in Zion, Zion.
> Sound the alarm on My holy mountain.

In Terndrup's musical interpretation and inversion of the text, Joel 2 becomes a spiritual battle cry: the sounding of the trumpet becomes a call to the people of God who are visualized as an army on the move.

2:2

Verse 2 continues the discussion of the day of Yhwh that was introduced in verse 1. Here the day is described as one of darkness and clouds along with the introduction of another key element: 'Like blackness spread upon the mountains a great and powerful army comes' (2:2). The verse concludes by stating that nothing like this has ever been seen before, nor will anything like it be seen in the future.

The reference to darkness, clouds, and a powerful army has led to considerable commentary. The darkness and clouds have been understood by some as literal, as happened with the swarms of locusts in the Egyptian plague (Pusey; Gill), while others have interpreted it figuratively, pointing to coming trouble (Radak; Bewer). The verse next notes that a powerful army comes like dawn or darkness ('*arapel*) spreading on the mountains. This imagery has also been understood in various ways. A number of readers understand this as referring to locusts, who are depicted as an army (Julian of Eclanum; Rashi; Gill; Ewald; von Rad; Watts; Simkins 1993). Others see this as indicating a human army (likely the Assyrians or Babylonians), which is encroaching like the dawn (Cyril of Alexandria; Luther; Calvin; Wesley; Achtemeier; Sweeney; Hagedorn 2021). Still others suggest that this is a general description of coming trouble and may refer to either locusts or an army or indeed both (Cyril of Alexandria; Gill; Crenshaw; Assis). However one understands the referent of the imagery, Pusey notes, the verse as a whole gives a picture that describes 'the order and course of the Divine judgments; how they are terrific, irresistible, universal, overwhelming, penetrating everywhere, overspreading all things' (171).

Another question is how the events of chapter 1 might be connected with the scene portrayed in 2:2 and following in terms of both the nature of the threat and the timing of it. One approach sees the locusts in chapter 1 as a precursor for the day of Yhwh and military threat found in chapter 2, even if the imagery in the latter is still that of locusts (Crenshaw). A different yet related approach, as seen in the work of Wolff, suggests that chapters 1 and 2 are presenting different crises. The events of chapter 1 are located in the past, but in chapter 2 repentance is still possible, so the threat seems to be still in the future.

According to Wolff, it is no longer locusts that are a threat but an apocalyptic army, the likes of which have never been seen before. The oncoming invasion is thus interpreted eschatologically (Wolff). Others see both chapters referring to the same events—either military attacks (Ogden 1983) or a locust infestation (Barton). (For more on the various options for understanding the relationship of the events portrayed in chapters 1 and 2, see Hadjiev 2020.)

2:3–4

Verse 3 continues with imagery of destruction: fire devours before them, and a flame burns behind them. Readers again disagree on whether this refers to locusts or an army. Some commentators offer numerous historical and contemporary examples of the ravages of locusts (Pusey). Others see this as describing the fiery effects of an army, likely the Babylonians (Jerome; Luther; Wesley). As Wolff notes, fire is not usually an effect of drought but of invasion and war, which points to a foreign invasion. The verse continues by stating that the land before them is like the Garden of Eden, but after them it is a wilderness—reinforcing the destruction that takes place. The land before the arrival of the invaders is depicted as paradise, and subsequently it is a wasteland (Theodore of Mopsuestia; Rashi; Calvin). The invocation of the Garden of Eden is somewhat surprising, as this imagery is not common in the HB (see Gen. 2–3; Ezek. 28; Crenshaw; Barton).

In verse 4 we are given a description of the enemy: they have the appearance of horses, and they charge like warhorses. Some interpreters throughout history have suggested that this is speaking of a human army (Theodore of Mopsuestia; Calvin; Wolff). However, more common is the assumption that the text speaks here of locusts. We see this in medieval Jewish tradition, where this was understood as referring to locusts and the speed of their running and movement, both of which are compared to horses (Rashi; Radak; Malbim; cf. Nicholas of Lyra). Early Christian readers tended to agree that this verse speaks of locusts (Jerome; Julian of Eclanum). Some point out that a locust head is often compared to the head of a horse and that various languages refer to locusts with horse-related descriptions (e.g., 'little horse'; see Theodoret of Cyr; Gill).

Notably, similar imagery appears in Rev. 9:7, which speaks of a locust invasion as part of its apocalyptic rhetoric. There we read, 'In appearance the locusts were like horses equipped for battle,' though the text goes on to say they have faces like human faces. Nonetheless, given the points of contact between Joel and Revelation, most commentators assume the Apocalypse is influenced by Joel's language and imagery of locusts and horse-related language and is most likely dependent on the Greek of the LXX (Strazicich 2007).

2:5–6

The action and movements of this foe are described in verse 5: they leap on the tops of mountain like the rumbling of chariots; they are like a powerful army, devouring stubble like a flame. As with the previous verse, verse 5 also seems to be a source of inspiration for the imagery of Revelation 9. In Rev. 9:9 we read that 'the noise of their wings was like the noise of many chariots with horses rushing into battle'. The reference to leaping and being 'like' a powerful army has led some interpreters to suggest that Joel 2:5 is speaking of locusts (Gill). Others, however, see here a clear reference to a human army fortified with equipment and weapons (Nicholas of Lyra). Cyril of Alexandria posited that this referred to the Assyrians or perhaps the Romans, while Luther states that it is likely the Assyrians or Babylonians. Luther sees the Turks of his own day as the equivalent of these foreign powers, representing the 'scourge of God' that will bring devastation and ruin.

In verse 6 we read, 'Before them peoples are in anguish, all faces grow pale (*pa'rur*)'. Though similar language is found in Nah. 2:10, the final word has been a challenge for interpreters (Wellhausen). The LXX and Targum both translate this as referring to faces blackened like a cauldron or a pot. These renderings would be followed by numerous readers (Vulgate; Rashi; Gill). Drawing on this verse, Basil the Great noted that in baptism one's inner self is no longer like a blackened kettle (*Concerning Baptism* 1.2; Ferreiro). Among modern readers, rather than 'blackened', the Hebrew term is most often understood as referring to the people growing pale in fear (Crenshaw; NRSV).

2:7–9

Verse 7 states that the enemies charge like warriors and scale walls like soldiers; each of them keeps to its own course, and they do not turn from their path. Rashi and Ibn Ezra suggest that this means the enemy is single-minded in its focus, and there is no straying from their plan and path. Jerome sees this as a description of a locust invasion and notes that he has seen the orderliness of locusts in his own day:

> Columns of locusts come and fill the air between heaven and earth, they flit about with such great order by the beck and call of God that they take on the likeness of mosaic pieces that are fixed in the pavement by the hand of an artist. They hold fast to their own place and do not veer off in another direction even by a pinprick. (277)

The description of the enemy's approach continues in verse 8: they do not jostle one another, and each keeps on its own course. The LXX understands this to mean that no one stands aloof from his brother—they attack in unity and with focus. According to Radak, this is a portrayal of locusts described as men in line with the description in verse 7. The verse concludes by stating that 'they burst through the weapons and are not halted' (NRSV). The Hebrew here is complex and has been understood in various ways. In the Targum, we read that the enemy goes and kills and does not take money. Rashi follows this reading, suggesting that this refers to soldiers who were hired or who took bribes (cf. Radak). The Vulgate, meanwhile, posits that they fall through windows and are not harmed (cf. Jerome). A more common reading is that this relates to the fact that the enemy can withstand weapons—whether it is a human army or locusts, they are not easily cut down by weapons and swords (Ibn Ezra; Luther; Gill).

In verse 9 we are told that the enemy leaps upon the city, runs upon walls, climbs houses, and enters windows as a thief. This verse clearly describes an enemy that can penetrate a city, though again there is disagreement as to the subject. Calvin suggests this refers to the Assyrians, for whom cities are no impediment (cf. Wesley). However, others suggest this verse gives a realistic description of the various ways locusts can invade a city (Crenshaw).

2:10

In verse 10 we read that 'the earth quakes before them, the heavens tremble. The sun and moon are darkened, and the stars withdraw their shining'. Some readers have understood the quaking and trembling as literal; Abarbanel, for example, suggests that this refers to the destruction of the Temple, while Bewer takes this to mean an earthquake and storm. Likewise, the darkening of the sun and moon has been understood as pointing to the darkness brought from a swarm of locusts (Gill). However, most have interpreted this figuratively as referring to coming trouble (Jerome; Radak). Indeed, a number of commentators go to surprising lengths to make clear that this is presented in a hyperbolic fashion and strive to dampen readers' expectations that these events will literally take place (Cyril of Alexandria; Theodore of Mopsuestia; Nicholas of Lyra; Luther). Calvin says this language is used to arouse the feelings of the people, while Wesley refers to this as 'divine hyperbole'.

Modern commentators have noted that the imagery of verse 10 seems to move beyond just locusts. Indeed, the prophet seems to be drawing on well-established traditions and imagery of what happens during times of divine judgment (Isa. 13, 34; see Crenshaw; Barton). Some see this as proto-apocalyptic imagery, and this may be corroborated by the fact that the imagery of the darkening of the sun, moon, and stars is picked up in the NT, including Mark 13:24 and Matt. 24:29, with apocalyptic overtones (Strazicich 2007). This imagery has also been associated with Joel in visual representations of the book and the prophet as seen for example in one of the relief sculptures on Amiens Cathedral (Figure 30). While Joel is not a character in the book

FIGURE 30   *Joel with sun and moon; Amiens Cathedral, France.*
Used with permission from Stuart Whatling.

bearing his name, here the artist places him alongside textual elements and memorable imagery within the book as a way of helping the audience visualize the prophet.

2:11

In verse 11 we are told that God utters his voice 'at the head of his army', which is a vast, numberless host. Elements of Jewish tradition were uncomfortable with God being depicted at the head of an enemy army. Thus, this clause has been interpreted by some as God speaking through the prophets of an approaching army (Radak; Rashi). A not dissimilar approach is taken by Cyril of Alexandria, who focuses on the power of the divine word: 'It is absolutely impossible that whatever God orders to take place would not come into effect' (284). However, others see here an indication that it is God rather than the enemy that is bringing this judgment on Israel (Luther; Calvin; Ewald). For those who see locusts as the encroaching foe, this verse makes clear that the locusts are no longer heralds of the day of YHWH but 'agents of His will' (Bewer: 104).

Verse 11 concludes by connecting this imagery to the day of the LORD: 'Truly the day of the LORD is great; terrible indeed—who can endure it?' (2:11). This imagery has been understood as divine retribution (Mezudath David), as well as being interpreted eschatologically, referring to the second coming of Christ (Gregory the Great, *Morals on the Book of Job* 3.17.54). Modern commentators have pointed out that the day of the LORD is presented here as a theophany, noting points of contact with other biblical texts where divine appearance is connected with the day of the LORD (Hab. 3:3–12; Nah. 1:2–6; see Achtemeier; Sweeney).

2:12

The tone of chapter 2 changes in verse 12, which instructs the people to return to the LORD with a right heart, as well as with fasting, weeping, and mourning. With this, the chapter moves from warning to penitence (Jerome; Luther). While no wrongdoing is mentioned, this has often been understood as a call to repent as destruction is at hand (Cyril of Alexandria; Radak; Darby). The mention of fasting and weeping has also been noted by interpreters. Aquinas drew on verse 12 as part of his larger argument that fasting is indeed an act of virtue (*ST* II-II, q. 147, a. 1). Others have commented that while these outward signs are important, they need to come with a right heart, which is mentioned first in the verse (Luther; Gill).

2:13–14

The themes of contrition and return continue in verse 13. To begin, the people are instructed to rend their hearts and not their clothing. From antiquity, this was seen as a call to heartfelt penitence and fasting in Jewish tradition (m. Ta'anit; Rashi). Indeed, Radak relays one interpretation that says if you rend your hearts, you will not need to rend your garments. Similar sentiments are found in the Christian tradition, where rending the heart is seen as indicating something deeper and inward that affects one's actions (Julian of Elcanum). Some readers interpret rending garments as an oriental or Hebrew custom and thus understand the prophet's words as aimed at a particular Jewish practice (Calvin; Luther). Others point out that rending garments is not forbidden, but comparatively a contrite heart is what God desires (Gill). Crenshaw compares this to the idea of circumcising the foreskin of the heart in Deut. 10:6 and Jer. 4:4.

The prophet next instructs the people to return to the LORD, 'for he is gracious and merciful, slow to anger, and abounding in steadfast love' (2:13). This is a common formula that occurs eight times in the HB, the most similar found in Jonah 4:2 (Bergler 1988; Sweeney). In the Palestinian Talmud, this verse is used as one of the key Scripture texts relating God's nature as merciful and slow to anger (y. Ta'an. 2:1). Because of this resonance with other biblical texts, a number of interpreters have commented on these points of contact and have suggested various relations between biblical passages (Radak; Calvin; Ewald). Verse 13 ends by noting that because he is gracious, God relents from punishing. In order to avoid the appearance of God changing his mind, the Targum renders the final part of this verse with the following: 'he draws back his Memra from bringing evil'. Gill offers a similar reading: God does not change his mind 'but alters the course of his providence'.

The imagery of 'rending your hearts and not your garments' has been picked up in liturgical and cultural expression. The phrase is used by Felix Mendelssohn in the oratorio *Elijah* alongside a number of other texts from the HB (Dowling Long 2017). Here the verse is used as part of a call to repentance, set during the time of the prophet Elijah, who is calling the people to forsake their idols.

Mendelssohn also draws on Joel's programmatic proclamation that God is slow to anger, merciful, and gracious. The imagery from Joel 2:13 is thus transposed here to a different biblical story, where it is used as part of a call to repentance and a return to the Lord—pointing to the versatility of Joel's imagery. The wording of 2:13 also appears in Thomas Tomkins's 1622 choral piece entitled 'Turn unto the Lord', where the verse is extracted and used alongside Ps. 100:5, which also speaks of God's mercy.

Similar themes of turning and relenting are found in verse 14. The verse is posed as a question: 'Who knows whether he will not turn and relent and leave a blessing behind him?' The Targum translates this as referring to a person who repents and is blessed by God rather than God himself turning, again avoiding the attribution of a changed mind to God. However, most readers understand this as describing God relenting from bringing punishment. Even so, the fact that the verse is framed as a question is a reminder of God's divine freedom: calling out to God is no guarantee of a response (Wolff; Crenshaw).

2:15–16

In verses 15–16, the prophet commands the people to blow the trumpet in Zion in order to call a fast and a solemn assembly. Athanasius comments that the trumpet is a warning call that the fast is to be done in a holy manner (*Festal Letters I* [Ferreiro]). The prophet declares that all the people—young and old—are to be assembled. Even infants are included either to arouse pity and encourage greater penance from their parents (Calvin) or because they are not exempt from the ravages of war and so should be part of any entreaty to God (Crenshaw). Whatever the case, the verse seems to give a picture of 'everyone of every age and situation participating in repentance, everything else left aside' (Theodore of Mopsuestia: 114; cf. Gill). A number of interpreters take this as an invitation and command to fast and repent in order to gain God's mercy (Leo the Great, *Sermon 88.1*; Jerome; Aquinas). Verse 16 concludes with a call to 'Let the bridegroom leave his room, and the bride her canopy', imagery that has led to diverse commentary. In the Palestinian Talmud, this is said to refer to the Torah and ark being brought into public on fast days (y. Ta'an. 2:1). Others see this as pointing to the fact that the bride and groom must deny themselves pleasures and commit to mourning with the rest of the community (Gill; Radak). Another approach notes that bride and groom were exempted from war in Deut. 24:5, and yet even these are called, along with children and the elderly, to join the solemn assembly (Jerome; Pusey).

2:17

After calling all the people to assemble and fast, the prophet instructs the priests to position themselves between the vestibule and the altar and weep (2:17). Commentators have often made note of the location of the priests in this verse. Some suggest that they are positioned in the same spot where they would normally offer sacrifices but will now instead weep and pray for mercy (Radak; Gill). Others highlight that the priests are located between the Temple entrance hall and the great altar, thus standing between the people and God (Calvin; Ewald; Wolff). The priests, we read, are to call out to God, asking him to spare his people. Indeed, for God's own sake, he should spare his people so that they are not a mockery among the nations (2:17). Cyril of Alexandria sees this as evidence that a military foe is in mind—surely locusts do not bring reproach and mockery from other nations (Cyril of Alexandria). Luther points out that the prophets often urge God and attempt to persuade him based on his own glory, and so in this sense Joel sits firmly in the prophetic tradition. Interestingly, the text is still silent on any wrongdoing on the part of the people (Crenshaw). It is not clear that turning or returning to God necessitates repentance; this may also be seen as a call to intercession and placing hope in God during a time of tribulation (Barton). Nevertheless, the lack of detail in the text allows for it to be used in a number of contexts, including the liturgical traditions of both Judaism and Christianity (Simkins 2016).

The instruction to fast and weep in these verses has been employed in musical and liturgical traditions. Thomas Tallis wrote a motet for five voices in 1575 based on Joel 2:12–17, entitled 'In Jejunio et Fletu' (In Fasting and Weeping), part of a larger collection of motets entitled *Cantiones Sacrae* written by Tallis and William Byrd. It is a sung response at matins for the first Sunday of Lent, where the themes of fasting and weeping are fitting content for Lenten liturgy (Dowling Long and Sawyer 2015).

2:18

The tone of the chapter (and some say the entire book) shifts dramatically in 2:18 (Wolff; Mason 1994). Here we are told that God became jealous for his land and took pity on his people. Uncomfortable with the idea of God being jealous, the Targum changes this so that the verse speaks of God sparing the land. However, the notion of God being jealous or zealous (*qane'*) is found elsewhere in the prophets referring to God (Wolff). While God does not have passions like a person, these feelings are attributed to him like a father (Calvin). This zealousness indicates that God has heard and responded to his people (Jerome; Rashi; Radak). Indeed, the lament of the people in the previous verses seems to have worked, and we see here 'the speedy course of mercy' (Cyril of Alexandria; cf. Barton). In recent years, readers have noted that it is the land for which God is jealous and the potential ecological implications for reading these verses in light of this. Horrell comments, 'Perhaps the fact of devastation of the land is, by itself, indication of a situation of desperate need, when the people need to mourn and lament, in the hope of bringing about an act of restoration and mercy on God's part' (Horrell 2010: 97; cf. Braaten 2006).

An ivory carving from the seventh–eighth century CE, likely originating in Syria or Palestine and now held in the Louvre, depicts the prophet Joel holding a scroll, on which part of Joel 2:18 is shown in Greek (Figure 31). This image

FIGURE 31   *The Prophet Joel, ivory; Louvre, Paris (seventh–eighth century CE). The scroll contains part of Joel 2:18 in Greek.*

Marie-Lan Nguyen/Wikimedia Commons/CC BY 2.5.

'shows Joel outside a great city, robes flowing wildly, his left foot forward dramatically, looking up and pointing with his right hand to heaven; on a scroll in his left hand are the Greek words for "The lord was jealous for his land, and had pity on his people" (Joel 2:18)' (Sawyer 2021: 284). Given that this verse brings a change of tone in the book, with promises of God's provision to come in the following verses, it is fitting that this image depicts the prophet in a more confident and positive manner than do many other portrayals of the prophet, particularly those which focus on the calamity of Joel 1.

2:19–20

The divine response is cataloged in the following verses. In verse 19 we are told that God will send grain, wine, and oil and will no more allow the people to be a mockery among the nations. The Targum connects these two ideas, stating that the shame of hunger will be removed. Israel's harvest is thus a sign that God has not abandoned his people (Gill; Pusey). More recent scholarship has noted the importance of the concepts of honor and shame in verse 19 and following—both the shame of the people and God's honor seem to be at stake and in view (Romerowski 1989; Simkins 1994).

God states in verse 20 that he will remove 'the northerner' (*hatsfoni*) far from them, a cryptic clause that has led to significant commentary. The LXX translates this northerner literally as the one from the north, while the Targum speaks of people who come from the north. In the Vulgate, this term is rendered as the northern enemy, and this idea is followed by a number of modern translations, which opt for 'northern army' (KJV; NRSV). As has been the case throughout this chapter, commentators have been divided on whether this relates to locusts or an actual army. While Rashi says the northerner may refer either to locusts or the Assyrians, Radak and Ibn Ezra both contend that the verse refers to locusts. Although some early Christian readers agreed that this verse concerns a coming locust invasion (Julian of Eclanum), most interpret this as referring to a physical army, either the Assyrians or the Babylonians who would attack from the north (Jerome; Theodore of Mopsuestia; Isho'dad of Merv).

This diversity of opinion regarding 'the northerner' would continue through the centuries. The assumption of a human army would prevail in the medieval and Reformation eras (Nicholas of Lyra; Luther; Calvin). However, in the early modern period, interpreters began to once again consider that locusts are in view, even if symbolically representing an invading army (John Wesley; John Gill; Wellhausen; Bewer). Modern commentators have echoed Rashi's careful interpretation and are less confident in making a definitive identification, as the locusts and human armies seem to be thoroughly entwined in the chapter (Crenshaw; Sweeney). Noting commonalities with the language of a northern enemy found in Jer. 1 and Ezek. 38, Wolff suggests this imagery may have mythic origins (cf. Achtemeier).

Spiritual readings of the first half of verse 20 have also been put forward. An interesting reading is found in the Babylonian Talmud, specifically in tractate Sukkah. Drawing on a phonetically similar word, the northerner was interpreted by the Sages as 'the hidden one', which is noted as one of the seven names of the evil inclination and which is always 'hidden' in the heart of humanity. The evil inclination was an early Jewish attempt to account for evil in the world. In this reading of Joel, the hidden impulse to do evil will be removed from the people (b. Sukkah 52a). A number of early Christian readers, meanwhile, interpreted the northerner as Satan or the devil (Cassiodorus, *Exposition of the Psalms* 36.35 [Ferreiro]; Cyril of Alexandria).

This northerner, we read, will be driven to a parched land, 'its front into the eastern sea, and its rear into the western sea,' and a foul smell will rise up (v. 20). Most readers are in agreement that the western sea refers to the Mediterranean and that the eastern sea refers to the Dead Sea (Jerome; Luther; Wesley; Barton). Radak is in the minority, positing that the latter refers to the Sea of Galilee. Jerome notes that cases of locusts stretching from sea to sea, and their stench filling the land, were well known in his time.

2:21–22

Verse 21 instructs the soil to not fear, but rejoice, because God has done great things. While Radak glosses this so that it refers to the inhabitants of the land, it is interesting that it is the soil that is addressed (Calvin). The following verse gives a similar instruction to the animals because 'the pastures of the wilderness are green; the tree bears its fruit, the fig tree and vine give their full yield' (2:22). The promises in these verses seem to reverse the threats to the land and animals found in 1:12 and 1:20 (Jerome; Ibn Ezra). Cyril of Alexandria describes this as an 'earthy' description to aid the people (cf. Luther). Figurative readings of this imagery have been common in both Judaism and Christianity. In relation to the fruitful trees and vines, the Jewish Sages noted that in Messianic times, barren trees in Israel would bear fruit (b. Ketub. 112b). Meanwhile, Tertullian suggests that the trees of verse 22 are a type of the cross, from which Christ would bring life (*Answer to the Jews* 12 [Ferreiro]).

2:23

In verse 23, the children of Zion are told to rejoice and be glad, 'for he has given the early rain for your vindication, he has poured down for you abundant rain, the early and the later rain, as before'. The various references to rain in this verse have been of most interest to readers. As the words for 'rain' and 'teacher' are similar in Hebrew, the Targum translates the first potential reference to rain as a 'teacher of righteousness' that will be given to the people. This would be followed by various other traditions, including the Vulgate, which renders this as a 'teacher of justice'. Rashi suggests that this is a reference to the prophets, who teach the people to return to God, while Abarbanel posits that this points to the Messiah. A number of Christian readers saw this teacher of righteousness as pointing to Jesus as the ultimate teacher (Aquinas, *ST* III q. 9, a. 4; Gill). With the discovery of the Dead Sea scrolls in the twentieth century, readers took note of the prominent figure of the Teacher of Righteousness found in the Damascus Document and other Qumran texts, and attempts were made to link this figure with Joel 2. Modern scholars are largely skeptical of such a connection (Wolff). Indeed, from the medieval period, interpreters began to suggest that this first clause was another reference to rain rather than to a teacher (Ibn Ezra; Luther; Calvin; Bewer). This remains the most prominent reading in contemporary commentaries and translations (Crenshaw; NRSV).

The reference to early and latter rain is often understood as the rains that come at planting and harvest time in Israel, referring to God's provision for his people (Pusey). According to the Talmud, the former rain is a blessing and cannot always be assumed. Tractate Ta'anit recounts a miracle that took place one year when grain grew in eleven days due to this early rain (b. Ta'an. 5a).

Meanwhile, the notion of 'latter rain' has been influential in Christianity. The Latter Rain Movement developed as a precursor to, and later as an outgrowth of, the Pentecostal traditions in the twentieth century. Drawing on Joel 2:23 along with a number of other texts (see also the commentary on Hos. 6:3), the contemporary outpouring and 'new wave' of the Holy Spirit are seen as the 'latter rain' of God, first given at Pentecost (Acts 2) and now believed to be ushering in the last days and the return of Jesus (Isgrigg 2019). Known for their belief in spiritual revivals, supernatural experiences, and prophetic activity, the Latter Rain Movement continues to influence contemporary charismatic and neo-charismatic groups. Indeed, the name 'Joel's Army' has been applied to those who are committed to living out the 'godly lifestyle' of prayer and fasting as laid out in Joel 2.

Verse 23 ends by noting that this rain will come 'as before'. In the Mishnah, Rabbi Meir reads the final clause as 'at the first (month)' and so uses this verse to suggest all of the month of Nisan is part of the rainy season (m. Ta'an. 1:2 [Neusner]). Wolff suggests that 'as before' points to Israel's earlier days of their relationship with God and his sustaining provision for them.

2:24–25

The themes of provision and replenishment continue in verses 24–25. In verse 24 we read that the threshing floors will be full of grain, and the vats of wine and oil will overflow. While these statements can be read literally to refer to God's provision, spiritual readings are also common (Gill). Within Christianity, the reference to grain and wine has led to figurative associations with the Eucharist (Cyril of Alexandria).

God speaks again in verse 25, stating that 'I will repay you for the years that the swarming locust has eaten, the hopper, the destroyer, and the cutter, my great army, which I sent against you'. The reference to locusts again raises the issue as to whether these should be understood literally or figuratively. The Targum offers a figurative reading, noting that God will repay the people 'in place of the years in which you were pillaged by peoples, tongues, governments, and kingdoms, the great retribution of my army which I sent against you'. Similar readings are found in the Christian tradition, where this is understood as referring to destroying armies (Theodore of Mopsuestia). However, others see here a literal reference to the damage inflicted by locusts as the Jewish commentator Ibn Ezra suggests. Why are these called God's great army? According to Julian of Eclanum, 'Surely this is not because [palmer] worms are related in any fashion to the eternal power of God, but because by their service and devastation in the affliction of things it carried out the work of revenge' (210). The fact that the locusts are listed here in an order different from that found in chapter 1 makes unlikely a reading of the former based on the stages of locust development (Crenshaw).

The imagery of 'restoring the years' has been generative in both cultural and religious contexts. This turn of phrase is the inspiration for the title of Annie E. Holdsworth's *The Years That the Locust Hath Eaten* (1897). Holdsworth was a popular novelist of the late nineteenth century, and this particular work portrays the sacrifices a young woman makes in an unhappy marriage from which she cannot escape. While the content of the book of Joel is not present in the work, this turn of phrase from the prophet offers a useful image for the novelist to describe something that has been stolen in life and cannot be easily replaced. The phrase occurs elsewhere in literature, including Thomas Wolfe's *The Web and the Rock*, where it is used in a metaphorical way to describe loss and emptiness (see Freedman and Willoughby 1992).

This imagery is also common in Christian teaching and sermons, from the nineteenth-century preacher C.H. Spurgeon (1886) to more contemporary contexts (Smith 2014). Spurgeon's sermon, entitled 'Truth Stranger than Fiction', is a reflection on the power of God to redeem what has been lost. He notes,

> It will strike you at once that the locusts did not eat the years: the locusts ate the fruits of the years' labour, the harvests of the fields; so that the meaning of the restoration of the years must be the restoration of those fruits and of those harvests which the locusts consumed. You cannot have back your time; but there is a strange and wonderful way in which God can give back to you the wasted blessings, the unripened fruits of years over which you mourned. The fruits of wasted years may yet be yours. It is a pity that they should have been locust-eaten by your folly and negligence; but if they have been so, be not hopeless concerning them.
>
> (Spurgeon 1951)

As with much of Spurgeon's preaching, the text is believed to have immediate relevance—it is the life of the Christian believer with which he is concerned, in particular the lost fruits from the years of sin and disbelief that God can restore if only people will repent.

2:26–27

In verses 26–27, the people are told that they will eat in plenty and will praise the name of the Lord who has done wondrous things. Following the Sages, Radak connects the two elements and suggests these 'wonders' refer to God causing produce to grow especially fast. God's people will never again be put to shame but will know that their God is in their midst and that there is no other God. The pagan deities the people have worshipped in the past do not provide for them, only YHWH (Radak). This promise to be in their midst has been understood by some Christian readers as a promise of the incarnation, when God would dwell with his people (Cyril of Alexandria).

In 1914, Edward Elgar set Joel 2:21–24, 26 to music in an anthem for Thanksgiving, using the *Authorised Version*. Here the imagery of abundance in the natural world is combined with giving thanks to God for his provision.

2:28

(Joel 2:28 in English translations is 3:1 in Hebrew versions [see introduction to this chapter]. This extends through 2:32, which is 3:5 in the Hebrew. In what follows I use the English versification.)

A new section is evident in 2:28, where God declares that afterward he will pour out his spirit on all flesh. Sons and daughters will prophesy, and old and young men will see dreams and visions. Readers have long noted that a new section begins in verse 28. Luther commented that the 'real prophecy' begins in this verse, while Calvin suggests that we see here a message of 'higher things' after the earlier message of earthly blessing (cf. Wellhausen; Darby). A number of modern scholars understand 2:28 and the ensuing section as part of a collection of oracles that emerged at a later time, likely at some distance from the historical prophet (Barton).

Verse 28 and those following have had a significant impact and history of reception, not least because they are quoted and alluded to in several places in the New Testament. The most well known of these is the quotation by Peter in Acts 2:17–21, which offers a full quotation of this text that is very close to the LXX of Joel. We also have allusions to 2:28 in Acts 10:45 and Titus 3:6, which speak of the spirit being poured out. Not surprisingly, early Christian commentators were quick to draw on Joel 2 when discussing Acts and the broader notion of the spirit (including comments from early Christian authors Chrysostom, Ambrose, Tertullian, Justin Martyr, Origen, and others; see Ferreiro).

The explicit use of Joel in Acts 2 leads to a number of questions, including what is meant by the declaration in 2:28 that these things will happen 'afterward'. In Jewish tradition, some voices did suggest that this temporal marker should be understood as pointing to the Messianic age. However, the great medieval commentators are unsure: Rashi states that this refers broadly to a future time, while Radak suggests it points to a time when the people will have repented and turned back to God. As Ibn Ezra notes, if a Messianic era was in view, the text would reference the end of days.

Christian readings have been heavily influenced by the quotation from Acts 2, where Luke seems to offer an 'actualized reading of the prophetic books' that is common in this period (Troxel 2015: 4; cf. Strazicich 2007). Luke, the author of Acts, sees a new era of salvation history being inaugurated in these events, as Joel's words are fulfilled in the events of Pentecost (Fitzmyer 1998). And yet the relationship between the past and the present of the NT has been difficult to navigate. Some interpreters focus on the historical context of Joel and understand 2:28 as pointing to a time after the exile (as in the work of the eighteenth-century English cleric John Wesley). Other readers pass over the issue quickly:

Luther opines that the prophet simply skips here from his own time to the time of Christ. However, a number of Christian commentators would struggle with how to relate Peter's use of the text to the historical sense of the passage. Jerome, for example, notes that Peter sees Joel as fulfilled with Jesus and Pentecost. And yet he also comments that it is difficult to untangle how this relates to the time of the prophet, the apostles, and the future. Theodore of Mopsuestia likewise wrestles with this issue. While he normally prefers a literal reading, in this case Peter's use of Joel forces him to note a connection. He resolves this by suggesting that the HB gives a shadow, and the NT presents the reality, bringing clarity (cf. Origen, *On First Principles* 2.7.2; Isho'dad of Merv). Christian readers have also noted that Acts 2 is not the end of the story. For many, Pentecost is a fulfillment of Joel's words, but the prophet also speaks of a future time—whether this is the second coming of Christ or a future judgment (see Aquinas, *ST* XP, q. 88, a. 3; Gill).

Works of art in the Christian tradition often fuse the horizons of these texts, bringing together the prophet Joel and the events of Acts 2. An example of this is Ludwig Glötzle's depiction of Joel in Salzburg Cathedral. Here the prophet is seen reclining, holding a scroll and quill, as he receives a vision that includes Jesus, Peter, and a dove representing the Holy Spirit (Figure 32).

FIGURE 32   *Ludwig Glötzle, Vision des Propheten Joel von der Ausgießung des Heiligen Geistes—Gesamtansicht; Salzburg, Dom Sankt Rupert und Virgil, Heilig-Geist-Kapelle (1888).*
© Bildarchiv Foto Marburg.

A similar collapsing of time can be seen in Hans Brosamer's 1562 wood-cut from a Luther Bibel (Figure 33). Placed just under the title of the book of Joel, the image shows Peter in the background speaking to a crowd, with the prophet in the foreground pointing (literally) to a crowded gathering as the spirit descends on them in the form of a dove. Here Joel and Pentecost are brought together, with the prophet pointing to the fulfillment of his own prophetic message.

The reference to the coming of the spirit in Joel 2:28 and its use in Acts has also proven to be inspirational in music, as seen in Edward Elgar's oratorio *The Kingdom* (1901–06). Elgar's piece brings to life the birth of the church, and Joel's words are used in the depiction of the outpouring of the spirit on those gathered at Pentecost. In fact, Elgar uses the imagery from Joel twice: first put on the lips of the chorus prior to and announcing the spirit's com-ing and then again from Peter as an explanation of the events that are taking place, as happens in Acts 2. Like their counterparts in Christian commentary

FIGURE 33   *Hans Brosamer, Joel and Pentecost, woodcut from the Luther Bibel (1562).*
Courtesy of Pitts Library Digital Archive/ Emory University.

noted earlier, Glötzle, Elgar, and other artists attempt to bring the Hebrew prophet Joel into conversation with the story of Pentecost. In doing so, they highlight the rich tradition within Christianity of reading the New Testament in light of the Old. And yet, as resonant as these connections might be for Christians, such works of art also run the risk of collapsing the prophetic text into the Christian story.

Verse 28 begins with God declaring that he will pour out his spirit on all flesh. What is this spirit? While the Christian association of this text with the coming of the Holy Spirit is most well known, there are other ways in which this has been understood. Theodore of Mopsuestia comments that the people in the OT did not think of the spirit as a separate person but as an aspect of God's care. Thus, this refers to God giving his wealth and care to all. In the early modern period, Ewald would posit that this refers to 'a new higher spirit [which] must make itself felt, the spirit of the perfected true religion' (136; cf. Bewer). Many modern commentators see this reference to the spirit as pointing to God's vital power or force (Crenshaw). As Wolff notes, 'the pouring out of God's spirit upon flesh means the establishment of new, vigorous life through God's unreserved giving of himself to those who, in themselves, are rootless and feeble, especially in the approaching times of judgment' (66). The imagery of the spirit is also used in the HB in relation to the empowerment of prophets (1 Sam. 10:10), and the rest of verse 28 would indicate that this might also be in view here (Barton).

What does it mean to pour out this spirit on all flesh? For Rashi, this means those whose heart is as flesh, that is, open and receptive. Tertullian, meanwhile, reminds us that while Scripture often speaks disparagingly of flesh (e.g., Rom. 7:18), we should also be aware of cases like Joel where the flesh is ennobled (*On the Resurrection of the Flesh* 10 [Ferreiro]). These readings notwithstanding, most readers see here a reference to the inclusiveness of God's spirit (Radak). And yet a recurring question is how inclusive this really is and whether the mention of *all* flesh includes Gentiles. Christian readers frequently interpret Joel 2:28 as indicating that salvation is now available to all people beyond just Judaism (Cyril of Alexandria; Calvin; Wesley; Pusey; Darby). Modern commentators take a more limited view: that Joel's reference to all flesh refers in this instance to everyone in Israel (Wolff; Watts; Crenshaw; Barton). In this sense, the spirit being given to all points to the direct communication that the chosen people will have with God—going beyond current cultic practices, even if these practices are referenced elsewhere in the book (Achtemeier).

We next read that 'your sons and daughters will prophesy'. Radak suggests that this refers to those like Samuel who prophesied in childhood, while for

John Gill, the reference to daughters brings to mind the four daughters of Philip the evangelist noted in Acts 21:9. For Cyril of Jerusalem, the fourth-century theologian, Joel's promise is a reminder that 'The Holy Spirit is no respecter of persons, for he seeks not dignities but piety of the soul' (*Catechetical Lecture* 27:19 [Ferreiro]). Not surprisingly, in the Reformation period, Luther took this to mean that 'All will be teachers and priests of God' (106). Calvin, however, disagrees; not everyone will be a prophet—but in comparison to ancient times, the gift would be more common. The spirit is given to the people here not to inspire obedience, as seen in Ezekiel 36, but to indicate that this will be a nation of prophets, reconfiguring the relationship with and access to God; this is, then, a challenge to the privileging of certain individuals (Wolff).

Verse 28 concludes by noting that the old men will dream dreams, and the young men will see visions. Julian of Eclanum notes that dreams are looked down upon in Deut. 13:1–5; why are they here a gift from God? Both are Scripture—which means sometimes dreams can have merit if there is testimony to corroborate them, but otherwise they should be rejected. Luther, meanwhile, comments that the revelation of the Holy Spirit was needed in this way at this time, but revelation is now available through Scripture—and we do not need the same signs that were then needed. Wesley disagrees; the dreaming of dreams was fulfilled in the prophet's day but is also now available to all (cf. Pusey). Contemporary scholars have focused on what these various forms of inspiration say about Israel's relationship with God rather than the forms themselves. As Crenshaw notes, 'The significance lies in the immediacy with which all of them relate to YHWH, rather than in the different modes of inspiration' (165).

Because of its use in the NT, and especially the quotation in Acts 2, this verse has had a significant afterlife in religious and cultural contexts. As noted earlier, early church leaders cited this verse often, and it was formative for the early church in terms of language and ideas (Dodd 1952). Beyond invoking this text to discuss the giving of the spirit, this verse has also been used to criticize the church and its exclusion of women—examples of this include the Montanists of the second–third centuries CE and the later Anabaptist movement (Trevett 1995). Pentecostals have likewise drawn on this verse to advocate for women in ministry as well as the gift of prophecy and the significance of the Holy Spirit in the contemporary church (Robinson and Ruff 2012; cf. Peterson 2017).

The imagery of this verse has also been picked up in broader cultural contexts. George Bernard Shaw used the idea of 'dreaming dreams' to speak of artists and thinkers (*Man and Superman*; *Geneva*; see Tiemeyer 2017). Further, in Dryden's *Absalom and Achitophel*, 'Achitophel urges Absalom to rebel against his father, David, by (anachronistically) applying Joel's words to his surrogate, calling him "the young men's vision, and the old men's dream'" (Freedman and Willoughby 1992: 406).

This verse has also been fertile ground for composers and musicians. Lelia (C.H.) Morris (b. 1862) wrote a hymn entitled 'A Tidal Wave Is Drawing Near', which speaks of the gospel being taken around the world. She draws on Joel 2 in a verse that states:

> A tidal wave of gospel power by prophets long foretold,
> When God his Spirit shall outpour upon the young and old;
> Your daughters and your sons shall prophesy with courage bold,
> 'Tis coming, 'tis coming, 'tis coming by and by.

In this instance, the imagery of Joel 2:28 is transposed to an imminent future, describing a time when the message of Christianity is shared by those prophets filled with God's spirit—young and old, daughters and sons.

2:29

The description of the outpouring of God's spirit continues in verse 29, where we read that this will include male and female slaves. Most readers have understood this as a continuation of the inclusive language of the previous verse, demonstrating the universal nature of this outpouring (Pusey; Bewer). Within this, some have offered more specific readings. The medieval Jewish interpreters suggested that this refers to slaves who embrace the Torah (Ibn Ezra) or those who voluntarily come to the aid of Israel (Radak). Luther, meanwhile, takes this as a 'very obvious passage against the ghostly papist priesthood' (108). Some modern commentators see this reference to servants and slaves as pointing to social upheaval and revolution (Wolff). Indeed, Joel's vision of a world that overcomes unjust power dynamics continues to inspire readers in the present around gender, class, and other issues (Claassens 2014a).

2:30–31

Verses 30–31 offer striking imagery, with the former declaring that God will show 'portents in the heavens and on the earth, blood and fire and columns of smoke'. The arresting imagery continues in verse 31 as we read that the sun will be darkened and the moon turned to blood before the coming of the great day of the LORD. It is not immediately clear how this relates to the giving of the spirit in verses 28–29, and interpreters approach these verses in various ways (see Barton). One approach focuses on intertextual connections, particularly in the NT. A number of early Christian readers saw this imagery as connected with the events surrounding Jesus's death as outlined in Matt. 27:45–54, an episode that also upset the order of the natural world (Cyril of Alexandria; Theodore of Mopsuestia; cf. Pusey). Luther takes the reference to fire as another chance to connect this text with Pentecost and the tongues of fire in Acts 2:3, while others point out that the imagery of the moon turning to blood recurs in Rev. 6:12.

Another approach understands this imagery as relating to cosmic and earthly signs accompanying the coming of the day of the LORD (Achtemeier). Some Jewish readers understood these signs as figurative prophecies of warning (Rambam), while in the Christian tradition, a common trope is that these are signs of the last days and the consummation of the world (Basil the Great, *Homilies on the Hexaemeron* 6.4 [Ferreiro]; Darby). Naturalistic readings have also been offered as readers have tried to describe this imagery in terms of natural events; thus, pillars of cloud are the byproducts of volcanos, the sun going dark is an eclipse, and columns of smoke can refer to fires (Ewald). Finally, another common approach has been to understand this as imagery related to the devastation of warfare (Crenshaw). Interpreters have thus connected these verses to war with Gog and Magog (Radak), the conflict between Hezekiah and the Assyrians (Julian of Eclanum), and the destruction of Jerusalem (Gill; Wesley).

2:32

The chapter concludes by noting that everyone who calls on the name of the LORD will be saved, and in Mount Zion and Jerusalem will be those who escape (2:32). In the Palestinian Talmud, this verse is used as proof that God hears the cries of his people everywhere (y. Ber. 9.1). Christian engagement with this verse has been shaped by the fact that the apostle Paul uses Joel 2:32 in Rom. 10:13 (and perhaps 1 Cor. 1:2) when speaking of the universal availability of salvation to all who call on the name of the Lord (Rodgers 2017). Drawing on Paul, Augustine sees in Joel a reference to the future inclusion of Gentiles (*Sermon 56.1* [Ferreiro]), while Jerome does likewise, quoting Gal. 3:28 to reinforce the inclusive nature of the gospel. For Luther, this verse indicates that all the elements in the preceding verses point to the revelation of the Gospel and the ingathering of all peoples (cf. Wesley). Calvin offers a more nuanced reading. Noting that Joel is cited by Paul in Romans 10 referring to Gentiles, Calvin suggests that Paul takes Joel's words differently from what the prophet originally intended. This same idea is found in later interpreters as well: while the prophet Joel refers to the deliverance of Israel, the language allows for it to be used in broader ways by Paul and others to include Gentiles (Bewer; Wolff; Crenshaw).

The verse concludes by noting that some will escape in Mount Zion and Jerusalem. The allusion to those who escape has been understood as referring to a remnant, other examples of which can be found throughout Scripture and history (Rashi; Calvin; Pusey). The language is very similar to that found in Obad 17, and one suggestion is that Joel here draws on and reworks the material from Obadiah (Bewer; Wolff; Sweeney; cf. the commentary on Obad 17).

———

Joel 2 plays an important role in the liturgical traditions of both Judaism and Christianity. Joel 2:15–27 serves as the *haftarah* in Ashkenazic tradition for Shabbat Shuvah, along with Hos. 14:2–10 (see also commentary on Hosea 14). Shabbat Shuvah takes its name from the call to return in Hos. 14:1, and it is the Sabbath that occurs between Rosh Hashanah and Yom Kippur, focused on repentance and return. As Fishbane notes, 'Both Hos. 14:5–8 and Joel 2:17–27 give unequivocal testimony to the divine blessings that may follow personal and public acts of contrition and, in so doing, provide models for future behavior' (2002: 281).

Joel 2 also features prominently in Christian liturgy. In the Revised Common Lectionary, Joel 2:1–2, 12–17 is read during Lent on Ash Wednesday, where it is found alongside Isa. 58:1–12, Ps. 51:1–17, 2 Cor. 5:20b–6:10, and Matt. 6:1–6, 16–21 (see Achtemeier). All of these texts speak of repentance and reconciliation, but the readings from Isaiah and Matthew in particular share much in common with Joel 2, including references to trumpets, true repentance, fasting, and prayer. Joel 2:21–27 is also read on Thanksgiving Day in both the United States and Canada in Year B, where it is read alongside Ps. 126 and Matt. 6:25–33, with the former speaking of Zion's fortunes being restored. Finally, Joel 2:23–32 is the Old Testament reading for Proper 25 (Year C, Season after Pentecost), along with Ps. 65; Sir. 35:12–17; Jer. 14:7–10, 19–22; 2 Tim. 4:6–8, 16–18; and Luke 18:9–14. A number of these readings highlight God's care for and responsiveness to all people, a theme that resonates with Joel's promise of the spirit being poured out on all flesh.

Joel 3

The book of Joel concludes with an oracle that speaks about the restoration of Judah and Jerusalem, along with God's judgment on the nations. The threat of catastrophe earlier in the book seems to be reversed in this final chapter as God comes to the rescue of his people (Prinsloo). A key feature of this chapter is that it has a number of resonances with other biblical texts, notably Obadiah, Amos, and Isaiah (Müller 2008). Readers have also noted that the chapter has apocalyptic and eschatological overtones (Plöger 1968; Hadjiev 2020). For these and other reasons, many modern readers see the material from the latter part of the book, including chapter 3, as a later addition (Barton; Jeremias 2007), though others advocate for a broad literary unity (Wolff; Bergler 1988; Assis).

English translations follow a different versification than Hebrew traditions. Because of the different ordering of Joel 2 (see comments in chapter 2), what is offered as chapter 3 in English translations is chapter 4 in Hebrew traditions. This commentary follows English translations in referring to this as chapter 3.

3:1

Chapter 3 begins on a hopeful note. Verse 1 points to a time ('in those days and at that time …') when God will restore the fortunes (*'ashuv et-shevut*) of Judah and Jerusalem. However, from antiquity the phrase 'restore the fortunes' has also been understood as 'return the captivity' of exiles, a reading that can be found in the Greek LXX, the Aramaic Targum, and the Latin Vulgate. Medieval

Hosea, Joel, and Obadiah Through the Centuries, First Edition. Bradford A. Anderson.
© 2024 John Wiley & Sons Ltd. Published 2024 by John Wiley & Sons Ltd.

Jewish commentators followed this reading and understood the referent in various ways. According to Radak, this is eschatological, and the return from captivity refers to the Messianic era. Ibn Ezra, meanwhile, suggests that this alludes to the reign of Jehoshaphat when neighboring nations brought tribute and captives were returned (2 Chr. 17:10ff).

Early Christian readers likewise understood this as referring to captivity and offered various interpretations. Jerome translates the phrase in question as 'convert the captivity', indicating that Jews who have converted will be part of a remnant in the last days. Theodore of Mopsuestia, meanwhile, continues his more historical reading, suggesting that this refers to the return of captives from Babylon. These various trajectories would continue in later Christian interpretations. Martin Luther, for example, follows Jerome in reading this chapter as relating to the Kingdom of Christ and the church. The terrible thing that will come on the nations is actually the gospel, and enemies will become friends. Luther thus interprets the reference to captivity as pointing to redemption from the captivity of death. John Calvin offers both a literal and spiritual reading: this restoration speaks of the return of the Judahites from captivity but also points to the Kingdom of Christ—in both senses this is about God's redemption of the world. John Gill echoes Radak in suggesting this is about the end times and the future restoration of Israel (cf. Darby). John Wesley, the founder of Methodism, moves in the opposite direction, positing that this simply refers to the return of the Jews from exile during the time of Cyrus. Meanwhile, modern translations and commentators are in broad agreement that this should be read as 'restore the fortunes', pointing to a great restoration similar to that seen in Zeph. 3:20 (Wolff; cf. NRSV; NIV).

3:2

In verse 2, we see that the restoration of Judah and Jerusalem is linked to judgment on 'the nations' (Ewald; Harper). God, we are told, will gather the nations in the valley of Jehoshaphat, and there he will render judgment on them. Because of the eschatological and apocalyptic tone of this chapter, a common approach throughout history has been to connect the events here recounted with that of Gog and/or Magog in Ezekiel 38 (for more on these traditions, see Tooman 2011; Strine 2017). Radak, for example, takes verse 2 as a reference to those nations that are inspired to join Gog and Magog against Israel. Gill suggests that this refers to the Turks, who he says are also spoken of as Gog and Magog in Ezekiel. E. B. Pusey takes a broader approach, though still eschatological in nature, indicating that this points to all nations working under the Anti-Christ against God and his church. Contemporary commentators note that 'the nations' is used here as a broad category, a common designation in Jewish writings of the postexilic period (Barton; Timmer 2015).

Of more interest has been the identification of the 'valley of Jehoshaphat'. Some suggest that the reference to Jehoshaphat is meant to encourage the people and remind them that God will provide for them as he did during Jehoshaphat's time (Calvin). Taking this further, others posit that the Valley of Beracah, the location of Jehoshaphat's famous victory over nations including Edom in 2 Chr. 20, is the intended location or is at least being invoked in some way (Ewald; Pusey; Sweeney). Another tradition, which seems to have developed in the first few centuries BCE, is that this refers to the Kidron Valley near Jerusalem (Eusebius; see Merx 1879). This may be related to the Christian idea that Christ's return will take place on the Mount of Olives, and so the general area was understood to have an eschatological connection (Nicholas of Lyra). Indeed, Aquinas uses 3:2 as part of his discussion of the last judgment; while there is much we do not know about the last judgment, he notes, we cannot rule out the valley of Jehoshaphat as the location (*ST* XP, q. 88, a. 4). Finally, others have suggested that no specific location is intended—or if a location is in mind, it is otherwise unknown. The name Jehoshaphat is a combination of the name YHWH and the word 'to judge'. Thus, some traditions simply refer to this as the valley of God's judgment, eschewing the reference to the proper name of the king (Targum; cf. Rashi; Gill). Indeed, modern readers by and large take the 'Valley of Jehoshaphat' as symbolic, pointing to God's judgment on the nations (Wellhausen; Wolff; Barton; Crenshaw).

The connection of this verse with the Kidron Valley remains strong in both Jewish and Christian traditions. On a wall at the base of the Mount of Olives, which is now a vast Jewish cemetery, a plaque commemorates verses 1–2 in both Hebrew and English (Figure 34). Here the connection of the Kidron Valley with the valley of Jehoshaphat is made explicit—and the presumed eschatological significance of this location has made this the most famous and sought-after Jewish burial ground in the world.

Verse 2 concludes by noting that God will judge the nations because they have scattered his people and divided his land. While for many this relates to the Babylonian captivity and destruction, other interpretations have been put forward. The scattering of the people has been understood by some as a reference to the Roman leader Titus and his siege of Jerusalem in 70 CE (Radak; Gill). Others have read this eschatologically: according to Abarbanel, this refers to the future battle with God and Magog, which he understands as a war between Christians and Muslims for Eretz Israel; as such, these two groups will be punished for trying to divide the holy land (see *Miqra'ot Gedolot*).

FIGURE 34   Plaque with text from Joel 3:1–2 (Heb. 4:1–2) at the Mount of Olives Jewish Cemetery, Jerusalem.

Used with permission from Jason Fiedler.

3:3

Verse 3 continues the description of the nations challenging God and his people, offering further context for why judgment is forthcoming (Simkins 2016). Here we read that the nations have cast lots for the people, traded boys for a prostitute, and sold girls for wine. The imagery of casting lots is also found in Obadiah 11 in relation to Edom and Jerusalem, which is another point of connection between the two books (Wolff). There has been disagreement as to how to understand the reference to trading a boy for a prostitute. The LXX renders this as 'gave the boys to whores', a reading that is followed by Jerome. The Targum suggests that a boy is traded for a harlot's hire, indicating that it is the price that is the key issue (cf. Ibn Ezra; Crenshaw). Some of the Sages used this verse to illustrate the horrors that followed the Babylonian conquest of 70 CE, including the selling of children and separation of families (Lam. Rab. 1.46). Many Christian readers have focused on the fact that defenseless persons are sold for a low price, the proceeds of which are then spent for vile purposes by Israel's enemies (Theodore of Mopsuestia; Calvin; Wolff).

The reference to 'casting lots' in this verse has been a point of departure for reflection on the relation of this practice to gambling—and the permissibility of the latter in the contemporary world. Many such discussions point to the fact that casting lots was a way of making decisions in the ancient world, and was even used as a way of discerning the divine will, as happened with the early church (Acts 1:23–26). Thus, casting lots is often determined to be fundamentally different from gambling—even if in the case of Joel 3:3 it is understood to be put to evil purposes (Gambling vs. casting lots 2004).

3:4

Verse 4 begins with a reference to specific nations and peoples: 'What are you to me, O Tyre and Sidon, and all the regions of Philistia? Are you paying me back for something?' A recurring question is why Tyre, Sidon, and Philistia are mentioned. (The LXX offers a different reading of the second half of the verse, speaking to Tyre, Sidon, and all 'Galilee of the Gentiles' [cf. 1 Macc. 5:15].) In premodern contexts, a number of readings were suggested. Rashi points to the gift of cities that Solomon gave to Hiram, king of Tyre, and with which the king was displeased (1 Kgs 9:11); here the payback refers to Tyre's perceived mistreatment in a previous era (cf. Ibn Ezra). Others posit that this refers to the time of the Assyrians and Babylonians when the neighbors listed here also made incursions into the holy land along with these larger empires (Julian of Eclanum; Nicholas of Lyra). Radak interprets the question as rhetorical, castigating these neighbors for plundering the land for no reason other than their own advantage (cf. Cyril of Alexandria; Calvin).

In the modern era, scholars have noted that the Phoenicians and Philistines—peoples connected to western and coastal areas near Judah—were known to be part of slave trading in the Persian era, to which verse 4 might refer; for many, this is an indication that verse 4 and those following may be a later addition (Harper; Wolff; Barton). Sidon was destroyed by Artaxerxes III of Persia in 343 BCE and Tyre by Alexander in 332 BCE—so 343 BCE is seen by some as the latest date for the compilation of the book (Achtemeier). The verse concludes by noting that God will turn the deeds of these nations back on their own heads and will do so swiftly. Similar language of 'returning deeds upon your heads' is found in Obadiah 15, which is another point of contact between these prophetic books (Crenshaw).

3:5–6

The list of transgressions continues in verse 5, where God states that 'my' silver and gold have been taken, and the rich treasures carried off into 'your' temples. Some readers have asserted that this relates to the vessels taken from the

Jerusalem Temple, likely during the Babylonian conquest (Jerome; Abarbanel; Luther; Assis). Others speculate that this refers not to the Temple but to other riches stolen from the people in the land and taken away to foreign palaces (Harper; Pusey). A key issue noted by some is that the silver and gold are God's, just as the land and the people also belong to him (Wolff).

Verse 6 outlines a further offense: these enemies have sold the people of Judah and Jerusalem to the Greeks. The term used for Greeks (*yevanim*) is one that is generally used in later biblical texts to refer to Greek-speaking lands (Wolff). Many commentators connect this verse to verse 4, as the Tyrians and other merchants near the sea were believed to have sold Israelites to foreign nations (Cyril of Alexandria; Nicholas of Lyra). Modern interpreters have noted the well-established slave trade involving these nations and Greece (Harper; Pusey; Watts). The verse concludes by noting the result: the people have been taken so far from home that they cannot return (Radak; cf. Calvin; Wesley).

3:7–8

The following verses foretell a reversal of fortune: God will rouse those who have been taken to faraway lands to leave those places, and these deeds will be brought back upon the heads of the perpetrators (v. 7). There have been some that have read this reference to 'rousing' in a spiritual manner; Luther, for example, says that the rousing of the people is the revelation of the gospel through preaching. However, most understand this as indicating that those who have been forced to leave the holy land will return and have retribution on those who have inflicted this on them (Ibn Ezra; Jerome).

Verse 8 offers more detail on this change in circumstances as God says that he will 'sell your sons and your daughters into the hand of the people of Judah, and they will sell them to the Sabeans, to a nation far away' (3:8). The identity and location of the Sabeans (*sheba'im*) have interested interpreters through the centuries. The LXX obscures this by rendering the term as 'captivity', suggesting that their sons and daughters will be sold as captives far away but without naming the location. In Jewish tradition, Rashi says that this relates to the children of Sheba, without offering further context, while Radak and Abarbanal posit that this refers to a location southeast of Israel, perhaps Cush or part of Arabia. In early Christian tradition, various possibilities were put forward, including India and Ethiopia, the latter because of the connection between Solomon and the Queen of Sheba (Jerome; Julian of Eclanum). Beginning in the early modern period, a consensus began to emerge that this refers to some part of Arabia, likely southern or southwest Arabia (Luther; Gill, quoting Strabo; cf. Ewald; Harper; Pusey; Wolff; Barton; Sweeney).

3:9

In verse 9, the prophet offers a proclamation to be made among the nations: prepare for war; stir up the warriors and soldiers. This call to war has been understood in various ways, in part because it is not clear whether the call to preparation is directed at the nations or if the nations are being informed of Judah being stirred for battle (see Crenshaw and Barton for discussion). Some traditions understand this as the former, with the nations being assembled for their eventual defeat by Israel's God (Calvin; Harper). Mezudath David, the work of the early modern Jewish rabbi David Altschuler, draws on the associations made earlier in the chapter to suggest that this refers to the war of Gog against Jerusalem. Abarbanel proposes that the term 'arouse' suggests the resurrection of the dead: even the enemies of Israel will be raised up for this final battle. Alternatively, others have posited that this is a call to Judah and Jerusalem to prepare for battle, with the nations being made aware of this (Gill). In the modern era, scholars such as von Rad have understood the call to prepare for war as indicative of a holy war, invoking the deity in order to sanctify a battle (cf. Crenshaw).

3:10

The call to arms continues in verse 10. Here the prophet gives instructions to 'Beat your plowshares into swords and your pruning hooks into spears'. Tools normally used for farming are to be turned into instruments of war— this is also clear in the LXX, which offers the image of sickles being turned into barbed lances (cf. Targum; Achtemeier). As Cyril of Alexandria notes, 'this [is] the time not for farming but for settling accounts for God, who has been dishonored' (309; cf. Jerome; Theodore of Mopsuestia). The imagery here is very close to that found in Isa. 2:4 and Mic. 4:3, where swords are turned into plowshares. Readers have offered various reasons for this reversal. According to Radak, the message from Joel is earlier—these weapons are needed because the war will be great. Afterward, they will do the opposite, as Isaiah prophesied.

Luther, meanwhile, cites the words of Jesus in Luke 22:36 to suggest that this imagery is to be understood spiritually and metaphorically in Joel, while the invocation in Isaiah should be read literally. Modern scholars tend to see this as an intentional contrast with Isa. 2 and Mic. 4; this is not an original expression from Joel but an ironic use of prophetic tradition (Wolff; Crenshaw). Simkins (1991) notes that this does not necessarily mean this idea is drawn from written traditions; Joel uses different terminology to the other prophetic voices, which might suggest this was a reworking of oral traditions.

Verse 10 concludes with a note that the weak will say, 'I am strong.' According to Abarbanel, even the weakest in society will see themselves as strong so that they can participate in the battle. Harper concurs, glossing this as 'Let the coward be a hero!' (135). A number of Christian readers have interpreted this spiritually: God's battles are fought by the weak through suffering, as seen in 2 Cor. 12:10 (John Cassian, 'Conference 7.5.8–9' [Ferreiro]; Luther; Gill). This imagery ('and now, let the weak say, "I am strong"') is also used in the Christian worship song 'Give Thanks with a Grateful Heart', written in 1978 by Henry Smith (Hosanna! Music). This use mirrors the spiritual reading noted earlier as a sign of God's working through weakness.

3:11–12

Verse 11 calls the nations to come quickly and gather. The first term (*'usu*) is used only here in the HB; Rashi notes that this can be understood as 'hasten' but speculates that the word actually relates to the homonym 'iron', giving the sense that the nations are gathered like a block of iron. The verse ends with a call for YHWH to 'bring down your warriors' (3:11). From antiquity it has been noted that this can be understood in two ways: either God leading his warriors 'down' into battle or God bringing down and defeating his foes (Jerome; cf. Gill). The Targum follows the latter understanding, indicating that God will destroy the might of the warriors. This reading is also taken in up in other traditions, including the Vulgate (cf. Rashi; Wolff). Others suggest this is a request for God to call down his own warriors, and both Jewish and Christian readers have understood this as a reference to God's mighty angels (Ibn Ezra; Pusey; Rudolph 1971).

The call to the nations continues in 3:12 as they are instructed to rouse themselves and come to the valley of Jehoshaphat. There, God says, 'I will sit to judge all the neighbouring nations.' Readers have long noted the connection between the name Jehoshaphat ('the LORD judges') and the judgment of God in this verse (Isho'dad of Merv). Some have offered spiritual readings; Luther claims

FIGURE 35   *Thomas Seddon, Jerusalem and valley of Jehoshaphat from the Hill of Evil Counsel (1854–55).*

Photo credit: © Tate.

that this refers to the nations being gathered by the word of God. However, more common is the assertion that this points to God's condemnation and punishment of the nations who have violated his land and people (Wolff). As noted in verse 2, a popular interpretation is that the valley of Jehoshaphat refers to the Kidron Valley near Jerusalem, and this idea is found in artistic representations such as Thomas Seddon's nineteenth-century painting, 'Jerusalem and valley of Jehoshaphat from the Hill of Evil Counsel' (Figure 35).

The nineteenth-century American pastor and hymn writer D. S. Warner used several verses from Joel 3, including verse 12, as the inspiration for his song entitled 'The Valley of Judgment'. Here the notion of God's judgment on the nations is interpreted spiritually as a call to hear God's truth and respond to the gospel:

> God is sitting in the awful valley,
> Near His final judgment seat;
> And His present mighty truth is calling
> Every nation at His feet.

Harking back to the imagery of verse 10, we see in the third stanza of Warner's hymn that the shaping of the plowshares into implements of war are also spiritualized as these are envisioned as 'holy weapons':

> Bring the mighty down to utter nothing,
> Let the weakest say, 'I'm strong,'
> Beat your plowshares into holy weapons,
> Press the battle'gainst the wrong.

3:13

There is a change of addressees in verse 13 as the text now speaks to the people of Judah. The people are told to 'put in the sickle, for the harvest is ripe. Go in, tread, for the wine press is full. The vats overflow for their wickedness is great'. Here agricultural and harvest imagery is used to describe warfare and punishment (Theodore of Mopsuestia; Rashi). Radak suggests that the overflowing vats refer to bloodshed. Clarifying this metaphorical language, the Targum renders the verse with 'Put the sword into them, for the time of their end has arrived; go down and tread their warrior dead like grapes'. Calvin and Wesley both emphasize God's eventual defeat of Israel's enemies, whose wickedness has reached its 'full measure'. Modern commentators have noted that treading grapes is also used in the context of military imagery in Isa. 63:1–6 (Crenshaw). Indeed, if the first clause is understood as referring to a pruning knife used for harvesting grapes, then the entire verse can be understood as drawing on vintaging imagery (Achtemeier). Some contemporary readers have also highlighted the rhetoric of this verse, noting that it is hard to reconcile this harsh rhetoric with the imagery in 2:28 of the spirit being poured out on all flesh (Barton).

Although Joel's imagery of the harvest seems to imply warfare and punishment, Christian hymn writers have employed this language for their own rhetorical ends, notably in relation to evangelism and the spreading of the gospel. Eben Rexford's (d. 1916) song 'O Where Are the Reapers?' uses the imagery of both sickles and the harvest:

> O where are the reapers that garner in
> The sheaves of the good from the fields of sin?
> With sickles of truth must the work be done,
> And no one may rest till the 'harvest home.'

Rexford and others put Joel into conversation with Jesus's declaration in Matt. 9:37 that 'the harvest is plentiful but the workers are few', drawing on the theme of harvest.

3:14

Verse 14 begins with a repeated phrase: 'Multitudes, Multitudes (*hamonim, hamonim*), in the valley of decision!' The term *hamonim* can be translated as 'multitudes' or as 'noise'. The LXX represents the latter, stating that 'noises rung out' (cf. Cyril of Alexandria). The Targum, meanwhile, suggests 'army upon army' (cf. Vulgate: 'Nations, nations!'). Calvin follows this reading, proposing that the prophet repeats 'Multitudes' as a herald. Harper brings the two ideas together, proffering 'multitudes roar', and speculating that this is giving a picture of the war cry of battle (cf. Crenshaw).

The second half of verse 14 continues by stating that 'the day of the LORD is near in the valley of decision'. While the exact meaning of the 'valley of decision' is not made clear, from the time of Eusebius this was understood to refer to the Kidron Valley, located between Jerusalem and the Mount of Olives. The reference to the day of the LORD reminds the reader of the use of this theme earlier in the book. As Wolff notes, the day of the LORD turns outward on Israel's enemies as opposed to the threats to Israel's well-being in previous uses in Joel. Here, within an eschatological framework, the day of the LORD is both judgment (on the nations) and salvation (for Israel) (Claassens 2014a). The Christian songwriter Michael Card uses Joel 3:14 in a song entitled 'Who Can Abide?' (1992), which speaks of the return of the Lord and the 'day' of his coming. Card draws on the imagery of the 'valley of decision', which he uses as a reference to judgment at the time of God's return and the 'final call'.

3:15

In verse 15 we are told that the sun and moon are darkened, and the stars withdraw their shining. Various reasons have been put forward to explain the darkening of these lights. In one rabbinic text, it is suggested that as a king extinguishes torches when in mourning, so God extinguishes the moon and stars when mourning for Israel (PesK 15.3 [Neusner]). Other readers understand this as relating to judgment in some way. According to Ibn Ezra, all becomes dark on the Day of Judgment. Abarbanel, meanwhile, explains this darkening as God stripping the heavenly princes of their power in his judgment. Jerome states that the lights are withheld as all of creation is frightened when seeing God's judgment.

Reformation and early modern readers understood this as figurative language but explained in various ways. For Luther, this speaks of the darkening of the sky during warfare, though it is used here metaphorically by the prophet. Gill reads this allegorically to refer to all those 'antichristian princes and nobles ... and clergy of all ranks' who have 'lost their glory'. Modern interpreters have noted that this language is very similar to that found in 2:10, which also occurs in the context of the day of the Lord. Simkins thus suggests that 'Yahweh's judgment on the nations corresponds to his destruction of the locusts' (1993: 449).

3:16

In verse 16 the day of the Lord imagery continues as we read that the Lord roars from Zion while the heavens and earth shake. The Lord, however, is a refuge for his people, a stronghold for the people of Israel. Calvin writes that God is depicted here as a lion protecting his people. Indeed, the image of the Lord roaring is similar to that found in Amos 1:2 and Jer. 25:30, and scholars have suggested that Joel may be drawing from these other traditions (Wolff). The heavens and earth shaking has been understood as God bringing retribution on the nations (Rashi) as the fear of the nations who quake before Israel's God (Ibn Ezra) or as a reference to an earthquake (Radak). For Luther, this points to the fact that all of creation witnesses to God's action.

3:17

The final section of the book outlines Judah's restoration and blessing. Here the dramatic action of the previous verses segues into a picture of peace and stability (Barton). Because of the idyllic language, some modern commentators see these final verses as coming from a later editor (Harper; Wolff).

In verse 17 we read that God will dwell in Zion, his holy mountain. The Targum alters this so that it speaks of God causing his *shekinah* to dwell in Zion. Christian readers, meanwhile, have interpreted this spiritually.

Luther and others understand this as referring to God dwelling in the spiritual Jerusalem and the church (cf. Gill; Wesley). Calvin, however, reiterates that God is not limited to any one place, but he resides in Zion because of his covenant with Abraham. The verse concludes by noting that Jerusalem will be holy, and 'strangers shall never again pass through it'. For some readers, this indicates that Israel and Jerusalem will no longer suffer harm from strangers (Radak). Modern interpreters have noted that the exclusive tenor here seems to conflict with the generous pouring out of the spirit in 2:28–32 (Claassens 2014a; Simkins 2016).

3:18

The picture of restoration continues in verse 18, where we read that 'on that day the mountains shall drip sweet wine, the hills shall flow with milk'. The use of 'on that day' suggests to some an eschatological frame of reference (Crenshaw). Various interpretations have been put forward regarding the imagery of wine and milk. Some read this figuratively, as with Jerome, who sees here a reference to spiritual virtues and graces. Others understand this as physical abundance that comes from God (Theodore of Mopsuestia; Julian of Eclanum; Isho'dad of Merv; Calvin). Indeed, reading this in the context of the larger book, one can see here a reversal of the food shortage from earlier in the text (2:19–26) (Wolff). More recently, ecological readings have highlighted the role of the land in this restoration imagery. We see here that 'the non-human creation acts as a mediating voice between YHWH and the people … the earth is a conduit for the blessings of fertility or the sorrow of famine' (Marlow 2009: 156).

Verse 18 continues by noting that the stream beds of Judah will flow with water, and a fountain will come from the house of the LORD, and water the 'Wadi Shittim' (*nahal ha-shittim*). There has been considerable disagreement as to how to understand the final clause, as the word *shittim* is both the name of a place (east of the Jordan) and the word for acacias (Jerome; Wolff; cf. LXX: 'brook of rushes'). In relation to the latter, it has been suggested that this might refer to the Kidron Valley, which has been called the valley of Acacias (Achtemeier). Meanwhile, Rashi notes that while this can be understood literally to refer to the place Shittim, it can also be read figuratively, meaning that God will atone for the sin at Peor—worshipping Baal-Peor (Num. 25)—which in rabbinic tradition was blamed on the water of Shittim; this water will thus be renewed (cf. Jerome). Spiritual readings are also common: noting that Shittim is far from Jerusalem, a number of readers focus on the fact that this spring from the Temple will water far-off places, representing God's blessings going far and wide (Theodore of Mopsuestia; Calvin; Prinsloo). Christian readers have also interpreted this stream as Christ or the promise of the gospel (Nicholas of Lyra; Luther; Gill; Wesley). Still others note that the Wadi Shittim cannot be identified and that, as the valley of Jehoshaphat noted earlier in the chapter, this may be a symbolic name and reference (Barton).

3:19–20

The theme of 'the nations' returns in verse 19, though here focus lies specifically with Egypt and Edom. Egypt will be a desolation and Edom a wilderness 'because of the violence done to the people of Judah, in whose land they have shed innocent blood'. In a number of rabbinic texts, a connection is made between the references to violence and the shedding of blood. In Sifre to Deuteronomy, we read that all acts of violence perpetrated by the nations of the world on Israel are seen as though they have shed innocent blood (333.4; cf. Gen. Rab. [Neusner]). In Christian tradition, commentators like Gill extend the shedding of innocent blood to include the persecution of Christians, such as the Waldenses and Albigenses.

Why are these nations singled out? According to Radak, we can identify Egypt with Ishmael (and thus the Arabs), while Edom represents Rome. Mezudath David, meanwhile, argues that Egypt was the first country to oppress the Israelites, and Edom was the last; we thus have here a representation of Israel's enemies from first to last. Abarbanel likewise connects Edom with Rome, suggesting that the innocent blood refers to the destruction of the second Temple by the Romans. Similar approaches are found in Christianity. While aware of figurative readings in Jewish tradition, Jerome suggests a literal understanding of Egypt and Edom makes the most sense. Pusey agrees and offers extended examples of the ruination that came upon Egypt and Edom. Wolff, meanwhile, believes that Edom and Egypt are used for heuristic purposes as representative of Israel's enemies. Readers have also noted several points of contact with the portrayal of Edom in Obadiah. For example, Obadiah 20 speaks of the desolation of Edom (Isho'dad of Merv), while Edom is also associated with violence in Obadiah 10 (Harper). Juxtaposed with Egypt and Edom, Joel 3:20 informs us that Judah and Jerusalem will be inhabited forever, for all generations, returning to the themes of restoration found in verses 17–18 (Radak).

3:21

The book concludes with an enigmatic reference to the avenging or cleansing of blood. The NRSV translates the verse as 'I will avenge their blood (*niqeti damam*), and I will not clear the guilty (*lo'-niqeti*), for the LORD dwells in Zion' (3:21). Readers have long wondered, however, whose blood is being avenged, and how this relates to the refusal to cleanse in the final clause (see Barton). We see this clearly in the ancient versions. The LXX understands this to say that God will avenge their blood, and this will not go unpunished. This reading seems to understand the blood as that shed by the nations, which will be avenged—perhaps pointing back to Egypt and Edom in verse 19 (Crenshaw). The Vulgate, meanwhile, interprets this as God saying he will cleanse their blood, which he had not cleansed. The implication here is that a more thorough cleansing of the people will accompany Israel's restoration (cf. Harper). We see these same trajectories at work in the history of interpretation. Rashi understands this verse to mean that even if God cleanses the nations of their other sins, he will not cleanse them of the bloodshed of the children of Judah. Wolff concurs, noting that God demonstrates that he is Israel's God by judging the nations. Calvin, meanwhile, follows the Vulgate's reading, arguing that God will cleanse that which he had not previously cleansed as part of Israel's ultimate restoration.

The book of Joel ends with a final proclamation that the LORD dwells in Zion. This has long been understood as having eschatological implications. According to the midrash Mekhilta to R. Ishmael, this speaks of the coming glory of Israel when God dwells in Zion and Judah is inhabited (Neusner). Taken together, the final verses can be understood as bringing closure to the book, speaking of Israel's agricultural and political restoration, and highlighting God's dwelling among his people (Assis 2013).

Obadiah: Introduction and Overview

At twenty-one verses, Obadiah is the shortest book in the Hebrew Bible. And yet, as far back as Jerome, it was noted that the book's difficulties seem to be in inverse proportion to its size ('quanto brevis est, tanto difficilis', Jerome [Migne] 1845: 1100). A number of key questions have played an integral role in the interpretation and use of Obadiah: What is the historical setting of this short work? How does Obadiah relate to other books in the canon of the Hebrew Bible? And how should one make sense of the message of the book, particularly the harsh language and imagery found in these verses directed toward Israel's neighbor Edom? This introduction offers a brief overview of the reception of Obadiah followed by a closer look at these key issues.

A Brief History of Obadiah's Interpretation

Obadiah is a part of the prophetic tradition of the Hebrew Bible, located in the Book of the Twelve, or the Minor Prophets. In the Hebrew MT, Obadiah is the fourth book of this collection, located between Amos and Jonah, while in the Greek LXX it is the fifth book in the Twelve, found between Joel and Jonah. The LXX and Aramaic Targum offer translations that are relatively close to the traditions passed down in the Hebrew of the Masoretic text. The Targum would go on to play a particularly important role in Jewish tradition, where it is often consulted and studied alongside the Hebrew text and the major commentators (see the rabbinic Bible, featuring the Aramaic Targum, in Figure 36).

Hosea, Joel, and Obadiah Through the Centuries, First Edition. Bradford A. Anderson.
© 2024 John Wiley & Sons Ltd. Published 2024 by John Wiley & Sons Ltd.

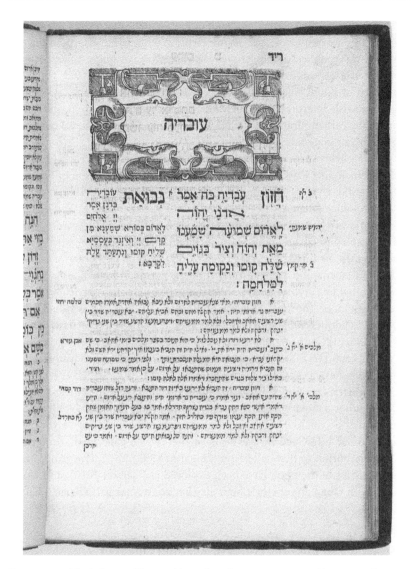

FIGURE 36 *Obadiah in Rabbinic Bible, with Hebrew text, Aramaic Targum, and commentaries.*

By permission of the Governors and Guardians of Marsh's Library © Marsh's Library.

Early rabbinic interpreters of Obadiah highlighted intertextual resonances between this work and the rest of the Hebrew Bible while also pointing out contemporary political ramifications of the text. Accordingly, links between Obadiah and Genesis (and thus Esau and Edom) are often noted, while the castigation of Edom is also seen as a cryptic reprimand of Rome, a common trope in Jewish interpretations of Edom. Such connections are found in the Talmud, the early midrashic text Genesis Rabbah, and the medieval commentator Rashi, among others.

Obadiah likewise received a fair amount of attention in the early Christian tradition, including works from patristic theologians such as Jerome, Theodore of Mopsuestia, Cyril of Alexandria, and Ephrem the Syrian. While historical and grammatical matters are discussed, the Church Fathers—and, indeed, their medieval successors—also read Obadiah with an eye toward spiritual and Christological issues, with many interpreting the book (or parts of it) in figurative fashion as relating to the church and the ultimate victory of God.

In the Reformation and the early modern period, commentators such as Martin Luther began to associate Obadiah more closely with particular historical circumstances. The most common of these was the idea that Obadiah makes reference to Edom's complicity in the events of 587 BCE, where Jerusalem fell to the Babylonians (Luther). This concern for historical context would dominate for several centuries as scholars read Obadiah with an eye toward historical and contextual issues.

The modern era witnessed further questions reflecting the current state of biblical studies: scholars began to question the unity of the book (Wellhausen); form critics began to investigate the possible *Sitz im Leben* of the book (Wolff); those interested in the Book of the Twelve gave further attention to its contribution to that collection (Nogalski 1993); the literary and poetic characteristics of the book have been explored (Anderson 2010); and works dealing with Obadiah's rhetoric have also begun to emerge (O'Brien 2008).

Historical and Literary Issues in Reading Obadiah

One of the more intriguing aspects of the reception history of Obadiah is how readers have understood the book's historical setting and the circumstances to which it might refer. The book itself gives few overt clues as to its setting or origins.

A common reading in early Jewish and rabbinic tradition was that this book represents the words of the character named Obadiah found in 1 Kings 18 during the time of the prophet Elijah. A servant of King Ahab, this Obadiah assisted the prophets of YHWH by hiding and feeding them during a time of persecution by Ahab's wife Jezebel; in this case the prophet and his message would be situated in the ninth century BCE. This interpretation is widely represented in Jewish tradition, including the Babylonian Talmud, Josephus (*Ant.* 8:316), and Rashi. If Obadiah was from the time of Ahab, this would make him the earliest of the Twelve Prophets. Why, then, was he not placed first in the collection of the Twelve? A Talmudic tradition holds that it was because Obadiah was a proselyte, and the others were Israelites by birth (b. Sanh. 39b; cf. Abarbanel). A number of visual representations of Obadiah throughout history have associated him with the steward of 1 Kings, including relief sculptures in Amiens Cathedral, which depict Obadiah alongside both Elijah and the king (Figure 37).

The Church Fathers were aware of this association with the character in 1 Kings, and some put this reading forward as an option (Jerome). However, other early Christian commentators place Obadiah in the period of Assyrian dominance, presuming the prophet to be a contemporary of Hosea, Amos, and Isaiah, an assumption likely made because of the book's placement toward the

Figure 37   Obadiah and Elijah before King Ahab; Amiens Cathedral, France.
Used with permission from Stuart Whatling.

beginning of the Book of the Twelve (Ephrem the Syrian). Still others suggest a date closer to the destruction of Jerusalem at the Babylonian conquest (Theodore of Mopsuestia).

In the Reformation and the early modern periods, those commenting on Obadiah began to ask further questions concerning the historical setting and context of the book. The Reformation commentators, for example, began to look for a more particular historical context in which to contextualize the book of Obadiah. Martin Luther was convinced that Obadiah prophesied after the Babylonian captivity and believed Obadiah to be using Jeremiah as a source. Drawing on parallels with Ps. 137:7, Luther sees the destruction of Jerusalem at the heart of Obadiah's message. He writes: 'Against the Edomites he prophesies that the vengeance of God would occur because the Edomites were quite delighted at the time of the Babylonian captivity that the Jews were being grievously afflicted and led into captivity. Yet, because the Edomites were brothers of the Jews, they should have showed compassion' (194). John Calvin was not as comfortable offering a specific historical context. Instead, he speaks of a general era when the Edomites 'rose up against the Israelites and distressed them by many annoyances'. Like Luther, Calvin also cites Psalm 137 and says that it is unlikely that Obadiah was as early as Isaiah. But the most he is willing to concede is that Obadiah may have been a contemporary of Jeremiah. Nevertheless, when Luther and Calvin are taken together, we see a noticeable shift in situating Obadiah nearer to the Babylonian conquest.

The commentators of the ensuing centuries would continue to focus on historical aspects of the text, narrowing in on issues of authorship, redaction, and dating. A variety of settings were put forward that placed Obadiah in contexts ranging from the ninth to the fifth centuries BCE. Some scholars in the nineteenth century held to a date on the earlier end of this spectrum (Keil; Pusey). Nevertheless, the influence of such readings was not widespread; in more contemporary works, the preponderance of interpreters would situate the prophet near the beginning of the exilic era, not far removed from the events of 587 BCE (Rudolph 1971; Fohrer 1975; Wolff; Renkema; Raabe).

Further readings have emerged over the years that have called into question some of the historical assumptions related to the interpretation of the book. Bartlett and others have questioned whether Edom played any role in the events of 587 BCE, arguing that Obadiah portrays a widespread misrepresentation of the Edomites (Bartlett 1982; Ben Zvi 2005). While some are sympathetic to this view and to Bartlett's concerns, they maintain that Obadiah must be reacting to *something* and most revert to the events surrounding 587 BCE as the most likely reason for the castigation of Edom (Raabe; Renkema).

Issues of structure and unity have long played an important role in readings of Obadiah. While the unity of Obadiah was assumed in premodern exegesis, the Church Fathers, as well as Calvin and Luther, noted a tension by interpreting verses 17–21 as eschatological and referring to the church as opposed to their more 'plain sense' engagement with verses 1–16. This is especially clear in the work of Luther, who finds the final verses of the book so difficult that he sees a figurative reading as the only plausible interpretive option.

This issue was taken in new directions in modern scholarship. The German orientalist Johann Gottfried Eichorn (1824) questioned the unity of the book, locating the prophet after 587 BCE, but positing that the final verses (17–21) were added much later, at the time of Alexander Jannaeus. Ewald (1875) would offer a reconstruction based on an exilic prophet that drew on a number of older oracles (cf. Driver 1909). Since Wellhausen, scholars have noted two distinct sections in the book: verses 1–14, 15b dealing with Edom's punishment and coming from the prophet, and verses 15a, 16–21 concerning Israel's restoration in the context of the nations, added at a later date (cf. Duhm 1916; Wolff), with further suggestions that verses 19–21 might be yet another addition (Bewer). Many such readings posit that the first section of the book comes from the exilic period (from the prophet himself), while the final section(s) come sometime later in the postexilic era, which would suggest more than one hand in its creation (Barton; Jeremias 2007). Assis (2016) has argued for a threefold division of the book, where the three sections represent different historical periods but each of these from the life of the prophet: verses 1–9 reflect a setting before the destruction of Jerusalem; verses 10–14, 15b speak to the events of 587 BCE and were written shortly after; and verses 15 a, 16–21 were written not long after the previous section, as with the hope of restoration as Judah's land was appropriated by its neighbors. This reading attempts to account for the structural issues in the book while retaining a coherent prophet and historical context.

Not everyone has been convinced by such reconstructions, and others have focused instead on the cohesion and unity of the text. In the nineteenth century, T. T. Perowne inveighed against such source critical division of Obadiah: 'This kind of criticism, always arbitrary and precarious, seems nowhere more out of place than in the brief prophecy of Obadiah' (15). Others have agreed that there are distinguishable sections within the book but have argued that the book needs to be read as a unity, whatever its redactional history (Snyman 1989; Raabe; Renkema).

Obadiah and the Hebrew Bible

The different ordering of the Twelve as found in the MT, the LXX, and other traditions suggests that the place of Obadiah within this collection was not a fixed one. Beyond its location in this collection, the fact that Obadiah is placed among these prophets means that readers, commentators, and homilists alike have been keen on pointing out possible connections. Early Christian interpreters in particular presumed that Obadiah was an early pre-exilic prophet, and the book's placement near the beginning of the Twelve seems to have informed this understanding (as with Ephrem the Syrian). Recent interest in the shape of the Book of the Twelve has also affected research on Obadiah: those who have argued for a redaction of the Twelve based on keywords and literary motifs have seen such moves at work in Obadiah, as have those who posit a thematic, narrative-like structure to the Twelve (House 1990; Nogalski 1993).

Beyond the Book of the Twelve, Obadiah's relationship to the broader prophetic tradition has been a significant matter in the reception of the book. Of particular import has been the recognition that Obadiah has much in common with Jer. 49, another oracle concerning Edom. The relationship of these texts was commented on in premodern sources, including the Babylonian Talmud, Jerome, and the *Glossa Ordinaria*; these sources either simply note the similarities between these passages or comment on the supernatural nature of more than one prophet receiving the same message. The relationship between Jeremiah 49 and Obadiah has remained a lively issue in modern commentaries, though no consensus has emerged—indeed, there are some who advocate for the priority of Jeremiah (Bewer; Raabe), others who suggest Obadiah was the original (Caspari 1842), and others still who suggest a common shared text that lies behind these texts but which is now lost to history (Wolff). Beyond this close connection with Jeremiah, Obadiah has commonalities with Isaiah and Ezekiel, as well as Joel, Amos, and Malachi, particularly in the use of keywords and phrases regarding Edom.

Finally, Obadiah's relationship to the Torah has been the subject of considerable commentary through the years, particularly Genesis, Numbers, and Deuteronomy. As noted earlier, premodern readers (notably in the Jewish tradition but also in Christian readings) frequently made a connection between Obadiah and Genesis because of the references to Esau and Edom. Such literal and historical connections became tenuous in the late modern period with the critique of the historical veracity of the ancestral narratives. Nevertheless, key verbal, thematic, and rhetorical connections between Obadiah and the Torah have again in recent years been explored, such as the reference to Edom in the oracle from Balaam found in Numbers 24 (Rouillard 1985) and the depiction of the descendants of Esau in Deuteronomy 2 (Anderson 2022).

Theological, Thematic, and Rhetorical Issues in Interpreting Obadiah

A number of themes can be found in the book of Obadiah, including divine justice and retribution. There have been readers throughout history that have used Obadiah to vilify 'others' and to justify divisions. As noted earlier, there is a long tradition of using Obadiah to denigrate Esau (and thus Edom). For example, Esau did not learn from his parents, Rashi notes, while Obadiah became righteous in spite of his evil contemporaries Ahab and Jezebel. Another rabbinic tradition comments that Esau was considered the greater by his parents, but God saw Esau and his descendants as lowly, as pronounced in Obadiah (PesK 3.13, 18). While it is not always clear whether the rabbis are speaking of Esau or using him figuratively, there is nevertheless a recurring theme of using Obadiah to belittle the character Esau and in turn others who might be associated with him. Early Christian interpreters also found reasons to castigate others using Obadiah. Jerome, among others, understood the figurative meaning of the book as relating to the Day of Judgment for all heretics. He has very strong words for those who, like the Edomites in Judah, have brought hardship to the church. In eighteenth-century England, the Baptist clergyman and commentator John Gill could write that Edom is 'a type of the enemies of Christ and his kingdom, and especially of the Roman antichrist'.

However, readers have also used this book in a variety of other ways through the centuries. For example, an important aspect of ancient Jewish interpretation read Obadiah in light of contemporary politics, notably concerning Rome. This reading follows the rabbinic tendency to equate Edom with the enemies of God in a symbolic manner. In the case of Obadiah, it is understood that the prophet is referring to how Rome, though it sees itself as large and lofty, will be brought down and made small, an event that will coincide with the reestablishment of God's people. Hence, Obadiah points in a figural manner to Rome and the eventual downfall of this oppressor (e.g., Lev. Rab. 13:5). When read in this light, Obadiah can be seen as an anti-imperial text, a call to end oppression, and a statement of eschatological hope. This eschatological understanding may have influenced the inclusion of the final verse of Obadiah as a verse that is recited on Rosh Hashanah (see below for liturgical uses).

Similarly constructive readings are found in the Christian tradition. There are a number of Church Fathers who read Obadiah pastorally. The book has been read as a warning against pride, as a chance to reflect on the nature of justice, and as an opportunity to consider notions of judgment and mercy. For example, Jerome offers an extensive warning about being deceived by pride, while Theodoret of Cyr notes that the case of Edom should teach us to truly rejoice when others rejoice and mourn when they mourn. Ambrose makes similar claims but takes the challenge personally: he prays that he, as a bishop, will truly hear those who come to him and suffer with those who suffer (*Concerning Repentance* 2.8; see Ferreiro).

Like their Jewish counterparts, Christians have also read the book figuratively and eschatologically. For instance, the restoration of Israel and the defeat of Edom point, for many Christian interpreters, to the ultimate victory of God through Christ and the church. Some of this figurative commentary is based on verse 21 and its mention of 'saviours' or 'deliverers', often equated with the apostles (Augustine, *City of God*). Like the Jewish reading concerning Rome, Christians have also used Obadiah as a chance to critique those in power: in seventeenth-century England we find the Puritans writing in a more popular style and using Obadiah's denunciation of Edom as part of the castigation of the royalist party. Here Obadiah functions as protest literature against the monarchy ('Dammee Cavaliers Warning Piece', 1643).

Contemporary readers of Obadiah have noted the harsh tenor of the book, including its stark rhetoric and violent imagery used in relation to Edom. Robert Carroll, for example, refers to the book's 'savage xenophobia' (1990: 496–97). Julia O'Brien (2008) has also explored the ideological underpinnings of recurring issues in the book and critiques its use of motifs such as brotherhood and land. Drawing on research suggesting that Edom had little to do with the downfall of Judah and Jerusalem, O'Brien sees the book's kinship language serving ideological ends, particularly regarding land; that is, Judah did not really conceive of Edom as a brother, but the terminology is used to underscore Edom's behavior. Thus, O'Brien makes the case that Obadiah is ostensibly using kinship language while in fact reinforcing the otherness of Edom. The danger is that those who read Obadiah as Scripture might find license in this book for denouncing others in like manner and that Obadiah would be seen as a model for how others can be treated (cf. Wacker 2012).

Looking at the text through the lens of gender, Claassens (2014b) has pointed out the complex issue of Obadiah and its impact. On the one hand, the text vilifies the other, something that a feminist reading needs to keep in mind, as this happens too frequently to women and other marginalized communities. Further, such 'othering' can often happen to innocent bystanders while the truly guilty (such as Babylon) are left to their own devices. Indeed, in a postcolonial world, we have to question texts that prioritize one group over another, particularly those that advocate a God-given right to a land at the expense of others. For all these reasons, Obadiah needs to be read with care. On the other hand, Obadiah can be read as a response to the trauma which was experienced by the Judean community. In fact, Claassens writes,

> Trauma theorists would say that the act of naming injustice and voicing the anger toward nations that violate their neighbors, as found in Obadiah, is an important step on the road to healing. In a contemporary context, one might say that Obadiah's candid quest for revealing acts of injustice resembles the various manifestations of truth and reconciliation commissions that have done important work in countries such as South Africa, Chile, Indonesia, and Ireland, to ensure that acts of injustice and human right violations are not forgotten. In terms of a gender perspective, naming injustice is a primary feminist concern; righteous anger serves as an impetus to work for change. (2014b: 320)

Offering a similar reading from an African perspective, Adu-Gyamfi (2015) has argued that Obadiah can offer hope for those who are victims of ethnic hatred in African contexts, as God is ultimately on the side of those who have been wronged.

Thus, the book of Obadiah has been understood and used in various ways: as a force for liberation and healing for those who have suffered trauma and subjugation or as a tool of oppression that further marginalizes those who are considered 'other'.

Liturgical and Cultural Engagement with Obadiah

Despite its length, Obadiah is well represented in Jewish liturgical traditions. The entire book of Obadiah serves as a *haftarah* reading in the Sephardic tradition, where it is read alongside the Torah reading concerning the reunion of Jacob and Esau (Gen. 32:4–36:43, *Vayishlach*). The juxtaposition of these readings is interesting as they 'stand at two opposite points in the historical spectrum of relations between Jacob/Israel and Esau/Edom' (Fishbane 2002: 42). Verse 21, meanwhile, is used during Rosh Hashanah, the Jewish New Year celebration. In this context, the verse is part of the *Musaf* recitation, which celebrates the coming of God's kingdom. Verse 21 is also found in the daily morning liturgy, at the end of the *Pesukei de-Zimrah* service, a selection of texts read before the Call to Worship. In both of these cases this verse occurs alongside Zech. 14:9, which also speaks about the kingdom of God (see Fisbhane).

Obadiah is conspicuously absent from the various liturgical traditions of Christianity. This is not to say that the book is ignored in the Christian church. Indeed, there are many examples throughout history of sermons and writings that draw from this prophetic work, and the prophet is revered in several Eastern traditions, including the Eastern Orthodox Church, which celebrates the prophet on 19 November (Figure 38). Nevertheless, the tone and size of the book have meant that it has had less representation in liturgy, hymnody, and other ecclesial forms of worship than other prophetic books.

In Western literature, Obadiah makes occasional appearances, though these are often quite limited. As noted earlier, Obadiah is referred to in a seventeenth-century Puritan piece, where the royalist party is castigated in a manner similar to Edom ('Dammee Cavaliers Warning Piece', 1643). Christopher Smart, writing in the mid-eighteenth century, refers to Obadiah in *Jubilate Agno*, amidst a flurry of biblical references. The name Obadiah also occurs in literature, though direct connections to the biblical prophet are not always obvious: the appellation is ascribed to characters in works ranging from Laurence Sterne's *Tristram Shandy*, to Flannery O'Connor's short story *Parker's Back* (O. E. Parker, the O. E. standing for Obadiah Elihu), to Obadiah Stane in the comic book series *Iron Man*. Obadiah is also the name of one of the islands in Clive Barker's young adult series *The Books of Abarat*.

FIGURE 38   *Amos and Obadiah; Russian icon, eighteenth century.*
Unknown/Wikimedia Commons/Public Domain.

As with other prophets, Obadiah is represented in a good deal of religious art, from illuminated Bibles, to woodcarvings, to ecclesial statues and artwork. General representations, particularly in Bibles and ecclesial contexts, provide little that might distinguish Obadiah from other prophets. Several of these depict the prophet pointing, while others include a bird in the background, presumably the eagle mentioned in verse 4 (Figure 39).

There are, however, several medieval depictions that are very specific in their portrayal of the prophet. We might first note a depiction found in the twelfth-century Winchester Bible. At the beginning of the book of Obadiah there is an image of the prophet entitled *visio abdia*. Yet the depiction is of Obadiah providing food to those prophets whom he had hidden away as outlined in

FIGURE 39   *Prophet Obadiah with a bird, in the nave of the basilica of San Giovanni in Laterano, Rome, Italy.*

Sailko - Own work/Wikimedia Commons/CC BY 3.0.

1 Kings 18. A second noteworthy occurrence is found in a collection of engravings from Amiens Cathedral (thirteenth century). Along with depictions of the rest of the twelve prophets, we find here a fourfold depiction of Obadiah. Again, these depictions all come from the story of Obadiah, the servant of Ahab, as recounted in 1 Kings 18. Examples on the cathedral include Obadiah feeding the prophets whom he had hidden from Ahab and Jezebel (Figure 40), as well as Obadiah meeting Ahab alongside Elijah (Figure 37). There is a further portrayal of Obadiah on another side of the Cathedral, and it too has Obadiah feeding the hidden prophets. There are, then, several premodern representations of Obadiah that equate the prophet with the servant of King Ahab. As noted earlier, this was a common tradition in both early Judaism and Christianity, and it seems to have had a significant influence on the visual reception of the book.

Moving to the sixteenth and seventeenth centuries we find depictions of Obadiah, which look to portray the content and message of the book. Several woodcarvings from this period are particularly acute in their renderings. Images of falling cities and eagles, which are to be brought down from the heights, are common in such illustrations (see Figure 45).

When we come to the contemporary era, a number of depictions of Obadiah are striking in their emotional resonance. Among his many other pieces of work, Marc Chagall has devoted attention to Obadiah, again conjuring much

FIGURE 40   *Obadiah feeding hidden prophets, Amiens Cathedral, France.*
Used with permission from Stuart Whatling.

in a simple pencil sketch ('The Vision of Obadiah', ca. 1955). While this Chagall image retains the notion of a city on a hill, perhaps with people fleeing from it, the depiction of the prophet is far from congratulatory or triumphalistic, lacking the pointing finger common in previous depictions. Rather, the prophet sits, his head slightly bowed, and there is an element of ambiguity and even reflectiveness introduced in Chagall's Obadiah. What might be the most evocative of the contemporary representations of Obadiah is found in John Singer Sargent's 'Frieze of the Prophets', a mural of the Twelve Prophets at the Boston Public Library (see Figure 3 given earlier). Again, far from a prophetic voice that exults in castigating its neighbor, Singer Sargent's partially robed Obadiah seems to be in pain, huddled close to the ground with head bowed. We are not given access as to what motivates this response, whether it is the plight of his fellow people or the severity of the message he has to deliver. Whatever the case, Singer Sargent clearly focuses on the humanity of the prophetic figure, something that we are much more apt to ascribe to Jeremiah, the weeping prophet, than to Obadiah, the vitriolic one. The sketches and drafts of this work (now at Harvard Library) reinforce the fact that the artist was intent on depicting this dimension of the prophetic vocation (see Figure 41; for more on Singer Sargent's prophets, see Promey 1998).

Taken together, the visual representations of Obadiah reflect the diversity of ways in which the book has been read and understood through the years.

FIGURE 41 *John Singer Sargent, study for the prophet Obadiah, Boston Public Library; charcoal sketch, 1890–95.*

Used with permission from © President and Fellows of Harvard College.

The Book of Obadiah: Commentary

Verse 1a

The book of Obadiah begins with a two-word phrase in Hebrew, *hazon ovadyah*, most often translated 'The vision of Obadiah'. Readers have spent significant energy on the word 'vision'. Jerome would state that Obadiah's 'vision' means that he experienced God like those prophets who had a more visually stimulating revelation such as Isaiah and Ezekiel (Isa. 6:1; Ezek. 1:1). However, Theodore of Mopsuestia explains that this is no different than the phrase 'the word of the LORD': 'Scripture calls God's activity "word of the LORD" in reference to the spiritual grace by which the prophets received the revelations of the future, and in the same way by *vision* he refers to the divine revelation by which in fact they received the knowledge of the unknown' (176). Theodoret of Cyr highlights that this introductory phrase emphasizes the divine, rather than human, element of the message.

The reformer John Calvin likewise introduces his commentary by focusing on this divine aspect of the vision: 'he did not bring forward his own dreams, or what he conjectured, or discovered by human reason, but that he adduced only a celestial oracle' (422). The sixteenth-century Englishman John Rainolds, meanwhile, commented that a vision 'is a doctrine revealed from God, so called because God revealed them so evidently, and delivered them for such certainty, as though they had presently seen before their eyes the things which they foretold'. E. B. Pusey likewise noted that the term *vision* is appropriate as the prophets were often called 'seers': 'Probably the future was unfolded to him in the form of sights spread out before his mind, of which he spoke in words given

Hosea, Joel, and Obadiah Through the Centuries, First Edition. Bradford A. Anderson.
© 2024 John Wiley & Sons Ltd. Published 2024 by John Wiley & Sons Ltd.

FIGURE 42   *The Vision of Obadiah, from the Bible of Jean XXII (vellum); fifteenth century. Ms H 7 fol.110v.*

NPL - DeA Picture Library/Bridgeman Images.

to him by God' (353). Along these lines, a number of medieval manuscripts depict Obadiah asleep in bed, with God opening the sky like a window to speak to the prophet—in these cases the vision is understood as a dream (Figure 42).

The Hebrew name Obadiah is most often understood to be a combination of words meaning 'servant of YHWH'. It has been posited that Obadiah is a title ('servant of YHWH') rather than a name, similar to suggestions that Malachi should be understood as 'my messenger' rather than a proper noun; however, the case is not a strong one as Obadiah is otherwise well attested as a name in the HB (1 Kgs 18; 1 Chr. 3:21; 7:3; 8:38; Ezra 8:9; Neh. 12:25; see discussion in Ben Zvi 1996). The name Obadiah is used to refer to a number of different characters in the HB, and the use of this name elsewhere has led to speculation as to whether or not any of these other Obadiahs should be identified with the prophet of the book under discussion. An early rabbinic tradition held that this prophet was the same Obadiah mentioned in 1 Kings 18. The Obadiah in 1 Kings is a servant of King Ahab during Elijah's ministry and who, the text tells us, hid one hundred prophets during a time of persecution by Jezebel. Thus, in the Talmud, Rabbi Yitzhak says, 'For what reason did Obadiah merit prophecy? It is because he concealed one hundred prophets in a cave, as it Is stated: "It was so, when Jezebel cut off the prophets of the Lord, that Obadiah took one hundred prophets, and hid them, fifty men in a cave, and fed them with bread and water"' (b. Sanh. 39b).

This was a common reading in rabbinic Judaism, and we find it picked up and expanded on elsewhere. Rashi draws on this tradition as he follows the Talmudic connections of Obadiah with the character of 1 Kings. However, Rashi also makes a connection with events from Genesis, based on Obadiah's reference to Esau, the twin brother of the patriarch Jacob, and Esau's progeny, Edom (Genesis 25–36):

> Why is Obadiah different that he was chosen to prophesy concerning Edom and did not prophesy any other prophecy? Our Sages of blessed memory stated: Obadiah was an Edomite proselyte. Said the Holy One, blessed be He: From them and in them will I bring upon them. Let Obadiah, who dwelt between two wicked people, Ahab and Jezebel, and did not learn from their deeds, come and impose retribution upon Esau, who dwelt between two righteous people, Isaac and Rebecca, and did not learn from their deeds. (Rashi)

An interesting dimension is added here in the statement that Obadiah was an Edomite proselyte, a trope known in early rabbinic interpretation (Lev. Rab. 18.2). Thus, the harsh message toward Edom comes from none other than one of their own. Following a Talmudic tradition, Abarbanel expands on this, stating that his status as a convert is the reason that Obadiah is not placed first in the collection of the Twelve, even though he would be the earliest in this reconstruction: it is because he is a proselyte, and the others are all of Israelite origins (see *Miqra'ot Gedolot*; cf. b. Sanh. 39b). This association is seen in a number of visual representations of Obadiah, which depicted him as Ahab's servant, often feeding the hidden prophets (see Figure 43, as well as Obadiah: Introduction and Overview for further discussion). Ibn Ezra, meanwhile, departs from the tradition, saying that we cannot equate the two Obadiahs simply because the name also appears in 1 Kings. He seems to suggest a later date for the prophet.

FIGURE 43   *Initial V with Obadiah feeding the prophets, Winchester Bible illumination, twelfth century.*
English School/Bridgeman Images.

While the linking of Obadiah with 1 Kings 18 is the most common association, other interpretations were known in antiquity. In the *Lives of the Prophets*, we read that Obadiah was from the district of Shechem, and was a disciple of Elijah, though in this case Obadiah is equated with the captain of Ahaziah that is spared by Elijah in 2 Kgs 1:13–18. This tradition says that Obadiah left the service of the king and went on to prophesy (Hare 1985). In early Christianity there was some diversity of opinion on this matter. Jerome is happy to follow Jewish tradition, concurring that it was Obadiah's brave act of hiding the prophets in 1 Kings 18 that led to him being given the gift of prophecy (cf. the medieval commentators Nicholas of Lyra and Hugh of St. Victor). Ephrem the Syrian, however, locates Obadiah in the eighth century, noting that he was from the tribe of Ephraim and was a contemporary of Hosea, Joel, Amos, and Isaiah. Cyril of Alexandria notes a number of similarities with

Joel and suggests that the two books may be from the same (pre-exilic) period, though his commentary also speaks at length about the circumstances relating to the Babylonian conquest.

Like Ibn Ezra, Martin Luther takes issue with the assumption that this Obadiah is the same character from the time of Elijah, and Jerome comes in for special criticism: 'this is much like the dreams of old women—like many other points of Jerome whenever he makes rash judgments about sacred matters'. Luther instead claims that 'it seems certain that he prophesied after the Babylonian captivity and that he took his prophecy from Jeremiah' (193; cf. Marbury 1649). Calvin is more circumspect on the matter, saying that we do not know for sure but that Obadiah likely comes after Isaiah and shares much in common with Jeremiah.

> It appears that Jeremiah (ch. xlix.) and this Prophet made use of the same thoughts and nearly the same words, as we shall hereafter see. The Holy Spirit could, no doubt, have expressed the same things in different words; but he was pleased to join together these two testimonies, that they might obtain more credit. I know not whether Obadiah and Jeremiah were contemporaries, and on this subject we need not bestow much labour. (418–19)

However, throughout his commentary Calvin makes general reference to the humiliation of Edom in relation to the Babylonians.

By the late nineteenth century, there were a host of understandings that had emerged within critical scholarship. C. F. Keil (1871) posited a setting for the prophet in the early ninth century during the reign of Jehoram, while Carl Paul Caspari (1842) and E. B. Pusey (1885), among others, put forward the reign of Uzziah in the mid-eighth century as the context (cf. G. L. Robinson 1926). Following Luther, a growing number of scholars would suggest a date just after the destruction of Jerusalem in 587 BCE (Rainolds; Gill; Perowne), and yet others, including Wellhausen, placed the book or parts of it in a postexilic setting, ca 450 BCE and later (cf. Bewer; Elliott 1884). In the twentieth century, such diversity was less evident, and the majority of critical scholarship situated the prophet and the book in the exilic or early postexilic period (see Raabe).

In the spirit of form criticism, Hans Walter Wolff suggested that Obadiah was a *Kultprophet*, and his original message would have given hope to those left behind in Jerusalem after the Babylonian conquest: 'In Obadiah we see one of the cultic prophets who gave the broken and dejected congregation of Zion the assurance that its prayers had been heard—an assurance in the form especially of a threat of judgment on its enemies' (Wolff 1986: 19). This is not to say that the original message of the prophet is what we now see before us in Bibles: Wolff is among those who offer redactional and source-critical reconstructions concerning how the message was shaped and revised before it found its form in the text as we now have it (see discussion in Obadiah: Introduction and Overview and on verse 15).

Obadiah is a name ascribed to several medieval rabbis in the Jewish tradition (the most well known of these being Obadiah Sforno), and in the Christian tradition the Latin form Abdias is connected to a work of New Testament Apocrypha known as Pseudo-Abdias, falsely attributed to a disciple by the same name found in the collection. The Hebrew name has seen a resurgence in the last century as both a first name and a surname, particularly in Israel, including Rabbi Ovadia Yosef, who served as the Sephardi Chief Rabbi of Israel (1973–83). The Assemblies of Yahweh, a Christian movement that developed in the mid-twentieth century in Bethel, Pennsylvania, has an educational institution called the Obadiah School of the Bible.

Verse 1b

Following the superscription, we are told that a report has been heard concerning Edom. The Greek LXX translates this in the singular, 'I have heard', which is the form found in Jer. 49:14. However, the Hebrew uses the plural, 'we have heard', and a number of readers have made note of this plural usage. Ibn Ezra and Radak comment that 'We have heard a report' can be understood as Obadiah aligning himself with former prophets who also spoke against Edom (cf. Pusey; Rainolds). Bewer suggests that the plural 'we' may refer collectively to the prophet and the people in this context, while Barton notes that this could point back to an earlier prophecy to which Obadiah is referring. While most translations render the next word as 'concerning Edom', some traditions understand the Hebrew preposition as indicating that this is directed '*to* Edom', implying that Edom is the intended audience of the message from Obadiah (LXX).

This report from the LORD, we are told, has been sent out via a messenger among the nations. The Church Fathers often found spiritual meaning in this: Ephrem suggests that the messenger is to be understood with a mystical meaning, referring to Emmanuel who announced peace to the nations. Isho'dad of Merv, meanwhile, notes that God sent his angels (as this is the same word as messengers) to gather the nations in order to come against Edom (cf. Raabe). The Reformers pointed out the military nature of the language used here. Luther comments that Obadiah is using military metaphors to frighten Edom—envoys, reports, and battle all indicate that destruction is imminent.

Calvin focuses on the fact that this report is from the LORD, which indicates that this is not happening by chance: 'wars are not stirred up at random, but by the secret influence of God' (422).

Verse 2

In verse 2 we read that Edom has been made small and is despised among the nations. While the mention of Edom seems naturally to refer to Judah's neighbor, some rabbinic texts understood this as instead speaking about Rome (b. ʿAbod. Zar.10a; Lev. Rab. 13:5). This relates to a long-standing tradition that saw Edom as symbolic of the enemies of the people of God, particularly Rome and later Christianity (Pesiq. Rab. 15:25). Cohen (1967) suggests it was Rabbi Akiba who first connected Edom and Rome in this way. In this sense, the message of Obadiah is a message of hope 'for an end to this brutal hegemony and a restoration of national religious service' (Fishbane 2002: 43). Bakhos (2007) has challenged the consensus concerning the ubiquity of this association in rabbinic literature and has pointed out that Esau and Edom function in a number of different ways in this corpus. Whatever the case, this connection was well known among Jews and Christians; Radak and Ibn Ezra explicitly make this association, and even the English Christian writer and cleric John Perowne comments in the nineteenth century, 'The persecutions which Christians have heaped upon them [Jews] go far, it must be confessed, to justify the reference, and it is scarcely surprising that with modern Jews it is a canon of interpretation that by the Edomites are meant the Christians' (23).

A number of Jewish sources use the phrase 'small among the nations' to make a connection with the story of Jacob and Esau in Genesis. The midrashic text Genesis Rabbah notes that here God contradicts Isaac and Rebekah: while the parents called Esau their 'great' (that is, elder) son, God says Edom is small among the nations (Gen. Rab. 44:11 [Neusner]). Rashi, drawing on traditions found in the Babylonian Talmud, says Edom is small and despised because it does not have its own language or script (cf. PesK 3.13, 18; for more on the question of Edomite language and script, see Crowell 2021).

Those reading from Christian perspectives also understood this reference to Edom in diverse ways. Ephrem the Syrian comments that the Edomites will be punished for how they treated their brothers; however, in a spiritual manner, he notes, this refers to the fact that 'the devil is made least, as the words which follow are extremely suitable to him as well' (Ferreiro: 121). Both Luther and Calvin focus on how Edom had become arrogant without reason—Seir was nothing special as a region, they note, and Edom was no better than any other nation. Pusey likewise suggests that Edom never did 'anything of moment' of its own accord. John Rainolds, the sixteenth-century Englishman of Puritan leanings, connects the Edomites to the enemies of the church and notes that 'the papists are the Idumeans' (5). John Gill concurs, noting that the Edomites refer to 'the Romish antichrist': 'The Jews generally understand, by Edom, Rome, and the Christians in general; which, if applied only to the antichristians, is not amiss.' In a manner quite different from his predecessors, Perowne speaks to the complexity of Jews and Christians sharing the Old Testament as Scripture. He warns against disassociating the text from its Jewish roots yet hopes that both Jews and Christians are able to find some meaning in the text.

The text of verses 1–2 refers to Edom in both feminine and masculine forms (see Raabe). Wacker sees in the feminine language 'a rhetorical discrediting device frequently found especially in the prophetic literature' (2012: 406), which matches the language of humiliation used in relation to Edom in these opening verses.

Verse 3

Verse 3 describes the Edomites as those of proud or arrogant heart, who live in the clefts of the rock. The Targum translates proud as 'wicked' and then adds 'for you are like an eagle who dwells . . .' The eagle is found in verse 4 in the MT, but here the Targum adds it to verse 3, perhaps using the well-known symbol of the Roman eagle to reinforce the connection of Edom with Rome (Cathcart and Gordon). In the Talmud, the Sages used verse 3 as a chance to discuss the similarities in wording between Obadiah 3 and Jer. 49:16, noting the slight differences in the passages to suggest that two prophets might have the same message but transmit it in their own way (b. Sanh. 89a). Rashi understands the clefts of the rocks to be referring to Edom relying on the support of the ancestors (Abraham and Isaac).

The Church Father Theodore of Mopsuestia gives a plain sense reading:

> Since the Idumeans inhabited mountain country, he means something like this: You excessively exalted your thinking, living as you do in recesses of rocks, and in your own estimation you made a splendid and spacious dwelling. You also had the idea that there would never be anyone capable of removing you from your current prosperity. For this you will suffer what has been said so as to gain a realization that it was vain for you to think yourself something when divine counsel is working against you. (179)

Others would offer similar interpretations, focused on geography and geological features (Luther). Pusey, for example, discusses the natural habitat and various aspects of the history of the mountainous regions of Edom, including the difficulty of attack. Noting later developments at Petra and the natural majesty of the place, he comments: 'In man's sight Edom's boast was well-founded; but what before God?' (356). Wolff focuses on the phrase 'You say in your heart, who will bring me down to the ground?' (v. 3) and points out that the Hebrew term *lev*, 'heart', signifies here 'the total personality, with its self-awareness' (34). The text thus presents a 'reflective soliloquy' on the part of Edom. He goes on to note that this sort of arrogance is also assigned to Babylon (Jer. 50: 29, 31), in which case Edom is deceiving itself: it is no Babylon.

Along with a number of geographical observations, Jerome offers a figurative interpretation, seeing this verse as directed against heretics: while a rock can be used to refer to something solid in Scripture (Ps. 40:2; Matt. 16:18), here the fissures represent heresies that cause rupture in the church. Rainolds also makes figurative associations, noting that the papists resemble not only the beast of Revelation in its cruelty but also the pride of Edom as seen in Obadiah: 'for these also have their dwelling in the clefts of the rocks, persuading themselves that this is the rock on which the church of God is built' (8). Modern readers have tried to locate more precisely which rock (*sela'*) the text refers to here. Bewer notes that it might point to Mount Seir as a region or specifically to the location of the place named Sela.

Illustrations of Obadiah frequently present the prophet as speaking to a mountainous region, attempting to place the prophet within the 'narrative' of the book bearing his name and drawing on the imagery within the text of high places (see Figure 44).

Verse 4

In verse 4 we read: 'Though you soar aloft like the eagle [or "vulture"; Heb. *nesher*], though your nest is set among the stars, from there I will bring you down, says the LORD.' The Sages used this verse as a way to indicate that although Esau was related to the patriarchs, he was not really one of them (y. Ned. 3:8; cf. Rashi on v. 3). Leviticus Rabbah makes another interesting connection between Genesis and Obadiah, this time in relation to Jacob's dream of a ladder ascending to the heavens in Gen. 28:12. Here the Sages note that Jacob saw the princes of the world ascending this ladder, including Babylon, Media, and Greece. He

FIGURE 44   *Obadiah overlooking city on a hill, from German Bible; Christoph Froschauer, sixteenth century.*

Courtesy of Pitts Library Digital Archive/Emory University.

also saw the one representing Edom, whose ascension seemed to have no end. Jacob says,

> 'Lord of the ages! Will you say that he too is subject to decline?' Said to him the Holy One, blessed be he, 'Jacob! Even if you see that he reaches heaven, I shall bring him down.' That is in line with the following verse of Scripture: 'though you make your nest as high as the eagle, and though you set it among the stars, I will bring you down from there (Obad 4)'. (Lev. Rab. 29:2 [Neusner])

The mention of the other great empires and the seemingly endless ascension of 'Edom' would suggest that this refers to Rome and the rabbis' belief that this empire too would one day be humbled.

If Jewish readings focused on Esau and Rome, Christian interpretations have tended toward the spiritual and pastoral. Jerome uses this verse to comment on the fall of Lucifer. Like Edom, Lucifer exalted himself (Isa. 14:13–14) and so was brought down. Luther offers here a brief reflection on trusting God rather than flesh: 'we see scattered throughout all Scripture that He calls us back from the arm of the flesh, from confidence in ourselves, to place our hope in Him' (196; cf. Calvin). Pusey also comments on arrogance and humility, noting various other biblical texts where God humbles the proud and exalts the humble (Job 20:6, 7; Isa. 14:13). For Pusey, this applies to his contemporary Christians as much as it does ancient Edom: 'They who boast of being Christians, and are on that ground self-satisfied, promising themselves eternal life, and thinking that they need not fear Hell, because they are Christians and hold the faith of the Apostles, while their lives are altogether alien from Christianity, are such Edomites' (356–57). Noting some of the same intertextual links as Pusey, Wolff suggests that this indicates a later interpolation, which attempts to make Edom look like the Babylonian king of Isaiah 14.

Verse 4 has also led to interesting interpretations and contemporary applications through the years. In the seventeenth century, the Englishman Edward Marbury would compare Edom's vain pride with that of the Spanish Armada of 1588, which was unsuccessful in its attempt to infiltrate England. In spite of Spain's 'strength of ships . . . and men', he notes, 'God gave us victory, and declared that no strength prevaileth against the Lord.' For Marbury, this episode was a reminder that 'our trust is not in the strength of our dwellings, but God is our rock; on the clefts of this rock we dwell safe, so that Faith, and not presumption do build our nest' (Marbury 1649). Several centuries later, Gordon Lindsay, the well-known evangelical and 'end times' author, would postulate that the use of 'eagle' and 'among the stars' predicted America's space exploration: the Eagle is not only the national symbol of the United States but also the name of the first manned lunar spacecraft (*God's Plan of the Ages as Revealed in Bible Chronology*, 1971).

A number of visual representations of Obadiah also draw on the imagery of this verse and include depictions of an eagle or other birds in order to bring to life this short prophetic work (Figure 45).

Verses 5–6

In verses 5 and 6 we are presented with a series of metaphors, statements, and questions that highlight Edom's destruction. The Hebrew of verse 5 is difficult, which has led to a variety of approaches. The Targum tries to make sense of the first clause by translating it thus: 'If thieves were to come to you, plunderers by night, *how would you sleep until they had stolen* all they wanted?' (see also

FIGURE 45   *Detail of Obadiah from Luther's Bibel (woodcut), Johann Melchior Bocksberger, illustrator. Sixteenth century.*
Courtesy of Pitts Library Digital Archive/Emory University.

Rashi). The Targum, along with the Vulgate, seems to understand the Hebrew *damah* (normally understood as 'cut off, destroyed') as meaning 'to sleep' or 'be silent' (cf. Radak). This is also seen in Luther's commentary, via the Vulgate, where the reformer goes to great lengths to demonstrate how such a reading fits: 'This properly means to reduce something to silence and to nothing, to demolish some kingdom or people to such an extent that scarcely traces remain to be seen, that they keep their silence and dare not utter a sound' (196; cf. Calvin). Others suggest that this awkward syntax is an exclamation inserted into the first half of the verse: 'how you have been destroyed!' (NRSV). Pusey follows this reading, noting that this is a 'burst of sympathy' from the prophet: 'In the name of God, he mourns over the destruction he fore-announces' (357).

Many interpreters understand verses 5–6 as suggesting that even thieves have limits to the damage they do, while Edom's desolation will be total (Theodore of Mopsuestia; Cyril of Alexandria; Calvin; Barton). Ephrem offers a more specific reading, connecting Edom's downfall with the Babylonians; this, however, is not a comment on the origins of the book—rather, Ephrem sees this as a prophecy predicting Edom's destruction: 'He prophesies that the people of Esau had to be pillaged by the Chaldeans with incredible zeal and then even deported to captivity. Nebuchadnezzar of Babylon fulfilled this prediction after he thoroughly destroyed Edom and moved its inhabitants elsewhere' (Ferreiro: 122). While Ephrem attributes Edom's downfall to Nebuchadnezzar, most contemporary scholars think that it was Nabonidus that brought Edom's kingdom to an end (Crowell 2007).

Verse 5 ends with a reference to grape pickers who, like the thieves noted previously, would normally leave something behind. Bewer suggests that the reference to vintagers is intentional, conjuring the many vineyards that would have dotted the landscape around Mount Seir.

A number of commentators note that the hidden things searched out in verse 6 must relate to the hiding in the clefts of the rock, from verse 3 (Raabe). Not only are the people hiding, but they are hiding treasures and wealth, and these, too, will be found out (Calvin; Pusey). Rainolds takes this as an opportunity to comment on the taking back of the property and riches of the churches and monasteries in early modern England so that these things might once again be properly put to use.

Verse 7

The NRSV translates verse 7 with the following:

> All your allies have deceived you,
>   they have driven you to the border;
> your confederates have prevailed against you;
>   those who ate your bread have set a trap for you—
>   there is no understanding of it.

In this verse the focus shifts to Edom's allies—these, too, will turn on Edom. Indeed, these allies will deceive Edom, just as Edom has been deceived (v. 3), and just as Edom has 'set' itself up in the stars (v. 4), their confederates have 'set' a trap under them, suggesting a poetic turn of events (Anderson 2010). The similarities with Jeremiah 49 are readily apparent, as Jerome and many other readers noted from antiquity (cf. Dicou 1994; Raabe; Renkema).

The Hebrew of the MT states that these allies have chased Edom to the border. The Targum says these allies have 'banished you beyond the frontier', using a term related to being driven into exile (Cathcart and Gordon). Luther notes a similar phrase is found in Isa. 5:8 with the sense that the Edomites will be sent off their own land, left without territory.

While the reference to 'bread' is found in the Hebrew of the MT, neither the LXX nor the text from Murabbaʿat includes this imagery, which leads Wolff to conclude that its presence in the Hebrew is a later addition. The broader idea, however, is also present in the Targum, where we find 'those who eat at your table'. Perowne suggests 'thy bread they make a snare under thee' with the sense that table fellowship is used against them. The importance of meals for political treaties and alliances is well known in the ancient world (Raabe). Jerome builds on the mention of bread, but in his case it is the Eucharist that comes to mind: even those that have broken sacred bread can turn out to be heretics if they question Scripture and follow the ways of the flesh, as did the Edomites.

The trap (*mazor*) that has been set for Edom is an obscure term in the Hebrew, and interpreters have long struggled with how to make sense of it; the LXX, Peshitta, and Vulgate render it as 'ambush', while the Targum speaks of a 'snare'. Rashi renders the Hebrew *mazor* as 'wound' and so understands the second half of the verse as 'your food they lay as a wound under you' (cf. b. Sanh. 92a). He takes the mention of food as a chance to draw on the stories from Genesis: 'Even your food your brother Jacob made for you was a wound, for he gave you bread and a pottage of lentils, and thereby you despised the birthright.' Calvin likewise offers a reading of a 'wound under thee', saying it is 'as when one hides a dagger between the bed and the sheet' (433). An alternative reading of *mazor* is 'foreigner', in which case the text can be read 'will set foreigners in your stead' (McCarter 1976; see also Symmachus).

The themes of comeuppance and the treachery of betrayal at the hands of friends recur frequently in the literature. Theodore of Mopsuestia submits that what is happening to Edom is simply what Edom has done to others: 'those who accepted you in friendship and shared a repast with you are the ones who devise traps for you, plotting your downfall, since on account of your overweening folly you do not know how to distinguish real friends from enemies' (180). Pusey comments, 'Destruction is more bitter, when friends aid in it' (358) and notes this probably refers to Moab, Ammon, Tyre, and Sidon. Calvin notes that this, too, can happen to the people of God: David feels let down by a man of peace in Ps. 16:9, and Jesus himself was betrayed by a friend. The difference is that 'the ungodly mutually cheat one another' (434), while the godly can trust that God's ways will win out in the end.

In the depiction of Obadiah by Melozzo da Forlì on the vaulted ceiling in the Sacristy of St. Mark Basilica of Santa Casa, Loreto (ca. 1477–82), Obadiah holds an engraving that quotes part of Obadiah 7 that speaks of these allies who will turn on Edom (Figure 46). Along with the prophet's pointing finger, this depiction seems to reiterate the retribution to come on Judah's neighbor Edom, which is seen as the heart of Obadiah's message.

Figure 46   *Melozzo da Forlì, Obadiah, Sacristy of St. Mark Basilica of Santa Casa, Loreto (ca 1477–82).*
Sailko – Own work/Wikimedia Commons/CC BY 3.0.

Obadiah 7 cryptically ends with the phrase 'there is no understanding of it' (NRSV), and there has been disagreement as to what this might refer. The Greek reads 'there is no understanding in them (*autois*)', suggesting Edom's enemies, while the Aramaic opts for 'no understanding in you', indicating Edom. Luther says this is similar to the German sentiment *Du Narr, du merkst nicht* ('You fool, you do not understand'), and Edom's foolishness is trusting these 'friends'. Radak and Calvin agree that it is the foolishness of the Edomites that the prophet chides. Others have posited that this is a later scribal gloss referring to the preceding term: 'there is no sense to it' refers in fact to the word *mazor* (Wellhausen; Fishbane 2002).

Verse 8

Verse 8 introduces several significant issues, including the wisdom of Edom and the first reference to 'Mount Esau', a collocation unique to Obadiah that brings together the traditions of Mount Seir and Esau. The Targum removes this appellation and refers instead to Esau's citadel or city, and a good deal of art that represents Obadiah depicts a city or urban context (cf. v. 9; 21). Wellhausen noted a syntactical and poetic shift here, including a break in the use of 'you' prominent in the previous verses, which might suggest that this is a supplement to the first seven verses.

The connection between Edom and wisdom seems to be an ancient one. Jeremiah 49:7 also mentions wisdom in relation to Edom, as does Bar. 3:22. The LXX places Job in Edom, and the Testament of Job says that he is of the sons of Esau (1:5). The fact that Eliphaz is said to be from Teman is yet another connection (Job 2:11). Pusey, among others, notes a number of these connections. Some have thus suggested that there was an Edomitic wisdom tradition similar to that found in Israel (Pfeiffer 1926), though recent research has questioned this assumption (Crowell 2008).

Genesis Rabbah makes an interesting connection between wisdom in Obadiah 8 and Jacob's preparations to return to the land of promise after his time living with Laban. The Sages note that Jacob sent Esau a present, 'so as to blind him, as it is said, "For a gift blinds the eyes of the wise" (Deut 16:19). And the word "wise" refers only to the Edomites, as in the following verse: "I will destroy the wise men out of Edom" (Obad. 8)' (Gen. Rab. 75:13 [Neusner]). Meanwhile, in Lev. Rab. 5:7, the mention of Edom's wisdom is seen to demonstrate that the nations have Sages, as does Israel. However, another midrash makes the point that while there is wisdom among the nations, this does not mean there is Torah among the nations—there is a difference (Lam. Rab. 65.1 [Neusner]).

A number of Christian readers explain that human wisdom is being compared to godly wisdom (Jerome). Calvin likewise states that this verse refers to true wisdom but notes that this gift of God can easily be turned to serve the self. Care needs to be taken so that wisdom does not become cunning and cruel, as happened with Edom. Luther suggests this continues the progress of Edom's humiliation: there will be a removal not only of safe spaces, hidden treasures, and allies, but indeed those wise men and warriors who may be able to offer assistance in this difficult period will also be taken away (Ps. 33:10). Theodore of Mopsuestia brings these two ideas together and suggests that Edom's wisdom is in fact knowledge of warfare and martial arts. Tebes (2009), drawing on archaeological finds, argues that Edom's wisdom refers to skill in craft or metalwork.

Verse 9

Verse 9 continues the theme of Edom's disgrace, focusing now on its warriors and then the populace at large. Proposals have argued that the mention of the warriors of Teman refers to a city or region and have put forward various possible locations for Teman within Edomite territory (Glueck 1940; de Vaux 1969; Bewer; cf. discussion in Raabe). More common is the idea that Teman is an example of synecdoche, a device of which Obadiah is fond (Calvin; Wolff). Instead of Teman, the Targum refers here to the 'inhabitants of the south', a change common in how the Targum translates other prophetic texts that refer to Teman (Jer. 49:7; Ezek. 25:13; see Cathcart and Gordon; cf. Rashi). This is also reflected in the Vulgate, which speaks of the 'valiant men of the south'. Radak posits that these mighty men are a reference to the blessing given by Isaac to Esau in Gen. 27:40, which states that Esau shall live by the sword. Ibn Ezra also draws on Genesis (36:11), noting that Teman, the son of Eliphaz, son of Esau, was known for his might. Luther likewise makes this connection with Teman, suggesting that the grandson of Esau named this place after himself, 'as princes and kings sometimes do'. He goes on to interpret this verse as 'Your mighty men will become fearful . . . this properly means that fear which generally pervades an army that is about to be cut to pieces and sees no way of escape' (198).

The fact that 'everyone from Mount Esau will be cut off' again points to poetic justice in this short book, as Edom is also accused of cutting off Judah's fugitives in verse 14 (Anderson 2010). Several commentators connect the two parts of the verse: as dismay and fear grow, the people flee, only to be cut off (Theodore of Mopsuestia; Rashi). The judgment here is much stronger than in earlier verses—Edom is not just to be made small; it is to be slaughtered (Ibn Ezra; Wolff). Wellhausen suggests that the word for 'slaughter' (*miqatel*) is a late Hebrew word, showing Aramaic influence on the book.

Verse 10

In verse 10 there is a shift of focus from Edom's punishment to their offenses, which will lead to Edom being cut off forever. The Hebrew refers to the violence (*hamas*) done to brother Jacob (cf. Amos 1:11). The LXX renders this as 'slaughter' but also adds 'and impiety' to the equation (cf. Jerome). Similarly, the Vulgate refers to the slaughter and iniquity done against Jacob. The twentieth-century German scholar Hans Walter Wolff translates *hamas* as 'murder'.

Various interpretations of this verse have been put forward. The Palestinian Talmud references this verse in relation to intentions and indicates that this refers to Esau, who intended to kill Jacob (y. Pe'ah 1:1). Accordingly, an evil intention is as good as an evil deed. Meanwhile, Radak interprets this violence as the destruction of the second Temple, citing Ps. 137:7 and Lam. 4:22 as confirmation; because of this, Edom will be punished at the end of days.

Similar diversity can be seen in Christian tradition. Ephrem observes that this prophecy is speaking of the total obliteration of Edom, and he sees this as having taken place during Roman rule. In the commentary attributed to Hugh of St. Victor, we see the various senses of Scripture at work: the historical sense of this verse relates to Edom's destruction, while the figurative sense points to the rooting out of heretics in the church, and the tropological relates to the destruction of the flesh. Calvin notes the importance of singling out Edom's wrongdoings: 'what brought them [the Israelites] chief consolation was to hear, that they were so dear to God that he would undertake the defence of their wrongs and avenge them' (438).

In this section the kinship theme of the book is strongest, and Edom is castigated because of how they treated their brother. Kinship terminology is used elsewhere to represent treaties and alliances (Fishbane 1970), though the reference here to Jacob and Esau by name also serves to call attention to the 'fraternal bond', thus highlighting the cruelty of the act (on development and meaning of kinship in relation to Edom, see Bartlett 1977; Tebes 2006). Pusey notes the correlation here with Deuteronomy 23, where Israel is told not to abhor the Edomites because they are kin. 'Edom did the contrary to all this' (360). However, O'Brien (2008) has pointed out the various ways in which such kinship language can be used and argues that Obadiah's reference to Edom as 'brother' is in fact being used here for ideological purposes (see discussion in 'Obadiah: Introduction and Overview').

Readers have long drawn on the kinship imagery in this verse to describe their own contemporary contexts. The Puritan Edward Marbury would comment in the seventeenth century, 'For a Turke to oppresse a Christian, an Infidell a Believer, is but a trespasse against humanity; for Hebrews to strive, and one Christian to afflict another, woundeth Religion also' (Marbury 1649). In 1915, British pastor John Pinkerton penned an article in the *Expository Times* on the idea of 'national hate'. Drawing on Obadiah, Pinkerton outlines the intense hatred between Israel and Edom, who ostensibly had much in common and were more kin than enemies. Pinkerton draws an analogy with his home country England and their adversaries in the First World War, Germany. Like Israel and Edom, he argues, England and Germany have more in common than they realize, seeing as they are both 'descended from a common Teutonic stock' (Pinkerton 1915: 300). Pinkerton argues that countries that hate others are doomed, as is seen in the fate of Edom, which disappeared from history. Similar themes of kinship and enmity are highlighted by Biwul (2017), as he explores similarities between Obadiah and contemporary Nigeria, noting commonalities around their social, religious, and economic contexts. Biwul suggests that the long-standing generational hostility that goes back to the ancestors leads to the unfortunate events we find in Obadiah; better, he argues, that common brotherhood and nationhood are nurtured in places like Nigeria before things come to the point they do in Obadiah.

Verse 11

In verse 11 Edom is accused of standing aside on the day when strangers entered the gates of Jerusalem and took its wealth—and then of being just like the other nations. This is the first mention of the term *day* in the book, and it occurs ten times within verses 11–14. Radak relates this to later Roman incursions. He offers a detailed explanation regarding Titus and his army, claiming that many in the army were actually Edomites; these rejoiced at the destruction of Jerusalem and handed over refugees to the Romans. Luther, however, asserts that verse 11 offers definitive proof that this prophecy concerns the Babylonian destruction, 'for Jerusalem was never captured before the captivity of the Chaldeans' (199). The strangers are never identified, though most contemporary readers see the Babylonians as the most likely candidate. Luther goes on to note that the casting of lots was for the right to destroy the Temple. Others commented on this casting of lots: Radak suggests the casting of lots was for the captives of the city, while Gill and others see it as referring to the plunder of the city, an interpretation that can be seen in some visual representations of this verse (see Figure 47).

In being just like the other nations, Theodore of Mopsuestia comments that Edom 'adopted the role of adversary' (181) rather than that of a brother. It was bad enough for the Assyrians and Babylonians to shed Israel's blood in this manner, but the text emphatically chastises Edom's participation, as they are from the same blood (cf. Raabe: 'with the force of *et tu, Brute*'). Their standing aside is as violent as those who entered the gates when they 'took pleasure in a spectacle so mournful' (Calvin: 440). As Wolff points out, while the text seems to speak of all Edom, it in fact refers to those in Jerusalem. He suggests Obadiah 11 refers to 'freebooter Edomite reconnaissance patrols, who were friendly towards the Babylonians and hostile towards the people of Jerusalem' (54).

For Bartlett, this verse is an example of why the crimes of which Edom is accused in Obadiah are overstated (Bartlett 1982). There is very little direct biblical evidence of such involvement on the part of the Edomites and no evidence outside the biblical material (cf. Lipschits 2005; O'Brien 2008). On the other

" And cast lots upon Jerusalem."—*Obadiah* i. 11.

FIGURE 47   Casting lots for Jerusalem. Unattributed image.
Unknown/Wikimedia Commons/Public Domain.

hand, scholars argue, this tradition emerging from nowhere seems unlikely (Raabe; Renkema). Becking has suggested a further way of looking at the matter:

> This tradition [of Edom's involvement] can be labelled as a 'claimed tradition'. Although the Edomite atrocities during the conquest of Jerusalem are most probably non-historic, the tradition arose as the result of a process of transposition. The memory of the Edomite occupation of Southern Judah functioned as the source of this process. . . . The shame of losing these territories was revengefully transposed to and enveloped into the bitter memory of the ruination of Jerusalem.
> (Becking 2016: 3; cf. Crowell 2021)

Whatever the case, it is clear from Ps. 137:7 and 1 Esd. 4:45 that a tradition about Edom's complicity in these events grew and developed over time.

Verse 12

The chastisement of Edom continues in verse 12, which expands on the themes of kinship and Judah's day of misfortune and distress. The use of tense in verses 12–14 has been the subject of considerable debate through the years; while the previous verses are clearly about the past, these verses use a present negative command. The Targum renders these events in the past (Targum: 'How you gloated . . . how you rejoiced . . .'), and most modern versions translate in the past tense to match the previous verse ('But you should not have gloated over your brother . . .', NRSV; cf. RSV; KJV). The most common way to navigate this tension is to understand the prophet as placing himself in the past, speaking to Edom about its behavior (Wellhausen; Rudolph 1971; Raabe).

Verse 12 begins by noting that the Edomites should not have 'looked on' during their brother's day of misfortune. Rashi connects this to the previous verse, stating that they 'should not have looked and stood from afar'. Both Luther and Calvin note the metaphorical sense of 'seeing' which is employed here, where Edom lies in wait or is rejoicing at what is seen (cf. NRSV: 'gloated over'). Rainolds compares this to those who go to see those who have been hanged, 'to fill their eyes with that cruel sight' (29). A number of commentators point to the progression in this verse: 'the complacent looking on deepens into malicious joy, and malicious joy finds expression in derisive mockery' (Perowne: 32). The word *day* is used in this verse to describe Judah's destruction. Here metonym is used, as 'day of your brother' means 'your brother's ruin' (cf. Ps 137:7, 'the day of Jerusalem'; see Raabe). For Christian readers such as Theodoret of Cyr, this points forward to the day of YHWH, a day of final judgment which is still to come.

The noun *nakro* is a hapax legomenon and has been interpreted in various ways. While most modern translations understand this as 'disaster' or 'misfortune' (cf. Job 31:3; Wolff), a number of Jewish interpreters understood this as Judah being 'delivered', in which case it means delivered into the hands of the enemy (Rashi; Malbim; citing 1 Sam. 23:7). Others translate this as Judah becoming a 'stranger' (Perowne; Pusey; Raabe). Ibn Ezra suggests 'a day that was strange to him, a day the likes of which he never recognized' (175). Calvin offers 'alienation' as an alternative, which he says might refer to exile (cf. Radak). The next clause in the Hebrew, read literally as 'to make great the mouth', is understood as referring to speaking proudly and jeering (Calvin; cf. Ps. 35:19–21; Isa. 57:4). Gill connects this to the Edomite taunt in Ps. 137:7: 'Raze it, raze it to the ground' (cf. Wolff).

Ambrose offers a spiritual reading of this verse, using it as an opportunity to discuss humility and pastoral duty: we are to mourn with those who sin or find themselves in difficult situations, rather than rejoicing over them or passing judgment on them (Ambrose, 'Concerning Repentance' 2.8.73). Later readings would focus more on Edom. Calvin observes that this verse serves as evidence in case Edom ever charges that God has been too severe with them: 'they in many ways sought such a ruin for themselves' (442). Edom was delighted as the ruin of Judah was not something they could do themselves; now that the Babylonians have undertaken the destruction, the Edomites 'could not forbear expressing their joy' (Gill). Rainolds compares this account with the affections and actions of Hagar, who, in Gen. 21:15–16, cannot bear to see the death of her child. The Edomites, on the contrary, rejoice in the afflictions of their kin. Not only does Edom wish this on Judah, but they cannot keep it to themselves and so speak proudly against them (Rainolds).

Verse 13

The following verse continues the admonition of Edom and returns to direct divine speech. In this verse the warnings include entering 'the gate of my people', as well as further gloating and looting on the day of Judah's calamity. Edom's actions in this verse are reminiscent of verse 5 and the mention of thieves (Wolff).

The MT uses the singular 'gate', while the versions amend this to the plural 'gates' to match verse 11. The gates here are frequently taken as referring to Jerusalem (cf. Mic. 1:9; Perowne) and, coupled with the taking of goods, have been understood as a key indicator that Obadiah refers to the Babylonian conquest of 587 BCE. Several commentators note that this verse indicates greater participation on the part of Edom, who entered the gates along with the Babylonians, taking part when they should have abstained (Calvin; Gill).

The final clause chastises Edom for looting 'his' wealth or army (*hayil*) on the day of his calamity (NRSV; NASB). The Targum and Rashi translate 'stretch out your hands' on their goods (cf. Ibn Ezra; Radak). However, the Hebrew can be understood as either 'goods' or 'army'. Thus, the LXX states that Edom should not 'join in the attack on their force', while the Vulgate proffers 'you shall not be sent out against his army' (cf. Douay-Rheims). Jerome comments on this reading and connects this to verse 14 where he equates those who are trying to escape with fleeing troops.

Verse 14

Verse 14 offers the final elements in this list of warnings offered by the prophet. Two further aspects are introduced here—standing at the crossroads (*haper-ek*) in order to cut off escapees, and the handing over of survivors. Isho'dad of Merv suggests the sense of the verse is that they have the people cornered. This cutting off and handing over of the people is reminiscent of Amos 1:6 and 9, where Edom is spoken of in relation to slave trade, along with Philistia and Tyre. Escapees and survivors together seem to signal all those who remain (Josh. 8:22; Jer. 42:17; Raabe). Edom has 'cut off' survivors, so it in turn will be cut off (vv. 9–10), hinting at the law of retaliation that is made plain in the following verse.

The Hebrew noun *perek* (NRSV: 'crossroads') is unusual: a number of commentators make note of this term, which is variously understood as 'breach' (in the city wall), 'narrow pass', 'escape route', or 'fork in the road' (see Raabe: 184). The LXX renders this as 'openings' or 'passes' (cf. Wolff), while Rashi interprets this as 'gaps', those places by which the people hoped to escape. Wellhausen says we simply do not know what the word means.

One can sense in the reception of this verse the consternation that interpreters feel about Edom's actions. Cyril of Alexandria writes that the prophet speaks of Edom's inhumanity, and divine judgment is thus imposed on those that truly deserve it. Theodore of Mopsuestia agrees; all of this, he opines, conveys the satisfaction and indeed the role that the Edomites played in the ruin of their brothers, and is the basis for Edom's eventual destruction. Luther highlights the insidious nature of the action here—not content with plunder, those who seek refuge are willfully cut off. Calvin observes this was something the Assyrians or Chaldeans would not have been able to do, unfamiliar as they were with the territory. But the Edomites, those close neighbors, knew the lay of the land and 'could stand at all the outlets' (444; cf. Ibn Ezra; Bewer). Pusey connects the treacherous actions of Edom here with the rebuke in Ezek. 35:10–11 and suggests this cutting off is part of Edom's desire to take Israel's land for their own and 'displace God's people'.

Verse 15

As noted in the introduction, verse 15 has been a crux for reflection on the potential literary development of Obadiah. Since Julius Wellhausen's conjecture in the nineteenth century, a number of modern scholars have suggested that verses 1–14 and 15b are a unit but that 15a fits better with 16–21. These latter verses are assumed to come from a later, postexilic date (Duhm; Bewer; Rudolph; Wolff; Barton). This inversion of verse 15 allows for a more consistent thematic flow in the book and also accounts for the use of second-person singular terms as found in the earlier parts of the book and in 15b. However, the ancient versions and the text preserved at Wadi Murabba'at support the reading of the MT, which argues against such a reconstruction (Watts 1969; Stuart 1987; Raabe). Wolff and Raabe offer helpful summaries that come to diverging conclusions.

In verse 15 we are introduced to the day of Yhwh and the explicit mention of recompense and retribution upon the nations. This sense of poetic justice is at the heart of the book as a whole (Anderson 2010). The Targum mitigates the proximity of the Lord by amending this to 'the day that will come from the Lord . . .' The day of Yhwh was a well-known expression, as seen in Isa. 13:6, 9; Ezek. 13:5; Joel 1:15; Amos 5:18, and elsewhere (Renkema; Raabe; cf. the commentary on Joel 1). This phrase has come to be equated with eschatological concerns in part because many HB texts that make use of this collocation place it in the (undetermined) future (Nogalski 1993). For some earlier commentators, this day of the Lord has only partially been fulfilled. Gill suggests Edom's day of the Lord came to pass some five years after the destruction of Jerusalem but also notes that the day of the Lord 'is not far off upon the Pagans, Mahometans, and all the "antichristian" states'.

While it is unclear how rigorously *lex talionis* might have been enforced in Israel and Judah, if it all, it is clear that the principle of retribution summarized in this idea was known (Exod. 21:23–25; Lev. 24:19; Jer. 50:29). The law of retributive justice was well known throughout the ancient world, as Pusey notes, including in Aristotle's *Ethics*. The notion of retribution in Obadiah 15 was also used in the Babylonian Talmud as a basis for the principle of come-uppance (b. Giṭ. 40a). Cyril of Alexandria comments on the element of divine justice in this verse: 'the divine nature measures out each person's failings and imposes a penalty that is completely commensurate with whatever sins each is guilty of committing' (141). Paulinus of Nola makes reference to this idea of recompense in a poem: 'Be mindful on that day of the sons of Edom, and change their role with ours, so that they may in disarray witness the day on which your people will dwell in Jerusalem's ancient city' (*Poem* 9.39; see Ferreiro: 122). Hugh of St. Victor, meanwhile, relates it to an adage: he who makes a pit falls into it.

The introduction of the nations in verse 15 takes some of the emphasis off of Edom and points to the more universal aspects that will emerge in the final verses of the book. Theodore of Mopsuestia notes this presence of the nations, commenting that retribution is coming for all who have harmed God's people, but Edom in particular will be singled out. Calvin makes a similar point but also discusses the fact of Judah's punishment: it may be that the Israelites are indeed being punished, but God is the judge of all people—no one escapes punishment. God starts in his own house, Calvin notes, but justice eventually comes for all nations. Matthew Henry concurs: 'Though judgment begins at the house of God, it shall not end there.' Pusey points out that this same language is used in Joel 3:7 and suggests that Joel's use has been applied here to Edom by the prophet; Wolff makes a similar observation but assumes priority lies with Obadiah.

Verse 16

In verse 16 we read: 'For as you have drunk on my holy mountain, all the nations around you shall drink; they shall drink and gulp down, and shall be as though they had never been' (NRSV). The LXX makes a minor change at the end of the first part of the verse, understanding the Hebrew *tamid* (often translated as 'continually') as the similar *temed* ('wine')—'all the nations shall drink wine'. Some Hebrew manuscripts read *saviv*, 'around' ('the nations around you', NRSV), which points to the difficulty of the verse. The Targum offers an expanded interpretation, stating that 'as you *rejoiced over the laying low* of my holy mountain, so all the peoples shall drink *the cup of their punishment* unceasingly, and they shall drink and be *swallowed up* . . .' (cf. Rashi).

There are four ways in which the first element of the verse has generally been understood: (1) it refers to the Edomites, who drank and rejoiced on the holy mountain (LXX; Targum). Cyril of Alexandria takes this language of drinking to mean that 'you mocked and jeered at the people of Israel, drinking and dancing and making the misfortunes of your brethren the occasion of festivities, so all the nations will drink and dance over you' (141–42; cf. Jerome; Calvin). This corresponds to the rest of the book, where the second person is always used in relation to Edom and seems to continue the theme of retribution. In this case, the first reference to drinking is literal, while the second 'drinking' is figurative and refers to punishment. As Calvin notes: 'this latter drinking is to be taken in a sense different from the former' (447). (2) Alternatively, Edom's drinking has been understood as punishment, which has already been meted out to Judah's neighbor. Ephrem the Syrian understands the first clause as relating to Edom already having drunk from the cup of wrath, while the wrath for the nations is yet to come. In this case, both examples of drinking are figurative. (3) Like Ephrem, Isho'dad of Merv also sees Edom having already 'drunk' its punishment at the hand of David. However, while he understands the first reference to drinking as metaphorical, he reads the second use as literal: as kings celebrate victory with libations, so the nations will celebrate at Edom's expense. (4) Finally, the text can be read as referring to Judah, who has drunk its cup of wrath, the same that will happen for the nations (Ibn Ezra; Perowne; Bewer; Raabe). In this case the two uses of drinking refer to punishment, and similar language is used elsewhere to refer to Jerusalem's fate (e.g., Jer. 51:7; Isa. 51:17–23). Wolff and others suggest that the cup of wrath imagery was part of the lament liturgies and thus fit well in the context of Obadiah (cf. Raabe: 202–42 for an extended discussion of the imagery of the cup of wrath).

Luther sees in this verse a cycle of judgment enacted through peoples and nations, which in turn leads to more sin, which itself will need to be corrected:

> God Almighty always punishes the old sins of a kingdom by means of new sins of other people whom He rouses to act . . . Thus, the Tartars and the Goths with their new sins rose up against the old sins of the Romans, who had oppressed the Jews in so many ways. Today the Turk is powerful. However, if the earth will not immediately pass away, another stronger country will rise up that will be stirred by the judgment of God to subdue the Turk, etc. (200)

Like Luther, Pusey sees the nations as continually enacting this wrath on other nations, each becoming in turn as it had never been: 'To swallow up, and be swallowed up in turn, is the world's history' (363).

Some have taken this verse as an opportunity to expound on the dangers of drinking alcohol and other vices. Hugh of St. Victor comments that the verse refers historically to Edom, allegorically to heretics and idolaters, and tropologically to the animal lusts, which each of us must control. Rainolds provides an excursus in a sermon to speak about 'the harm which proceedeth of excessive drinking. And although I have less cause to fear this vice in Christian men', he writes, 'much less in Englishmen, least of all in Oxford, yet the great plenty of winesellers lately increased causeth me to dread, lest by degrees we come unto it'. After discussing the theme of wine in the Bible, he concludes, 'Let us therefore, hence learn that our prophet, by the metaphor of drinking representing the endless and unspeakable troubles of the wicked, commendeth unto us sobriety and modesty in the use of God's creatures, lest that we draw upon us plagues spiritual and temporal' (Rainolds: 34).

Verse 17

In verse 17 the tone shifts, and the final few verses of the book speak of the restoration of God's people. Verse 17 refers to Mount Zion as a place of escape, followed by the statement that the 'house of Jacob shall take possession of those who dispossessed them' (NRSV). It is probable that Joel 3:5 draws on this verse, which similarly speaks of Mount Zion and escape (Barton).

The mention of 'those that escape' brings to mind verse 14, where the Edomites cut off those that tried to escape. The LXX, meanwhile, renders this as *soteria*, 'there will be salvation', a move that corresponds with the mention of 'saviors' in verse 21 (cf. Vulgate). The Targum retains the idea of escapees/deliverance but indicates that it is these survivors, rather than Mount Zion, which will be holy (cf. Radak). This notion of a remnant is developed by Ibn Ezra, who comments that some understand this as referring to a future remnant, others to those saved in the time of Hezekiah, and still others to those who escaped during the destruction of the second Temple. Bringing this together with the theme of lament, Wolff believes the text has in mind the remnant that remains and which gathers for the service of lament in Jerusalem following the Babylonian conquest.

Modern scholars have questioned whether the reference to holiness in relation to Mount Zion is a later interpretive gloss, particularly as it is missing in some medieval manuscripts (Elliger 1959; Wolff). The ancient versions, however, support the MT (Gelston). The reference to salvation in the Greek and Latin texts was a launching point for various readings of this verse in the Christian tradition, as was the mention of holiness. 'There is Obadiah', Theodoret of Cyr writes, 'who prophesies the cause of salvation to all in Zion. From there God will disperse holiness into the entire inhabited earth through the saving cross' (Ferreiro: 124). Jerome suggests that one possible meaning for Mount Zion becoming 'holy' is the reintroduction of the Temple and the Holy of Holies in particular, which took place after the return from exile. Others would see in this move from deliverance to holiness a progression from salvation to sanctification (Matthew Henry).

The final word of verse 17 is understood as a form of the noun *morash* in the Masoretic tradition. This reading indicates that the house of Jacob will repossess 'its possession'. However, several ancient variants understood this to be a participle from *yarash* and translated as 'those who had possessed them', or 'their dispossessors', which would more clearly suggest Edomitic presence in parts of Judah. This rendering is followed by the LXX, Vulgate, Syriac, as well as the text from Wadi Murabba'at. Accordingly, Obadiah 17 refers either to the house of Jacob 'possessing its possession' or 'dispossessing their dispossessors'.

The latter reading is followed by the NRSV (cf. Wolff), while the NIV and NASB follow the MT (cf. Raabe; Renkema). To what does this 'possession' refer? Following the Targum, Rashi seems to have material goods in mind as he interprets this verse as referring to the physical possessions of those who dispossessed the Israelites. More common is the idea that this refers to the land of Judah. Cyril of Alexandria comments on the inversion that takes place here: while Edom thought they would possess the descendants of Jacob, they are instead dispossessed (cf. Radak).

Luther noticed a marked change in the text here; while to this point his commentary has at least attempted to address historical questions, here he sees 'another kingdom, which we can understand in no other way than as the spiritual kingdom of Christ spread among all nations through the Gospel' (200; cf. Gill). Noting that there are two kingdoms of which we need to be aware— the earthly Israelite kingdom and the kingdom of Christ—he notes this verse speaks of the latter: 'from the people of Israel the apostles and other disciples of Christ would come who were going to make subject to themselves the whole world by a new preaching of the Gospel and thus were going to establish a new and eternal kingdom' (201). Calvin makes a similar interpretive move, noting that this verse points to the future restoration of the church. It also teaches that 'Whenever then God inflicts wounds on his church, prepared at the same time is the remedy; for God designs not, nor does he suffer, that his own people should be wholly lost' (448; cf. Rainolds).

In a sermon entitled 'Possessing Possessions', the English pastor Charles Spurgeon drew upon Obadiah 17 in a message delivered in London in 1890. Spurgeon has no doubt that this text was fulfilled at some point in history, as Israel was restored and Edom was destroyed. However, he notes that 'the former fulfilment of a promise does not make it useless . . . the promise may be presented again, and it will again be honoured'. He proceeds to offer a spiritual reading for his church, imploring his listeners to fully possess the spiritual blessing and promises in their own lives. For Spurgeon, Obadiah's prophecy in verse 17 concerning possession is an exhortation to Christians to embrace the fullness of their spiritual lives, to help lead others to salvation, and to live lives of holiness.

Verse 18

In verse 18 we return to the theme of Edom's destruction, and, drawing on the imagery of a consuming fire, we find reference to the house of Jacob (a fire), the house of Joseph (a flame), and the house of Esau (consumed stubble).

The Hebrew states that 'the house of Jacob shall be a fire'; the Aramaic Targum clarifies this with 'The people of the house of Jacob shall be strong as fire', and similar interpretive additions are made throughout the verse. The MT says that there will be no 'survivor' (*sarid*) from the house of Esau, which again reminds the reader of the survivors handed over in verse 14. The LXX instead notes that there will be no 'fire bearer' (*purphoros*) for the house of Esau, likely indicating someone who would lead the troops into battle (Hesychius; Bewer). As Gill comments in the eighteenth century,

> not so much as a torch bearer left, one that carries the lights before an army, as the Septuagint and Arabic versions; which versions, and the custom alluded to, serve very much to illustrate the passage. It was a custom with the Greeks, as we are told, when armies were about to engage, that before the first ensigns stood a prophet or priest, bearing branches of laurels and garlands, who was called 'pyrophorus', or the 'torch bearer', because he held a lamp or torch . . . hence, when a total destruction of an army, place, or people, was hyperbolically expressed, it used to be said, not so much as a torch bearer or fire carrier escaped; hence this phrase was proverbially used of the most entire defeat of an army, or ruin of a people.

The Greek term *purphoros* was corrupted in some traditions to *purophoros*, and so some understood it as having to do with one who carries wheat or corn (Jerome is aware of both readings; see Ellicott [1884], 'wheat bearer').

Why are both Jacob and Joseph mentioned, and how should we understand the reference to the 'house of Joseph'? Some suggest that this is simple parallelism, and the two (Jacob and Joseph) are not to be distinguished; others note that by synecdoche this implies the entirety of the former kingdom of Israel, an inclusive gesture (Amos 5:6; 6:6; cf. Keil; Raabe; Wolff), and an idea that is already present in texts including Isa. 8:14 and Ezek. 35:10. In this sense, the verse implies an idealized version of the future including both north and south, which will be expanded on in the final verses.

The Sages discussed how best to understand this verse, particularly whether or not the 'house of Esau', which is to be consumed, refers to all of Esau's descendants. In the Babylonian Talmud this is understood to refer only to those who act as Esau acted (b. 'Abod. Zar.). Rashi, meanwhile, drawing on Pirqe R. El. (37), cites Num. 24:18 as corroboration for this verse, as Balaam foretold of Edom's destruction.

In Genesis Rabbah this verse is cited at several points in the story of Jacob. First, in this midrashic engagement with Jacob's encounter at the Jabbok, the stranger is said to have produced fire with his finger. Jacob retorts, 'From this do you expect to frighten me? The whole of me is made up of such a substance: "And the house of Jacob shall be a fire"' (Gen. Rab. 77:2). Second, at the height of his ordeal with his brother Esau, this verse is used to comfort Jacob: 'A single spark from your [forge] and one from your son's and the two of you will burn them up' (Gen. Rab. 84:5; [Neusner]). In both cases, this verse is seen to ascribe strength and victory to Jacob himself.

Christian readers also gave a good deal of attention to this verse. Jerome comments on the reference here to Jacob and Joseph to note that both Judah and the ten tribes of the north will together devour Edom. He goes on to note that the spiritual understanding refers to the church's eventual victory and vindication, particularly for those who remain faithful. There will be no remnant of Esau left because all will turn to Christ. As was the case in verse 17, Luther sees a literal interpretation of this verse as impossible, as the tribes of Joseph never return after their banishment, and Judah never took possession of Edom. Thus, this must 'refer to the preaching of the Gospel among all nations by the apostles and other disciples. By this preaching all nations have devoured—that is, have become incorporated with—the kingdom of Christ spiritually' (202). Luther notes that Arabia Petra, the land of the Edomites, would go on to be the home of many holy men, including St. Anthony, thus fulfilling this prophecy. Calvin expounds on the imagery of fire and puts this into the context of the exile: though they might assume the flame had died out, 'yet a fire would be kindled' that would consume Edom (450). For Calvin, this again shows God's love for his people (and his church) in spite of the harsh reality for the Edomites. Others would point to a historical fulfillment of this verse as having taken place in the Hasmonean period (Perowne; Pusey) and a spiritual fulfillment in the preaching of the apostles, who preached the word 'which is like fire' (Gill).

The verse ends by noting that 'the LORD has spoken'. Wolff suggests that the reference to God speaking may have been the original ending for Obadiah's words before the final verses were appended, while Renkema says this is better understood as validation of what the prophet has just said.

Verse 19

In verse 19, the text refers to a number of territories being possessed (using the Hebrew root *yarash*). The term *possession* is the same root found in verse 17 and is a trope found elsewhere in the HB in relation to Esau and Edom (Deut. 2:5, 22; Josh. 24:4; Num. 24:18; Isa. 43:10–11; Ezek. 35:10; Amos 9:12). What is presented as a positive idea in Deuteronomy and Joshua—that Esau and his descendants have been given their land as a possession—is inverted in Numbers and the prophets, as Edom is to be dispossessed of its possession (Anderson 2022). Obadiah offers the fullest account of this dispossession trope.

Synecdoche is used throughout the verse, and determining subjects and objects has proven difficult. Some have suggested that there is only one subject here—the house of Jacob or perhaps Jacob and Joseph from the previous verse—and all the other names are territories to be possessed. Wellhausen, for example, saw the Negev, Shephelah, Ephraim, and Gilead as direct objects to be possessed by Jacob, and the other names as later additions (variations of this are found in Wolff; Dicou 1994). Others have suggested two subjects—Judah and Benjamin—with the first three colons referring to Judah, and the final one referring to Benjamin. Perowne commented that only Judah and Benjamin remained at this time, and so the verse was directed to them: Judah gets everything to the west of the Jordan, and Benjamin gets Gilead to the east. The most common reading, including the ancient versions, is to see three different 'possessions'. In this case the first noun is the subject in each colon, and the second is the direct object (with the exception of the third colon, which continues the second). This is the general thrust of the versions and most modern translations, such as the NRSV (cf. Radak; Pusey; Rudolph 1971):

> [19]Those of the Negeb shall possess Mount Esau,
>   and those of the Shephelah the land of the Philistines;
> they shall possess the land of Ephraim and the land of Samaria,
>   and Benjamin shall possess Gilead.

Readers have long noted that the territories mentioned here are reminiscent of those laid out by Joshua at the conquest of Canaan (Jerome; Perowne; Rainolds). Cyril of Alexandria sees in this verse a reference to exiles returning from Babylon to possess Edom as a sign of blessing from God. Cyril invokes the exiles here as he believes that the land was devastated and emptied. However, these returnees would become so prosperous that the original land would be too small for them. Calvin makes a similar observation, as this verse indicates the exiles will have a land bigger and better than before, indeed, fulfilling what had been promised to Abraham but had never been fully realized. Calvin also notes, however, that this had never been fulfilled, and so he offers a figurative reading concerning the kingdom of Christ. Luther again cannot find a way to read this verse literally, and he also supposes a figurative reading focused on the early apostles going out from Jerusalem: 'Necessity compels us, then, to relate all of these references to the preaching of the Gospel' (202).

The first clause states that the Negev will possess Mount Esau—the latter, as noted in verse 8, a designation that is unique to Obadiah. As with previous verses, the Targum shows its aversion for metaphorical language: it fills in gaps by speaking of the conquerors as 'the inhabitants of' the Negev, the Shephelah, and so on, while the places possessed are the citadels, lands, and cities of these being overtaken. Rashi explains that the people of Judah were living in the south of *eretz Yisrael* at this time, and so they would possess Mount Esau, which is at the southern boundary. Modern readers have noted that reference to the Negev may also refer to the fact that Edomites had begun to have a more consistent presence in parts of southern Judah from the eighth to the sixth centuries BCE, and so it is the inhabitants of this region that will possess Mount Esau (Lipschits 2005; Tebes 2006).

Depictions of Obadiah frequently portray the prophet delivering a message to a city located on a hill, drawing on the imagery in the book of the high places of Edom and 'Mount Esau', which are to be dispossessed (see Figure 48).

FIGURE 48   Johann Christoph, Der Prophet Abdias (woodcut). From 'Biblia ectypa: Bildnussen auss Heiliger Schrifft Alt und Neuen Testaments', Christoph Weigel (author).
Courtesy of Pitts Library Digital Archive/ Emory University.

The second clause of verse 19 is verbless; as noted earlier, many assume that the reference to the Shephelah 'possessing' the Philistines is implied rather than being stated explicitly. The Shephelah invokes the central plains and its inhabitants: 'the strip of foothills west of the Judean highlands and east of the coastal plain of Philistia' (Raabe: 259). The coastal lands of Philistia were considered part of the traditional land promised (Num. 34:6; Deut. 11:24; Josh. 1:4; 15:33–47), which again has alerted readers to potential reference to the conquest traditions.

Given the structure of these verses, one expects the third colon to contain a subject, in this case Ephraim, and a direct object to be possessed, Samaria (Renkema). However, both nouns here have the direct object marker, suggesting that perhaps they should be seen as a continuation of the previous phrases. It could be, as Raabe notes, that the reader must supply the identity of the possessor in this case, and he suggests broadly the 'main part of Judah located in the central highlands' as the possible 'possessor' of both Ephraim and Samaria (cf. Barton).

As with the earlier Shephelah clause, commentators frequently assume that a reference to 'possessing' is missing but implied in the reference to Benjamin's possession of Gilead, with the former often understood as referring to the inhabitants of the tribal lands in the north. Gilead denotes to a stretch of land east of the Jordan River, associated with the Transjordan tribes Reuben, Gad, and Manasseh. Rashi indicates that Benjamin will join Manasseh as the land of Israel expands eastward. Some have suggested that 'Benjamin' is a corruption (Bewer; Wellhausen; Wolff); Gilead came under Ammonite rule in the Babylonian period, and so it has been put forward that Benjamin should be read as 'the Ammonites', producing a reading where the Gilead will possess the Ammonites (Duhm). However, Sweeney points out that there are links between Benjamin and Gilead (1 Sam. 11; 31), and it has the most natural association given the directionality of the other locations mentioned:

> Insofar as 1–2 Chronicles continually identifies Judah and Benjamin as the tribes who survived the Assyrian deportations of northern Israel and who constitute the remnant of Israel in the post-Assyrian period, this statement reflects the perspective of the late- or post-exilic period that Judah and Benjamin together would see to the restoration of all Israel to the land.
>
> (Sweeney: 296)

Raabe brings together the various locations and movements that are encountered in verse 19:

> Verse 19 concretizes and particularizes the general promise given in v 17b. The Judahites who were left in the land following the Babylonian deportations will fan out in all four directions. . . . The arrangement of subjects and objects makes

good geographical sense: the inhabitants of the Negeb move south (and east); those of the Shephelah move west; those of the central and main part of Judah possess the northern territory; and those of Benjamin proceed east. Apart from the first clause, the verse promises the repossession of Israel's entire land within the traditional borders.

(Raabe: 258; cf. Radak; Renkema)

Verse 20

The geographical references continue in verse 20, as do the complexities. A number of contemporary scholars suggest the verse is a later addition, commenting on and expanding verse 19 (Wolff; Renkema). A literal translation of the Hebrew reads:

> The exiles of this company [Halah?],
> of the sons of Israel
>   the Canaanites to Zarephath;
> and the exiles of Jerusalem who are in Sepharad,
>   will possess the cities of the Negeb.

As with verse 19, it is not entirely clear how many subjects and direct objects are found in this verse. Following the Sages, Rashi understands verse 20 as having two subjects—the two groups of exiles—both of which possess cities in the Negev (cf. Perowne). Other readings, however, try to make sense of two subjects with two separate 'possessions' (LXX, Targum). In this reading, a dropped phrase ('will possess') in the first clause is the reason for the lack of clarity in the text (cf. Pusey; Raabe; Renkema). The mention of 'exiles' in this verse has been picked up by those who advocate for understanding Obadiah as an exilic or postexilic text (Barton), as well as by those who see this as predicting the return of exiles in the future (Ephrem the Syrian; Nicholas of Lyra).

The first part of the verse speaks of the 'exiles of *hahel hazeh*'. This clause is difficult and has been understood in a variety of ways (see Barton). The LXX changes this to read 'the beginning of the migration' (cf. Peshitta), while the Targum renders the clause as 'this people'. Following some other ancient traditions (e.g., Vulgate), the word *hahel* has been understood as a defective spelling of *hayil*, 'company, army'. Rashi, for example, comments that the word is missing the *yod* and then harmonizes the Targum with the Hebrew text, noting how 'this people' (Targum) is an expression of a 'host' (Rashi). If this option is followed, 'this company or host' would seem to refer to those from

Judah mentioned in the previous verse, and the following clause ('of the sons of Israel') would then add further commentary on this description (Gill). The nineteenth-century *Speaker's Commentary* posits that the use of 'this company' means that Obadiah himself is writing as one of the exiles (cf. Perowne).

Others have posited that the term in question should be understood as a proper noun. Thus, some have suggested an emendation that would make this another place name, Halah, referring to the Assyrian city to which northern exiles were taken (as in 2 Kgs 17.6 and 1 Chr. 5.26; see BHQ; Duhm 1911; Renkema). This option has the advantage of offering a parallel location for the exiles referred to in the second half of the verse, who will return from Sepharad.

The reference to 'Canaanites' in verse 20 has been another point for discussion through the years. The LXX and Targum both interpret this as referring to the territory ('land of the Canaanites'; cf. Rashi; Theodore of Mopsuestia). However, a more common reading is that this is referring to those in exile as Canaanites, and these are to possess Zarephath, a city located on the northwest coast between Tyre and Sidon which is mentioned by Pliny and Josephus as being connected with glassmaking and wine (Gill). With this northern emphasis, modern scholars assume that the Phoenicians are in mind. Wolff remarks that the author/redactor 'seems to see Galilee and Phoenicia as prepared for the homecomers from exile who had once belonged to the Northern Kingdom' (68).

In medieval Jewish commentary, however, it became common to see these place names as referring to European locations. Ibn Ezra observes that some Canaanites relocated to Germany at the time of Joshua's conquest—and so Canaanites here refers to those from the land who relocated to Germany. Radak, meanwhile, identifies Zarephath with France (cf. Rashi and Nicholas of Lyra). As many Jews were later sent to Germany, Spain, and other locations by the Romans after 70 CE, this verse speaks of those Jews in exile who now find themselves in Germany, France, and beyond. Calvin is aware of both of these readings—he writes that Jewish tradition understands this as referring to the Germans and the Gauls.

The second part of the verse refers to the exiles of Jerusalem who are in Sepharad. While the LXX renders the term as *Ephratha* and the Vulgate opts for *Bosphorus*, a city on the Black Sea, the Targum and Peshitta famously render the location as *Spain*. Ephrem the Syrian and other early Christian leaders were also aware of this equation of Sepharad with Spain, noting that the verse refers to the 'transmigration to Spain' (cf. Isho'dad of Merv; Nicholas of Lyra). This latter reading of the text has had a long afterlife, as Jews from Spain and surrounding regions are referred to as Sephardim (Montefiore and Loewe).

The Jewish commentator Abarbanel rejected the association of Canaanites with Germany but saw the references to France and Spain as valid—this refers to those exiled to these far-flung lands (see *Miqra'ot Gedelot*). Luther comments on the tradition of reading Zarephath as France (which he ascribes to Nicholas of Lyra) but notes that 'this seems very inappropriate to me'. He then refutes Jerome's reading of Sepharad as Bosphorus, as well as the Jewish reading of Spain, and suggests instead that this refers to 'some inconsequential town in the land of Canaan' (204; cf. Calvin; Rainolds). While other locations for Sepharad have been offered in the modern period (Keil suggested Sparta), the most common is Sardis, in modern Turkey (see discussion in Barton; Lipinksi 1973).

That these exiles will take possession of the cities of the Negev (Targum: 'the land of the south', cf. v. 19) is again not a self-explanatory statement. Cyril of Alexandria sees this as referring to 'the Indian nations, since the Indians and their lands are furthest south' (144). However, most readers interpret the verse in two halves: if the first half of the verse presents exiles taking possession of land far to the north, the latter half can be seen to complement this, focusing on exiles returning to the southern regions (Raabe).

The Negev in the biblical period 'extended from the hills south of Hebron to Kadesh-barnea and that primarily centered in the Beersheba and Arad valleys' (Raabe: 259). Archaeological discoveries of the past century have shed light on the inhabitants of this region during the period in question and may explain the focus on the Negev in these verses. Material culture points to a significant presence of Edomites in the Negev from the late eighth to the sixth centuries BCE (Beit Arieh 1989; Tebes 2006). While it was formerly assumed that this was related to military incursions, further discoveries have suggested that this Edomitic presence in the Negev was driven by trade and economic opportunities. The existence of pottery that reflects Edomitic cultural traits but which was produced in the Negev points to long-term settlement rather than simply evidence of passing traders or military incursions (Bienkowski and van der Steen 2001). Textual evidence from the period also indicates cross-pollination between cultures. For example, Edomitic names are found in Judahite genealogies of this period (Knoppers 2001). Because of this, it has been suggested that this is a plausible historical context for the development—or at least consolidation—of notions of kinship between Judah and Edom/Jacob and Esau (Tebes 2006). Significantly, after the fall of Jerusalem, there was a northward expansion of semi-nomadic groups, including Edomites (Lipschits 2005). Accordingly, a strong Edomite presence developed in the Negev, and so it is envisioned that the returning exiles will (re)possess this part of the land, just as the residents of the Negev will possess Mount Esau (v. 19).

As Raabe notes, in spite of the complexity of this passage, 'the basic gist of the verse remains clear: even the Jerusalemites who dwell in the farthest regions will participate in Israel's restoration' (268). Readers frequently note that if verse 19 is concerned with those remaining in the land expanding and moving out to Israel's 'true' (and indeed extended) borders, verse 20 draws those in exile back into the equation.

Verse 21

The final verse of the book brings the prophet's message to a climactic finish. The NRSV reads, 'Those who have been saved [or "saviors"] shall go up to Mount Zion to rule Mount Esau; and the kingdom shall be the LORD's.' The Targum retains the idea of saviors, speaking of 'liberators' or 'deliverers' going up to Mount Zion. Other traditions, however, change this to a passive sense, referring to those who are saved. Thus, the LXX renders the first clause as 'The men who are rescued from Mount Zion' (cf. Peshitta; Aquila; Theodotion). These examples point to a difficulty in this verse, namely whether or not those saved/saviors are going *up to* Mount Zion or if they are going *down from* Mount Zion to Edom.

The only other plural use of this term (*moshi'im*) in the HB occurs in Neh. 9:27, which invokes Israel's early days. Indeed, 'savior' or 'deliverer' is a title used to describe the leaders in the book of Judges (e.g., Judg. 3:9; 15), and a number of commentators make this connection. Thus, just as the people had been delivered by saviors in the past, so too it would happen again. Ibn Ezra offers such an interpretation, explaining that these saviors are judges who will judge those who survive on Mount Esau. Radak, meanwhile, observes that these 'saviors' refer to a future Messiah and his colleagues, citing Mic. 5:4. Maimonides makes note of Num. 24:18 and its reference to the dispossession of Seir; bringing this into conversation with Obadiah, he notes that this will happen at the hands of the Messiah, as noted in Obadiah 21 (*Melachim uMilchamot* 11.1).

Christian readers have also made note of the fact that the book of Judges refers to Israel's leaders as 'saviors' (Luther). Citing this connection, Calvin makes an observation about the judges of Israel: 'the Prophet here reminds them that God had still in his hand redeemers, whenever it might please him to gather his people' (454). Rainolds notes that the first fulfillment of this text can be seen in figures such as Zerubbabel and others who returned to Jerusalem. These men are 'principle agents' and 'ministerial instruments', even if God alone is the true savior. In the Church of Latter Day Saints, the reference to saviors in this verse has been understood as fulfilled in those missionaries who leave their families for this important task of mission work (Gillum 2005).

However, for Christians, the occurrence of the term *saviors* also proved a natural launching point for Christological and apostolic interpretation. An example of this is found in Augustine's *City of God*. He writes:

> If, by that form of speech in which a part is put for the whole, we take Idumea as put for the nations, we may understand of Christ what he says among other things, 'But upon Mount Sion shall be safety, and there shall be a Holy One' (Obadiah 17). And a little after, at the end of the same prophecy, he says, 'And those who are saved again shall come up out of Mount Sion, that they may defend Mount Esau, and it shall be a kingdom to the Lord' (Obadiah 21). It is quite evident this was fulfilled when those saved again out of Mount Sion— that is, the believers in Christ from Judea, of whom the apostles are chiefly to be acknowledged—went up to defend Mount Esau. How could they defend it except by making safe, through the preaching of the gospel. . . . For Mount Sion signifies Judea, where it is predicted there shall be safety, and a Holy One, that is, Christ Jesus. But Mount Esau is Idumea, which signifies the Church of the Gentiles, which, as I have expounded, those saved again out of Sion have defended that it should be a kingdom to the Lord. This was obscure before it took place; but what believer does not find it out now that it is done?
>
> (Augustine, *City of God* 18.31)

Augustine reads this figuratively, interpreting Mount Zion as the place from where salvation will come, referring to the work of Christ. He also reads Edom as symbolic of the nations, and so Mount Esau is equated with the church of the Gentiles. Taken together, when salvation goes forth from Mount Zion, it is the apostles who go out with the gospel, bringing salvation and making Mount Esau safe. Accordingly, in Augustine's reading, rather than being overcome, Mount Esau is defended.

Jerome also reads the verse in relation to the early church sent out by Christ, those saviors who are sent out with the gospel and become shepherds of the people (cf. Hugh of St. Victor). Nicholas of Lyra notes that while some say these saviors were Ezra, Nehemiah, or the Maccabees, the Church Fathers identify these as the apostles, such as Peter and Paul. The identification of the apostles with these saviors who announce salvation would continue into the modern period (Gill; Perowne; Pusey).

These saviors, the Hebrew text says, will 'judge' Mount Esau. The LXX understands this as exacting punishment, and this idea is repeated often, from Rashi, to Ephrem, to Cyril. However, Raabe observes that to judge in this context refers to 'exercising authority and governing', which again might point back to the judges of pre-monarchic Israel. Wolff concurs, noting that to judge in the sense of governing always refers to people, not things; thus, it implies survivors who are ruled over. Indeed, some see here a sort of promise for Edom and a much more positive conclusion to the book than is often assumed (Augustine; Kellermann 1975; Renkema).

The rabbis used this verse to explain why Jacob did not go to meet Esau after telling him he would do so at the reunion of the brothers in Gen. 33:14, 17. In Genesis Rabbah we read,

> 'until I come to my lord in Seir' (Gen 33:14): R. Abbahu said, 'We have reviewed the entire Scripture and have not found that Jacob ever actually went to Esau at Mount Seir in his entire life. Surely it is not possible that the upright Jacob should have deceived him. But when will he come to him in point of fact? It will be in the age to come: "And saviors shall come up on Mount Zion to judge the mount of Esau (Ob. 21)"' (Gen. Rab. 78:14 [Neusner]; cf. y. 'Abod. Zar. 2:1).

A similar reading is found in the Zohar, where Obadiah 21 is seen as vindication for Jacob's actions in Genesis 33 (Zohar *Vayishalach*, 130). As noted in the introduction, these texts are also read together in liturgical settings, as Obadiah is the *haftarah* reading for *Vayishlach*, Gen. 32:4–36:43 (Fishbane 2002).

The final clause refers to the kingdom of YHWH. The Targum expands the final clause of the verse to read 'and the kingdom of the Lord shall be revealed over all the inhabitants on the earth'. The Targumist likely thought that God had always been ruling, but his kingdom had not yet been revealed to everyone (Cathcart and Gordon). Rashi comments that the final clause 'teaches you that His kingdom will not be complete until He exacts retribution on Amalek', likely a reference to the fact that Amalek is said to come from the line of Esau. *The Israel Bible* points to this verse as a Zionist prophecy concerning the restoration of the state of Israel, fulfilled in the twentieth century.

Theodore of Mopsuestia remarks on the closing of Obadiah: 'Through all the good experiences of the Israelites and the sufferings in payment of the penalty on the part of those who sinned against them, God emerges as true king, Lord and maker of all, doing with authority what he pleases in regard to his own and those seeming to be foreigners' (184). However, not surprisingly, Christians have often equated this reign of God with Jesus. Rainolds compares the earthly kingdoms with the heavenly: 'If the queen of Sheba thought Solomon's servants happy, that had him to rule them, how much more they which have a greater than Solomon, Christ Jesus . . . if we feel some taste of comfort in the government of Queen Elizabeth, what and how great shall we enjoy under him?' (Rainolds: 40).

When the larger contextual unit of verses 17–21 is read in light of the various place names and directional markers, the picture of Israel repossessing its land has been understood as idyllic: it not only employs archaic geographic and conquest-related terminology but also uses the language of territories that would cover the four corners of an idealized 'ancient' Israel (whatever historical realities lie behind these), as well as incorporating Edom (Cyril of Alexandria; Calvin; Renkema; Ben Zvi 1996). As Barton comments, this text speaks of 'the glorious restoration of preexilic (even pre-721) "land of Israel" and its annexation of neighbouring territories to produce a kind of "Greater Israel," whose boundaries would correspond roughly to those supposed in the Old Testament to have existed in the age of David' (Barton: 157; cf. Theodore of Mopsuestia; Pusey).

Concluding Reflections

This study has explored the use and reception of three Hebrew prophets—Hosea, Joel, and Obadiah. As part of this we have surveyed the use of these prophetic texts in commentaries and interpretive traditions, the impact of these texts in the religious traditions of Judaism and Christianity, and the social and cultural employment of these prophetic works in areas ranging from literature, to music, to the visual arts. In conclusion I offer a few personal reflections on the project and observations on the task of reception history.

The first observation relates to the volume of material that one finds in the reception of these texts and the challenge of giving shape to this material. Even for these more 'minor' prophets, the amount of material related to these prophets is astounding. As noted at the outset, what I have offered here are just snapshots and soundings of what is a much larger conversation—and even these are shaped and limited by my own interests and situatedness. Thus, what is offered here is an introduction and an invitation, and my hope is that others will continue to tell the story of how these prophets have been used and employed in various times and places: adding to, supplementing, and offering new perspectives on what is found in these pages.

A second observation relates to the diverse interpretations, conclusions, and uses one finds in the reception of these prophets. In the course of the project I often found myself feeling like a compiler of the Talmud or the *Glossa Ordinaria*, bringing together the various and sometimes opposing views of many Sages without offering any resolution or definitive answers. And yet, in many ways, this is fitting because one of the tasks of reception history is to alert us to the polyvalence of the Bible and the multivocality

Hosea, Joel, and Obadiah Through the Centuries, First Edition. Bradford A. Anderson.
© 2024 John Wiley & Sons Ltd. Published 2024 by John Wiley & Sons Ltd.

of interpretation. Who gets to determine what is an appropriate, or correct, approach to interpreting a text? What communities (religious, scholarly, or otherwise) can claim 'ownership' of this collection as well as how it is read, understood, and appropriated? Reception history reminds us that these are not easy questions, nor are they new. The Bible is and always has been a contested and complex text.

A final (and related) reflection is one that many of us know at an abstract level but which becomes especially clear when undertaking the task of reception history: the history of the Bible's reception is ultimately the exploration of a human practice—and the readers, interpreters, and artists examined in this study exemplify the full spectrum of humanity's potential and folly. On the one hand, we have seen difficult examples of how gender and religious identity have played a significant and sometimes harmful role in how these biblical texts have been used and understood down through the centuries. And yet, time and again, I have been surprised by the charity, imagination, insight, and scholarship of so many of these interlocutors throughout history. For every example that left me frustrated or disappointed, there were several others that caught me by surprise and challenged my assumptions about what I was expecting from these readers, commentators, and artists. This points to one of the real benefits of reception history, which is that it can allow us to view the past (and hopefully the present) with both critical and moral clarity, as well as with charity and appreciation.

Perhaps this is a fitting way to conclude: while the reception of these prophets points to the long and complicated history of how the Bible has been used and understood, it also serves as a reminder to this reader of the privilege of taking part in this ancient and ongoing conversation.

Glossary and Biographies

Abarbanel (Abravanel) (Isaac ben Judah) (1437–1508): medieval Jewish philosopher and commentator; born in Portugal

Altschuler, David: see *Metzudat David*

Ambrose (ca. 333–97): fourth-century Church Father and bishop of Milan; known as a teacher of Augustine

Aramaic: Semitic language closely related to Hebrew; language of the Targums

Aquinas, St. Thomas (1225–74): medieval church theologian, author of famous *Summa Theologica*; member of the Dominican order

Augustine of Hippo (354–430): influential Church Father and theologian known for writings including *Confessions* and *City of God*

Basil the Great (ca. 330–79): fourth-century theologian and bishop of Caesarea, known for establishing rules for monastic life

Hosea, Joel, and Obadiah Through the Centuries, First Edition. Bradford A. Anderson.
© 2024 John Wiley & Sons Ltd. Published 2024 by John Wiley & Sons Ltd.

Bewer, Julius August (1877–1953): German-American biblical scholar

Burroughs, Jeremiah (1599–1646): English Congregationalist and Puritan

Calvin, John (1509–64): influential French theologian and biblical commentator of the Reformation

Chrysostom, John (ca. 347–407): well-known preacher of the patristic period, bishop of Constantinople

Cyril of Alexandria (ca. 376–444): patriarch of Alexandria; theologian and biblical commentator

Darby, John Nelson (1800–82): Anglo-Irish theologian and Bible teacher; influential in the development of Brethren movements and Dispensationalism

Dead Sea Scrolls: name given to manuscripts discovered at Qumran near the Dead Sea, including biblical and other texts

Ephrem the Syrian (306–73): Syrian theologian, biblical commentator, and hymn writer; particularly influential in eastern Christianity

Ewald, Georg Heinrich August von (1803–75): German Protestant biblical scholar, orientalist, and theologian

Figural/Figurative interpretation: interpretation that focuses on metaphorical or typological dimensions, often juxtaposed with 'literal' interpretation

Genesis Rabbah (Bereshit Rabbah): midrash on the book of Genesis from the rabbinic period (300–500 CE)

Gill, John (1697–1771): English Baptist pastor, biblical commentator, and theologian

Glossa Ordinaria: medieval collection that includes glosses from the Church Fathers, as well as notes from medieval scholars such as Nicholas of Lyra

Haftarah: lectionary reading from the Hebrew Prophets that accompanies the reading from the Torah

Harper, William Rainey (1856–1906): American Baptist pastor, biblical scholar, and academic

Historical-critical approaches/historical criticism: academic approaches of the modern era primarily interested in historical questions such as authorship, sources, and redaction of biblical texts

Ibn Ezra, Abraham (ca. 1092–1167): influential Jewish biblical commentator and philosopher of the Middle Ages

Irenaeus (ca. 120–200): bishop of Lyons and early church theologian

Isho'dad of Merv (ca. 850): biblical commentator, bishop of Hdatta, and influential theologian of the Eastern Church

Jerome (Hieronymus) (ca. 342–420): biblical scholar, most known for his translation of the Bible into Latin (Vulgate) and his commentaries on the Bible

Josephus, Flavius (c. 37–100): Jewish author of the first century CE, including works such as the *Jewish War* and *Jewish Antiquities*

Julian of Eclanum (386–455): early church theologian and commentator; bishop of Eclanum, connected to the Pelagians

Lectionary: list of Scripture readings for liturgical use

Lives of the Prophets: Jewish legends concerning the prophets, likely from the first century CE

Luther, Martin (1483–1546): German Augustinian monk and later leader of the Reformation, known for theological writings and biblical commentaries

LXX: see Septuagint

Maimonides, Moses (Rambam) (1138–1204): influential medieval Jewish physician, philosopher, and commentator

Malbim (Meir Leibush ben Yehiel Michel Wisser) (1809–79): a nineteenth-century rabbi and biblical commentator

Masoretic Text (MT): standard Hebrew text of the Hebrew Bible, developed from the sixth to tenth centuries CE

Mays, James L. (1921–2015): American Old Testament scholar and biblical commentator

Metzudat David: text found in *Miqra'ot Gedolot* written by David Altschuler, a seventeenth-century Jewish commentator

Midrash Rabbah: rabbinic commentary on the five books of Torah and the Five Scrolls, from the third–fifth centuries CE. Includes Genesis Rabbah, Exodus Rabbah, etc.

Miqra'ot Gedolot **(Rabbinic Bible):** influential in Jewish tradition, this includes the Masoretic Text, Targum, and commentaries from Rashi, Ibn Ezra, Radak, and others in one volume; first edition printed in Venice (1524)

Mishnah: a collection of rabbinic sayings, later commented on in the Talmud

Nicholas of Lyra (1270–1349): medieval Franciscan teacher and biblical commentator

Origen (184–253): early Christian exegete and theologian, known for extensive use of allegory and figurative interpretation

Peshitta: Syriac translation of the Hebrew Bible, first century CE

Pesikta deRav Kahana: a collection of homilies and midrash from the fifth to sixth century CE

Pesikta Rabbati: a collection of midrashic materials on the Torah and prophets, ninth century CE

Philo of Alexandria (ca. 25 BCE –45 CE): Jewish philosopher from Alexandria; known for use of allegory in his biblical interpretation

Pirqe Rabbi Eliezer: eighth century CE midrashic work on the Torah

Pusey, E.B. (Edward Bouverie) (1800–82): English Anglican clergyman, professor of Hebrew at Oxford, and biblical commentator

Qumran: location near the Dead Sea where the first of the Dead Sea Scrolls were discovered

Radak (Rabbi David Kimhi) (1160–1235): medieval Jewish rabbi, grammarian, and biblical scholar

Rashi (Rabbi Shlomo ben Isaac) (1040–1105): important French Jewish rabbi, well known for commentaries on the Bible and Talmud

Saadia Gaon (882–942): influential Jewish scholar of the Bible, Talmud, and philosophy

Septuagint (LXX): ancient Greek translation of the Hebrew Bible; popular in the early church

Spurgeon, Charles Haddon (C. H.) (1834–92): influential English Baptist pastor of the nineteenth century

Talmud: collection of sayings from the rabbis, presented as commentary on the Mishnah (fourth–sixth century CE); found in two forms: the Palestinian (or Yerushalmi) Talmud and the Babylonian (Bavli) Talmud

Tanakh: acronym for Jewish ordering of the Hebrew Bible (Torah, Nevi'im, and Ketuvim)

Tanhuma: collections of midrash on the Torah

Targum: translations of the Hebrew Bible into Aramaic from the first centuries of the Common Era. Targum of the Prophets is known as Targum Jonathan

Theodore of Mopsuestia (ca. 350–428): theologian and biblical commentator of the early church, known for more literal interpretations in the Antiochene tradition

Theodoret of Cyr (393–457): Syrian bishop and biblical commentator

Theodotion (second century CE): Jewish scholar and translator of the Hebrew Bible into Greek

Vulgate: Latin translation of the Bible by Jerome, fourth century CE

Wellhausen, Julius (1844–1918): German orientalist and biblical scholar, known for his work on the source criticism of the Pentateuch and other parts of the Hebrew Bible

Wesley, John (1703–91): English clergyman and theologian, founder of Methodism; commentator on the Bible

Wolff, Hans Walter (1911–93): German Protestant theologian and biblical scholar; commentator on the prophets

Zohar: thirteenth-century work of Kabbalah mysticism

Abbreviations

ʿAbod. Zar.	ʿAbodah Zarah
AASOR	Annual of American Schools of Oriental Research
AB	Anchor Bible
ABD	*Anchor Bible Dictionary*
AJSL	*The American Journal of Semitic Languages and Literature*
ASV	American Standard Version
ATD	Das Alte Testament Deutsch
b	Babylonian Talmud
BASOR	Bulletin of the American Schools of Oriental Research
B. Bat.	Baba Batra
B. Meṣ.	Baba Meṣiʿa
BCE	Before the Common Era (= BC)

Hosea, Joel, and Obadiah Through the Centuries, First Edition. Bradford A. Anderson.
© 2024 John Wiley & Sons Ltd. Published 2024 by John Wiley & Sons Ltd.

Note: the bibliography is divided into three sections: (A) Versions, Translations, and Anthologies; (B) Commentaries and other frequently cited resources; and (C) General Bibliography.

(A) Versions, Translations, and Anthologies

Cathcart, Kevin, and Robert Gordon. 1989. *The Targum of the Minor Prophets*. Aramaic Bible 14. Collegeville: Liturgical Press.
Ego, Beate, Armin Lange, Hermann Lichtenberger, and Kristin De Troyer (eds.). 2005. *Minor Prophets*. Biblia Qumranica 3B. Leiden: Brill.

Ferreiro, Alberto (ed.). 2003. *The Twelve Prophets*. Ancient Christian Commentary on Scripture 14. Downers Grove: InterVarsity Press.

Fischer, B., R. Weber, and R. Gryson. 2007. *Biblia Sacra: Iuxta Vulgatam Versionem*. Stuttgart: Deutsche Bibelgesellschaft.

Gelston, Anthony. 2010. *The Twelve Minor Prophets*. BHQ 13. Stuttgart: Deutsche Bibelgesellschaft.

Glossa Ordinaria. 1603. *Bibliorum Sacrorum Cum Glossa Ordinaria, Volume 4*. Edited by Fugensis Strabus. Venice.

Ginzberg, Louis. 1909. *The Legends of the Jews. 7 Volumes*. Philadelphia: Jewish Publication Society of America.

Mann, Jacob. 1940. *The Bible as Read and Preached in the Old Synagogue, Volume 1*. New York: Ktav.

Mann, Jacob, and Isaiah Sonne. 1966. *The Bible as Read and Preached in the Old Synagogue, Volume 2*. Cincinnati: Hebrew Union College-Jewish Institute of Religion.

Montefiore, C., and H. Loewe (eds.). 1938. *A Rabbinic Anthology*. New York: Meridian.

Neusner, Jacob. 2007a. *Hosea in Talmud and Midrash: A Source Book*. Studies in Judaism. Lanham: University Press of America.

Neusner, Jacob. 2007b. *Micah and Joel in Talmud and Midrash: A Source Book*. Studies in Judaism. Lanham: University Press of America.

Neusner, Jacob. 2007c. *Habakkuk, Jonah, Nahum, and Obadiah in Talmud and Midrash: A Source Book*. Studies in Judaism. Lanham: University Press of America.

New English Translation of the Septuagint. 2009. Available at: http://ccat.sas.upenn.edu/nets/edition/

Rosenberg, A. J. 1986. *Mikraoth Gedeloth, The Book of the* Twelve Prophets, *Volume 1*. Brooklyn: Judaica.

Sperber, Alexander. 1962. *The Bible in Aramaic, Volume 3: The Latter Prophets according to Targum Jonathan*. Leiden: Brill.

Talmud: William Davidson Edition. Available online: https://www.sefaria.org/texts/Talmud

Ziegler, J. 1984. *Duodecim Prophetae*, Third Edition. *Septuaginta. Vetus Testamentum Graecum Auctoritate Academiae Scientiarum Gottingensis editum*. Göttingen: Vandenhoeck & Ruprecht.

(B) Commentaries and Other Frequently Cited Resources

Achtemeier, Elizabeth. 1996. "The Book of Joel." Pages 301–36 in *New Interpreter's Bible, Volume 7*. Nashville: Abingdon Press.

Allen, Leslie, C. 1976. *The Books of Joel, Obadiah, Jonah and Micah*. NICOT. Grand Rapids: Eerdmans.

Andersen, Francis I., and David N. Freedman. 1980. *Hosea*. AB 24. New York: Doubleday.

Aquinas, Thomas. 1911–1925 [1485]. *Summa Theologica*. Translated by Fathers of the English Dominican Province. New York: Benziger Brothers.

Barton, John. 2001. *Joel and Obadiah: A Commentary*. OTL. Louisville: Westminster John Knox.

Ben Zvi, Ehud. 1996. *A Historical-Critical Study of the Book of Obadiah*. BZAW 242. Berlin: de Gruyter.

Ben Zvi, Ehud. 2005. *Hosea*. FOTL. Grand Rapids: Eerdmans.

Bewer, Julius A. 1911. *A Critical and Exegetical Commentary on Obadiah and Joel*. ICC. Edinburgh: T&T Clark.

Bič, M. 1960. *Das Buch Joel*. Berlin: Evangelische Verlagsanstalt.

Calvin, John. 1846a [1559]. *Commentaries on the Twelve Minor Prophets, Volume 1: Hosea*. Translated by John Owen. Edinburgh: Calvin Translation Society.

Calvin, John. 1846b [1559]. *Commentaries on the Twelve Minor Prophets, Volume 2: Joel, Amos, Obadiah*. Translated by John Owen. Edinburgh: Calvin Translation Society.

Claassens, L. Juliana M. 2014a. "Joel." Pages 309–11 in *The Women's Bible Commentary: Revised and Expanded Edition*. Edited by Carol A. Newsom. Louisville: Westminster John Knox.

Claassens, L. Juliana M. 2014b. "Obadiah." Pages 319–20 in *The Women's Bible Commentary: Revised and Expanded Edition*. Edited by Carol A. Newsom. Louisville: Westminster John Knox.

Crenshaw, James L. 1995. *Joel*. AB 24c. New York: Doubleday.

Cyril of Alexandria. 2007. *Commentary on the Twelve Prophets, Volume 1*. Translated by Robert C. Hill. Fathers of the Church 115. Washington DC: The Catholic University of America Press.

Davies, Graham I. 1992. *Hosea*. NCBC 21. Grand Rapids: Eerdmans.

Dowling Long, Siobhan, and John F. A. Sawyer. 2015. *The Bible in Music: A Dictionary of Songs, Works, and More*. Lanham: Rowman & Littlefield.

Driver, S. R.1909. *An Introduction to the Literature of the Old Testament*. Edinburgh: T&T Clark.

Duhm, B. 1911. "Anmerkungen zu den Zwölf Propheten." *ZAW* 31: 161–204.

Duhm, B. 1916. *Israel's Propheten*. Tübingen: Mohr Siebeck.

Ewald, G. H. A. 1875 [1840–41]. *Commentary on the Prophets of the Old Testament, Volume 1*. Translated by J. Frederick Smith. Edinburgh: Williams and Norgate.

Fishbane, Michael. 2002. *The JPS Bible Commentary: Haftarot*. Philadelphia: Jewish Publication Society.

Fohrer, G. 1975. *Die Propheten des frühen 6.Jahrhunderts*. Gütersloh: Gerd Mohn.

Gill, John. 1748–63. *Exposition of the Old and New Testaments*. Available online: https://www.sacred-texts.com/bib/cmt/gill/index.htm

Gruber, Mayer I. 2017. *Hosea: A Textual Commentary*. LHBOTS 653. London: Bloomsbury T&T Clark.

Hare, D.R.A. 1985. 'The Lives of the Prophets.' *OTP* 2:379–84.

Harper, William Rainey. 1905. *A Critical and Exegetical Commentary on Amos and Hosea*. ICC. Edinburgh: T&T Clark.

Isho'dad of Merv. 1969. Commentaire d'Išo'dad de Merv sur l'Ancien Testament IV. Isaïe et les Douze. Translated by C. Can den Eynde. CSCO 304. Louvain: Peeters.

Jeremias, Jörg. 1983. *Der Prophet Hosea*. ATD 24.1. Göttingen: Vandenhoeck & Ruprecht.

Jeremias, Jörg. 2007. *Die Propheten Joel, Obadja, Jona, Micha*. ATD 24.3. Göttingen: Vandenhoeck & Ruprecht.

Jerome. 1845. *Libri Commentariorum (Commentaries on the Minor Prophets)*. PL 25. Edited by J.-P. Migne. Paris.

Jerome. 2017. "Three Books of Commentary on the Prophet Hosea to Pammachius." Pages 148–261 in *Commentaries on the Twelve Prophets, Jerome, Volume 2*. Edited by Thomas P. Scheck. Translated by Maria Veritas Marks and Thomas P. Scheck. Ancient Christian Texts. Downers Grove: IVP Academic.

Julian of Eclanum. 2021. *Commentaries on Job, Hosea, Joel, and Amos*. Edited and Translated by Thomas P. Scheck. Ancient Christian Texts. Downers Grove: IVP Academic.

Keefe, Alice A. 2016. "Hosea." Pages 823–35 in *The Prophets: Fortress Commentary on the Bible*. Edited by Gale A. Yee, Hugh R. Page Jr., and Matthew J.M. Coomber. Minneapolis: Augsburg Fortress.

Keil, C. F. 1954 [1871]. *The Twelve Minor Prophets*. Translated by James Martin. Volume 1: Biblical Commentary on the Old Testament. Grand Rapids: Eerdmans.

Landy, Francis. 1995. *Hosea*. Readings. Sheffield: Sheffield Academic Press.

Luther, Martin. 1975 [1556]. In *Lectures on the Minor Prophets I: Hosea, Joel, Amos, Obadiah, Micah, Nahum, Zephaniah, Haggai, Malachi*. Edited by Hilton C. Oswald. Translated by Richard J. Dinda. Luther's Works 18. St. Louis: Concordia.

Macintosh, A. A. 1997. *A Critical and Exegetical Commentary on Hosea*. ICC. Edinburgh: T&T Clark.

Mays, James L. 1969. *Hosea*. OTL. Philadelphia: Fortress.

Nicholas of Lyra. 1603. In *Bibliorum Sacrorum Cum Glossa Ordinaria, Volume 4*. Edited by Fugensis Strabus et al. Venice.

Perowne, Thomas Thomason. 1824. *Obadiah and Jonah with Notes and Introduction*. Cambridge Bible for Schools and Colleges. Cambridge: Cambridge University Press.

Pusey, E. B. 1885. *Minor Prophets: With a Commentary Explanatory and Practical and Introductions to the Several Books, Volume 1*. New York: Funk & Wagnalls.

Raabe, Paul R. 1996. *Obadiah: A New Translation with Introduction and Commentary*. AB 24D. New York: Doubleday.

Rainolds, John [d. 1607]. *The Prophecy of Obadiah Opened and Applied, in Sundry Sermons*. Online: https://quod.lib.umich.edu/e/eebo/A10338.0001.001/1:3?rgn=div1; view=fulltext

Renkema, Johan. 2003. *Obadiah*. Translated by Brian Doyle. HCOT. Leuven: Peeters.

Rudolph, Wilhelm. 1966. *Hosea*. KAT 13.1. Gütersloh: Gerd Mohn.

Rudolph, Wilhelm. 1971. *Joel, Amos, Obadja, Jona*. KAT 13:2. Gütersloh: Gerd Mohn.

Simkins, Ronald A. 2016. "Joel." Pages 837–44 in *The Prophets: Fortress Commentary on the Bible*. Edited by Gale A. Yee, Hugh R. Page Jr., and Matthew J. M. Coomber. Minneapolis: Augsburg Fortress.

Stuart, Douglas. 1987. *Hosea-Jonah*. WBC 31. Waco: Word.

Sweeney, Marvin A. 2000. *The Twelve Prophets, Volume 1*. Berit Olam. Collegeville: Michael Glazer.

Theodore of Mopsuestia. 2004. *Commentary on the Twelve Prophets*. Translated by Robert C. Hill. Fathers of the Church 108. Washington DC: The Catholic University of America Press.

Wacker, Marie-Theres. 2012. "Hosea," "Joel," and "Obadiah." Pages 371–96, 406–10 in *Feminist Biblical Interpretation: A Compendium of Critical Commentary on the Books of the Bible and Related Literature*. Edited by Luise Schottroff and MarieTheres Wacker. Translated by Lisa E. Dahill *et al*. Grand Rapids: Eerdmans.

Watts, John D. W. 1969. *The Books of Joel, Obadiah, Jonah, Nahum, Habakkuk and Zephaniah*. CBC. Cambridge: Cambridge University Press.

Wellhausen, J. 1892. *Die Kleinen Propheten. Skizzen und Vorarbeiten, Volume 5*. Berlin: Reimer.

Wesley, John. 1754–65. *Explanatory Notes on the Bible*. Nashville: Abingdon. Online: https://www.christianity.com/bible/commentary.php?com=wes

Wolff, Hans Walter. 1974a. *Hosea*. Translated by Gary Stansell. Hermeneia. Philadelphia: Fortress.

Wolff, Hans Walter. 1974b. *Joel and Amos*. Translated by Gary Stansell. Hermeneia. Philadelphia: Fortress.

Wolff, Hans Walter. 1986. *Obadiah and Jonah*. Translated by Margaret Kohl. Minneapolis: Augsburg.

Yee, Gale A. 1992. "Hosea." Pages 195–202 in *The Women's Bible Commentary*. Edited by Carol A. Newsom and Sharon H. Ringe. Louisville: Westminster/John Knox Press.

Yee, Gale A. 1996. "The Book of Hosea." Pages 197–297 in *The New Interpreter's Bible, Volume 7*. Nashville: Abingdon.

(C) General Bibiography

Ackroyd, Peter R. 1963. "Hosea and Jacob." *VT* 13: 245–59.

Ackroyd, Peter R. 1968. *Exile and Restoration*. OTL. Philadelphia: Westminster.

Ackroyd, Peter R. 1992. "Obadiah, Book of." *ABD* 5: 2–4.

Adler, Rachel. 1998. *Engendering Judaism: An Inclusive Jewish Theology and Ethics*. Philadelphia: Beacon.

Adu-Gyamfi, Yaw. 2015. "God's Wrath and Judgment on Ethnic Hatred and Hope for Victims of Ethnic Hatred in Obadiah: Implications for Africa." *Old Testament Essays* 28:11–30.

Ahlström, G. W. 1971. *Joel and the Temple Cult of Jerusalem*. Leiden: Brill.

Albertz, Rainer, James D. Nogalski, and Jakob Wöhrle (eds.). 2012. *Perspectives on the Formation of the Book of the Twelve*. Berlin: De Gruyter.

Alt, A. 1959 [1919]. "Hosea 5,8–6,6: Ein Krieg und seine Folgen in prophetischer Beleuchtung." *Neue kirchliche Zeitschrift* 30: 537–68.

Anderson, Bradford A. 2010. "Poetic Justice in Obadiah." *JSOT* 35: 247–55.

Anderson, Bradford A. 2011. *Brotherhood and Inheritance: A Canonical Reading of the Esau and Edom Traditions*. LHBOTS 556. London: T&T Clark.

Anderson, Bradford A. 2016a. "The Intersection of the Human and Divine in Genesis 32–33." *Zeitschrift für die Alttestamentliche Wissenschaft* 128: 30–41.

Anderson, Bradford A. 2016b. "The Spatial Rhetoric of Obadiah." Pages 101–16 in *Obadiah*. Edited by Bob Becking. Readings. Sheffield: Sheffield Phoenix.

Anderson, Bradford A. 2021. "Family Dynamics, Fertility Cults, and Feminist Critiques: The Reception of Hosea 1–3 through the Centuries." *Religions* 12/9: 674. https://doi.org/10.3390/rel12090674

Anderson, Bradford A. 2022. "Edom's (Dis)Possession." *CBQ* 84: 261–80.

Andiñach, Pablo R. 1992. "The Locusts in the Message of Joel." *VT* 42: 433–41.

Arnold, Patrick M. 1989. "Hosea and the Sin of Gibeah." *CBQ* 51: 447–78.

Assis, Elie. 2006. "Why Edom? On the Hostility Towards Jacob's Brother in Prophetic Sources." *VT* 56: 1–20.

Assis, Elie. 2013. *The Book of Joel: A Prophet Between Calamity and Hope*. LHBOTS 581. London: Bloomsbury T&T Clark.

Assis, E. 2016. *Identity in Conflict: The Struggle between Esau and Jacob, Edom and Israel*. Siphrut 19. Winona Lake: Eisenbrauns.

Augustine, of Hippo. 1956. "City of God." Pages 354–430 in NPNF 2. Translated by Marcus Dods. Edited by Philip Schaff. Grand Rapids: Eerdmans.

Bakhos, Carol. 2007. "Figuring (Out) Esau: The Rabbis and Their Others." *JJS* 58: 250–62.

Balz-Cochois, H. 1982. *Gomer: Der Höhenkult Israels im Selbstverständnis der Volksfrömmigkeit: Untersuchungen zu Hosea 4, 1–5, 7*. Frankfurt am Main: Peter Lang.

Barrett, C. K. 1968. *The First Epistle to the Corinthians*. London: A&C Black.

Bartlett, John R. 1977. "The Brotherhood of Edom." *JSOT* 4: 2–27.

Bartlett, John R. 1982. "Edom and the Fall of Jerusalem, 587 B.C." *PEQ* 114: 13–24.

Bartlett, John R. 1992. "Edom." *ABD* 2: 287–95.

Batten, Loring Woart. 1929. "Hose's Message and Marriage." *JBL* 48: 257–73.

Baumann, Gerlinde. 2003. *Love and Violence: Marriage as a Metaphor for the Relationship Between Yahweh and Israel in the Prophetic Books*. Translated by Linda M. Maloney. Collegeville: Liturgical.

Becking, Bob. 2016. "The Betrayal of Edom: Remarks on a Claimed Tradition." *HTS Teologiese Studies / Theological Studies* 72.4. Online: http://dx.doi.org/10.4102/hts.v72i4.3286

Beit-Arieh, Itzhaq. 1989. "New Data on the Relationship Between Judah and Edom Toward the End of the Iron Age." Pages 125–31 in *Recent Excavations in Israel: Studies in Iron Age Archaeology*. Edited by Seymour Gitin and William G. Dever. AASOR 49. Winona Lake: Eisenbrauns.

Ben Zvi, Ehud. 1999. "A Deuteronomistic Redaction in/among 'The Twelve'? A Contribution from the Standpoint of the books of Micah, Zephaniah and Obadiah." Pages 232–61 in *Those Elusive Deuteronomists*. Edited by L.S. Schearing and S.L. McKenzie. JSOTSup 268. Sheffield: Sheffield Academic Press.

Ben Zvi, Ehud. 2021. "From 'Historical' Prophets to Prophetic Books." Pages 5–16 in *The Oxford Handbook of the Minor Prophets*. Edited by Julia M. O'Brien. Oxford: Oxford University Press.

Bergler, Siegfried. 1988. *Joel als Schriftinterpret*. Frankfurt: Peter Lang.

Bergmann, Neil W. 2013. "Ecological Appropriation of Joel." *Australian eJournal of Theology* 20/1: 34–48.

Bienkowski, Piotr, and Eveline Van der Steen. 2001. "Tribes, Trade, and Towns: A New Framework for the Late Iron Age in Southern Jordan and the Negev." *BASOR* 23: 21–47.

Bird, Phyllis. 1989. "'To Play the Harlot': An Inquiry into an Old Testament Metaphor." Pages 75–94 in *Gender and Difference in Ancient Israel*. Edited by Peggy Day. Minneapolis: Fortress Press.

Bitter, S. 1975. *Die Ehe des Propheten Hosea: eine auslegungsgeschichtliche Untersuchung.* Göttingen: Vandenhoeck & Ruprecht.

Biwul, J. K. T. 2017. "Brothers in Conflict: Reading the Prophet Obadiah against the Context of the Political and Religious Hostility and Violence in Nigeria." *Old Testament Essays* 30: 30–55.

Blank, Sheldon H. 1936. "Studies in Post-exilic Universalism." *HUCA* 11: 159–91.

Blenkinsopp, Joseph. 1996. *A History of Prophecy in Israel*. Revised Edition. Louisville: Westminster John Knox.

Bos, James M. 2013. *Reconsidering the Date and Provenance of the Book of Hosea: A Case for Persian-Period Yehud*. London: Bloomsbury T&T Clark.

Bosson, Nathalie. 2016. "Coptic Translations. Minor Prophets." Pages 671–77 in *Textual History of the Bible, The Hebrew Bible Vol. 1B: Pentateuch, Former and Latter Prophets*. Edited by Armin Lange and Emmanuel Tov. Leiden: Brill.

Bourke, J. 1959. "Le Jour de Yahvé dans Joël." *RB* 66: 5–31.

Braaten, Laurie. 2006. "Earth Community in Joel 1–2: A Call to Identify with the Rest of Creation." *Horizons in Biblical Theology* 28: 113–29.

Brenner, Athalya. (ed.). 1995. *A Feminist Companion to the Bible: The Latter Prophets*. First Series. Sheffield: Sheffield Academic Press.

Brooke, George J. 2006. "The Twelve Minor Prophets and the Dead Sea Scrolls." Pages 19–43 in *Congress Volume Leiden 2004*. Edited by A. Lemaire. Leiden: Brill.

Budde, K. 1925. "Der Abschnitt Hosea 1–3 und seine grundlegende religionsgeschichtliche Bedeutung." *Theologische Studien und Kritiken* 96–97: 1–89.

Budde, K. 1926. "Zu Text und Auslegung des Buches Hosea." *JBL* 45: 280–97.

Budin, Stephanie L. 2008. *The Myth of Sacred Prostitution in Antiquity*. New York: Cambridge University Press.

Burroughs, Jeremiah. 1863. *An Exposition of the Prophecy of Hosea* [1643]. Edinburgh: James Nichol.

Buss, Martin J. 1969. *The Prophetic Word of Hosea. BZAW 111*. Berlin: de Gruyter.

Cannon, W. W. 1927. "Israel and Edom: The Oracle of Obadiah – II." *Theology* 15: 191–200.

Cantalamessa, Raniero. 2008. "Pope's Preacher: God Desires Mercy, Not Sacrifice." Translated by Joseph G. Trabbic. Online: https://www.catholic.org/news/international/europe/story.php?id=28167

Carroll, Robert. 1990. "Obadiah." Pages 496–97 in *A Dictionary of Biblical Interpretation*. Edited by R. Coggins and J. L. Houlden. London: SCM.

Caspari, C. P. 1842. *Der Prophet Obadja*. Leipzig: Reihold Beyer.

Cathcart, Kevin J. 1992. "Day of Yahweh." *ABD* 2: 84.

Cazelles, H. 1949. "The Problem of the Kings in Osee, 8:4." *CBQ* 11: 14–25.

Chalmers, R. S. 2007. *The Struggle of Yahweh and El for Hosea's Israel.* Sheffield: Sheffield Phoenix.

Childs, Brevard S. 1979. "The Enemy from the North and the Chaos Tradition." *JBL* 78: 187–98.

Childs, Brevard S. 1979. *Introduction to the Old Testament as Scripture.* Philadelphia: Fortress.

Cohen, Gerson D. 1967. "Esau as Symbol in Early Medieval Thought." Pages19–48 in *Jewish Medieval and Renaissance Studies.* Edited by Alexander Altmann. Cambridge: Harvard University Press.

Cohen, Naomi G. 2007. *Philo's Scriptures: Citations from the Prophets and Writings: Evidence for a Haftarah Cycle in Second Temple Judaism.* Leiden: Brill.

Coote, R. B. 1971. "Hosea XII." *VT* 21: 389–402.

Coggins, R. and J. L. Houlden (eds.). 1990. *A Dictionary of Biblical Interpretation.* London: SCM Press and Philadelphia: Trinity Press International.

Credner, K. A. 1831. *Der Prophet Joel übersetzt und erklärt.* Halle: Waisenhaus.

Crowell, Bradley L. 2007. "Nabonidus, as-Sila, and the Beginning of the End of Edom." *BASOR* 348: 75–88.

Crowell, Bradley L. 2008. "A Reevaluation of the Edomite Wisdom Hypothesis." *ZAW* 120: 404–16.

Crowell, Bradley L. 2021. *Edom at the Edge of Empire: A Social and Political History.* Archaeology and Biblical Studies 29. Atlanta: SBL.

Davies, Graham I. 1993. *Hosea.* Old Testament Guides. Sheffield: Sheffield Academic Press.

Day, Peggy L. 2000. "Adulterous Jerusalem's Imagined Demise: Death of a Metaphor in Ezekiel XVI." *VT* 50: 285–309.

DeGrado, Jessie. 2018. "The qdesha in Hosea 4:14: Putting the (Myth of the) Sacred Prostitute to Bed." *VT* 68: 1–33.

de Vaux, Roland. 1961. *Ancient Israel: Its Life and Institutions.* Translated by J. McHugh. New York: McGraw-Hill.

de Vaux, R. 1969. "Teman, ville ou region d'Edom?" *RB* 76: 379–85.

Dicou, Bert. 1994. *Edom, Israel's Brother and Antagonist: The Role of Edom in Biblical Prophecy and Story.* JSOTSup 169. Sheffield: JSOT Press.

Dines, Jennifer. 2012. "Verbal and Thematic Links between the Books of the Twelve in Greek and their Relevance to the Differing Manuscript Sequences." Pages 355–70 in *Perspectives on the Formation of the Book of the Twelve: Methodological Foundations – Redactional Processes Historical Insights.* Edited by Rainer Albertz, James D. Nogalski, and Jakob Wöhrle. Berlin: De Gruyter.

Dobbie, R. 1955. "The Text of Hosea 9.8." *VT* 5: 199–203.

Dodd, C. H. 1952. *According to the Scriptures: The Substructure of New Testament Theology.* London: Collins.

Doob Sakenfeld, Katharine. 2004. "How Hosea Transformed the Lord of the Realm into a Temperamental Spouse." *Bible Review* 20:1. Online: https://www.baslibrary.org/bible-review/20/1/6.

Dowling Long, S. 2017. "Joel (Book and Person). Music." in *EBR* 14. Online: https://doi.org/10.1515/ebr.joelbookandperson

Eccles, Charles Stuart. 1776. *The Necessity of Humiliation: A Sermon*. Bath: R. Cruttwell.

Eichhorn, Johann Gottfried. 1824. *Einleitung in das Alte Testament*. Fourth Edition. Göttingen: Carl Eduard Rosenbusch.

Eidevall, Göran. 1996. *Grapes in the Desert. Metaphors, Models, and Themes in Hosea 4–14*. Stockholm: Almqvist & Wiksell.

Eisen, Arnold M. 2006. "The Call of the Shofar." *Times of Israel*. Online: https://jewishstandard.timesofisrael.com/the-call-of-the-shofar/

Elliger, K. 1959. *Das Buch der zwolf Kleinen Propheten*. ATD 25; Fourth Edition. Göttingen: Vandenhoeck & Ruprecht.

Elliott, Charles. 1884. "The Date of Obadiah." *The Old Testament Student* 3: 321–4.

Emmerson, G. I. 1984. *Hosea: An Israelite Prophet in Judean Perspective*. JSOTSup 28. Sheffield: JSOT Press.

Everson, A. Joseph. 1974. "The Days of Yahweh." *JBL* 93: 329–37.

Fischer, Eugene A. 1976. "Cultic Prostitution in the Ancient Near East: A Reassessment." *Biblical Theology Bulletin* 6: 225–36.

Fishbane, Michael. 1970. "The Treaty Background of Amos 1:11 and Related Matters." *JBL* 89: 313–18.

Fitzmyer, Joseph A. 1998. *The Acts of the Apostles*. ABD. New York: Doubleday.

Fohrer, G. 1966. "Die Sprüche Obadjas." Pages 81–93 in *Studia biblica et semitica Theodoro Christiano Friesen dedicatea*. Edited by Wilhelm C. van Unnik and Adam Simon van der Woude, Wageningen: H. Veenman.

Fredriksen, Paula, and Oded Irshai. 2006. "Christian Anti-Judaism: Polemics and Policies." Pages 977–1034 in *The Cambridge History of Judaism, Volume 4: The Late Roman-Rabbinic Period*. Edited by Steven T. Katz. Cambridge: Cambridge University Press.

Freedman, David Noel and Bruce Willoughby. 1992. "Joel." Page 406 in *Dictionary of Biblical Tradition in English Literature*. Edited by David Lyle Jeffrey. Grand Rapids: Eerdmans.

Fresch, Christopher J. 2017. "Textual History of the Minor Prophets." Pages 589–600 in *Textual History of the Bible, The Hebrew Bible Vol. 1B: Pentateuch, Former and Latter Prophets*. Edited by Amin Lange and Emanuel Tov. Leiden: Brill.

Fretheim, Terence E. 1984. *The Suffering of God: An Old Testament Perspective*. Philadelphia: Fortress.

Fuller, Russell E. 1997. "The Twelve." Pages 221–318 in *Qumran Cave 4.X: The Prophets*. Edited by Eugene Ulrich *et al.* DJD 15. Oxford: Clarendon.

Fuller, Russell. 2017. "Ancient Hebrew Texts (Minor Prophets)." Pages 601–10 in *Textual History of the Bible, The Hebrew Bible Vol. 1B: Pentateuch, Former and Latter Prophets*. Edited by Amin Lange and Emanuel Tov. Leiden: Brill.

'Gambling vs. casting lots.' 2004. *Baptist Board*. Online: https://www.baptistboard.com/threads/gambling-vs-casting-lots.25726/

Garratt, Samuel. 1854. *England's Sin and God's Warning. Two Fast Day Sermons Preached on the Fast-Day, April 26, 1854*. London: Wertheim and Macintosh.

Gillum, Gary P. 2005. "Obadiah's Vision of Saviors on Mount Zion." Pages 226–35 in *Sperry Symposium Classics: The Old Testament*. Edited by Paul Y. Hoskisson. Salt Lake City: Religious Studies Center, Brigham Young University, and Deseret Book.

Ginsberg, H. L. 1961. "Hosea's Ephraim: More Fool than Knave: A New Interpretation of Hosea 12: 1–14." *JBL* 80: 339–47.

Ginsberg, H. L. 1971. "Hosea." *Encyclopedia Judaica* 8: 1010–24.

Glenny, W. Edward. 2013. *Hosea: A Commentary Based on Hosea in Codex Vaticanus*. Septuagint Commentary Series. Leiden: Brill.

Glenny, W. Edward. 2016. "Minor Prophets: Septuagint." Pages 614–23 in *Textual History of the Bible, The Hebrew Bible Vol. 1B: Pentateuch, Former and Latter Prophets*. Edited by A. Lange and E. Tov. Leiden: Brill.

Glenny, W. Edward. 2021. "Textual History of the Minor Prophets: Hebrew Manuscripts and Versions." Pages 41–56 in *The Oxford Handbook of the Minor Prophets*. Edited by Julia M. O'Brien. Oxford: Oxford University Press.

Glueck, Nelson. 1940. *The Other Side of the Jordan*. New Haven: American Schools of Oriental Research.

Goldschmidt, Daniel. 1970. *High Holy Day Liturgy: Part II: The Day of Atonement*. Jerusalem: Koren.

Gordis, R. 1954. "Hosea's Marriage and Message." *HUCA* 25: 9–40.

Gordon, Cyrus H. 1936. "Hosea 2,4–5 in the Light of New Semitic Inscriptions." *ZAW* 54: 277–80.

Goshen-Gottstein, Alon. 2002. "Ben Sir"'s Praise of the Fathers: A Canon-Conscious Reading." Pages 235–67 in *Ben Sira's God*. Edited by Renate Egger-Wentzel. Berlin: de Gruyter.

Graetz, Naomi. 1995. "God is to Israel as Husband Is to Wife: The Metaphoric Battering of Hosea's Wife." Pages 126–45 in *A Feminist Companion to the Latter Prophets*. First Series. Edited by Athalya Brenner. Sheffield: Sheffield Academic.

'The Great Shofar and Rosh HaShanah'. 2023. *First Fruits of Zion*. Online: https://torahportions.ffoz.org/disciples/matthew/the-great-shofar-and-rosh-hash.html

Guillaume, Philippe. 2007. "A Reconsideration of Manuscripts Classified as Scrolls of the Twelve Minor Prophets (XII)." *The Journal of Hebrew Scriptures* 7. https://doi.org/10.5508/jhs.2007.v7.a16

Hadjiev, Tchavdar S. 2020. *Joel, Obadiah, Habakkuk, Zephaniah*. London: Bloomsbury T&T Clark.

Hagedorn, Anselm C. 2021. 'Joel'. Pages 411–23 in *The Oxford Handbook of the Minor Prophets*. Edited by Julia M. O'Brien. Oxford: Oxford University Press.

Hanson, Paul D. 1975 *The Dawn of Apocalyptic*. Philadelphia: Fortress.

Hayes, John H. 1968. "The Usage of Oracles against Foreign Nations in Ancient Israel." *JBL* 87: 81–92.

Heschel, Abraham Joshua. 1962. *The Prophets*. New York: Harper and Row.

Hiebert, Theodore. 1992. "Joel, Book of." *ABD* 3: 873–80.

Hvidberg, F. F. 1962. *Weeping and Laughter in the Old Testament: A Study of Canaanite-Israelite Religion*. Leiden: Brill.

Holladay, William L. 1966. "Chiasmus, the Key to Hosea XII 3–6." *VT* 16: 53–64.

Holm, Thomas. 2014. "Hosea 4 End Time Prophesy Is Being Fulfilled TODAY." Online: https://thejosephplan.org/hosea-4-end-time-prophesy-is-being-fulfilled-today/

Holt, E. K. 1995. *Prophesying the Past: The Use of Israel's History in the Book of Hosea.* JSOTSup 194. Sheffield: Sheffield Academic.

Holtz, S. E. 2012. "Why Are the Sins of Ephraim (Hos 13, 12) and Job (Job 14, 17) Bundled?" *Biblica* 93: 107–15.

Horrell, David. 2010. *The Bible and the Environment: Towards a Critical Ecological Biblical Theology.* London: Equinox.

House, Paul R. 1990. *The Unity of the Twelve.* JSOTSup 97. Sheffield: Almond.

House, Paul R. 2005. "Obadiah." Pages 542–44 in *Dictionary for the Theological Interpretation of the Bible.* Edited by Kevin J. Vanhoozer. Grand Rapids: Zondervan.

Huffmon, Herbert B. 1959. "The Covenant Lawsuit in the Prophets." *JBL* 78: 285–95.

Isgrigg, Daniel D. 2019. "The Latter Rain Revisited." *Pneuma* 41: 439–57.

Jackson, Wayne. 2020. "My People Are Destroyed for a Lack of Knowledge." ChristianCourier.com. Access date: May 4, 2020. https://www.christiancourier.com/articles/771-my-people-are-destroyed-for-a-lack-of-knowledge

Jeffrey, D. L. (ed.). 1992. *A Dictionary of Biblical Tradition in English Literature.* Grand Rapids: Eerdmans.

Jeremias, Jörg. 1997. *Die* Reue Gottes. *Aspekte alttestamentlicher* Gottesvorstellung. Neukirchen-Vluyn: Neukirchener Verlag.

Jones, Barry Alan. 1995. *The Formation of the Book of the Twelve: A Study in Text and Canon.* SBLDS 149. Atlanta: Scholars.

Keefe, Alice A. 2001. *Woman's Body and the Social Body in Hosea.* JSOTSup 338. London: Sheffield.

Keefe, Alice A. 1995. "The Female Body, the Body Politic and the Land: A Sociopolitical Reading of Hosea 1–2." Pages 70–100 in *A Feminist Companion to the Bible: The Latter Prophets (First Series).* Edited by Athalya Brenner. Sheffield: Sheffield Academic Press.

Kelle, Brad E. 2005. *Hosea 2: Metaphor and Rhetoric in Historical Perspective.* Atlanta: SBL.

Kelle, Brad E. 2009. "Hosea 1–3 in Twentieth Century Scholarship." *CBR* 7: 179–216.

Kelle, Brad E. 2010. "Hosea 4–14 in Twentieth Century Scholarship." *CBR* 8: 314–75.

Kellermann, U. 1975. *Israel und Edom. Studien zum Edomhass Israels n 6.–4. Jahrhundert v. Chr.* Münster: Habil.-schrift.

Kim-Farley, Robert J. 2020. "Sow the Wind, Reap the Whirlwind: Katrina 15 Years After." *American Journal of Public Health* 110: 1448–9. Online: https://doi.org/10.2105/AJPH.2020.305881

Knoppers, Gary N. 2001. "Intermarriage, Social Complexity, and Ethnic Diversity in the Genealogy of Judah." *JBL* 120: 15–30.

Krier, T. 2016. "Hosea (Book and Person). Literature." *EBR* 12: 442–3.

Kuan, Jeffrey K. 1991. "Hosea 9:13 and Josephus, Antiquities IX, 277–287." *PEQ* 123: 103–8.

Kuhl, C. 1934. "Neue Dokumente zum Verständnis von Hos. 2, 4–15." *ZAW* 52: 102–9.

Lange, Armin, and Matthias Weigold. 2011. *Biblical Quotations and Allusions in Second Temple Jewish Literature*. JAJS 5. Göttingen: Vandenhoeck & Ruprecht.

Lescow, Theodor. 1999. "Die Komposition des Buches Obadja." *ZAW* 111: 380–98.

Leith, Mary Joan Winn. 1989. "Verse and Reverse: The Transformation of the Woman Israel in Hosea 1–3." Pages 95–108 in *Gender and Difference in Ancient Israel*. Edited by Peggy Day. Minneapolis: Fortress Press.

Lemaire, A. 2005. "Essai d'interprétation historique d'une nouvelle inscription monumentale Moabite." *Comptes-Rendus de l'Académie des Inscriptions et Belles-Lettres* 2005: 95–108.

Lipinski, E. 1973. "Obadiah 20." *VT* 23: 368–70

Lipschitz, Oded. 2005. *The Fall and Rise of Jerusalem: Judah under Babylonian Rule*. Winona Lake: Eisenbrauns.

Lipshitz, Abe. 1988. *The Commentary of Rabbi Abraham Ibn Ezra on Hosea*. New York: Sepher-Hermon Press.

Lohfink, Norbert. 1961. "Zu Text und Form von Os 4:4–6." *Biblica* 42: 303–32.

Loya, Melissa T. 2008. "Therefore the Earth Mourns: The Grievance of Earth in Hosea 4:1–3." Pages 53–63 in *Exploring Ecological Hermeneutics*. Edited by Norman C. Habel and Peter Trudinger. Atlanta: Society of Biblical Literature.

Lundbom, Jack R. 1979. "Poetic Structure and Prophetic Rhetoric in Hosea." *VT* 29: 300–8.

Macintosh, A. A. 2001. "Hosea: The Rabbinic Commentators and the Ancient Versions." Pages 77–82 in *Biblical Hebrew, Biblical Texts. Essays in Memory of Michael P. Weitzman*. Edited by A. Rapoport-Albert and G. Greenberg. JSOTSup 333. Sheffield: Sheffield Academic Press.

Macwilliam, Stuart. 2011. *Queer Theory and the Prophetic Marriage Metaphor in the Hebrew Bible*. Sheffield: Equinox.

Marbury, Edward. 1649. *A Brief Commentarie or Exposition upon the Prophecy of Obadiah, Together with Usefull Notes Delivered in Sundry Sermons*. London: George Calvert. Online: https://quod.lib.umich.edu/e/eebo2/A89517.0001.001?rgn=main; view=fulltext

Marlow, Hilary. 2009. *Biblical Prophets and Contemporary Environmental Ethics*. Oxford: Oxford University Press.

Mason, Rex. 1994. *Zephaniah, Habakkuk, Joel*. Old Testament Guides. Sheffield: JSOT Press.

May, H. G. 1932. "The Fertility Cult in Hosea." *AJSL* 48: 73–98.

Mazar, A. 1982. "The 'Bull Site': An Iron Age I Open Cult Place." *BASOR* 247: 27–42.

McCarter, P. Kyle. 1976. "Obadiah 7 and the Fall of Edom." *BASOR* 221: 87–91.

McEntire, Mark. 2021. "The Minor Prophets in Modern Culture." Pages 385–95 in *The Oxford Handbook of the Minor Prophets*. Edited by Julia M. O'Brien. Oxford: Oxford University Press.

McKenzie, S. L. 1986. "The Jacob Tradition in Hosea xii 4–5." *VT* 36: 311–22.

Merx, A. 1879. *Die Prophetie des Joel und ihre Ausleger*. Halle: Buchhandlung des Waisenhauses.

Morris, Gerald. 1996. *Prophecy, Poetry and Hosea*. Sheffield: Sheffield Academic Press.

Moughtin-Mumby, Sharon. 2008. *Sexual and Marital Metaphors in Hosea, Jeremiah, Isaiah, and Ezekiel*. Oxford Theological Monographs. Oxford: Oxford University Press.

Mowinckel, Sigmund. 1958. *He that Cometh*. Translated by G. W. Anderson. Oxford: Basil Blackwell.

Mroczek, Eva. 2016. *The Literary Imagination in Jewish Antiquity*. Oxford: Oxford University Press.

Mueller, William R. 1961. "Donne's Adulterous Female Town." *Modern Language Notes* 76: 312–14.

Müller, A. K. 2008. *Gottes Zukunft: Die Möglichkeit der Rettung am Tag JHWHs nach dem Joelbuch*. WMANT 119. Neukirchen-Vluyn: Neukirchener Verlag.

n. a. 2006. "Solemnity of the Most Sacred Heart of Jesus." *Homily Service* 39: 7, 42–45. DOI: 10.1080/07321870600623196

Nogalski, James D. 1993. *Literary Precursors to the Book of the Twelve*. BZAW 217. Berlin: de Gruyter.

Nogalski, James D. 2011. *The Book of the Twelve: Hosea-Jonah*. Macon: Smyth and Helwys.

Nogalski, James D. and Marvin A. Sweeney (eds.). 2000. *Reading and Hearing the Book of the Twelve*. SBLSymS 15. Atlanta: SBL.

Nulman, M. 1993. *The Encyclopedia of Jewish Prayer: Ashkenazic and Sephardic Rites*. Northvale, NJ: Jason Aronson.

Nyberg, Henrik S. 1935. *Studien zum Hoseabuch*. Upsala Universitetsårsskrift 6. Uppsala.

Obed-Edom Obadiah Lyrics. 1996. ApologetiX. Online: https://www.newreleasetoday. com/lyricsdetail.php?lyrics_id=51554

O'Brien, Julia M. 2008. *Challenging Prophetic Metaphor: Theology and Ideology in the Prophets*. Louisville: Westminster John Knox.

Ogden, G. S. 1983. "Joel 4 and Prophetic Responses to National Laments." *JSOT* 26: 97–106.

Onye, Anthonia. 2022. "Do Women Have a Voice? Yes!" *Anabaptist World*. Online: https://anabaptistworld.org/do-women-have-a-voice-yes/

Östborn, Gunnar. 1956. *Yahweh and Baal: Studies in the Book of Hosea and Related Documents*. Lund: C. W. K. Gleerup.

Pajunen, Mika S. 2021. "The Minor Prophets in the Judean Desert Manuscripts." Pages 57–68 in *The Oxford Handbook of the Minor Prophets*. Edited by Julia M. O'Brien. Oxford: Oxford University Press.

Paton, L. B. 1896. "Notes on Hosea's Marriage." *JBL* 15: 9–17.

Paul, Shalom M. 1968. "The Image of the Oven and the Cake in Hosea 7: 4–10." *VT* 18: 114–20.

Paul, Shalom M. 1995. "Hosea 7:16: Gibberish Jabber." Pages 707–12 in *Pomegranates and Golden Bells: Studies in Biblical, Jewish, and Near Eastern Ritual, Law, and Literature in Honor of Jacob Milgrom*. Edited by David P. Wright, David N. Freedman, and Avi Hurvitz. Winona Lake: Eisenbrauns.

Peterson, Paul S. 2017. "Joel (Book and Person). Christianity." *EBR* 14. Online: https://doi.org/10.1515/ebr.joelbookandperson

Pfeiffer, R. H. 1926. "Edomitic Wisdom." *ZAW* 44: 13–25.

Pinkerton, John. 1915. "National Hate." *The Expository Times* 26/7: 299–302.

Plöger, Otto. 1968. *Theocracy and Eschatology*. Translated by S. Rudman. Oxford: Blackwell.

Prinsloo, W. S. 1985. *The Theology of the Book of Joel*. BZAW 163. Berlin: De Gruyter.

Promey, Sally M. 1998. "The Afterlives of Sargent's Prophets." *Art Journal* 57/1:131–44.

Raabe, Paul R. 1995. "Why Prophetic Oracles against the Nations?" Pages 236–57 in *Fortunate the Eyes That See: Essays in Honor of David Noel Freedman in Celebration of His Seventieth Birthday*. Edited by Astrid B. Beck *et al.* Grand Rapids: Eerdmans.

Réau, L. 1955–1959. *Iconographie de l'art chrétien. 3 Volumes*. Paris: Presses Univ. de France.

Rendtorff, Rolf. 1998. "Alas for the Day! The 'Day of the Lord' in the Book of the Twelve." Pages 186–97 in *God in the Fray: A Tribute to Walter Brueggemann*. Edited by Tod Linafelt and Timothy K. Beal. Minneapolis: Fortress Press.

Robeck Jr, Cecil, and Amos Yong (eds.). 2014. *The Cambridge Companion to Pentecostalism*. Cambridge: Cambridge University Press.

Robinson, George L. 1926. *The Twelve Minor Prophets*. New York: Harper.

Robinson, Thomas A. and Lanette D. Ruff. 2012. *Out of the Mouths of Babes: Girl Evangelists in the Flapper Era*. New York: Oxford University Press.

Rodgers, Peter. 2017. "Joel (Book and Person). New Testament." *EBR* 14. Online: https://doi.org/10.1515/ebr.joelbookandperson

Romerowski, S. 1989. *Les Livres de Joël et d'Abdias*. Vaux-sur- Seine: Edifac.

Rouillard, H. 1985. *La Péricope de Balaam (Nombres 22–24). La Prose et les 'Oracles'*. Paris: Gabalda.

Rowley, H. H. 1956. "The Marriage of Hosea." *Bulletin of John Rylands Library* 39: 200–33.

Rudnig-Zelt, Susanne. 2006. *Hoseastudien: Redaktionskritsche Untersuchungen zur Genese des Hoseabuches*. Göttingen: Vandenhoeck & Ruprecht.

Samuel, Maurice. 1940. *The Great Hatred*. New York: Knopf.

Sawyer, John F. A. 2009. *A Concise Dictionary of the Bible and its Reception*. Louisville: Westminster John Knox.

Sawyer, John F. A. 2021. "The Twelve Minor Prophets in Art and Music." Pages 279–95 in *The Oxford Handbook of the Minor Prophets*. Edited by Julia M. O'Brien. Oxford: Oxford University Press.

Schügel-Straumann, Helen. 1995. "God as Mother in Hosea 11." Pages 194–218 in *A Feminist Companion to the Latter Prophets*. First Series. Edited by Athalya Brenner. Sheffield: Sheffield Academic.

Scholz, Susanne. 2021. "Reading the Minor Prophets for Gender and Sexuality." Pages 300–12 in *The Oxford Handbook of the Minor Prophets*. Edited by Julia M. O'Brien. Oxford: Oxford University Press.

Secunda, Shai. 2022. "Wandering Jews." *Jewish Review of Books*. Online: https://jewishreviewofbooks.com/jewish-history/12399/wandering-jews/

Seow, C.-L. 1982. "Hosea 14:10 and the Foolish People Motif." *CBQ* 44: 212–24.

Seow, C.-L. 1992. "Hosea." *ABD* 3: 291–7.

Seow, C.-L. *et al.* (eds.). 2009–. *Encyclopedia of the Bible and Its Reception*. Berlin: De Gruyter.

Setel, T. Drorah. 1985. "Prophets and Pornography: Female Sexual Imagery in Hosea." Pages 86–95 in *Feminist Interpretation of the Bible*. Edited by Letty M. Russell. Philadelphia: Westminster.

Shepherd, Michael B. 2011. *The Twelve Minor Prophets in the New Testament*. New York: Peter Lang.

Sheppard, G. T. 1980. *Wisdom as a Hermeneutical Construct*. BZAW 151. Berlin: de Gruyter.

Sherwood, Yvonne. 1996. *The Prostitute and the Prophet: Hosea's Marriage in Literary-Theoretical Perspective*. JSOTSup 212. Sheffield: JSOT Press.

Simkins, Ronald A. 1991. *Yahweh's Activity in History and Nature in the Book of Joel*. Lewiston: Mellen.

Simkins, Ronald A. 1993. "God, History, and the Natural World in the Book of Joel." *CBQ* 55: 435–52.

Simkins, Ronald A. 1994. "Return to Yahweh": Honor and Shame in Joel." *Semeia* 68: 41–54.

Siquans, A. 2020. "Anti-Jewish Polemic and Jewish Bible Interpretation: Two Examples from Origen and Ephrem the Syrian." Pages 55–70 in *Volume 2 Confronting Anti-semitism from the Perspectives of Christianity, Islam, and Judaism*. Edited by Lange, A., Mayerhofer, K., Porat, D. and Schiffman, L. Berlin: De Gruyter.

Smith, Colin. 2014. "God Can Restore Your Lost Years." *The Gospel Coalition*. Online: https://www.thegospelcoalition.org/article/god-can-restor-your-lost-years/

Snyman, S. D. 1989. "Cohesion in the Book of Obadiah." *ZAW* 101: 59–71.

Spencer, Nick. 2016. "They Shall Reap the Whirlwind": How Churchill Harnessed Christianity in the Service of War." Online: https://www.democraticaudit.com/2016/12/20/they-shall-reap-the-whirlwind-how-churchill-harnessed-christianity-in-the-service-of-war/

Spurgeon, C. H. 1886. "Truth Stranger than Fiction. Sermon Delivered on Lord's Day Evening, May 30, 1886." Online: https://www.ccel.org/ccel/spurgeon/sermons35.xx.html

Spurgeon, C. H. 1890. "Possessing Possessions". Online: https://www.spurgeon.org/resource-library/sermons/possessing-possessions/

Spurgeon, Charles H. 1893. "Hosea 2:23: God's People, or Not God's People." Online: https://www.preceptaustin.org/spurgeon_sermons_on_hosea_2

Spurgeon, C. H. 1951. The *Treasury of the Old Testament. Volume 4: Jeremiah to Malachi*. Grand Rapids: Zondervan.

Stark, Michael. 2020. "The Root of Immorality" (Sermon). Online: https://www.sermoncentral.com/sermons/the-root-of-immorality-michael-stark-sermon-on-national-sin-246251?page=1&wc=800

Strazicich, John. 2007. *Joel's Use of Scripture and Scripture's Use of Joel*. Leiden: Brill.

Strine, C. A. 2017. "On the Compositional Models for Ezekiel 38–39: A Response to William Tooman's *Gog of Magog*." *VT* 67: 589–601.

Tammuz, Oded. 2016. "Hosea 10,13b–14b: A Warning about a Rebellion." *BN* 170: 35–50.

Tebes, Juan Manuel. 2006. "You Shall Not Abhor an Edomite, for He is Your Brother": The Tradition of Esau and the Edomite Genealogies from an Anthropological Perspective." *Journal of Hebrew Scriptures* 6. https://doi.org/10.5508/jhs.2006.v6.a6

Tebes, Juan Manuel. 2009. "The Wisdom of Edom." *BN* 143: 97–117.

Terndrup, Craig. 2011. "Blow the Trumpet in Zion". *The Forerunner.* Online: https://www.forerunner.com/blog/blow-the-trumpet-in-zion

Thompson, J. A. 1955. "Joel's Locusts in the Light of Near Eastern Parallels." *JNES* 14: 52–5.

Tiemeyer, Lena-Sofia. 2006. *Priestly Rites and Prophetic Rage: Post-Exilic Prophetic Critique of the Priesthood.* FAT 2.19. Tübingen: Mohr Siebeck.

Tiemeyer, Lena-Sofia. 2017. "Joel (Book and Person). Literature." *EBR* 14. Online: https://doi.org/10.1515/ebr.joelbookandperson

Timmer, Daniel. 2015. *The Non-Israelite Nations in the Book of the Twelve: Thematic Coherence and the Diachronic-Synchronic Relationship in the Minor Prophets.* Leiden: Brill.

Tooman, William A. 2011. *Gog* of *Magog*: Reuse of Scripture and Compositional Technique in Ezekiel 38–39. FAT II.52. Tübingen: Mohr Siebeck.

Tov, Emanuel. 2003. "Approaches Towards Scripture Embraced by the Ancient Greek Translators." Pages 213–28 in *Der Mensch vor Gott: Forschungen zum Menschbild in Bibel, antiken Judentum und Koran: Festschrift für Hermann Lichtenberger zum 60. Geburtstag.* Edited by Ulrike Mittmann-Richert, Friedrich Avemarie and Gerbern S. Oegema. Neukirchen: Neukirchener Verlag.

Trevett, Christine. 1995. *Montanism.* Cambridge: Cambridge University Press.

Trotter, James M. 2001. *Reading Hosea in Achaemenid Yehud.* JSOTSup 328. Pp. 242. Sheffield: Sheffield Academic Press.

Troxel, Ronald L. 2015. *Joel: Scope, Genre(s), and Meaning.* Winona Lake: Eisenbrauns.

Van Dijk-Hemmes, Fokkelien. 1989. "The Imagination of Power and the Power of Imagination: An Intertextual Analysis of Two Biblical Love Songs: The Song of Songs and Hosea 2." *JSOT* 44: 75–88.

Vatke, Wilhem. 1835. *Die biblische Theologie wissenschaftlich dargestellt: I. Die Religion des Altes Testaments.* Berlin: Bethge.

Vernes, Maurice. 1872. *Le peuple d'Israel et ses espérances relatives à son avenir depuis les origines jusqu'à l'époque persane (Ve siècle avant J. C.).* Paris: Sandoz et Fischbacher.

Volz, Paul. 1898. "Die Ehegeschichte Hoseas." *ZAW* 6: 321–35.

Von Rad, Gerhard. 1968. *The Message of the Prophets.* Translated by David M. Stalker. London: SCM.

Vriezen, Th. C. 1941. "Hosea 12." *NThSt* 24: 144–9.

Wacker, Marie-Theres. 1989. "God as Mother? On the Meaning of a Biblical God-Symbol for Feminist Theology." *Concilium* 206: 103–11.

Wacker, Marie-Theres. 1996. *Figurationen des Weiblichen im Hosea-Buch.* Freiburg: Herder.

Weems, Renita J. 1989. "Gomer: Victim of Violence or Victim of Metaphor?" *Semeia* 47: 87–104.

Werse, Nicholas R. 2019. *Reconsidering the Book of the Four. The Shaping of Hosea, Amos, Micah, and Zephaniah as an Early Prophetic Collection.* BZAW 517. Berlin: de Gruyter.

Wheeler, Brandon. 2021. "The Minor Prophets in Islam." Pages 253–66 in *The Oxford Handbook of the Minor Prophets.* Edited by Julia M. O'Brien. Oxford: Oxford University Press.

Whitt, William D. 1991. "The Jacob Traditions in Hosea and their Relation to Genesis." *ZAW* 103: 18–43.

Willi-Plein, Ina. 1971. *Vorformen der Schriftexegese innerhalb des Alten Testaments.* BZAW 123. Berlin: de Gruyter.

Wolff, Hans Walter. 1977. "Obadja - ein Kultprophet als Interpret." *EvT* 37: 273–84.

Yee, Gale A. 1987. *Composition and Tradition in the Book of Hosea.* Atlanta: Scholars.

Yee, Gale A. 2001. "She Is Not My Wife and I Am Not Her Husband": A Materialist Analysis of Hosea 1–2." *BibInt* 9: 345–83.

Yona, Shamir. 2006. "Rhetorical Features in Talmudic Literature." *HUCA* 77: 67–101.

Yoo, Y. J. 1999. "Israelian Hebrew in the Book of Hosea." PhD Dissertation, Cornell University.

Biblical and Ancient Texts Index

Hosea, Joel, and Obadiah Through the Centuries, First Edition. Bradford A. Anderson.
© 2024 John Wiley & Sons Ltd. Published 2024 by John Wiley & Sons Ltd.

General Index

Hosea, Joel, and Obadiah Through the Centuries, First Edition. Bradford A. Anderson.
© 2024 John Wiley & Sons Ltd. Published 2024 by John Wiley & Sons Ltd.